Date: 8/10/21

BIO RUSSELL
Rice, Christina,
Mean...moody...magnificent! :
Jane Russell and the

MEAN . . . MOODY . . . MAGNIFICENT!

MEAN . . . MOODY . . .
MAGNIFICENT!

Jane Russell and the Marketing
of a Hollywood Legend

Christina Rice

UNIVERSITY PRESS OF KENTUCKY

Scholarly publisher for the Commonwealth,
serving Bellarmine University, Berea College, Centre
College of Kentucky, Eastern Kentucky University,
The Filson Historical Society, Georgetown College,
Kentucky Historical Society, Kentucky State University,
Morehead State University, Murray State University,
Northern Kentucky University, Spalding University,
Transylvania University, University of Kentucky,
University of Louisville, and Western Kentucky University.
All rights reserved.

Editorial and Sales Offices: The University Press of Kentucky
663 South Limestone Street, Lexington, Kentucky 40508-4008
www.kentuckypress.com

Unless otherwise noted, photographs are from the author's collection.

Library of Congress Cataloging-in-Publication Data

Names: Rice, Christina, 1974– author.
Title: Mean . . . moody . . . magnificent! : Jane Russell and the marketing of a
    Hollywood legend / Christina Rice.
Description: Lexington, Kentucky : University Press of Kentucky, [2021] |
    Includes bibliographical references, filmography, and index.
Identifiers: LCCN 2021006503 | ISBN 9780813181080 (hardcover) | ISBN
    9780813181103 (pdf) | ISBN 9780813181097 (epub)
Subjects: LCSH: Russell, Jane, 1921–2011. | Actors—United
    States—Biography.
Classification: LCC PN2287.R82 .R53 2021 | DDC 791.43/028092 [B]—dc23

This book is printed on acid-free paper meeting
the requirements of the American National Standard
for Permanence in Paper for Printed Library Materials.

Manufactured in the United States of America.

Member of the Association
of University Presses

For my daughter Gable,
who is neither mean nor moody,
but always magnificent.

Contents

CONTENTS

The journey with Jane was a very different one than with Ann Dvorak. Whereas Ann was a bit of an enigma, and primary source documents related to her proved difficult to track down, Jane was a hyper-documented open book. She was the product of endless controversy due to Howard Hughes's marketing of her and her films, so interest has been high for decades, and she received a lot of press coverage. Jane lived to be almost ninety and always made herself available for interviews, so letting her speak for herself in these pages was easy. I found Jane to be so no-nonsense and unconcerned with keeping up appearances that she turned out to be a consistently reliable narrator, which is a gift for a biographer. However, writing about Jane Russell also proved to have its own unique challenges. She was exceedingly outspoken, particularly as she got older, and sometimes spouted off right-leaning political views that didn't always paint her in a positive light. Still, they are part of her story and could not be ignored.

Jane's stated beliefs were frequently out of alignment with her actions, which I found extremely maddening. Here was a proud, lifelong Republican who was also a staunch supporter of government child welfare programs; she once had to aggressively lobby Congress to save a bill funding foster care that had been passed by the Carter administration but nearly killed under Reagan. Jane actively favored a career over a life of domesticity and agreed that women should be compensated equally to men, but often derided feminism as a lot of nonsense. She told at least one journalist that homosexuality was unnatural, but she eagerly accepted an invitation to a screening of *Gentlemen Prefer Blondes* preceded by a Marilyn and Jane drag performance. She once described herself as a "mean-spirited, right-wing, narrow-minded, conservative Christian bigot," but close friends dismissed these comments as Jane just being her outspoken self and not expecting to be taken seriously. Jane understood the power of her celebrity to help accomplish the goals of her WAIF foundation, formed in aid of adopted children, but never seemed to grasp how her comments could affect the many nameless individuals who admired her.

Recently I was having dinner with a group of friends who were all gay men. The subject turned to Jane and one of them mentioned how he had idolized her as a youth. She had become a gay icon, largely due to the "Ain't There Anyone Here for Love?" number from *Gentlemen Prefer Blondes*, and he had gravitated to Jane, picturing her as someone fierce and fabulous who would accept him for who he was. When he later learned of her views of the LGBTQ community, he was devastated. The conversation about Jane continued, but I noticed he became silent, his expression solemn. Had Jane been

Preface

When my book on Ann Dvorak was published in 2013 after fifteen years of tears and toil, I was determined to be done with writing movie star biographies. The commitment was too great and the uphill battle too brutal. To ensure I wouldn't subject myself to another Dvorak-like odyssey, my husband even introduced me to the editor of the *My Little Pony* comic book series, and I ended up writing more than twenty-five issues, much to the delight of my young daughter. While I was able to pay homage to my love of classic film in the pony world of Equestria (King Vorak, a character I created was even mentioned in the finale of the *My Little Pony* television series), should have known the urge to write about the women of Hollywood's gold age would overcome common sense.

Only a few months after *Ann Dvorak: Hollywood's Forgotten Rebel* published, I reached out to Patrick McGilligan with the University Press Kentucky for thoughts on who would be a good subject for a second bo was leaning toward Aline MacMahon, whom I had been introduced to v researching Ann Dvorak, but Patrick was in favor of someone with name recognition than Ann, not less! Had I ever considered Jane Russ had to admit I hadn't. Sure, I adored her opposite Marilyn Monr *Gentlemen Prefer Blondes* and had managed to suffer through *The* once, but did I really want to spend a few years immersed in the world Russell? There was no denying she still had a lot of name recognition. A in addition to her film star status, a generation had grown up watchi advocate for the comfort of "full-figured gals" in Playtex bra comm was surprised to discover that other than her 1985 autobiography, r had been written about Jane. I was vaguely aware of Jane's con Christian beliefs, which generally did not line up with my own wo and which I suspected had turned off other writers. This aspect of h give me pause, but after mulling over the project for almost a yea decided this exceedingly complex woman was a challenge I wanted there, I have no doubt she would gladly have pulled up a chair and thrown back a few drinks with us. I also think she would have been genuinely perplexed as to why my friend could have been so affected by anything she had to say. She never seemed to understand how contradictory she could be, and that her words really did resonate with others.

Ultimately, my feelings for Jane are conflicted. I love watching her on-screen. There, she is a larger-than-life personality, a true product of the golden age who is often a complete joy to behold. Off-screen she is equally fascinating, often admirable and sympathetic, while at the same time perplexing and disappointing. In other words, the movie star turned out to be devastatingly human. Still, writing this book is a journey I am glad I took, and the life and career of Jane Russell are interesting and worth exploring.

While the Ann Dvorak odyssey left me emotionally drained, I felt the opposite with Jane. One of the things I found most admirable about Jane was her self-confidence. That aspect of Jane seems to have rubbed off on me, and I look forward to discovering my next book project, whatever or whoever it may be.

Introduction

Another long day in Arizona was wrapping up and Jane just wanted to go to sleep. After all, if she didn't get her nine hours in she could be a bear. However, she was well aware that here in the small Hopi village of Moenkopi, she needed to be on her best behavior, both charming and accommodating. Only nineteen, she had been given a huge break in the fall of 1940, handpicked by eccentric multimillionaire Howard Hughes to co-star in his latest big-screen production, *The Outlaw,* a retelling of the legend of outlaw Billy the Kid. With Howard Hawks, one of Hollywood's most capable and versatile directors, at the helm, Jane knew this was the opportunity of a lifetime. Normally a no-nonsense type of gal, she was starting to understand that being Howard Hughes's latest discovery was going to require tolerating a certain amount of, well, nonsense.

A group of photographers had been invited to join the cast and crew on location and it soon became apparent to most what they were there to photograph. "Pick up those buckets, Jane!" "Bend over and pretend you're using the axe, Jane!" Over and over, the photographers found creative and not so subtle ways to shoot down the front of Jane's peasant blouse, presumably at the request of Russell Birdwell, the PR guru who had been hired by Hughes to promote the film. Some of the photogs even climbed up on rocks in order to angle their cameras downward to get the perfect shot of her cleavage. Jane, young and naive, was clueless about what was taking place. "I had no idea what they were seeing," she would later say of where the photographers' cameras were pointing.[1] However, she soon got wise to what was happening.

The breaking point came when one of the photographers came to her room on location one evening. It wasn't even a room, really, just a large tent. The cameraman would later recall that when he asked Jane to put on a low-cut satin nightgown, she seemed "unfazed."[2] She obligingly struck several suggestive poses—leaning over the sink to brush her teeth, leaning forward while reading a magazine, throwing her chest out while stretching in the entryway.

Photographer Gene Lester later said Jane was unfazed by his request that she jump on the bed for a photo. This was far from the truth. (Gene Lester via Getty Images)

The shoot culminated with Jane, at the photographer's request, jumping up and down on the bed. But she was far from unfazed—after the photographer left, she finally broke. Jane knew she had been hired because of her looks, and more specifically her body, but bouncing on a bed in a dirty Arizona tent in her nightgown was too much. As panic set in and the tears came, she got dressed and went to see the one person on set she knew she could trust.

Jane had unexpectedly lost her father three and a half years earlier, and in her eyes Howard Hawks had quickly filled that role, at least for the brief time they would be working together on this film. Yes, "Father Hawks" would provide a shoulder to cry on and put a stop to this. However, when she went to her director, she was not consoled as she had hoped. Instead, Hawks looked impassively at Jane's tear-stained face and responded with zero emotion. "Look, you're a big girl, and you've got to protect yourself. If someone asks you to do *anything* that's against your better judgment, say NO! Loud and clear. . . . You're in charge of you. No one else."[3]

With those few words, Howard Hawks freed Jane Russell. She was smart enough to know that her physical attributes would be her bread and butter if she continued a career in films, but she was now empowered. She was the one who could—and would—draw the line, the one who would determine when enough was enough, even when it came to Howard Hughes. Jane would never again allow Hollywood to make her feel that uncomfortable.

By the early 1950s, Jane Russell should have been forgotten: at best a curious footnote in the annals of Hollywood history, and at worst a complete joke. Her career was launched on what is arguably the most notorious advertising campaign in cinema history, for Howard Hughes's *The Outlaw*. Posters for the film proclaimed the brooding brunette heroine of the film to be "mean . . . moody . . . magnificent," and advertisements invited filmgoers to "tussle with Russell." Completed by early 1941, *The Outlaw* didn't premiere until 1943, and its wide release was delayed; the film gradually rolled out between 1946 and 1950. Throughout the 1940s, Jane Russell was nicknamed the "motionless picture actress" and would have only three films projected in theaters the entire decade. With such an inauspicious and prolonged start to a career, most aspiring actresses would have given up and faded away. But not Jane. Instead she carved out a place for herself in Hollywood and became one of its more recognizable figures.

Confident, unapologetic, and a mass of contradictions, Jane was once described by an interviewer as a person who "says what she thinks and has about as much subterfuge as a mirror." That same writer went on to say of Jane's famous face, "In repose it is aloof, giving the split second impression that this is a haughty creature. The illusion is dispelled the minute she speaks, and then her face is saucy and friendly and filled with humor. The contrast makes an interesting face, but the most fascinating thing about it is the smolder. That's the only word for it—a kind of smolder that comes from the eyes, top-tilted and dark amber in color, that seem to reflect an inner fire."[4] Jane was such a force of nature that she could hold her own on-screen opposite the likes of Robert Mitchum, Clark Gable, Vincent Price, Bob Hope, and Marilyn Monroe. More a movie personality than a serious actress, Jane could electrify a screen and was a true star of the old studio system. Despite a movie career that was stalled for nearly a decade, Jane's filmography is respectable, if not sterling, and she had the opportunity to work with some of Hollywood's most talented directors, including Howard Hawks, Raoul Walsh, Nicholas Ray, and Josef von Sternberg.

Over half a century after appearing in her last film, Jane Russell still has name recognition, but for the casual film fan, she is primarily known for three things: the uproar over *The Outlaw* and its signature images of Jane snarling while lounging on piles of hay; co-starring with Marilyn Monroe in *Gentlemen Prefer Blondes;* and Playtex bra commercials. All three are certainly milestones in the varied life and career of Jane Russell, but there is more to her than an often-touted 38-24-26 figure and a slew of adjectives used to describe her bustline.

Though never overly ambitious, Jane grew restless if not busy. During those early years when her film career was at a standstill, she transformed herself into a musical performer, a genre she pursued until the end of her life, appearing on the air alongside such notable radio personalities as Kay Kyser and Bob Hope, recording singles, and singing live. Later she would become a familiar actress in live theater, including one turn on Broadway in Stephen Sondheim's *Company.* Jane was also comfortable with television, appearing on scripted shows as well as on programs as varied as *Person to Person, What's My Line?,* and *Lifestyles of the Rich and Famous.*

In direct contrast to her many smoldering on-screen portrayals, Jane Russell was a woman of deep religious faith. Never subscribing to any particular denomination (though she was known to speak in tongues), she proudly and publicly heralded her devotion to the Bible and the Lord. Later, she would have a secondary career as a Christian vocalist, recording albums and touring. It can be difficult to reconcile how this devout off-screen personality could coexist with the cinema sexpot persona promoted by Howard Hughes, but Jane herself had no trouble managing the contradiction because a successful career in Hollywood enabled her to advocate for something she cared deeply about: orphaned children.

The side effects of an abortion in 1942 left Jane unable to conceive later on. She would ultimately adopt three children with husband Robert Waterfield, but the drawn-out process of adoption in the United States left Jane frustrated, leading her to visit orphanages overseas. These efforts were thwarted due to laws restricting international adoption. Jane did an end run around the rules, bringing home a boy surrendered to her in England by a desperate mother, an action that caused an international uproar and prompted the FBI to open a file on her. The whole experience left Jane so enraged that she created the WAIF foundation, which for many years served as the fund-raising arm of the International Social Service (ISS) agency. WAIF turned out to be Jane's true calling. During its forty-plus years, the organization raised hundreds of thousands of dollars, lobbied Congress to change laws, and matched tens of thousands of orphaned children with families. For Jane, the success of WAIF overshadowed any on-screen achievement.

On the surface, Jane Russell seems to have lived a charmed life, but it was one that contained many obstacles, and Jane was never completely free of demons. In what seemed like a storybook marriage, the movie star wed a professional football player. It was a pairing rooted largely in animal magnetism, and while the marriage did last over twenty years, it was fraught with friction, frustration, and at times physical abuse. When her second marriage was cut tragically short, the blow nearly destroyed her. Her third husband proved to be a savior of sorts, but Jane never really recovered from the loss of her second partner, and her methods of coping sometimes yielded unfortunate consequences.

Despite her personal demons, however, the life and career of Jane Russell are full and fascinating. Yes, she did know Marilyn and had one of the longer (platonic) relationships with Howard Hughes, but there is so much more to explore. More than just the "mean . . . moody . . . magnificent" broad film fans were introduced to with *The Outlaw*.

1

From Bemidji to Burbank

Jane Russell may have lived in Bemidji only for nine days following her birth at St. Anthony's Hospital on Dewey Avenue, but the small Minnesota town had no qualms later claiming her as a native daughter. Jane's parents, Geraldine Jacobi and Roy Russell, had been living in Edmonton, Canada, but for the birth of her firstborn daughter, Geraldine sought the comfort of the Jacobi family vacation home across the border. When the due date neared, she packed her bags, leaving Roy behind to continue earning a living at a brokerage firm. Once in Bemidji, she waited . . . and waited . . . for a baby who did not seem terribly concerned with being born. As the due date came and went, Geraldine remarked to the doctor, "It seems like nine months since I last saw my husband and this monster has nine legs and never stops kicking!"[1] On June 21, 1921, at 6:15 a.m., the "monster" finally arrived, all nine pounds and eleven ounces of her thrashing and screaming.[2] As her mother later commented, "I think she has been kicking ever since."[3] Jane Russell had entered the world.

Jane's full legal name has often been cited as Ernestine Jane Geraldine Russell, with her known name sandwiched between those of her mother and her beloved Aunt Ernie. Perhaps she added the other names in tribute to these two women who played such a dominant role in her life, or maybe the change was the whim of a Hollywood press agent in 1941. No matter how the extended moniker came into being, on that summer morning in 1921 the baby was named simply Jane Russell because, as Geraldine would later recall, she thought it would "look well in lights!"[4]

Jane was reportedly named after stage actress Jane Cowl, and while this tie to the theater may have had some influence on Geraldine, it's also true that the name Jane appeared multiple times on the Jacobi family tree. Jane Strode, the original Jane in the family, made the journey from England to Canada sometime in the mid-1840s. According to Jacobi family lore, Strode's husband dropped dead of exhaustion shortly after the family arrived in Montreal, leaving his widow in a foreign land with two young daughters.

Desperate and with no means to get back to England, Strode remarried within weeks, much to the disapproval of her English family members, who disinherited her and used the money to build a church in Shepton Mallet.[5] Strode's daughter, also named Jane, married David Hyatt when she was sixteen; the union quickly produced three daughters and a son, including Jane Russell's maternal grandmother, Amelia Hyatt, who was born in Kingston, Ontario, in 1871.[6]

Amelia would marry Gustave Jacobi, who was born to Prussian immigrant Ernest Jacobi and Ellen Stevenson of Ireland. Ernest was the son of renowned artist Otto Reinhold Jacobi (1812–1901), who at one point was the Prussian court painter. When Otto's prominence in the court diminished and it became apparent that his son might be called to serve in the Prussian military, Otto made arrangements for the family to immigrate to North America. He became a celebrated artist in Montreal, but later moved the family to the small township of Ardoch, Ontario, near Malcolm Lake. Across the lake resided the Stevenson clan, which had received land as a grant from Queen Victoria. The Jacobi and Stevenson families became doubly intertwined: siblings Ernest and Louisa Jacobi married siblings Ellen and James Stevenson. Gustave was born in October 1866, almost nine months to the day following the wedding Ernest and Ellen.[7]

The Jacobis and Stevensons, taking advantage of land grants being issued by the US government, relocated to North Dakota in the 1880s. Both young families first settled in Grand Forks and then later moved north, where they founded the town of Ardoch, named after their previous home in Ontario. James Stevenson served as the town's first postmaster and Ernest Jacobi operated the local store. When Amelia Hyatt came to Ardoch to visit the Stevensons' daughter Janet, it was only natural that she would socialize with the Jacobis. And so Amelia Hyatt (eighteen) met and fell for Gustave Jacobi (twenty-three). The pair married in 1889 in Amelia's hometown of Kingston, but set up housekeeping back in North Dakota, eventually settling in Grand Forks. Their first child, Jane's mother Geraldine, came two years later, followed by five more children between 1893 and 1905.

Being the oldest of six could certainly be trying at times, but Geraldine valued the large noisy household and would pass this appreciation of a big family on to her only daughter. She was especially close to her sister Ernestine, or Ernie, two years her junior. Ernie was high-spirited, daring, and dramatic, while Geraldine was more reserved, keeping a watchful eye on her younger sister, and instead saving her own love of drama for the stage. An especially

Jane, age three, with her mother, Geraldine Jacobi, at their Burbank home, circa 1925.

gifted orator, she won declamation contests in high school, which encouraged her parents to enroll her at the Emerson College of Oratory in Boston. Ernie would be sent to the Frances Shimer Academy for young ladies in Chicago. In Boston Geraldine began studying painting with artist Mary Bradish Titcomb, an interest Jane Russell would also later adopt. In exchange for the lessons, Geraldine modeled for Titcomb, who dressed her in a "beautiful blue-green silk Mandarin coat, with a little Chinese hat to match, and placed a tea cup and saucer in my lap."[8] The resulting painting, entitled *A Portrait of Geraldine J.*, was displayed in the Corcoran Gallery of Art in New York, the World's Fair in San Francisco, and later, after President Woodrow Wilson purchased it, in the White House. Today the painting is on display in Wilson's former home in Washington, DC.

In between college terms, Geraldine would reunite with the family, frequently catching up with the Jacobis at their summer vacation home in Bemidji or reconnecting with relatives in Montreal. During Geraldine's senior year at Emerson, famed stage actor George Arliss came to Boston in his signature role of Disraeli in the play of the same name. The production, at the Plymouth Theatre, required a large number of extras, so students at local theater schools were tapped to fill these roles. Geraldine was selected to appear onstage as one of the "Diplomats, English and Foreign Naval and Military Officers, Lords and Ladies, Liveried Servants, etc."[9] Specifically, Geraldine played a lady-in-waiting, which she described as "the most wonderful experience of my young life."[10] From there Geraldine launched a modest career as a stage actress, appearing with stock companies in both New York and Redding, Pennsylvania. Her career started showing some promise when she received a credited part in a traveling production of a show titled *Daddy Long Legs*, which, according to its advertisements, was guaranteed to make viewers "want to give to the apple women on the corner, or pencil vendor a piece of change after having seen it."[11] The show made stops in, among other places, Ohio, Illinois, Indiana, and Maine. While the *Daddy Long Legs* company was in Kalamazoo, Michigan, Geraldine managed to squeeze in a marriage ceremony to Roy Russell.

Roy William Russell was a second-generation American and native of Grand Forks, North Dakota. His father, William Douglas Russell, had been born in Embro, Ontario, to Alexander and Elsie Russell of Scotland. Following William's birth in 1860, the family migrated to North Dakota and operated a farm, where Alexander ruled with an iron fist that frequently made contact with William. One day when William was seventeen, he decided he'd endured enough abuse and walked off the farm, never to return.[12] He made his way to Casselton, North Dakota, where he encountered Lena Abentroth. Born in Poland in 1865, Lena had come to North Dakota with her parents when she was thirteen. William was instantly smitten with her and married her in 1884. Early on in their marriage, William had eased his way into a profitable liquor business, something his straitlaced wife was opposed to. To appease her, the pair moved to a farm in Grand Forks, though William kept one hand in the liquor business until Prohibition put a stop to that. In Grand Forks the Russells expanded their family with the birth of Roy in 1890.

Growing up in Grand Forks, Roy Russell and Geraldine Jacobi were certainly aware of each other. After all, Gustave Jacobi was William Russell's banker and, as Amelia Jacobi noted, he was "the handsomest man in town."[13] As adolescents the eldest children of the Jacobi and Russell clans became high school sweethearts, though no one seemed to think the relationship was serious. When Geraldine moved to Boston to attend Emerson, she presumably was leaving Roy Russell behind forever, though the pair exchanged birthday cards each year, having been born a year and two days apart. Roy had been conscripted into the army during World War I, and he and

Jane with her father, Roy Russell, circa 1925.

Geraldine met again when the *Daddy Long Legs* company arrived in Kalamazoo near the camp where he was stationed. He had the audacity to show up at Geraldine's room, where the sight of him in uniform caused her to faint. Once she recovered, Roy revealed that he had never stopped loving her—she had spoiled him for any other woman and he had been keeping her photo facedown in his trunk in a futile attempt to forget her. Fearful he would be sent into battle at any moment, he asked her to marry him that very night. She accepted, although she had some secret reservations: "He didn't lack courage — he was just void of ambition."[14]

Each wrote of their intentions to their parents, hoping to receive family blessings. Instead Roy's mother expressed outrage that he would consider marrying an actress, proclaiming she would rather see her son in a coffin. Geraldine didn't fare much better. Viewing Roy as "no good," Gustave wept when he received his daughter's telegram, shot off a quick response that he did not approve of hasty war marriages, and ordered her back home.[15] Fearing that Geraldine's parents could probably talk her out of marrying him, Roy took no chances and wasted no time. He met Geraldine after a performance in March 1918 with a marriage license in hand, a taxi waiting, and an Episcopal minister standing by. They were wed around midnight.

One night together was all the newlyweds had. The next morning Roy brought Geraldine to the train station so she could depart with the theater company. The minister and his wife also showed up to give their blessing: "Good-bye Mrs. Russell and God bless you!"[16] Roy went back to the camp. During a lull in the touring schedule around Easter, the new Mrs. Russell returned to Grand Forks, where the Jacobi family was waiting with open arms and wedding gifts, including a diamond ring from Gustave. The Jacobi family bonds were tied too tightly to be broken that easily.

In the ensuing months, Geraldine visited Roy in between theater engagements until the influenza pandemic of 1918 reached epic proportions, causing theaters to be shut down. Geraldine returned to Grand Forks to wait out the epidemic, and soon discovered she was pregnant. By the time performances were allowed to resume, she was visibly showing. Describing herself as a "very dumpy person," Geraldine was unable to continue in the role of Julia Pendleton.[17] Although sorry to leave the stage, Geraldine was thrilled by the impending birth, which was news that became brighter when the Armistice was declared before Roy shipped out to Europe.

Finally able to start their life together, the couple soon relocated from Grand Forks to Edmonton, Canada, where Roy had secured employment at a brokerage firm, Mason & Hickey. Geraldine was reunited with her beloved sister Ernestine, who had recently wed her own high school sweetheart, Bob Henry. She too was expecting her first child. The Jacobi girls were once again together and, for a time, living under the same roof. Each gave birth, just days apart, to baby boys they nicknamed Billie. By the next year, happiness had turned to tragedy when both babies died prematurely, Geraldine and Roy's

Jane, age two, during a trip to North Dakota to visit family.

from infantile convulsions brought on by gastroenteritis.[18] While crawling around their property, the boy had put something rotten in his mouth and had ingested part of it before Geraldine was able to remove it.

Following the devastating loss of her golden-haired firstborn, Geraldine was beside herself with grief. Despite advice from actress and friend Minnie Maddern Fiske that she fill the void by having another child, Geraldine decided she needed the distraction of the stage and prepared to leave for New York, where Fiske had offered to introduce Geraldine to her agent. But before she could make the trip, Geraldine discovered she was pregnant again. As it would turn out, her acting career was effectively over, though during the course of the pregnancy, she was invited to give recitals at various churches and universities, something she believed ingrained a love of performing in Jane. Ultimately, as her due date approached, she traveled to Bemidji to spend those last weeks of pregnancy in familiar surroundings waiting for Jane to finally decide to enter the world. Roy and Geraldine would go on to have four more kids, all sons. As the only girl, Jane would always be referred to as "Daughter" by the family.

After Jane was born, Roy quit his job at the brokerage firm, and he and Geraldine got into the construction business as suppliers. The venture went badly, and the young family ended up declaring bankruptcy. Things had been equally difficult for Ernestine and Bob Henry, who packed their bags and decided to try their luck in sunny Southern California. Figuring they had nothing else to lose, Roy, Geraldine, and baby Jane sailed from Vancouver to San Francisco. There they secured a Ford "Tin Lizzie" and drove to Los Angeles, arriving in April 1922. For two people raised on the North Dakota prairie, the coasts, mountains, and redwoods of California were jarring. Geraldine recalled being unimpressed with Southern California in comparison to the Bay Area because it was less green and a rush of floods that season was bewildering. Still, the orange groves were amazing and the sun shone warmly, so the couple had no regrets about the move, even though Roy had a hard time finding work at first. Until they got on their feet, the Russells stayed in the guesthouse at Ernestine and Bob's place in Glendale.

Eventually Roy secured a position as an office manager with the Andrew Jergens Company. Soon the family was in a position to purchase a home. Geraldine happened upon a small house for sale in the far end of Burbank near the hills. Located at 1018 Angeleno Avenue, the house was modest and lacked many modern amenities, but to Geraldine, "it was cute as a bug's ear; and it has a little fenced back yard."[19] The couple paid $5,000 for the house and moved in shortly thereafter. Young Jane was thrilled when Roy constructed a sandbox for her in the little yard.

In the four years they had been married, Roy and Geraldine had endured trial and tragedy as they sought to establish their place in a postwar world. Now at last, in the San Fernando Valley, they felt secure enough to lay down the roots that would guide and shape their young daughter.

2

Valley Girl

They may not have realized it at the time, but when the Russells relocated to the San Fernando Valley, it was to become a true home for them. This is where four more children would be born and raised, where Geraldine would become firmly rooted in the community, and where Roy would live out the remainder of his short life. Even after emerging on the national stage as a movie star, Jane would remain in the Valley; she resided there for nearly six decades.

Jane's precociousness was evident early on: when she was three and asked about her age, she would respond that she was actually five, already displaying the cool confidence that later came through in her screen roles. Geraldine, drawing on her previous experience, started giving private elocution and drama lessons, work she genuinely loved. Young Jane would often sit in on the lessons, intently watching Geraldine and her students. If one of the pupils had trouble with a particular inflection, Jane was always quick to chime in, pitch perfect. Whenever Jane herself was in the mood to perform, a favorite was a number called "The Dead Pussycat," which was always accompanied with tears rolling down her face.[1]

Firmly settled in Southern California, the Russells spent the rest of the decade growing their family. Between 1924 and 1929, Geraldine would give birth to four sons: Thomas (1924), Kenneth (1925), James "Jamie" (1927), and Wallace "Wally" (1929). Jane's four younger brothers would keep her grounded, never allowing her to become conceited or bigheaded even after she became a glamorous movie star recognized around the world. It's true they may have dished out good-natured chiding about her film star status but, as one of Jane's cousins later remembered, "They looked up to her, they loved her. She always called them 'buddy,' 'little buddy.' They adored her."[2] Despite this mutual affection, sharing a house with four boys could certainly have its trying times. When Geraldine took the brood grocery shopping, she'd sometimes run a second errand with Jane, leaving the boys in the car with the food.

Jane the tomboy with an unidentified friend.

They would promptly devour any sweets their mother had bought. Jane would see the empty bags and burst out crying, "Now you see why I hate my brothers!" For the most part, though, fights between the siblings would be smoothed over quickly—and usually by Jane. "Many of the squabbles she settled herself," Geraldine recalled. "Squabbles I knew nothing about."[3] Despite her later status as an international sex symbol, Jane was a tomboy in her youth, more comfortable in jeans and sweatshirts than satin and sequins. "I played with the boys on their baseball teams," she later recalled, "and rode horses with them generally in one of my brothers' shirts and a pair of slacks."[4]

Ernestine and Bob Henry had been just as busy procreating, eventually outpacing the Russells by having seven children total. Like Jane, her cousin Patricia Henry, or "Pat," was the family's only daughter, so she and Jane felt like sisters, though Geraldine and Ernestine weren't always sure what to make of their two girls. "I was more of a tomboy than Jane, because her brothers were younger than she was and some of mine were older," Pat later mused. "But our mothers were ladies to their fingertips and they really didn't know how to handle these two girls that weren't 'ladies.'"[5] Pat Henry would be the first of many women Jane would forge a tight bond with during her life. The Russell and Henry families were extremely close, preferring to spend all their time together, so much so, in fact, that when Roy gave Geraldine $50 one summer to rent a cabin in the mountains, she and the kids instead went and stayed with the Henrys in Glendale until the money was gone.[6]

When Jane was old enough, she was enrolled in Joaquin Miller Grammar School, less than a mile from the Burbank home. After only a week of kindergarten, Jane's teacher contacted Geraldine for a conference. As the big sister, it seemed, Jane had grown accustomed to being in charge. Said the exasperated teacher, "She will not mind her own business, nor will she keep her hands off the other children; she goes from table to table saying, 'No, no, dearie, you don't do it that way.' The first thing the poor child has to learn is to let the other children alone."[7] This doesn't seem to be a lesson Jane ever took completely to heart, as she was known to completely redecorate the home of a friend or family member—not because she'd been asked to do so, but because she believed it needed to be done.

Joaquin Miller Grammar School was where Jane received her first taste of acting; she participated in the school plays "without being urged."[8] Geraldine may have dreamed of her daughter's name in lights, but she kept that to herself. "I guess Mother always knew that I'd end up acting," Jane once said. "But she never tried to force me to learn anything."[9] Jane also tried her hand at dancing, studying under Cecelia May Fisher, whom Jane recalled as being the "best teacher in Burbank." However, the lessons were short-lived. "It didn't take me long to realize that I would never set the world on fire as a dancer."[10]

Geraldine may not have pushed drama on her daughter, but music was another matter. As Jane later said, "She has never told any of us kids what we were to do—except to learn to play some musical instrument. I play the piano after a fashion, and all the boys are talented musicians. Music is just about Mother's main hobby. Since she had the beginning of a fair orchestra right in her own home, she invited some of the neighborhood kids to join us. And the first thing you know we were giving concerts all over the Valley, for ladies' clubs, the Y.M.C.A. and private parties."[11] Music was indeed a family affair. When guests of music instructor Susie Allen Olmstead attended her students' recitals, they were entertained by all five Russell children.[12]

By the end of the 1920s, the Russell family was firmly rooted in Southern California. Even the stock market crash in 1929 did not have an impact on the family fortunes; Roy's position with the Jergens Company remained stable. Roy and Geraldine may have stopped having kids, but that did not stop the household from expanding. Following the death of Roy's mother Lena, his father William relocated and moved in with the family. This addition stretched the Burbank house beyond its limits, and the Russells realized they had to move to a place with much more space. Little Jane Russell was going to be leaving the only home she'd ever known.

In 1933 the Russell family moved from a small house on an equally small lot in Burbank to seven acres in nearby Van Nuys, which at the time was sparsely populated and made up of agricultural ranches. The parcel, near Woodman Avenue and Sherman Way, backed up against the Tujunga Wash, which had left the land vulnerable to be used as a dumping ground for rusty cars and other debris. Geraldine shrugged her shoulders at the land's imperfections and declared it perfect. After all, they needed to excavate in order to build a house, so the dug-up dirt could be used to cover the trash. "You *would* pick out a dump!" was Roy's reaction, but the dump was indeed covered up and in its place rose a single-story house, designed to look like a Mexican hacienda with palm trees planted around to give it a patented, yet non-native, Los Angeles flair.[13] They named the place La Posada, Spanish for "journey's end." Or so Geraldine thought. "La posada" actually translates as "the inn," but with eight people in the household the name wasn't inappropriate.

The early 1930s were an idyllic time for the family at La Posada. Roy had been promoted to general manager of Andrew Jergens West Coast plant; so despite the Great Depression, the family was fairly well off. Geraldine and Roy each had a car and a palomino saddlebred; the horses were named Flash and Silver. For the kids there were two cow ponies, and the family also kept cows and chickens. Managing such a large household was so great a task that

At eleven, Jane was already showing signs of the confident beauty movie audiences would come to know.

a married couple was employed full-time to help Geraldine. During the summer the boys would sleep under the stars, and Jane had fond memories of riding the horses for miles up and down the wash. She became so proficient at riding that it never posed a problem later on when she was required to be on horseback for a film. However, whenever Roy and Geraldine went riding together, he did not want anyone else to accompany them. With such a packed house, it was the only time he had his wife to himself.

There was no shortage of stability and love in the family, even if the patriarch had a hard time verbalizing it. Once, when Geraldine and the kids had been vacationing in Bemidji for an extended period of time, they came home to a house that had been completely repainted. "I'm not going to tell you that I love you," Roy stated. "I'm painting it on the wall."[14] On another occasion, Geraldine and Ernestine took the kids to stay at Crater Camp in Malibu Canyon in order to escape the heat of the San Fernando Valley. Roy warned his wife that she'd be too scared and lonesome to make it through the night. According to Geraldine,

> When we were all in bed and the tent was locked, I heard a car stop by the creek. Someone was coming down the path. My heart stood still; then in the moonlight, I saw it was Roy. He just about ate me up. *He* was the one who couldn't stand it! We dragged a mattress outside and slept on the ground under the trees. Oh, it was wonderful—the sky, the stars and the trees! It was at times like these that I was assured of the freshness of his love, for he was one who could not easily say the things a woman longs to hear.[15]

Jane's first marriage would find her with a man who had an equally hard time expressing his feelings.

Jane's shapely figure would ultimately catapult her to film stardom, but growing up, she was so thin and tall that it made her self-conscious. "Jane came home from school," Geraldine remembered, "and announced to my surprise that all the sleeves of her dresses were to come down to her wrist and all the skirts were to come to her ankles. What now? There was no explanation offered. Sometime later, I discovered some boy had laughed at her and called her a rake, so she was now going to cover up those long gangly legs and arms."[16] During this time Jane was such a tomboy that after the theatrical version of *Little Women* was released in 1933, some of the kids at school started calling Jane "Jo," which was okay by her. Jane was never one to be starstruck but was so impressed with Katharine Hepburn's performance as Jo March that she wrote the actress a fan letter, though she never received a response.

As the eldest child, Jane was certainly expected to help her mom out with the Russell boys, but she didn't let any obligations at La Posada put a damper on her fun. After starting the seventh grade in Van Nuys, Jane became close friends with a girl in her class named Pat Alexander. For a time, the pair became inseparable, planning near-identical outfits in an attempt to look like

Jane and Geraldine at La Posada, the family home in Van Nuys. Mother and daughter would always have a close relationship.

twins. They would often go for long hikes in the Hollywood Hills, helping themselves to the milk left on the porches of the small vacation cabins that peppered the landscape at the time. Occasionally Geraldine would decide movies were a bad influence and off limits, and that's when Jane and Pat would ditch school, make their way over to Hollywood, and spend the day at a theater, often viewing three double features. Once they even made it to the RKO lot by hopping a fence that separated the studio from what is now called the Hollywood Forever Cemetery. Little did Jane know then the role that studio would play in her future.

Even though Jane was a tomboy who more than held her own in a house full of brothers, from a young age she desperately wanted to fall in love, later noting that she was "born married. It was all I waited for."[17] She would often lie on the grass at La Posada at night looking for shooting stars and making wishes to find the love of her life. Even so, the first time a boy tried to kiss her, during a weekend party, she froze and then got Pat to make a hasty exit with her. It was at that same party that a fourteen-year-old Jane first laid her eyes on Robert "Bob" Waterfield, a junior at Van Nuys High School. This first sight of the athletic Waterfield sent shivers up and down Jane's spine in a way she had not experienced before. However, as she watched him standing at his post by a doorway as a steady stream of girls, one by one, wandered up and then briefly disappeared outside with him, Jane was less enchanted.

Jane had initially felt out of place at Van Nuys High School, but finally found her way. She became more involved in school, even joining the drama club. On one occasion she co-starred as Aunt Elizabeth in a Jack Benny spoof the school produced.[18] Another play, entitled *Short Sleeves*, co-starred Jane's classmate James Dougherty, who a few short years later would marry a sixteen-year-old waif named Norma Jeane Baker, now known the world over as Marilyn Monroe.[19] For a brief period toward the end of high school, Jane and two classmates formed a singing trio called the Pitch Pipers that performed on the local KRDK radio station.[20]

At some point during high school, Pat Alexander and her family moved away. The loss of her closest friend threw Jane into a tailspin, so Geraldine shipped her daughter off sixty-five miles east to a farm in Fontana where Aunt Ernestine was now living with Bob and the kids. The Henrys had not weathered the Depression as well as the Russells and were even forced to borrow money from Roy and Geraldine. When they could no longer afford to live in Los Angeles County, they purchased cheap land in Fontana. When Jane became despondent, Geraldine figured Aunt Ernie would keep Daughter preoccupied with the many chores needed to keep the farm running, not to mention attending to its nine inhabitants. Plus she would be able to spend time with her cousin Pat, with whom she still remained close.

The family was glad to have her, though Ernestine admitted Jane could sometimes be a handful. She'd often find ways to cut corners on chores, such as piling things up high in one corner rather than putting them away or scraping food off dirty dishes and stacking them at the bottom of the refrigerator rather than washing them. When Ernestine smelled smoke on Jane's breath, she'd order the purse opened—and the cigarettes would be confiscated without comment and flushed down the toilet. "To make a big deal out of it would have been foolish," said Ernestine.[21] Jane and Pat also engaged in a bizarre game of "playing dead," in which they would lie lifelessly on Highway 99 until an approaching car would come to a screeching halt. "Meantime," Ernestine later recalled, "they'd scamper off to the orange grove, giggling their fool heads off while the petrified passengers hunted for sprawling bodies. This was their notion of a rib-tickling joke."[22]

Jane stayed with the Henrys long enough to be enrolled in school, which was turning out to be not her forte. She'd often ditch class with cousin Pat and hitch a ride to the more exciting nearby city of San Bernardino. In most instances they would get caught, though Ernestine often punished only her own daughter because "Pat taking the rap made Jane feel terrible."[23] Despite the workload and Ernestine's discipline, Jane enjoyed her time in Fontana—it would not be the last time she found refuge there. Still, Jane was happy to return to La Posada, where she was greeted warmly by the family, including Grandpa Russell, who often served as a movie theater companion.

The summer of 1937 lazily wore on. Jane remembered that season being the one in which she was instructed to eat dinner at the dining room table instead of in the breakfast room with her rowdy brothers. Geraldine had decided it was time for her tomboy of a daughter to finally start acting like a lady. This was also the summer Grandpa Russell taught her how to drive a car. Despite its pleasant beginnings, however, that summer would come to a nightmarish end, irrevocably altering the lives of the Russell family in the worst possible way.

3

Daughter Grows Up

After the birth of Thomas, Geraldine had a spiritual awakening of sorts, something that would come to dominate her life as well as her children's. She started reading the Bible frequently, attributing any positive happening in her life to the Lord's work. When she was pregnant with her youngest, Geraldine began experiencing severe intestinal issues that persisted even after the baby was born. Eventually she visited Lilian Yeomans, a physician turned drug addict turned faith healer, whom Geraldine believed cured her. From then on she stopped seeing medical doctors, instead putting her fate in the Lord's hands. That faith would come to be tested.

In June 1937 Roy Russell started experiencing extreme stomach discomfort. Even though Geraldine had decided to put all her faith in the Lord in times of medical distress, Roy went to a steady stream of doctors before finally being diagnosed with a gallstone too big to pass on its own. Surgery to remove the stone was scheduled on June 30, and even though Roy was not yet fifty, he was fearful, commenting to his wife, "The Lord will heal you and the children, but He won't heal me."[1]

The night before the surgery, extended family was invited to La Posada for an evening of food and songs. When Roy and Geraldine went riding in the wash, they even let the kids come along. In the morning Roy insisted on preparing for the worst, advising Geraldine on how to handle their finances if he did not make it through the surgery. While under sedation and on his way into the operating room, he grabbed Geraldine's hand and said, "Kiddy, I'm too young to die." Geraldine responded, "Well you're not going to die, dear. But remember that whether we live or whether we sleep, we are the Lord's. You love the Lord and I love the Lord and we belong to each other through eternity!" Holding his wife's eyes with his own, Roy answered, "I hope you will remember that."[2]

The surgery was successful and after a week in the hospital, Roy was allowed to return to La Posada, where he convalesced under the constant

Jane during her junior or senior year at Van Nuys High School.

supervision of nurses. A little over two weeks later, the nurses felt Roy no longer needed professional care. On the evening of July 17, Roy found himself in
pain, with a fluctuating temperature. Geraldine monitored his condition
throughout the night. In the early morning hours, he started having trouble
breathing. As Geraldine later recalled, "I crooked my arm under his head and
raised it so that he could breathe better and, instantly, he had a stroke. I

couldn't look at him. His eyes bulged. His tongue flew out, and his face turned purple. I laid him quickly down, ran to the telephone, and called the doctor."[3] It was no use. Roy Russell was dead at age forty-seven.

The doctor arrived immediately and confirmed the death, ordering a nurse to stay with Geraldine. Instead she proclaimed she was fine and got in the car to drive to her parents' house. Amelia and Gustave had relocated to Glendale to be near their children and grandchildren, something Geraldine was extremely grateful for at that moment. Before reaching the Jacobis', she stopped off at the home of one of Roy's colleagues, notifying them of his death and asking for prayers. When she finally arrived at her parents' with the news, both Gustave and Amelia broke down in tears. Whatever misgivings they had had about their daughter's choice nearly twenty years earlier had faded, and they now grieved openly. Geraldine remained stoic. After her visit with her parents, she made the long trip home to La Posada, where she would need to inform her five children that their father was no longer alive. When she arrived they were all awake and eating breakfast. Geraldine started the conversation by extolling the virtues of the Lord and acknowledging all he had provided. She then let them know that the Lord "has taken our daddy."[4] The younger boys didn't understand the euphemism, so when one asked for an explanation, Jane burst out, "He's dead, you fool!"[5] This response was something they would all always remember. Jane had turned sixteen less than a month before. Wally, the youngest of the brood, was eight.

At the funeral Geraldine wore white and insisted the children do so as well, believing Roy would not have wanted them to mourn. Throughout the whole process Geraldine had remained calm, claiming to have achieved an inner peace. Her behavior was odd enough to prompt Ernestine to comment, "You don't look like anyone's widow. You look like someone's bride. Your face is glowing."[6] That evening Jane called a friend and asked him to go riding with her in the wash. They rode in the moonlight for hours, not saying a word. "The huge full moon did its best to throw a silver sheen on the black landscape, but to me everything seemed dark with grief."[7] A family friend chastised her for not staying at home with the family, but Geraldine understood.

Still retaining her iron control, Geraldine began a practical assessment of her financial options, which included cashing in Roy's life insurance policy. Instead of a lump sum, she opted to collect a monthly amount of only $137 in order to make the money last as long as possible. She also needed to sell the palominos, whose upkeep could not be sustained on the reduced income. It was only when Geraldine was washing Roy's saddle for the last time that she finally broke down, weeping as she never had before. "I felt as if I were selling Roy instead of the saddle," she later remembered.[8]

After the horses were sold, "we lost the lovely couple that took care of us," Jane recalled.[9] Prior to his death Roy had advised Geraldine to sell La Posada, but she was determined to hang onto it as long as possible. Besides, the ranch contained an orchard with plenty of fruit-bearing trees, and they had kept the cows so the kids could have milk, so at least the land could sustain the family. This meant that all effort was directed to the outside of the ranch while the interior of the house became, as Geraldine put it, "unspeakably dirty. But all the land was irrigated. All was cultivated. Everything was provided for outside."[10] Initially, the family tried to raise some extra cash by renting a room to a "business man" for $17.50 a month.[11] However, when a local minister put Geraldine in touch with a couple looking for a place to house their elderly blind mother, she agreed, using the $50 a month rent she received to hire a cook. This proved to be an excellent move. As Jane admitted, her mother "was never a very good cook." This lack of culinary talent was most definitely a family trait. Jane would always quickly fess up to being a terrible cook, often joking, "The first thing I say to a man is 'Can you cook?' because if he can't, we can't go any further."[12] Soon an older German woman moved in, along with Geraldine's elderly Aunt Jane, and the cook's son, who had suffered some mental instability but thrived at the ranch. "So we were a motley lot," Geraldine remembered, "all of us living on one hundred and thirty seven dollars a month. But we were all blessed, and the Lord provided for the three old ladies, the cook, her son, my five children and myself."[13]

With the paid domestic help gone, the kids needed to pitch in around the house more than they were used to. This was especially true of Jane as the oldest: it fell on her to take on the Sisyphean task of doing the laundry and ironing for a home overflowing with people. La Posada did not have modern luxuries like an electric washer and dryer, so Jane spent one precious day of each weekend bent over a wash bin. She was irritated by the lost day more than the work itself, which she had grown accustomed to while staying at Aunt Ernie's in Fontana.

Despite the devastating loss and increased responsibilities at home, Jane was blossoming from a skinny tomboy into a beautiful and vivacious young woman. She continued to be active at Van Nuys High School and developed a core group of girlfriends with whom she would remain close her entire life. Having to hold her own in a house full of younger brothers had kept Jane level and given her a confidence that seldom wavered when it came to inter-

Jane with brothers (*left to right*) Tommy, Wally, Ken, and Jamie at La Posada. Jane would always credit them with keeping her grounded once she became an international movie star.

acting with other people. As her cousin Pat Henry relayed, "She has a magnetism and a charisma that you just couldn't believe. We would go up to Lake Arrowhead just looking for something to do when the next thing you know she's met somebody and we'd be tearing it in their sailboat because she never met a stranger."[14] Jane got along famously with men, not only because of her looks but because of her ability to be so at ease with them. Jane viewed growing up in a predominantly male household as "lovely because I understand men. I understand boys. They can cry, they can have the same feelings that women do."[15] At the same time, Jane never had trouble fostering and maintaining meaningful relationships with other women, though "the women that make a big fuss and carry on a lot bore me to tears because I was raised with boys."[16] Despite Jane's general ease with men, there turned out to be one who was able to pull Jane out of her comfort zone.

One day, not long after observing Robert Waterfield and his revolving harem at the party during her freshman year, Jane officially met him at school when she walked past where he was stationed as a hall monitor. He asked for her hall pass, and then for a date. She responded, "That depends . . . on where, when, and why," her heart beating in her throat, despite her cool facade.[17] He responded by standing still, "looking down at me, absolutely quiet, completely

sure of himself, and then he moved away without a word, with all his gang following him. I was impressed as only a dizzy kid of fourteen can be impressed."[18]
She may have found his behavior off-putting, but couldn't ignore how undeniably attracted she was. "He's no good for you, Janie," her friends warned. "But
that didn't stop me," she said. "He was the main school figure and he had a
gang of stooges who always traveled with him."[19] She was also intuitive enough
to know that falling at his feet like the other girls at school was not the way to
deal with Robert Waterfield. Instead, "I saw to it that I joined that gang. I saw
to it that I was wherever he was. I went in for sports, I went in for groups of
pals, I went in for anything that I thought would attract and hold his interest."[20] Despite her discreetly chasing him "for more than a year and a half," Jane
and Robert never actually went out on a date before he graduated in 1938. This
was only a temporary setback, as far as Jane was concerned.[21]

Robert Staton Waterfield was born in Elmira, New York, on July 26,
1920, the only child of Staton Waterfield and Frances Gallagher. He was
called Bob by most, but Jane usually referred to him as Robert. By 1923 the
family had relocated to Van Nuys, where Staton worked a variety of jobs,
including mechanic, salesman, and ice deliveryman, changing addresses
every couple of years in the process.[22] Staton found more secure work at the
Van Nuys Moving and Storage Company, so the Waterfield family moved to
16002 Hartland Street, where they seemed to have finally settled down.
However, in March 1930, when he was thirty-eight, Staton died unexpectedly
of what was ruled acute cardiac dilatation.[23] Robert was four months shy of
his tenth birthday. Having such a horrible commonality caused Jane to later
muse, "I lost my own father in 1937, and I'm not sure now that that wasn't
one of the things that brought us together."[24] The devastating upheaval may
have also been why Waterfield would ultimately come to loathe change of any
kind. Frances was able to support her son by working long hours as a nurse,
which also enabled her to break ground on a housing lot two doors down at
16014 Hartland a few months after her husband's death. The extended hours
Frances put in to support them meant Robert grew accustomed to spending
a lot of time alone, the polar opposite of how Jane was raised. At the same
time Frances made Robert the center of her world, and while there was never
a lack of love in the Russell household, there were too many people for anyone ever to be the center of attention.

Waterfield would later perform spectacularly on professional football
fields, something many assumed was largely due to a natural ability evident
early on. On the contrary, Waterfield later admitted, "During my high school

days, I was quite small, weighing under 150 pounds. I loved playing, but I was far too light to do very much. My final year at Van Nuys, I did make the varsity, played tailback on the single wing."[25] He may not have been the top varsity football star, but he did excel in gymnastics during high school and was able to beef up physically during the summers, helping Frances with finances at the same time by working in a concrete-pipe yard, which was "pretty good for the back muscles, and they paid me two bits an hour."[26] Waterfield enjoyed his one year of high school football immensely, but "playing college football was far from my dreams—not only because of my size, but also because my father had died when I was 10 and I figured I had to get a job."[27] He found work on the assembly line at the Douglas Aircraft facility in Santa Monica, just five miles from the University of California, Los Angeles. College didn't seem to be in the cards for him, but "I was a real college football fan, tho. Every time it was possible, I'd sneak off to watch UCLA practice."[28] Robert may have thought his school days were over, but "my mother didn't feel that way. She kept after me to get more education."[29] With Frances's encouragement, Waterfield finally enrolled in UCLA in 1940 after a two-year break, attending on a gymnastics scholarship. Any misgivings he may have had about his football abilities hadn't stopped him from continually practicing his passing and kicking skills during the educational hiatus, which caused him to "get pretty arm heavy and leg weary at times, but I guess it paid off."[30] It did: by 1941 Waterfield had made the UCLA varsity football team. A career on the field finally seemed possible.

Serious, brooding, and distrustful of unfamiliar people, Waterfield was described by a sports journalist as "a reserved, taciturn young man who dislikes crowds and parties and enjoys life most when he is with a few old friends or off by himself with a gun or a fishing rod."[31] Jane herself reinforced this description of Waterfield by nicknaming him Old Stone Face. "He's not a gregarious guy," she once commented. "He's a horror to try to get out at parties. His best friends are his old friends, those he went to school with. When I bring friends to our house, it takes about ten meetings before Bob will warm up to them."[32]

Despite sharing the same high school halls for a spell, and Jane's attempts to run in the same circles as Robert, the pair didn't actually connect until Jane was a senior in high school and Waterfield had already graduated. He later described the fateful meeting matter-of-factly: "We got to know each other one day on the beach at Santa Monica. It was a year or so after I got out of high school. We went out on a date together that night and she's been my girl ever since."[33] Geraldine's preferred retelling of the meeting is more dramatic: "Who should wander down the beach, as if he owned the Pacific, but this same Bob Waterfield! He comfortably plunked himself on the corner of her beach blanket. Jane's heart pounded out of her bathing suit, and that started it."[34] Of the beach encounter, Jane herself would later recall that when the two made eye contact, "I felt like a bird hypnotized by a green-eyed snake, and the snake won."[35] This fateful meeting on the sand of Santa Monica Beach officially launched a tumultuous relationship that would last almost three decades. According to Jane, when the pair kissed for the first time later that night, it was "perhaps the most exciting moment I've ever experienced. The sensation it produced stayed with me for more than twenty years, and had things been a little different, it may have stayed with me for the rest of my life."[36]

Jane had experienced her fair share of crushes over the years, but with Waterfield she had finally fallen and fallen hard. After the meeting on the beach, Geraldine confirmed, "From then on, it was no one but Bob."[37] Initially Jane and Robert continued to circle each other cautiously, with Jane figuring out the best way to navigate a relationship with her brooding Romeo. Waterfield seemed to enjoy the thrill of emotional combat, something Jane was not accustomed to but would soon learn to engage in. During this early courting period, Waterfield tested the boundaries of the new relationship by continuing to see other women. Rather than giving him a reaction, Jane chose to remain cool and find alternate beaus to occupy her time, though she never cared seriously for any of them: she had eyes only for Robert. Thus was established an early pattern of Jane and Robert deliberately trying to hurt each other. Jane's response did the trick, though, and Robert agreed to commit himself fully to her . . . at least for the time being. On the day she graduated from high school, "we made love. His way. My first. It was my eighteenth birthday."[38]

The football hero and the movie star seemed like a match made in heaven, and on a superficial level these two physically beautiful people did seem to be well suited. Animal magnetism was one of the things that brought the couple together, and that connection sustained their relationship to some extent. However, Jane's outgoing personality never seemed to jive especially well with Waterfield's introverted nature. Additionally, she always seemed to be at a disadvantage because "I knew I was five times as in love with him as he was with me, but that didn't matter either, so long as he would speak to me and let me be somewhere near him."[39] Even after Jane's big publicity push for *The Outlaw* began, marking the beginnings of her career as a film actress, a film writer noted that Jane seemed more interested in talking about Waterfield than her career. During the interview, which took place at the beach, Jane gazed dreamily at Robert as he worked out, making comments like "Isn't Bob graceful?" in response to questions about her acting.[40] Echoes of Jane's relationship with her father appeared in the relationship, as Waterfield was not one to express his feelings openly. Jane once revealed, "I'd beg and tease him, 'Why can't you love me a little?' Bob would answer, not with the adoring phrases that I wanted to hear, but by saying, 'Who says I don't? I'm here aren't I?'"[41]

The relationship with Waterfield kicked off a streak of independence in Jane that prompted her to start pushing Geraldine away, first in the form of a letter reading, "Mother, you will never have any regrets for the way you have brought me up; but now I'm a person, and you're a person, and I have to live my life and make my decisions just as you live and make your decisions."[42] Jane soon stopped participating in the community concerts Geraldine had been organizing. "I finally bowed out," Jane recalled, "because you get tired of playing *The Bells of St. Mary's* all the time. Besides, I was too busy having fun with my own gang."[43] The next change for Jane was one that wounded Geraldine to the core. The family matriarch had remained exceedingly spiritual over the years, something she sought to ingrain in her children. Much to her disappointment, the day came when Jane felt she no longer needed spiritual guidance. As Geraldine ruefully recalled:

One evening, church had just nicely started when I heard the rattling of the Ford pipes out in front of the church. I knew it was Bob calling for her; as he kept rattling those pipes, she became more nervous every minute. Finally, she turned to me and said, "How long do I have to keep up this farce?"

I answered, "Go Jane, and I'll never ask you to come to church again."

She was gone like a flash, and that was the last of Daughter's churchgoing for four years. The boys were terribly troubled and full of misgivings for Daughter, but I reassured them that she could not hide from God.[44]

In addition to church, Jane had also grown weary of school and was failing at least one class. Geraldine may have conceded religion (for the time being), but foregoing high school graduation was unthinkable. "There's nothing much to say about my school days," Jane later noted, "except that I wanted

Jane with the other contestants hoping to be crowned San Fernando Valley Mission Fiesta Queen, 1939. (Los Angeles Times Photographic Archives [Collection 1429]. Library Special Collections, Charles E. Young Research Library, UCLA.)

to quit and go to work when my father died in 1937. That was the one time Mother had her own way. I graduated with my class."[45]

As Jane was nearing the end of high school, she experienced her first bit of publicity when the Van Nuys 20–30 Club sponsored her as its nominee for queen of the annual San Fernando Valley Mission Fiesta. During the one-month campaign, Jane received a lot of local press coverage, got to show off her singing talents, and made numerous public appearances at community events in an attempt to sell the most tickets to the fiesta (the criterion for being crowned). Despite being proclaimed the most "photogenic" of the group of hopefuls, Jane lagged behind Eloise Burns of San Fernando, who had the highest ticket count and was therefore crowned Fiesta Queen of 1939. Jane resigned herself to serving on the queen's court but seemed to enjoy her first taste of media attention. The photographers who took a shine to Jane during the Fiesta Queen campaign marked an early indication of what was soon to come.

4

Accidental Aspiring Actress

After Jane had graduated from high school, her focus was on finding a job. Her relationship with Robert Waterfield had matured to the point that they actually got engaged, but starting a family was far from the couple's mind. He was focusing his attentions on UCLA and Jane, despite her newfound independence, still felt an obligation to Geraldine and her four brothers. However, before Daughter entered the workforce, Geraldine decided six weeks with relatives in Canada would do her some good. Jane ventured north without reservations and in great spirits, but soon longed to return to her fiancé. As Geraldine put it, "All would have worked out as scheduled, but Cupid already had gotten his arrow into her. A forlorn, lovesick girl was just miserable away from Bob."[1] It seems absence had made the heart grow fonder on both sides, as Waterfield sent multiple letters to Canada imploring Jane to come home. Although her Canadian relatives attempted to distract Jane, all of her attention was focused on Van Nuys and Robert Waterfield. Geraldine finally relented and allowed her to come home early.

Back home, Jane immediately found retail work at Roos Bros., Inc., a men's clothing retailer on Hollywood Boulevard just west of Vine Street.[2] As to her long-term plans, Jane was undecided, but Geraldine certainly had some ideas. She convinced Jane to sign up for acting classes at the Max Reinhardt Workshop, located at 5939 Sunset Boulevard. Launched by Reinhardt, a noted theater and film director, and his wife in 1938, the school was "dedicated to the discovery and development of talent for stage, screen, and radio."[3] Jane enrolled at Geraldine's urging, but once it became clear that she would not even meet Reinhardt or his wife—they did not instruct first-term students—she quickly lost interest. On many days, she would skip class, opting to head across the street to the old Warner Bros. lot, where part of the studio had been converted into the Sunset Bowling Center.

During her brief tenure at the Reinhardt workshop, Jane and a girlfriend ventured down the street to the Earl Carroll Theatre, where auditions were

A fresh-faced Jane at La Posada.

being held for the impresario's famed chorus. Jane passed the audition and was selected, much to the horror of her Reinhardt instructor, who shouted, "Do you want to be a cheap showgirl or an actress?"[4] The acting coach wasn't the only one appalled by this prospect. When Jane told Geraldine about the offer, "my heart sank. I knew that to forbid it would be fatal, so I just said nothing but prayed."[5] Ultimately, Jane turned down the opportunity—not because it was undignified, but because the position was for a traveling troupe that would be spending Christmas in New York. She could not bear the thought of being away from Robert Waterfield. Plus, "Bob didn't approve of the stage door Johnnies."[6] As 1939 came to a close, Jane had decided to become neither an actress nor a cheap showgirl.

Show business didn't appear to be in the cards, and Jane was still convinced that she wasn't the academic type, though Geraldine disagreed. "She thought I needed more schooling," Jane later recalled, "and since I still felt acting was pretty silly, we decided I might attend a school of design and perhaps learn to be a designer."[7] Figuring design school was better than nothing, Geraldine forked over the tuition money for Jane to enroll shortly after the New Year in 1940. However, as Jane was on her way to the school, tuition check in hand, she decided to make a detour to visit her friend Pat Dawson (there were a lot of women named Pat in Jane's life), who was enrolled in classes at Maria Ouspenskaya's School of Dramatic Arts. Ouspenskaya, a diminutive but stern actress who had studied under Stanislavski in Russia, had enjoyed a moderate stage career in New York before coming to Hollywood in the mid-1930s. She landed parts in notable films such as *Dodsworth* (Samuel Goldwyn Productions, 1936), *Waterloo Bridge* (MGM, 1940), and *The Wolf Man* (Universal Pictures, 1941), usually playing humorless matriarchal types. In January 1940 she transformed a large residence located at 2027 North Vine Street into a drama school. Classes, which took place in both stories of the house, included body work with Adolph Bolm and voice and diction with Margaret Prendergast McLean. Ouspenskaya herself worked with the students for two hours each afternoon.[8] Though Jane claimed she was merely stopping by to say hi to her friend, there also must have been an element of interest or curiosity that caused her to visit the school, located around a half mile north of Hollywood Boulevard in a residential area. When she set foot inside the house, something about the atmosphere flicked a switch inside her as she "watched the students walk by with plays under their arms talking about diction and directors. The bug bit me again. I forgot all about not wanting to be an actress. I marched into the office right then and gave them the check that was meant for designer school."[9]

While studying at Ouspenskaya's, Jane received training in diction and dance, though her abilities in the latter had not improved with age—she admitted she had two left feet. "I was just awful!"[10] When Jane first began, Madame Ouspenskaya proclaimed, "You've got talent and great promise!" Jane's lack of ambition soon overshadowed talent and promise, however, causing an exasperated Ouspenskaya to moan, "Jane—you're the most indifferent and discouraging pupil I've ever had. You won't develop your talents. What *am* I going to do with you?"[11] Still, Jane continued to enjoy the atmosphere and appreciated the time the elder actress spent with the students. A few years later, after she broke into the movies, Jane ran into Ouspenskaya, who commented that she had the potential to become a fine actress except she had no energy. Jane had a hard time disagreeing. Jane stayed at Ouspenskaya's school for six months, but "certainly didn't feel ready for any starring role."[12] However, Pat Dawson's mother, who had been employed at Warner Bros. and was married to Academy Award–winning editor Ralph Dawson, decided to use her connections to help Jane get representation. Jane was dragged to the office of Charles Feldman, one of the more established and successful agents at the time. She found him charming. He humored her, but then explained that he repped only established actors. Jane found that catch-22 logic—having to be established in order to get an agent to help you get established—baffling and once again started to become disillusioned with acting.

If visiting Pat Dawson at Ouspenskaya's school was the springboard to Jane pursuing an acting career, it was a visit to another Pat that proved to be a catapult. Jane's dear friend Pat Alexander was back in town and employed at a diner near Hollywood and Vine. While working a shift, Pat was noticed by local photographer Tom Kelley, who thought she had potential as a model and invited her to come to his studio. Kelley went on to have a long and successful career in Hollywood as an independent photographer, but is now best known for his nude images of Marilyn Monroe, which showed up on the controversial/celebrated Golden Dreams calendar—and the centerfold of the inaugural issue of *Playboy* magazine. Pat Alexander's first reaction to the proposition was to proclaim she would not pose nude. Kelley laughed and assured Pat he wanted to use her for a line of sporting clothes. He added that his wife Natalie was always present at photo shoots. Pat then asked if she could bring a friend. Jane came to Kelley's studio with Pat and he opted to use her immediately. Jane began working regularly with Tom Kelley and would always credit him with helping launch her career.

Working with Kelley proved to be an education and an awakening of sorts, as he taught Jane tips and tricks to look good on camera. Kelley's mantra for his models was "If it's not uncomfortable, it'll be a lousy picture." As Jane later explained, "He showed me how to stand on my toes like swimming star Esther Williams, bend one knee in front of the other, raise my arms folded over my head and stretch my torso. It was positively the most awkward position one could get into." As it turned out, Kelley knew what he was talking about. "When I saw the shots, I was thrilled. I didn't look so skinny after all. Tom Kelley was some photographer!"[13] Jane had served as a photographer's model at least once before, posing stiffly in an ad for the Van Nuys J. C. Penney that ran at the back of the 1938 Van Nuys High School yearbook. The influence of a pro like Kelly was notable, and as a result Jane got additional work modeling clothes at Nancy's of Hollywood, a higher-end dress shop on Hollywood Boulevard just a few doors down from where she had previously worked at Roos Bros. Jane also appeared in at least one print advertisement, given the fictional backstory of being a student at University of Southern California who enchanted men with her flawless complexion, courtesy of Woodbury powder.[14] Seeing her tomboy daughter in print as a clothing model was especially gratifying for Geraldine, who admitted, "I had

Photographer Tom Kelley was instrumental in launching Jane as a model, ultimately paving the way for her film career. Jane always spoke highly of Kelley and stayed in touch with him, as is evident in this 1947 photo of the two. (Tom Kelley Studios, Ventura California)

so much fun watching the papers and cutting out the pictures of Daughter in the new creations every few days."[15] Kelley came to be especially fond of Jane and very protective of her. Though he excelled in full-body pinup photography, he did take some brooding close-ups of Jane, one of which he hung up in his studio.

At this point Jane may have not been overly ambitious about an acting career, but she wasn't averse to it either, so Kelley arranged a screen test for her at Twentieth Century-Fox. When Jane arrived, Betty Grable was in the midst of doing a wardrobe test. As Jane silently observed the process, she found herself once again actually interested in acting and wondering what it would be like to one day have a similar test done. When it was time for the screen test, the experience was underwhelming. "You sat in a chair—it was a stool. They turned you to the right, they turned you to the left, and they sent you home. You didn't say a word. There was no sound, nothing." As for the result of the test: "They called back and told Tom I was not photogenic."[16] When Tom Kelley relayed this to Jane, he laughed uproariously and hollered, "Those dumb shits! They could have come up with anything but that! If you aren't photogenic, the sky isn't blue!"[17]

Another man, whom Jane would later refer to only as Mr. X, also claimed to take an interest in her career. He took her to Paramount, where she was proclaimed too tall and shown the studio gates. In response to her frustrated tears, Mr. X promised he could get her into pictures—if Jane met him at his Beverly Hills home. She acquiesced, but when the inevitable come-on occurred, Jane laughed, declared she was in love with a six-foot-one football player, and continued laughing as she made her way out the door. Jane would later claim Mr. X was "the only honest-to-God Hollywood wolf I ever met."[18]

Jane may have been cool to the notion of acting when her mother was the one suggesting it, but now that she had a taste of modeling and the Hollywood studios, she felt differently. She suddenly wanted to be a part of the industry that was so prevalent all around her (though her efforts seldom matched these desires), and the rejections from Fox and Paramount sent Jane into a bit of a tailspin. On top of it, Waterfield had finally earned a place on the UCLA football team, and there he channeled most of his attention. Feeling alone and confused about what path her life should take, Jane decided to seek the refuge of Aunt Ernie's farm in Fontana to temporarily get away from Hollywood and clear her head. Little could she know that when she returned to Los Angeles her life would never be the same.

As it turned out, the movies were coming for her.

5

The Howards

In April 1940 Joseph Breen, head of the Production Code Administration (PCA), drafted an internal memo expressing concern over a Billy the Kid project in pre-production. At the time Breen's concern was that the film, based on a notorious real-life outlaw of the American West, would not adequately convey a deserved punishment for the film's protagonist.[1] This would not be Breen's last correspondence regarding the film that became *The Outlaw*. Far from it. However, as it played out over the next few years, on-screen justice for Billy the Kid would be the least of Breen's worries.

What would eventually become the Production Code Administration was an offshoot of the Motion Picture Producers and Distributors of America (MPPDA), founded in 1922. The MPPDA, the US film industry's self-regulating arm, came into being when religious groups and socially conservative community members cried foul at the not-so-Victorian story lines that were seeping into the increasingly popular motion pictures. Real-life Hollywood scandals didn't help these hostile attitudes, so when the US government threatened intervention, film producers opted for self-regulation, appointing former postmaster general Will Hays as the head of the MPPDA. An early attempt to stem the tide of tawdry came in the form of the "Don'ts and Be Carefuls," a 1927 list of rules crafted by the MPPDA that two years later morphed into the Motion Picture Production Code. The stated standards in the 1929 Code had been guided in large part by Martin Quigley, a Catholic who also happened to be editor of the prominent trade publication *Motion Picture Herald,* and Father Daniel A. Lord, a Jesuit priest. Filmmakers were encouraged to adhere to the rules of the Code but seldom did, instead treating them as mere guidelines that were easy to ignore. Rather than scrubbing movie screens clean, the studios instead ushered in a period now paradoxically known as the pre-Code era, when the existing Code was ignored and sex, drugs, and violence, along with self-assured, dynamic female characters, ruled the screen. This resulted in state censorship boards springing up all over the country and the Catholic Church forming the Legion of Decency. In 1934 outrage over (profitable) film content became loud enough that filmmakers could no longer rely on self-policing. The Code became the law of celluloid.

Joseph Ignatius Breen, a devout Irish Catholic, was hired to be the iron fist of the PCA once the Code started being aggressively enforced. As it turned out, for better or for worse, Breen was spectacularly good at his job and would remain at the helm of the PCA for over twenty years. Under Breen the PCA sought to nip any issues in the bud during the planning stages of a film, which was an attempt to save the studios costly post-production edits or prevent state censorship boards from editing prints. Since catching red flags at the script stage was a regular approach, it was not unusual for Breen to take note early on and express preliminary concerns, as he did with *The Outlaw*. A film about an unabashed gunslinger would have certainly caught the PCA's attention, but it was the name associated with the film that most likely made the hairs on the back of Breen's neck stand at attention: Howard Hughes.

The eccentric, brazen multimillionaire had entered the realm of film production a little over a decade before, most notably as the producer and director of *Hell's Angels* (1930), a landmark film for its use of aviation photography. Never taken seriously by the big studio moguls, who viewed him as an unsophisticated outsider, Hughes had pursued his cinema ambitions by launching his own production company, Caddo, and setting up shop in the heart of Hollywood. Soft-spoken but shrewd, Hughes proved to have a keen appreciation for talent, both in front of and behind the camera, which at times resulted in movie magic. Prior to *The Outlaw*, the last film Hughes had released was 1932's *Scarface*, an ultra-violent but brilliant drama about the gangs who terrorized Chicago during the Prohibition era.

For *Scarface* Hughes had employed screenwriter Ben Hecht and director Howard Hawks. Together they created a brutal but memorable pre-Code title, launching the film careers of George Raft and Ann Dvorak and adding to Paul Muni's on-screen clout. Even though the film was released at a time when the Code was being halfheartedly enforced, *Scarface* drew a lot of attention and ire for its violent themes and perceived glamorization of 1920s gangsters, which caused the PCA to try to strong-arm Hughes into making edits. Hughes, more than happy to put up a fight when it came to on-screen censorship, left Hawks alone during production, although ultimately he did make some concessions. Yet he backtracked on others, demonstrating his willingness to go toe-to-toe with industry censors.

Jane, the self-professed tomboy, on the verge of a career as a Hollywood glamour girl and unwitting thorn in the Production Code Administration's side, circa 1940.

Following the release of *Scarface,* Hughes turned his attention away from films, opting to concentrate on aviation, his true passion. In 1932 he founded the Hughes Aircraft Company in Glendale, California, which spearheaded countless innovations in aerospace. Throughout the 1930s Hughes would set multiple flying records, which brought him international fame. By the end of the decade, the shadow of war was looming and the aerospace industry was proliferating around the country. Nonetheless, in early 1940 Hughes determined the time was right to get back into the movies and decided Billy the Kid was the way to do it.

For the production, Hughes once again turned to Howard Hawks, hoping the versatile director could repeat the success of *Scarface* a decade before. Screenwriter Jules Furthman, who had worked with Hawks previously on *Come and Get It* and *Only Angels Have Wings,* was hired to pen the script, which was based on a Ben Hecht story. Given the results the last time the two Howards had paired up, Breen most likely braced himself for a film that would transport the bloodshed from the streets of Chicago to the dusty paths of the Old West. Howard Hughes, however, was not a man whose actions were easy to predict. As *The Outlaw* began to take shape, it became apparent that violence was not the issue that would rankle Joseph Breen.

The Outlaw, set to be distributed by Twentieth Century-Fox, was an incredibly loose interpretation of its source material; as Hawks explained to Breen, it would be "suggested by *one* of the legends, connected with 'Billy the Kid.'"[2] On a trip through New Mexico, Hawks had become aware of a fringe belief that Pat Garrett, the lawman credited with killing Billy the Kid, had instead shot someone else in the face, allowing the actual outlaw to escape south of the border with a girl he had fallen in love with.[3] Drawing on this conspiracy for inspiration, *The Outlaw* centers on the characters of Billy the Kid, Doc Holliday, and Pat Garrett, with a young Mexican maiden named Rio thrown in to provide some romantic interest.

For the role of Holliday, Hughes approved casting veteran actor Walter Huston, while Garrett would be played by Thomas Mitchell, winner of an Academy Award for *Stagecoach,* who had just appeared as Scarlett O'Hara's father in *Gone with the Wind.* For the two younger leads, Hughes was intent on casting unknowns. After all, he had a proven track record with novice actors, and had even managed to profit from hiring them. In the previous decade he'd signed Jean Harlow and Ann Dvorak to long-term contracts following their appearances in *Hell's Angels* and *Scarface,* respectively, and then sold Harlow's contract to MGM for $30,000 and Dvorak's to Warner Bros. for $40,000.

Once it was decided that *The Outlaw* would star two unknowns, a search was launched to find the perfect newcomers. During pre-production, Howard Hawks set up an office in the Hollywood building Hughes owned and operated from: 7000 Romaine Street. The director was spending so much time prepping the film and looking for his leads that he ended up having a cot moved into his office. In order to cast the widest net in his search for talent while maximizing time and money, Hawks decided to shoot the screen tests on sixteen-millimeter film (as opposed to the standard thirty-five-millimeter) in the basement of the Romaine building. As the director explained, "If we had made these tests in 35mm, I would have had to be away from my desk for a much longer period whenever I made a test, leaving the building and driving to whatever studio might be used. Instead, these 16mm tests were shot in an ordinary room located very conveniently in the basement of the Hughes building. When a test was scheduled I simply walked downstairs and made it, and was able to return to my office-work in a matter of minutes."[4] In addition to convenience and cost savings, Hawks believed the smaller cameras were better suited for the parade of inexperienced hopefuls who would be streaming in and out of the makeshift basement set, noting, "There is a greater feeling of informality on a 16mm test-set. The actors feel less strained. They turn in an easier, more natural performance because of it."[5] Shot by cinematographer Lucien Ballard, whom Hawks planned to use for principal photography, these tests were reportedly the first use of sixteen-millimeter sound stock by a major production.

An unusually large number of actors were tested for the role of Billy the Kid and Rio, though as Lucien Ballard later revealed, "They were testing a hundred boys and a hundred girls for the leads, as a publicity stunt of course."[6] If the Hollywood publicity machine is to be believed, the screen tests were all for naught when Jane Russell was serendipitously discovered by a dental hygiene–conscious Howard Hughes. As Hughes's long-time assistant Noah Dietrich later claimed, "One day I found Howard in a state of high excitement. 'Today,' he announced, 'I saw the most beautiful pair of knockers I've ever seen in my life.'" Dietrich continued, "He had been to the dentist, and the remarkable bosom belonged to the receptionist, a nineteen-year-old Van Nuys girl named Jane Russell. Howard signed her to a contract and designated her to play Rio, the girlfriend of Doc Holliday."[7] At the time Jane herself seemed to confirm the dental part of this story: "Dr. Creamer let me work part time as his office girl, arranging dental appointments with nervous patients. I got a steady $10 a week."[8] Decades later, however, Jane repudiated

Jane and Jack Buetel shortly after finding out they'd been cast in *The Outlaw.*

all of this as nonsense, commenting, "That's all Hollywood hype. I never worked for a dentist. After leaving school I worked for a chiropodist for about a week, and quit—I'd had enough of putting people's feet in warm water. And Howard Hughes was never a client."[9] Considering there are no listings anywhere for a "Dr. Creamer," and given the unlikelihood that Howard Hughes traveled to Van Nuys to get his teeth cleaned, this version of Jane's discovery is indeed probably Hollywood hype. It's more likely that Jane's modeling work with Tom Kelley brought her into the orbit of Howard Hughes.

Levis Green, a talent agent with the small Howard Lang, Ltd. Agency who always had his eyes peeled for fresh talent, would drop in on Tom Kelley to scope out the models as prospective clients. Green was well aware that the two Howards were searching for a fresh face who could fill the role of Rio. On one visit to Tom Kelley, Green spotted a photo hanging on the wall that transfixed him. Ironically, the photo of Jane Russell that caught Green's attention didn't even hint at her physical attributes; it was a tightly framed portrait of her face, looking as if she was on the verge of snarling. The dark intensity of Jane's expression appealed to Green, and he was convinced that the brooding girl in the photo should be tested for the part of Rio. There was one minor problem: Tom Kelley refused to reveal Jane's identity. He and his wife had grown genuinely fond of her and didn't feel that connecting her with a notorious playboy like Howard Hughes, or the agent, whom Kelley called "the Silver Fox," would be in her best interest.[10] Green responded by swiping the photo off the wall when Kelley's back was turned.

Green's intuition proved correct as both Hawks and Hughes immediately wanted to bring Jane in for a screen test, but first they needed to locate her. Now that it was clear the Howards were legitimately interested in testing Jane, Tom Kelley revealed her identity and offered to track her down at La Posada. Instead he approached Geraldine, who admitted, "The name Howard Hughes didn't mean one thing to me. I told him that Jane was with her cousin in Fontana, gathering and packing eggs and would be home Thursday."[11] Not wanting to wait one day, let alone several, Kelley wrangled Ernestine's number from her sister and began calling the farm, but this proved fruitless as well. As Jane's cousin Pat Henry later recalled, "We went up to the San Bernardino mountains to a church camp, and the church camp didn't have any phone at it. When the week was over and we came back to Fontana, my mother said, 'that photographer has been phoning everyday. He showed some of your pictures to Howard Hughes who is looking for a special type of girl and he thinks you're it.'"[12] In an excited frenzy, Jane rushed back to Los Angeles from Fontana and met with Levis Green, whom she liked immediately, although she did identify him as "a hustler. Obviously! He was a bachelor too, I found out."[13]

Green took Jane to meet with Freddie Schuessler, Hughes's casting director, who gave Jane a scene to learn and then turned her over to Howard Hawks, who met Jane in his small office in the Romaine Street building. The director provided Jane with the basic background of Rio, including the character's half-Irish, half-Mexican lineage, and instructed her to memorize her lines for a screen test the following Monday. Jane left Romaine Street and set about preparing for the opportunity of a lifetime.

As she began memorizing her lines, Jane got a brainstorm. Since Rio was half Mexican, Jane decided she should deliver the dialogue with a Spanish accent. She enlisted the aid of Eloisa "Elsie" Pachecco, a friend who lived nearby. Jane drove over to Elsie's house and the pair sat in the car with Elsie reading the lines of dialogue with a Spanish accent over and over as Jane mimicked her, word for word.[14] The night before the test, Jane was too excited to sleep. When she wasn't studying her lines, she was wondering if she was finally turning some kind of corner in her life. She may never have been overly ambitious, but when opportunity presented itself, Jane could embrace it and put in the work.

When she arrived at 7000 Romaine, Jane was escorted down to the basement where a makeshift set had been erected with a haystack and "a set of suitable Mexican architecture [which] was obtained from an independent 35mm studio."[15] There were four other prospective Rios waiting for their shot —all dressed exactly like Jane, in a simple peasant outfit with a long hair fall—along with five men vying for the role of Billy the Kid. Among the group were Leatrice Joy Gilbert, the daughter of actors Leatrice Joy and MGM matinee idol John Gilbert, and Will Fowler, the son of newspaper reporter Gene Fowler. (Will later abandoned acting for journalism and supposedly was the first reporter to appear at the Elizabeth Short, aka Black Dahlia, crime scene.) Jane quickly scanned the group of Billy hopefuls and decided a young man named Jack was the most handsome.

The scene used for the screen test was Rio and Billy's first encounter, with Rio trying to shoot him to avenge her murdered brother and Billy wrestling the gun away from her, then pinning her down on a bale of hay. The aspiring actors were paired up randomly and performed the scene as the others looked on. Jane was disappointed when she wasn't paired with the handsome boy, who instead did his test with Leatrice Joy Gilbert.[16] When it was Jane's turn, any nervousness melted away as soon as she was in front of the camera. "Honestly, the camera didn't bother me," she later remembered. "It was just a larger edition of Tom Kelley's, and the lights were so intense that the people standing around just faded away. It was just the boy and myself. I wasn't really nervous."[17] Under the direction of someone of Hawks's caliber, Jane's performance was convincing, Spanish accent and all. When she finished, the director was all smiles, and informed Jane that one of the crew had commented that she spoke pretty good English for a Mexican.[18] After completing the screen test, Jane was sent home to bide her time until casting decisions were made.

After a few days of anxious waiting, Jane was finally called back to 7000 Romaine Street on October 8, 1940. When she arrived, Howard Hawks took her into a screening room. As Jane later remembered:

My heart was in my throat. Mr. Hawks took me to a projection room and ran the film of all the tests that were shot the day I did mine. Mine was last. I sat there, feeling like I was hooked to an electric wire, and watched each girl. I was sure which girl had it. The one in the second test. She was so good, my heart sank. Then mine came on the screen. It's hard to describe the feelings I had. It was like watching someone else only knowing it was me. There was a softness about the girl on the screen that others hadn't had. To see your own likeness and feel it isn't you, to see beauty when you feel so unbeautiful, so plain, so average (as most teenagers do) was a shock.[19]

Despite the previous assessment by Twentieth Century-Fox, there was no denying that Jane looked stunning on celluloid. As far as Howard Hawks was concerned, Jane had the acting chops to pull off the role, but it was up to the other Howard to make the final decision. Jane didn't need to worry. According to cinematographer Lucien Ballard, "I made these tests in the haystack, used cross-lights so that her tits show big, and Hughes went wild for it. I didn't know it then, but he had a thing for tits; he had the scene made into a loop, and he'd run it over and over again."[20] Howard Hughes had found his next Jean Harlow, but this time he was not going to let her go to another studio.

Without saying a word, Hawks brought Jane from the screening room to his office. Already there was the handsome young man Jane had noticed earlier, who was introduced as Jack Buetel, an aspiring actor from Dallas. Jack was seated on the chair in Hawks's office, so Jane plopped herself down on the cot. She remembered that Hawks was "so calm and quiet, but his eyes were twinkling, bright blue" as he delivered the news the pair was hoping to hear: "Well, you two kids have the parts."[21] Upon hearing the announcement, "I flopped back on the cot in his office and Jack went 'Whoaaaaa!' and he [Hawks] said, 'That's just exactly how I want you to act in this picture. I want you to be perfectly natural.'"[22] Both were then handed a contract that would bind them to Hughes Productions for the next six years. Starting on

Jane and Jack Buetel look on as director Howard Hawks goes over the terms of their contract. The pair had been handpicked by Hawks to star in *The Outlaw*.

November 7, 1940, Jane would be paid $50 a week, with periodic options that would increase her salary to $400 per week by the end of the fifth year.[23] It was a modest contract, even for 1940, but Hawks assured them, "These will be torn up if the picture is a success."[24]

Jane was then sent to another part of the Romaine building, where Levis Green was waiting to sign her on as a client. Jane and Buetel thanked Hawks, and as she later recounted:

> As we walked out the door, there was a man standing in the hall with his hat tipped back. He was just leaning on the wall. Jack and I went down the hall, and Jack poked me and said "That's him!"
>
> I said, "Who?"
>
> "That's Howard Hughes!"
>
> And I turned around and looked at him and [waving] went "Oh!"
>
> And he just sort of nodded and we went off and that was our first meeting.[25]

As soon as she'd signed with Levis Green, Jane called La Posada, screaming, "Mom, I got it!" "Praise the Lord!" came the answer. When Green came on the phone to reiterate the good news, Geraldine again replied, "Praise the Lord!" to which Green answered, "I should say, praise the Lord!"[26]

Jane Russell left the Romaine Street building that afternoon with two contracts under her arm and all expectations exceeded. She was thrilled to be under the wing of Howard Hawks for the next few months, but wasn't quite sure what to make of the other Howard, the shy unassuming man she had encountered in the hallway.

Howard Hughes would be Jane's boss for the next thirty-five years.

6

Shooting an Outlaw

Jane's sudden good fortune may have prompted Geraldine to praise the Lord, but it mainly just amused her four brothers, who greeted their newly anointed film actress sister by shrieking, "You're gonna be a MOOVIE star. Woo, Woo!"[1] With them around, there was never a danger of Jane taking herself too seriously. After delivering the news to the family, there was one other person Jane needed to tell, but she doubted he would be praising the Lord. As she suspected, when Jane informed Robert Waterfield, he responded, "This is going to break us up. You know that, don't you?"[2] Jane soon found that Waterfield wasn't the only one unimpressed by her film contract. "None of my friends in the Valley are very excited," she commented at the time. "Most of them have families that are connected with the studios and I heard a lot of movie chatter long before I set foot in front of a camera. All us kids realized long ago that the movies were a rough game, and you had to expect plenty of disappointments."[3]

For the time being, Jane would have to put the misgivings of her friends and boyfriend aside while she dealt with her biggest concern: her closet. Shortly after signing Jack Buetel and Jane, Howard Hawks celebrated by throwing a party for the pair at the Mocambo nightclub on the Sunset Strip. When Jane received the invitation, it became painfully apparent to the lifelong tomboy that her wardrobe was nowhere near suitable for the glitz of Hollywood's nightlife. Desperate, Jane went to Greer Limited on Sunset Boulevard and found the perfect dress, which Geraldine remembered as "a splendid creation. The bodice was gray silk crepe, and the skirt was made of many-colored silk strands of cord which gave the effect of grass."[4] At $150 the gown was three times what Jane was going to be making a week, so she left the shop empty-handed, only to receive a call the next day that the garment's price had been drastically reduced. Jane's good fortune seemed to be on a streak.

When Geraldine dropped her daughter off at Howard Hawks's house for the evening, Jane made a mental note of her next purchase priority: a car.

Jack and Jane arrived at Mocambo "scared to death, but trying to keep their chins up," as Geraldine later recalled.[5] The club was oozing glamour, and Jane was officially introduced to Hollywood's jet set when Gary Cooper pulled her onto the dance floor. "Mother," she would relay the next morning, "when I danced across that floor, I would have died if I hadn't been wearing that dress."[6] The clothing splurge had been worth it. Having gone to Clark Gable's tailor, Buetel felt equally prepared—at least from a clothing standpoint. When the group, including Gary Cooper, left the club, everyone was greeted by eager fans. One of them asked Jane for an autograph, which she found baffling. Cooper handed her a pen. "Might as well get started," he stated matter-of-factly. "You're in it."[7]

At the end of the fairy-tale evening, Jack Buetel drove a bewildered Jane home, arriving at La Posada at 3:00 in the morning. Instead of reveling in the evening's events or going to bed, she grabbed the keys to Geraldine's car and rushed to see Robert Waterfield. Paranoid that one of the town's many gossip columnists had been lurking on the outskirts of the Mocambo's dance floor, "I wanted to tell him so he'd understand, before he read it in the papers."[8] She needn't have worried. Jane's first foray into Hollywood's nightlife seems to have gone undetected; her anonymity remained intact for the time being. Still, she felt compelled to constantly reassure Waterfield that the film contract would not change their relationship. Ultimately, he simply chose to ignore Jane's new profession altogether, and it was seldom a topic of discussion between the two.[9]

The morning after her evening at the Mocambo, Jane purchased a brand-new 1940 Ford Coupe. She'd wanted a convertible, but that price tag would have required her to wait until a few of the options on the Hughes contact were exercised. She was still in need of a new wardrobe, but since Jane had spent so much on the one evening gown, Howard Hawks took the lead on that particular issue, sending Jane to visit Slim Keith, a friend (and the future Mrs. Hawks) who had an impeccable sense of style. Slim was laid out in the hospital with a broken leg, but she made arrangements for Jane to meet with a buyer at the I. Magnin department store. On Howard Hawks's dime, Jane obtained some perfectly fitted dresses, a coat, and a tailored suit. Since *The Outlaw* would be shooting on location in Arizona at the end of November 1940, Hawks personally took Jane to Nudie's Rodeo Tailors in North Hollywood to be outfitted with appropriate western ware. Jane's director also started to give his prodigy a few pointers. "He wanted me to keep my voice low," she remembered, "and he said that girls should walk from the hips, not from the knees. He said I should take long strides."[10] Despite any issues with

The first photos of Jane released to the press were taken in the basement of Howard Hughes's Hollywood office building, where a makeshift set was constructed to conduct screen tests. (Los Angeles Herald Examiner Collection/ Los Angeles Public Library)

Robert Waterfield, the events of the previous month had Jane "on cloud nine."[11] She had a film contract, a new car, new clothes, and would be working under the watchful eye of one of Hollywood's most capable directors. All she needed to do now was actually make the movie.

Shortly before Jane departed for Arizona, word of her landing the role in *The Outlaw* became public knowledge when gossip columnist Louella

Parsons broke the news via her syndicated column on November 22. While Buetel was referred to merely as "a Texas boy," Jane was the lead of Parsons's column; "a brunette and a beauty," she was said to have caused Howard Hughes to confide in a friend, "I believe I have as big a find as I had in Jean Harlow in 'Hell's Angels.'"[12] Within days details about Jane's background, including her Minnesota lineage and work with Tom Kelley, were splashed across newspapers around the country, along with images of her and Buetel signing their contracts in Howard Hawks's office. A provocative solo image of Jane with her dress practically zipped down to her navel, which appears to have been hastily shot in the basement of the Romaine Street building, also started showing up in the papers, setting the stage for the type of publicity she was to get for the rest of her career. Jane Russell had officially arrived.

Jane's good fortune seemed to slip a bit when she missed a step at La Posada and injured her ankle.[13] The two-hundred-person movie crew arrived at location ahead of her, setting up a camp in Tuba City, Arizona, slightly north of Moenkopi, the Hopi village where filming would take place.[14] The bad ankle proved to only be a minor setback, however, and when Jane arrived in Flagstaff on November 27, 1940, she was greeted by "a welcoming committee of gun-shooting, sombrero-waving cowboys."[15] From Flagstaff she journeyed to Moenkopi, where she discovered there wasn't much for her to do in front of the moving picture cameras. Instead she was put to work in front of the still cameras: a slew of photographers, invited by the Hughes publicity machine, descended on her and produced an onslaught of images that would introduce Jane Russell to the world. It was during that location shoot that photographer Gene Lester coaxed Jane into jumping up and down on the bed in a satin nightgown. When she went crying to Howard Hawks about it, he essentially ordered her to keep a stiff upper lip and learn to say no when the situation warranted it. For the rest of her life, Jane would credit this bit of wisdom as "the best advice I ever got."[16]

Both Jane and Jack were extremely grateful to be under the wing of Howard Hawks; after he had successfully guided them into their roles during the screen test process, both trusted their director implicitly. Jane was not required on set while Hawks filmed the opening sequences of The Outlaw, including the introductions of Billy the Kid, Doc Holliday, and Pat Garrett, but she sometimes showed up anyway. "I watched a little. I loved the way he [Hawks] directed Jack," she later said.[17] The cast and crew got along well, despite the isolation of the location, which was so remote that the only way Jane could stay in touch with Geraldine and Robert Waterfield was via a radio

A welcoming committee greets Jane as she arrives in Flagstaff to film *The Outlaw*.

telephone. On Saturday nights, cast and crew would treat themselves to a night on the town. Jane later recalled, "We'd pile into buses and ride forever, it seemed, to Flagstaff to bum around. Everybody got loaded and we sang all the way back."[18] On one of these excursions, Jack and Jane received a taste of their newfound recognition when they were invited to participate in a La Cuesta celebration in which Jack was called upon to choose a festival queen.[19] As the location shooting progressed, all seemed to be going well, and the five-hundred-mile buffer between the two Howards suited Hawks just fine. Even though Howard Hughes had been fairly hands-off during the making of *Scarface*, Hawks still preferred distance between himself and his producer. However, as Hughes's longtime assistant Noah Dietrich explained, "Each day's shooting was flown to Hollywood in a special plane, and Howard viewed the film in his private projection room. His old instinct for interference began to assert itself."[20] What happened next depends on who is telling the story. Some say Hughes felt Hawks was not spending enough money on the film (or spending too much), or he wasn't capturing enough of Arizona's natural beauty in the scenes (specifically clouds). Others, in the Hughes camp, claimed their boss was fed up with Hawks's bickering with Walter Huston and Thomas

Mitchell over script changes, which was holding up production.[21] Jane later theorized that "Hughes identified with Billy the Kid and wanted him to be the antihero. Hawks wanted him to be smart-alecky. Hughes wouldn't hear of this. Hughes didn't want him cocky, but Hawks definitely did."[22]

Whatever the reasons, Howard Hughes had started interfering with the production. Howard Hawks, who had more than proved his worth as a director, with over two dozen films under his belt, was not about to tolerate Hughes's meddling, which he feared would only increase. After three weeks of shooting and dealing with Hughes's micromanaging, Hawks had had enough. He fumed at Hughes, "If you think you can do a better job, why don't you take over the picture yourself?"[23] With that, production was shut down and everyone was ordered to come home. Jane later remembered a bewildered Jack Buetel asking, "Where do I go? Do I go home to Dallas or Hollywood?"[24]

Jack and Jane were both devastated. Neither had experience in motion pictures, so Howard Hawks had been their safety net. Neither knew what to expect from the enigmatic Hughes, who did indeed decide to direct the picture. Even though Jane's experience of being directed by Hawks extended no further than the screen tests, she tried to absorb as much as she could from him. "I adored him," Jane later observed, "and got things from him I was able to use even though he was no longer there. He didn't take any shit off people. He knew what he wanted, and if he didn't get it, he removed himself."[25] As Hawks prepared to fly back to Los Angeles, he invited his young leads to join him. However, they were advised by unit manager Cliff Broughton that, as employees of Howard Hughes, they had better not travel with the departing director. As Jane would see time and again over the years, loyalty was very important to Hughes. The pair took the advice seriously and stayed behind until Hughes's people made the travel arrangements. As he was leaving, Hawks told his would-be protégés, "Don't worry about it kids, we'll work together one day."[26] In 1946 Hawks did try to cast Buetel in the John Wayne vehicle *Red River* but, as Jane explained, "Howard Hughes would not loan him because he was still angry at the fact that Hawks had left" *The Outlaw*.[27] Montgomery Clift was cast opposite Wayne instead, which helped launch his film career in spectacular fashion. As for Buetel, Jane would later bemoan, "The poor darling. He got screwed. He really did."[28]

Jane dutifully returned to Los Angeles, fearful that her big break had just evaporated. She was called in to Hughes's office, where she spent an awkward two hours with her boss as he tried to ask her in a roundabout way if her loyalty lay with him or Howard Hawks. Once Jane realized what he was

Residents of the Hopi village where early scenes of *The Outlaw* were shot observe Jane getting ready for a photo shoot.

getting at, she assured him that she was all his, professionally speaking. "Tremendously relieved," he finally sent Jane on her way.[29]

Years later she would recall waiting months for *The Outlaw* production to restart. However, industry trade publications reported within days that *The Outlaw* had resumed filming on soundstages under the direction of Howard Hughes.[30] Switching the director wasn't the only big change to take place. Hughes had also decided to replace Lucien Ballard, Hawks's hand-picked cinematographer who had shot the screen tests. Instead Hughes hired Gregg Toland, who had just finished shooting *Citizen Kane* with Orson Welles. Toland would come to be regarded as one of Hollywood's greatest cinematographers, but as Lucien Ballard later claimed,

So Gregg came to me—I thought he was one of the best in the business—and he said, "I've seen the footage you did, and there's not a thing in the film that I could do as well as you did." Gregg wanted me to stay on the film and get him started, so I did, and I stayed on shooting the second unit. And Hughes, I found out, was very interested in effects. Every day he'd call up and say, "How did you do so-and-so?" So from then on I used a lot of filters and things to keep him happy."[31]

A few days after filming resumed with Hughes at the helm, the director was seriously injured in an automobile crash. The accident, which occurred on Christmas Eve, (Hughes's thirty-fifth birthday), left him with a four-inch laceration on the forehead, a concussion, and numerous cuts and bruises.[32] Rather than shut production down, Gregg Toland was assigned directorial duties, with Jules Furthman assisting. Paul Harrison, a journalist who visited the set, reported the resulting chaos: "There they all were in a dramatic situation, with everybody arguing about how it should be played. After learning their parts the night before, the two youngsters [Jane and Jack] had been handed revised scripts. Furthman was showing the players what to do." The reporter continued, "Toland was sitting behind the camera in apparent discouragement after having protested that part of the action just couldn't be fitted to a previously shot scene. Assistant Director Sam Nelson was putting in a word of advice." Harrison concluded, "If they don't get it right finally, Hughes will retake it when he reassumes the direction. But when it's all over, those two kids will have picked up some odd notions about acting and the sanity of the cinema."[33]

For Jane and Jack, that last point would turn out to be an understatement. Jane confirmed the rotating directors, recalling that when Jules Furthman directed her introductory scene in a barnyard, the same scene used in her screen test, she drew from the direction Howard Hawks had given her earlier.[34] The days that Furthman was at the helm proved especially challenging as he "covered his lack of confidence and experience by bluster and bull-dozing."[35] Furthman vented much of his frustration on Jane, prompting her to admit, "He was like my grandfather. Grandpa never said I did anything good all my life."[36] On one occasion Furthman's abuse of the cast and crew was so extreme that Walter Huston felt the need to pull him aside to calm him down.[37] When Jane complained of a sore throat, Furthman had her admitted to a hospital and banned all visitors, including Robert Waterfield. When she returned to the set four days later, resentful of what she deemed an imprisonment, Jane was so irritated she was slow to cooperate. "For Christ's sake we're making a picture!" Furthman roared at her in front of everyone. "It was all very silly," admitted Jane.[38]

Hughes's return proved to not be much of an improvement. Although the director seemed to have a clear idea of what he wanted, he was incapable of

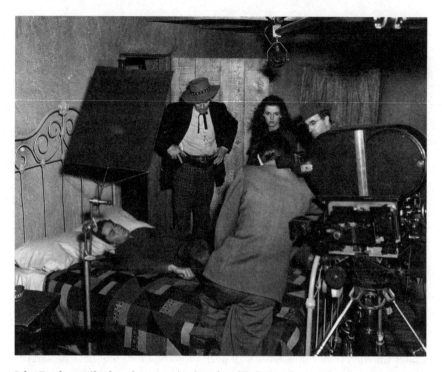

Jules Furthman (*back to the camera*), who often filled in as director on *The Outlaw,* preps
a scene with Jane, Jack Buetel (*lying in bed*), and Walter Huston (*left*).

conveying it to his cast, insisting on multiple takes of every scene—which to
everyone else appeared to be identical. Jack Buetel in particular suffered from
Hughes's idiosyncrasies. One of his scenes in a graveyard was shot over one hundred times, and in another Hughes told the actor not to raise his eyebrow so
much. It seemed Hughes had no trouble telling his actors what he didn't want
but could not explain what he *did* want. Under this mystifying direction, Buetel
became more and more stiff; as Jane later commented, Buetel becomes boring
as the film progresses.[39] Describing her experience for the film's publicity
team, Jane described Howard Hawks as an "imagist-artist" and Hughes as a
"precisionist-technician."[40] The technical aspects of the production, such as
camera angles, lighting, props, and effects, were Hughes's concerns, whereas
Hawks focused on his actors. Hughes didn't really know how to help his actors,
so he tried to compensate with the technical, something he felt he could control.
During the production, Walter Huston tried to help Jane and Jack with the
interpretations of their roles, often standing on the sidelines and subtly coaching
them, but there was only so much he could do with the inexperienced actors.[41]

Even though each production day dragged on with endless takes of the same scenes, Jane claimed Hughes "was very polite to all of us."[42] The other folks working on *The Outlaw* agreed, with one person commenting, "He doesn't pretend to be a czar on the set."[43] Hughes earned the respect of his crew—everybody called him Howard, not Mr. Hughes—yes his methods still perplexed most; editor Wally Grissell noted that the boss was often referred to behind his back as "Hardway" because "he does everything the hard way."[44] Jane and Jack, who didn't know any better, came to think this method was completely normal. Thomas Mitchell and Walter Huston, on the other hand, did know better. Huston didn't mind so much (and he certainly had no issue collecting the paychecks for all the extra days' work), going so far as to say that the real star of *The Outlaw* was Hughes. "To watch him work . . . his patience, his perseverance, his unshakable perfectionism was a show in itself." Thomas Mitchell, however, became increasingly enraged at having to reshoot scenes again and again. In one instance Mitchell finally lost his temper, marched up to Hughes (who had his nose buried in the script), and began screaming at him. When he finally ran out of steam, Hughes looked up calmly at Mitchell and asked, "Did you say something, Tommy?" This only sent the Oscar-winning veteran into a faster tailspin. Huston (whom Jane later described as "a buddy. He was wonderful") reacted to the scene by bursting into laughter, causing Jane and Jack to follow suit.[45]

His directing of actors left much to be desired, but Hughes had a brilliant mind for mechanics which, matched with his meticulous nature, served him well. With *The Outlaw,* this was apparent in some of the gunfire scenes, which come off convincingly. One scene in particular, in which Billy the Kid gets the tips of his ears shot off, is especially impressive. Unfortunately, this meticulousness did not translate when it came to his actors. Looking back, Jane described her boss as "a perfectionist but he didn't know how to deal with people."[46] As Jane got to know Hughes better, he struck her as being "perpetually lonely." Hughes was often unshaven and haggard looking on set, wearing rumpled clothing. Jane once remarked to him that he looked tired, and he was genuinely touched by her concern.

Hughes was perplexed by Jane's naturally outgoing nature, which caused her to mingle democratically with everyone on *The Outlaw* crew. "Has anyone ever told you not to be snobbish?" he questioned her one day, apparently looking for the roots of her perpetual socializing. As production wore on, Hughes became especially protective of Jane and kept a watchful eye on her. When Jane began having lunch regularly with Jack Buetel and his stand-in,

Hughes ordered his associate Lee Murrin to start escorting her to lunch. He also assigned Murrin as Jane's personal driver during filming, cautioning him to "drive carefully."[47] Hughes maintained an elaborate dressing room on set, which was strictly off limits to everyone (a curious intruder once prompted Hughes to display a rare show of temper), but once, after a particularly arduous two days of shooting, he took an exhausted Jane into his room to lie down, covered her with a blanket, and left.[48]

Despite Hughes's technical acumen, there was one area where his engineering prowess fell short. Jane may have initially been unaware of Hughes's obsession with her bustline, but she soon discovered his interest when he designed a bra for her to wear in *The Outlaw*. His concern was that the seams on her own brassiere would be visible under her blouse, whereas he wanted it to appear as if she wasn't wearing a bra (and therefore possessed breasts that defied gravity). Jane dutifully put on the Hughes's aerodynamic creation but absolutely hated it, feeling it was uncomfortable and flimsy. She took it off and threw it under a cot. Then she put her own garment back on, stuffing tissues under her blouse to hide the seams, and got ready to go back on set over the protests of the "poor wardrobe girl who said, 'I'm going to get fired!' I said, 'He'll never know the difference.' And he never did."[49] Over the years Jane would be asked ad nauseam about the Hughes wonder bra. She would always oblige with an affirmative answer (often accompanied by an eyeroll), but did give credit to Hughes for being ahead of his time in his quest for a seamless bra.

The switch from the location shoot in Arizona to a Hollywood soundstage was a welcome change for Geraldine, who was excited to see her daughter in action. "I didn't want to come," she told a reporter when visiting the set in early 1941. "I promised myself I wouldn't upset Jane by watching her work. But I just couldn't stand it any longer." She justified the visit to the *Outlaw* set by proclaiming, "I waited 19 years to see this."[50]

The monotony of filming was broken up one day when Jane had to visit the courthouse in downtown Los Angeles to get her contract with Howard Hughes approved. Because Jane was under twenty-one, a minor at that time, it was standard practice for a judge to sign off on such deals. Jane was permitted to leave the set for her court date and Geraldine, who needed to sign the contract, accompanied her. When Jane appeared before Judge Emmet H. Wilson, he was appalled by her appearance—she was still wearing her heavy makeup for filming. He refused to speak with Jane until she made herself "presentable" for the court. "There was a mad scurry," Geraldine later

A former actress herself, Geraldine Jacobi was thrilled that Daughter had been cast in *The Outlaw* and couldn't resist visiting Jane on the set.

recounted. "Someone went out and bought Turkish towels, and we worked in the washroom trying to get that make-up off. It was fatal with just cold water. Finally, after we had done the best we could, I took the veil off my hat. Daughter arranged it over her face and we approached the judge with fear and trembling. He let her pass, and the contract was approved; then we rushed back to the studio and the make-up man."[51]

"It took nine months," Jane later recalled of *The Outlaw* shoot. "It should have taken eight weeks." In reality, an assembled cut was completed by the end of March 1941, but Hughes was apparently unhappy with much of the footage and decided to invest an additional $127,000 in retakes.[52] It's not clear just how much footage was reshot, but there was no doubt about the ballooning budget. According to Noah Dietrich, Hughes had originally budgeted $400,000 for the film, but "*The Outlaw* ended up costing $3,400,000."[53] With *The Outlaw* finally in the can, Jane thought her work on the film was done.

In fact it was just beginning.

7

Motionless Picture Actress

In late 1939 Russell Birdwell was enjoying an evening at the famed Cafe Trocadero on the Sunset Strip. *Gone with the Wind* would soon be premiering, and as the press agent on that film, Birdwell certainly had cause to be proud of what he had accomplished for David O. Selznick's behemoth production. After all, he had managed to keep the movie on the front page for years with his brilliant "Search for Scarlett" campaign, which seemed to have every able-bodied woman in the country vying for the role of Scarlett O'Hara. Now he was on top of the world at one of Hollywood's celebrity hot spots, having a drink with MGM screen queen Norma Shearer.

When a tall, shy young man walked up to the table to engage Birdwell in conversation, the press agent was unimpressed. "He wore white tails alright," Russell later recalled, "but he actually didn't wear them. They wore him. The outfit looked as if he had inherited it from his grandfather and last wore it twenty years ago. The coat was too short, the pants were too short. His wrists stuck out. He twisted his neck so nervously that his collar appeared to be choking him. I wondered who on earth he could be, but Norma Shearer said something and I turned back to more pleasant subjects."[1] The stranger finally interrupted the conversation with a timid "May I see you?" Birdwell replied with an irritated "In a minute," though he hardly meant it. The man in the ill-fitting white tux skulked away at the rebuff.

"Don't you know who that was?" Shearer inquired with mild amusement.

"No."

"You should. It's Howard Hughes."[2]

Going forward, Russell Birdwell would definitely know who Howard Hughes was.

Russell Juarez Birdwell was born in Mexico City in 1903, but later claimed to have originated from Texas, which is where he did in fact grow up.[3] He started his career as a journalist working for the Newspaper Enterprise Association (NEA) syndication service, reporting mostly on the film industry.

He would go on to write novels and a memoir of his newspaper reporter days. He even tried his hand at film directing. However, his greatest success came as one of Hollywood's most infamous press agents. Always dedicated to his craft, he was once convicted of assaulting a *Los Angeles Times* photographer who got too close and tried to snap a photo of a client.[4] He was relatively private when it came to his personal life, but the publicity campaigns Russell Birdwell oversaw for films like *Gone with the Wind* (1939) and *The Alamo* (1960) made him so well known that an industry joke had an actress demanding, "Get me the press agent who handled Birdwell."[5] Countering his public successes in the film industry, Birdwell experienced his fair share of private tragedy; his father died when Birdwell was a teenager, his younger sister committed suicide when she was only twenty-one, and his only son was a quadriplegic following a birth injury and lived only to the age of twenty-two.[6] However, personal setbacks never seemed to impact Russell Birdwell's ability to sell a film.

By the time *The Outlaw* started shooting, Birdwell had officially been brought on by Hughes to publicize the movie. True to his reputation, Birdwell dreamed up advertising angles that matched Hughes's taste for all things sensational. The press agent's efforts to promote *The Outlaw* produced one of the most notorious marketing campaigns in Hollywood history, outshining the actual film and catapulting Jane Russell to international stardom.

From day one Howard Hughes made it clear that the discovery of Jack Buetel and Jane Russell was going to be the cornerstone of publicity for *The Outlaw*. Jane in particular would be a focal point of the $55,000 advertising budget supplied by Twentieth Century-Fox, which would be distributing the film.[7] Birdwell's tenure with Hughes began when Howard Hawks was still in the director's chair, so before he could turn his attention to Jane, the press agent needed to figure out who was to be credited for what. The final ruling was designed to appease all egos: *The Outlaw* would be credited as a Howard Hughes production, directed by Howard Hawks, and both Howards would receive co-credit for the discovery of Jane Russell and Jack Buetel.[8] With that bit of business out of the way, Russell Birdwell could turn his attention to selling *The Outlaw* and Jane to the public at large.

The press agent wasted no time, dispatching a slew of photographers to the Arizona location to shoot Jane. Gene Lester later recalled Birdwell's instructions: "Howard just signed a girl with the biggest chest in Hollywood. We want her boobs publicized. We don't care how you do it, just as long as you get her cleavage showing."[9] The photographers took their marching orders seriously, their mission made easier because Jane "had no idea what they were seeing" when they asked her to wield an axe, tie her shoes, or perform any number of other tasks, including riding a horse while wearing a bathing suit, that would yield the best view of her cleavage.[10]

One of the first publications to feature Jane's desert debut was *Pic*, a large-format magazine that not only ran sixteen interior photos taken by photographer Bob Wallace but also used a color shot of Jane lugging two large buckets on the cover of its February 4, 1941, issue. Jane was mortified when she saw the layout. Going forward, she vowed, she would be less naive and take Howard Hawks's advice to heart. After getting over the initial shock, Jane mainly just wanted to put those Arizona images behind her, but they proved to be prominent and persistent. "One weekend was all it took," she later lamented. "Those pictures came out for the next five years."[11]

Jane wasn't the only one who took issue with the *Pic* layout. The Catholic Legion of Decency immediately noted its objections, and gossip columnist Louella Parsons threw in her two cents: "I wonder where the Hays office was when the photographs on Jane Russell were released to a national picture magazine? The league of decency is up in arms—and rightly so." Parsons came to Jane's defense, though. "It is unfair to the little girl, who is a sweet child and who should not make her debut in a photograph as disgusting and suggestive."[12] Parsons's rival, Hedda Hopper, also injected her opinion, managing to enrage Levis Green by insinuating that Geraldine approved of the *Pic* layout. In a sternly worded letter, Green chastised Hopper: "We do want to call to your attention, the entire incorrectness of your statement regarding Jane Russell's Mother's approval of her daughter's pictures, in what we, the studio, and her Mother all considered very rotten and indecent."[13] Apparently Howard Hughes and Russell Birdwell had not communicated their intentions to Jane's agent. Hopper shrugged off the whole incident, writing back, "With all the publicity that Jane Russell is getting, I don't think any of the pictures have done her any harm at all. . . . While some of the photographs did make her look a little bit over-voluptuous, it helped put her across."[14] Geraldine was less tolerant about such photos of her daughter appearing on newsstands around the country, noting that Birdwell "had told me at the time not to be concerned about any photos taken of Jane, because all pictures had to be passed by his office and no pictures would be allowed if they were unseemly. . . . Well, it seemed afterwards that the pictures were just as objectionable as before. We felt as if Mr. Birdwell were selling a can of tomatoes, and didn't care what kinds of wrapper he put on the can."[15] Jane would echo the "can of tomatoes" sentiment countless times for the rest of her life.

During the first big publicity push for the yet-to-be-released *The Outlaw,* Jane was photographed all around Southern California. Here she is in 1942 showing off a gold nugget with Peggy McManus inside the Assay Office at the Knott's Berry Farm Ghost Town. (Courtesy of the Orange County Archives)

Around the same time *Pic* was hitting newsstands, the extremely popular *Life* magazine introduced Jane to over 3.25 million readers.[16] Proclaiming her "1941's Best New Star Prospect," *Life* ran a mere eight images of Jane.[17] The photos, taken by Bob Landry, were incredibly tasteful compared to the cleavage shots in *Pic,* but it all added up to a media onslaught by Russell Birdwell. This did not go unnoticed by the trade publication *Variety,* which noted that Jane was "getting a publicity buildup equaled only by that Warner Bros. put on for Ann Sheridan."[18] The promotion of Jane Russell proved to be intense right out of the gate, and would not let up for years. With *The Outlaw* presumably being released sometime during the first half of 1941, Birdwell and his staff were firing on all cylinders as they got Jane's picture splashed across magazines and newspapers around the county. Columnists sometimes referred to Jane as "a Dark-Haired Harlow," assuring the public that Jane's "physical assets are calculated to make the fans forget whatever talents she may lack."[19] *The Outlaw* advertising campaign received an additional boost when Jane and Jack were invited to appear on Louella Parsons's nationwide radio program *Hollywood Premiere* on May 2, 1941. Audiences received what would turn out to be an extremely early sneak preview of the film as the pair enacted a scene from *The Outlaw* before being interviewed by Parsons. Jane and Jack were paid in publicity instead of cash.

With 1941 rolling along and no *Outlaw* release in sight, MGM threw a large wrench into Howard Hughes's plans by releasing its own Billy the Kid movie, starring Robert Taylor, in the spring. Undaunted, Birdwell switched tactics by ordering his staff and the marketing people at Twentieth Century-Fox to cease using the name Billy the Kid and instead refer to the film's main character as "the most legendary of all western bad men."[20]

A decision was also made to focus the publicity of *The Outlaw* almost exclusively on Jane, and the easiest way to move forward on that plan was to take more pictures of her. Almost immediately after *The Outlaw* finished principal photography, posing for photos practically became a full-time job for Jane. She later noted of Birdwell, "He slapped a label on me and didn't know me at all. Pictures were taken every place you could think of, even at La Posada (but never showing our beautiful ranch house). It was me fighting with my brothers, me sitting on the fence talking to Mary the cow, me at the beach, in the water, climbing the rocks, visiting the pier, riding the roller coaster."[21] Birdwell and his crew dispatched Jane all over Southern California in the name of publicity. Some of the many places she appeared included Knott's Berry Farm's newly constructed Ghost Town, a "drive-in" gold mine near Newhall, and a Sigma Nu "Star Party" hosted by the University of Southern California at the Griffith Observatory and featuring co-eds dressed as their favorite film stars. Every event Jane attended included a photographer in tow. At one point Jane and Jack Buetel boarded a chartered plane to travel to Chet Ellicott's Slash E Ranch, a dude ranch in Idaho. The reporter who accompanied the pair was impressed that Jane "proved to be a regular American girl."[22]

Geraldine, chaperoning, was more excited about the dude ranch cuisine, noting, "Never before or since have I seen such a table. Mr. and Mrs. Ellicott were the owners and outdid themselves with hospitality. The steaks were the thickest and the juiciest, simply whoppers! Next day, the chicken just called for 'ohs' and 'ahs.'"[23] Jane also spent an afternoon at the Ambassador Hotel being sketched by noted illustrator James Montgomery Flagg, best known for his 1917 Uncle Sam army recruitment poster. Flagg appreciated Jane's ability to sit still for long stretches of time and noted that she "is beautiful, voluptuous and swarthy as a pirate's daughter." He was also impressed that Hollywood hadn't "gotten around to starving her into anemia as they did Garbo and hundreds of others and that cliche they pull—'the screen always makes 'em look fatter.'"[24] Less impressive to Flagg was the blitz of photographers that magically appeared when Jane emerged in a bathing suit.

The time and money Birdwell put into the various photo spreads immediately paid off, as Jane appeared on the covers of magazines with names like *Click, Pic, Spot,* and *See,* not to mention receiving consistent newspaper coverage. *Spot* even put Jane on the cover two months in a row, which the editor acknowledged was "bad journalism but good business."[25]

Perhaps most notably, Jane was sent to photographer George Hurrell, previously employed by MGM and Warner Bros., who came to be regarded as the godfather of Hollywood glamour photography. Using light and shadow in a way that spawned many imitations, Hurrell's striking portraits of movie stars are unmatched to this day. When Jane arrived at his studio, she greeted the legendary photographer with "I feel like a guinea pig," to which he responded, "You won't when we've finished with you."[26] The pair got along immediately. After spending so much time in front of cameras, Jane was getting to be an old pro and appreciated Hurrell's no-nonsense approach to his craft. "It's funny stuff, this bizness," she said at the time. "George is easy to sit for. He just says 'look there' and 'look there.' Some guys start talking about thoughts and so on, it's hard to follow them. You never think George is taking pictures, it's so easy."[27] Of his model, Hurrell said, "Jane's wonderful, so cooperative and interested. And a marvelous bony structure in the face—she's wonderful."[28] In their first session Hurrell photographed Jane lying on a fur rug, in some shots wearing a simple dress and in others a frilly satin and lace negligee. The images were classic Hurrell and oozed Hollywood glamour. But he was just getting started.

In the next session Hurrell took inspiration from the yet-to-be-released *The Outlaw.* "I'll shoot Jane Russell in a haystack!" he enthused.[29] Hurrell had

Under the capable lens of photographer George Hurrell, Jane shifted from sexy smolders to sweet smiles while posing on bales of hay. The haystack photos from *The Outlaw* publicity campaign would follow Jane for the rest of her life.

a substantial amount of hay brought in, but after the delivery trucks pulled away, he realized he had a problem. "We just had a haystack there," he later remembered. "But one funny thing about it is that I realized, 'She can't get up on the hay. She's going to keep falling off.' So I had to put steps under the hay, just to keep her up there. She was a great gal."[30] Hurrell would do a couple of sessions with the haystack. A black-and-white shoot had shown Jane barefoot in a simple dress seductively pulled down below her shoulders. Numerous images from this session would be printed and distributed, some with Jane glaring at the camera and others in which she smiles innocently.

The second haystack sitting ended up being partially art-directed by illustrator John Wentworth. Birdwell had hired Wentworth to design some of the poster art for *The Outlaw*. Sticking to the haystack theme, he proposed a large-scale advertisement that would have "COLOR—excitement—and plenty of SEX. I thought it a good idea to have a six-shooter languishing in her hand."[31] Wentworth also envisioned another poster inferring "that Jane is the 'OUTLAW' and here again—the startling effect of this sexy gal—looking right at you—has plenty of attention value."[32] Hurrell followed orders for the second set of haystack images, shot partially with Kodachrome, with Jane dressed in one of the peasant blouse and skirt combos she had worn in *The Outlaw*. In these Jane was either leaning back in the hay with her skirt pulled up to show her thighs or leaning forward with exposed cleavage, all while brandishing a handgun or two. In keeping with Howard Hughes's focus (and regarding Jane as more of a thing than a person), one of Birdwell's team thought, upon an initial viewing of the photos, that "the breasts looked sloppy."[33] Wentworth assured the critics, "We can apply air brush to change any breast lines that are not satisfactory and outline any other parts of the figure to make them more idealistic."[34] Personally, Wentworth viewed the photos as "ample."[35] Birdwell's team ultimately regarded the second haystack shooting as "highly successful," and hoped to have a publication layout chronicling the creation of billboard-sized advertisements, described as the birth of a twenty-four sheet.[36] One of the color images was immediately sent to *Esquire* magazine, which ran it as a large foldout in the June 1942 issue.

The Hurrell haystack photos would go on to become some of the most iconic and instantly recognizable in Hollywood history. They would also come to define Jane Russell for the rest of her career and beyond, marking the point where internally she would need to separate the on-screen siren with the off-screen Valley girl. Since she had taken to heart Howard Hawks's advice to say no, she claimed to feel empowered, yet frequently seemed to be straddling a very fine line between what made her uncomfortable and what she felt she was obligated to do for the sake of publicity and her career. The Hurrell images are certainly less crude and voyeuristic than the Moenkopi shots of Jane leaning over with an axe, but there's no denying how extremely provocative they are. Perhaps she felt comfortable enough with George Hurrell to let her guard down during the shoot. By that time he had already obtained name recognition and a sterling reputation as one of Hollywood's best photographers, adored by the likes of Joan Crawford and Norma Shearer. However, Jane claimed the photographer's status never came into play. "You know," she relayed years later, "I was photographed by so many people that year, that this was just another one. Mr. Hurrell was nice and all, but I didn't think about it until the pictures began appearing everywhere."[37] Since the specific content of the second photo shoot was being dictated in part by Russell Birdwell's office, it's possible Jane felt she needed to acquiesce, though at the time she claimed, almost defiantly, "I *posed* for the pictures, didn't I? And I liked them. I'm old enough to know what I'm doing."[38]

Ultimately, Jane appreciated that if she wanted to be a Hollywood star, publicity was part of the deal and something she would have to endure. Later on, having spent a lifetime being confronted with the image of herself as a smoldering brunette on a haystack, Jane felt no affection for the portraits, but she still understood their selling power. In her autobiography, published in the mid-1980s, she wrote, "I'd like a classy portrait on the jacket of this book, but my publishers convinced me that the thing in the haystack is the J.R. people want to read about. Hope they're right. How disgusting!"[39] Decades later, when asked what she had in common with Jane Russell the sex goddess, she would reply with an emphatic "Nothing!"[40]

Birdwell's crew continued to brainstorm creative ways to keep Jane Russell in the forefront of American consciousness. The results were hit or miss. After Jane attended a flower show in Pasadena, an enthusiastic suggestion was made to manufacture a perfume called "The Outlaw" that would release "all of the tempestuousness, etc., etc., which Jane exhibits in the picture of the same name."[41] That idea seems to have gone nowhere. Throughout 1942 the publicizing of Jane Russell was a daily topic of discussion at Birdwell & Associates, and while the team seemed to take advantage of every last photo op that came Jane's way, Birdwell was conscious of events that would not add to Jane's brand, so to speak. When Howard Hughes personally approved Jane's participation in the 1942 Los Angeles Open Golf Tournament, Birdwell reached out to him directly to advise against it, noting that "dozens of other starlets will be there, plus newsreel cameramen, and I don't believe it will be a good idea for (1) Jane to appear in company with a lot of unimportant names, and (2) for her to appear in a newsreel before our picture is out.[42]" Even Jane Russell's publicity sometimes had its limits.

With Jane's photos hitting print publications nonstop, copywriters wielded an assortment of adjectives to describe her. *Pretty, lovely,* and *attractive* were sometimes used, but more often than not readers were treated to a wide array of ways to highlight Jane's figure, especially her bustline: *voluptuous, buxom, bosomy, curvy, well-rounded, ample, breasty, Junoesque, extraordinarily physically endowed,* and so on. Additionally, reporters were always happy to point out that Jane carried 122 pounds on her five-foot-seven frame. However, as the months went by without the release of *The Outlaw,* a new favorite description for Jane emerged: motionless picture actress.

Undaunted, Birdwell and his crew chose instead to focus on other monikers courtesy of the press, such as "Sensational Cinderella," "Sultry Cinderella," "Perfect 36" and, in keeping with the Howard Hughes/Jean Harlow angle, "Dark-Haired Harlow" and "Hell's New Angel."[43] Still, some members of the public vented their frustrations at the lack of an actual on-screen Jane. As a professor at the University of Michigan wrote to Birdwell, "When is that account of yours, Jane Russell, going to appear in a picture? I am getting damn tired of looking at her on magazine covers and Esquire gatefolds. I want to see her *move,* even if it's in a Mickey Mouse. If she's going to be a flop you might as well let it happen now."[44]

If the well of ideas for new ways to promote Jane was starting to run dry, that was remedied on December 7, 1941, when the Japanese attack on Pearl Harbor officially pulled the United States into World War II. So many American men deployed overseas led to the rise of wartime pinup girls, and Jane would prove to be one of the most popular. Months before the US had become directly involved in the war, Jane had already been a favorite when she visited Camp Roberts in Northern California for an Army Day celebration. The military men seemed to instantly gravitate toward her, so promoting Jane as a pinup for the soldiers didn't require much effort from Birdwell. His office received multiple requests for images of Jane for army barracks, appeals for personal introductions and appearances, or just messages to inform Jane of military honors, such as being named the Long Beach Naval Reserves' Keep 'Em Flying Girl or the Sweetheart of the Muroc Bombing and Gunnery Range.[45] These developments seemed to inspire Birdwell, who took full advantage of wartime promotional possibilities and had Jane photographed registering automobile tires, getting her first sugar-rationing book, decorating a "Victory Window" at the I. Magnin on Wilshire Boulevard, doing a "Victory Exercise" routine, and participating in war-bond rallies, among countless other patriotic activities. She posed with Joe E. Brown Jr.

Jane during a personal appearance at Camp Roberts in April 1941. She may have been referred to as the "motionless picture actress" in the early 1940s, but she was a favorite with servicemen.

and members of his air force unit, who nicknamed themselves Russell's Raiders, and ventured into the shipyards on Terminal Island to pose for a naval "Serve with Silence" campaign, in which soldiers were advised that "a slip of the lip may sink a ship." Never one to pass up an opportunity for a good story, Birdwell flipped a typical wartime narrative by arranging a photo of a soldier knitting a sweater for Jane while looking longingly at an image of her. The press may have enjoyed taking jabs at Jane (and Howard Hughes) by calling her the "motionless picture actress," but throughout the war servicemen never tired of receiving the latest picture of their favorite pinup.

The photos were a point of aggravation for Geraldine, who noted, "The world was beginning to wonder, 'What kind of girl is this?'"[46] The only men who may have found the endless barrage of Jane photos tiresome were Jane's brothers (three of them enlisted), who had to deal with fellow servicemen ogling photos of their sister. Geraldine later commented that her sons "had more to fight than the Japs and Germans. They knew Daughter, and the tall tales and the pin-ups were hard to stand."[47]

Compared to the tedium of making *The Outlaw*, posing for endless photographs was easy. "It's a good thing I started modeling for Tom Kelley," Jane would often say.[48] That experience had prepared her for working with the likes of Russell Birdwell and Howard Hughes, for whom publicity sometimes seemed like a matter of life or death. Even when she wasn't posing in front of a camera, Jane was kept busy by Howard Hughes. He had her work with acting coach Florence Enright, of whom Jane said, "She had been on the stage for years and was a comedienne—sweet, wonderful, little woman. She would put you through the paces so that you felt perfectly natural in front of a camera, you didn't feel stilted."[49]

Jane wasn't the only one under contract to the enigmatic multimillionaire, so she became friendly with some of the others, including Faith Domergue and Jane Greer. She also became acquainted with a cool blonde actress, Carole Gallagher, who had briefly dated Howard Hughes. Jane and Carole hit it off immediately, and the pair moved together into a house on Barham Boulevard that belonged to Carole's grandmother. They got a kick out of dressing in identical suits and wearing long hair falls that cascaded down their backs. "We probably looked like a pair of hookers," Jane remembered, "but we thought we were the living end."[50]

Despite the publicity-driven workload, Jane was having the time of her life. She enjoyed the independence that came with earning a living and believed her freewheeling behavior was fine, as long as no one was getting

When she wasn't posing for thousands of photos, Jane studied acting with coach Florence Enright.

hurt. Additionally, her newly adopted lack of spiritual faith wasn't a problem, though Geraldine secretly agonized over it.

By mid-1942 Jane's romance with Robert Waterfield had cooled off. The pair may have had an unspoken agreement not to discuss Jane's film career, but nonetheless it was putting a strain on their relationship. During the filming of *The Outlaw,* when Hughes associate Lee Murrin would drive Jane home late at night, she would have him make a detour to Waterfield's house. Scratching the window screen to wake her fiancé up, she would reassure him that any illicit behaviors he had conjured in his mind were simply not true.[51] These gestures did little to diminish his growing irritability. During the filming even Howard Hughes noticed and became concerned when Jane arrived at work "upset by the conduct of her fiancé," who some of the crew knew to be "quite mad with jealousy."[52] When Jane moved to the Hollywood Hills, the pair seemed to grow apart even further, and she began quietly dating other men, including a football player on the USC team, UCLA's crosstown rival. She also went out on a date with actor John Payne, whose marriage to actress Anne Shirley was on the skids. Jack Buetel, who was friends with Payne, arranged the date at Jane's request. The actor, best known for his role in the perennial classic *Miracle on 34th Street,* was ten years Jane's senior and more intellectually inclined than Robert Waterfield. She found herself undeniably attracted to him.

One of the many requests for a personal appearance Jane received via Russell Birdwell's office was to attend the annual San Diego State College Blue Book Ball. Bob Lantz and Bob Menke of the college's Associated Student Body were relentless in their appeals to Birdwell & Associates to bring Jane to San Diego. They even set up a display in the college bookstore featuring a Jane Russell WANTED VERY MUCH ALIVE poster, which received a write-up in the *San Diego Union* and was reportedly seen by twelve hundred students.[53] Perhaps Birdwell viewed the two students as kindred spirits, and the newspaper story seems to have convinced him of the publicity potential. He agreed to send Jane to San Diego to be elected Sagebrush Sweetheart of the Blue Book Ball. Accompanied by Dale Armstrong, one of Birdwell's executives, and Aunt Ernestine, Jane boarded the 8:45 a.m. train on June 19, 1942, and headed south with a jam-packed itinerary in hand and the impression that all accommodations had been arranged and paid for by the students.

The organizers seemed to think everything went smashingly well, but Armstrong was less than enthralled. "The students tried their best but had had no experience in setting up such a deal and so were of no help. There was no money apparently, since whenever there were drinks students did not pick up the checks. Hotel accommodations were not paid for; students had made reservations but we had to pay the bill."[54] Armstrong also noted, without elaboration, that Aunt Ernie "was more a bother on the whole trip than help."[55] The excursion turned out to be a further bust as the story received

Jane poses with students at San Diego State College, where she was to appear at the annual Blue Book Ball. Jane, in the first trimester of an unplanned pregnancy, was ill during much of this venture.

scant coverage in the local newspaper and wasn't picked up by any other news outlets. Moreover, the trip was grueling for Jane. She was sick during the train ride, and after arriving in San Diego continued to be so ill that she passed out in her room at the Hotel del Coronado and missed some of the scheduled events. She was not, as Armstrong noted, at "her sparkling best."[56]

Emotionally, it was also not the best time to have to turn on the charm for a large group of college students as Jane had a lot on her mind. She was pregnant.

Jane was just shy of her twenty-first birthday, under contract to Howard Hughes, and the focus of an expensive marketing campaign for a film that had yet to be released. She certainly longed to have a large family at some point, but starting now was out of the question. Also, this was a time when "good girls" didn't have babies out of wedlock, so Jane felt she had no choice but to terminate the pregnancy. In an era when safe and accessible abortions simply did not exist, Jane's options were limited. She recounted the whole ordeal in her 1985 autobiography:

I didn't know anything about who to go to. Finally, after talking to an older girl I'd known at school (who knew her way around), I got the name of a doctor. Robert drove me over to a small clean enough building in Glendale somewhere, and I went cold turkey—no anesthetic—into hell. I've never had anything hurt like that since. I suppose Robert thought it his. I wasn't that sure. But he was still in school and marriage was out of the question. The abortion didn't take. I had to go back with Carol [*sic*]. It was the same horror all over again. When we got to our house, I found myself very sick for the first time in my life.

I had a raging fever and a terrified Carol called our doctor, who rushed me to the hospital. As he gave me my first anesthesia, he swore at the butcher who had done this, and I went out. When I came to, I asked Carol whether Robert had called. He hadn't. I said, "You'd better take me home to mother."[57]

The botched abortion proved to be a life-altering event. So much physical damage had been done that Jane would never be able to have children. She also came to believe that turning her back on the Lord had played a large role in her misfortune. From that moment on, Jane would embrace her spiritual faith vehemently and proclaim it loudly.

It's not clear if Russell Birdwell and Howard Hughes were aware of the situation, but Jane was too sick to even try to pretend everything was okay. Geraldine assumed the role of liaison between Daughter and Birdwell & Associates, explaining that Jane's ribs were taped and the doctor had ordered her to remain in bed.[58] Photo shoots, personal appearances, and acting classes were cancelled as Jane remained bedridden. However, when *Look* magazine wanted to run a multipage spread on Jane, it was too good an opportunity to pass up; the reporter was allowed to interview Jane at La Posada while she was recovering, and accompanying photos were taken.[59]

A month later Jane had recuperated enough that she was able to leave the house and resume the photo shoots. However, the effects of the ordeal, both physically and mentally, were picked up by the camera, and the team at Birdwell & Associates could not help but notice the change in Jane. After one disastrous shoot, Dale Armstrong commented that in the pictures "Jane shows the kind of care that she hasn't been taking care of herself lately." He hoped to get a different photographer and "Jane (looking half-way alive) together."[60] When Jane started pushing back on some of her obligations,

Jane at La Posada in late summer 1942. She had been unwell after the abortion, but put on a good show for the press.

During a break from her relationship with Robert Waterfield, Jane engaged in a brief but passionate romance with actor John Payne. Here they are shown arriving at the premiere of *The Pied Piper* in September 1942.

Armstrong felt compelled to notify Birdwell, "The picture situation with Jane is getting more critical. She looks like hell and despite the fact that I try to set the dates late in the day so she can get all possible sleep, it doesn't seem to do much good. Also, talking to Jane gets no where."[61]

The ordeal caused Jane to rethink her love life. She had been enamored with Robert Waterfield since she was fourteen, but was now starting to waver. He did come to visit her every day at La Posada, but only for around ten minutes, and always with a friend. He didn't seem to want to be alone with a sick woman. John Payne, on the other hand, phoned her every day during her recuperation. Payne, whom Jane described as a thinker, reader, and writer, showered attention and tenderness on her, in stark contrast to Waterfield. It was enough to trigger a serious change of heart. Jane broke off the engagement and gave the ring back to Waterfield, who promptly hocked it. She then started a serious relationship with John Payne.

Whose baby had Jane been pregnant with? The only thing she ever said in print was she wasn't sure it was Waterfield's. Jan Lowell, who with her husband worked with Jane on the early draft of the autobiography, revealed, "I know who it was. I said to her, 'Jesus, Jane, if you were going to screw around, you could have picked a better actor than John Payne.'"[62] Jane, however, claimed that she went out with Payne only the one time before the abortion and did not see him again until after. She was also dating the USC football player at the time. In any event, whoever the father was, Jane chose to not disclose his name publicly.

After two months of recuperating Jane was finally able to move back in with Carole and reenter the public spotlight in September 1942. She was often seen on the arm of John Payne, who was on the verge of being dispatched with the Army Air Corps. The pair, seemingly inseparable, was spotted around town in popular hangouts like the Ice Follies and at film premieres. Deep down Jane was still harboring some residual feelings for Robert Waterfield, but these were tempered when she discovered he had been dating another woman while she was practically at death's door. Jane threw herself headlong into an intense relationship with Payne. The pair even discussed marriage, joking that if they did tie the knot, she would legally be Jane Payne.

As Jane rejoined the living in the fall of 1942, the endless photo shoots were finally subsiding. Instead her days were filled with costume fittings and rehearsals for a live performance. A full year and a half after principal photography had wrapped on *The Outlaw*, it seemed the film was finally going to be released in theaters. In order to promote it, Jane and Jack Buetel would be personally introducing screenings with a live show. Given the pair's limited theater experience, they were subjected to a grueling schedule of rehearsals with Jules Furthman, who would be directing a skit. With the premiere seemingly on the horizon, Jane looked forward to putting the "motionless picture actress" label behind her.

But was Howard Hughes really ready to release *The Outlaw*? Only time would tell. No matter what happened, it was of minimal concern to Russell Birdwell. In the midst of one of *The Outlaw*'s many media pushes, Birdwell told Lee Murrin, "Just in case Howard should be concerned because so much national stuff is now breaking on Jane and 'The Outlaw,' you can assure that this type of thing will continue down through the months — and the years if necessary."[63]

Little did Birdwell know how prophetic those words would be.

8

Mean . . . Moody . . . Magnificent

The Outlaw had begun principal photography in December 1940, and a complete cut was ready by the end of March the following year. This was accomplished despite the abrupt departure of Howard Hawks, Howard Hughes's serious automobile accident, and his deliberate directing style. Yet it would be years before most audiences got a chance to view Hughes's offbeat take on the legend of Billy the Kid. Hollywood lore would attribute the delays largely to a legendary battle royale between Hughes and the Production Code Administration. The office of Joseph Breen was indeed mortified by the western opus, but the eccentric whims of Howard Hughes would play a role just as big, if not bigger, in the excessive delays in the rollout of *The Outlaw*. At the epicenter of the ballyhoo was Jane Russell, who would soon find herself grappling with the realization that being involved in a cinema controversy was maybe not a price she was willing to pay for a film career.

In the midst of production on *The Outlaw,* when Howard Hughes was still convalescing in the hospital following his Christmas Eve car crash, Geoffrey Shurlock and Al Lynch from the Production Code Administration visited the set. Jules Furthman, who was filling in as director, met with the pair and confirmed that many concerns the PCA had with the submitted script would be addressed. "Major difficulties" would be corrected; Furthman assured them, "There will be no suggestion of a sex affair between the two young leads" and "The sequence in the hayloft (already shot) will be trimmed with the hope of omitting any suggestions of a sex affair."[1] Considering that sexual interactions are the basis of Rio and Billy's relationship, it's not clear how this could actually be accomplished. When the completed cut was submitted to the PCA for approval at the end of March, Joseph Breen quickly realized that whatever Furthman agreed to had been completely ignored by Howard Hughes.

Breen personally reached out to Hughes by sending a letter via messenger to notify him, "The picture is definitely and specifically in violation of our

Production Code and because of this cannot be approved."[2] Breen clarified that the overarching reasons for the denial of a certificate of approval were twofold; "(a) The inescapable suggestion of an illicit relationship between the 'Doc' and Rio, between Billy and Rio; and (b) The countless shots of Rio in which her breasts are not fully covered."[3] Just in case there was any question as to which scenes were problematic, a list was drawn up:

Breast shots of Rio when she leans over Billy in bed.
Breast shots of Rio when Billy returns to cabin after finding sand in water containers.
Breast shots where Rio is tied to posts.
Breast shots—Rio at camp fire.
Breast shot—Rio sitting on rock.
Breast shot—Rio in water.
Breast shot—Rio on horse.[4]

Breen went on to advise Hughes that his decision could be appealed to Will Hays, who now bore the title of president, Motion Picture Producers and Distributors of America. Predicting Hughes would go this route, Breen immediately shot off a letter to Hays expressing his shock and outrage at the film he had just witnessed: "In my more than ten years of critical examination of motion pictures, I have never seen anything quite so unacceptable as the shots of the breasts of the character of Rio. This is the young girl, whom Mr. Hughes recently picked up and who has never before, according to my information, appeared on the motion picture screen. Throughout almost half the picture the girl's breasts, which are quite large and prominent, are shockingly emphasized and, in almost every instance, are very substantially uncovered."[5]

The screening of *The Outlaw* seems to have caused Breen to spend that night stewing over the state of women's breasts. The next day he fired off another letter to Hays: "In recent months we have noted a marked tendency on the part of the studios to more and more undrape women's breasts. In recent weeks the practice has become so prevalent as to make it necessary for us, almost every day, to hold up a picture which contains these unacceptable breast shots." He continued, "Yesterday we had the exhibition of breasts shots in the Howard Hughes picture, THE OUTLAW, which outdoes anything we have ever seen on the motion picture screen."[6]

After receiving the couriered letter from Breen, Hughes took it seriously enough to call a conference that same night with Furthman along with PCA representatives Shurlock and Lynch. It was determined that some of the problematic lines of dialogue could be easily altered, but the offensive breast shots could not be dealt with without completely reshooting many of Jane's scenes. Despite the daunting demands, however, Furthman was willing to try to fix the issues and asked to meet with Breen personally for discussion. That meeting did take place a couple of days later, though Hughes was conspicuously absent. Shortly thereafter Hughes received another letter from Breen suggesting no fewer than thirty-seven cuts of Jane in an attempt to eliminate the existence of her breasts.[7]

Hughes felt he had no choice but to appeal the decision.

In the ensuing weeks, Russell Birdwell and Hughes attorney Neil McCarthy traveled to New York to personally appeal their case to the board of directors of the MPPDA. At Hughes's instruction, oversized photos of all the major actresses of the time, including Betty Grable, Rita Hayworth, Marlene Dietrich, Irene Dunne, Norma Shearer, Loretta Young, Madeleine Carroll, and Claudette Colbert, were printed out and hung around the hearing room. Beside these images were blowups of Jane in *The Outlaw*. When it was time for Birdwell to plead his case for the film, he called up a mathematician with a pair of calipers who proceeded to measure the necklines of the actresses in Code-approved films versus Jane's, arguing there was no difference in the amount of skin exposed. That Jane was more fully endowed than the other actresses was something Birdwell did not bother to point out. The board sided with the PCA, agreeing *The Outlaw* was in violation of the Code and not deserving of a certificate of approval. However, the measurement argument was compelling enough that the number of required cuts was vastly reduced, targeting six scenes and approximately forty feet.[8] "I got credit for it," Birdwell would say of the stunt, "but it was Howard's idea."[9]

Believing Howard Hughes would fall in line and abide by the MPPDA's ruling, Breen approved issuing *The Outlaw* certificate number 7440, essentially giving the film the PCA's seal of approval. Breen did note that issuance of the certificate was provisional, based on Hughes implementing the cuts specified through the appeal process and emphasizing that the changes "will be made in *all* prints put into general release."[10] These cuts would also appease the Legion of Decency and the extremely hard-nosed New York Censor Board.

With provisional approval from the PCA, it appeared that Jane's film debut was nearly ready to hit theaters. Under normal circumstances, any of the major studios would have quickly released the film in order to turn a profit. Howard Hughes, however, was never one to engage in the expected. He may have had a hard time conveying his wants to actors, but he was extremely deliberate in how he directed and edited *The Outlaw.* The numerous shots of Jane's bustline included in the final film were quite intentional. One of the more notorious scenes had Jane leaning over a bedridden Billy the Kid. Jane later explained that Gregg Toland shot the scene, quickly realized the issue with Jane's cleavage being too visible, and moved the cameras for the rest of the takes. When it came time to cut the film, Hughes insisted on the first take, knowing full well the PCA would never approve. As the months of 1941 passed, Hughes's obstinance, matched with his perpetual tinkering of the film, continued to delay its release. All the while Russell Birdwell surged forward with the press campaign, joking with the Twentieth Century-Fox publicity directors that the film "would soon cease being a military secret."[11]

By early 1942 it appeared that *The Outlaw* was finally going to be unleashed on the world with premieres in London and Chicago, featuring personal appearances by Jane. The fact that war was raging in Europe seems to have finally occurred to someone, and Birdwell informed a member of the British Information Service that the premiere with Jane could not go forward "due not only to transportation difficulties in getting her back to this country but the problems of trying to get her a passport to get her out of the United States." Seemingly as an afterthought Birdwell followed up, "In addition to all of these problems there is the personal risk involved and this is something we think we should forgo at this time."[12] In response to the news that Jane could not travel to London, an associate involved in the premiere planning sent a telegram reading, "Was not aware premiere depended on Jane Russell's arrival."[13] The London opening remained cancelled as Birdwell turned his attention to an early 1942 premiere in Chicago.

World affairs seem to have been of less concern to Russell Birdwell than Jane's clothing as he prepared to send her and Jack Buetel to Chicago. Apparently the wardrobe Howard Hawks had helped Jane purchase prior to the location shoot at the end of 1940 wasn't to Birdwell's liking, as he noted to Lee Murrin, "Preparatory to taking Jane Russell to Chicago for the opening of 'The Outlaw' I am buying her four complete outfits so she can make a presentable appearance. As she stands today on the hoof she is the worst dressed woman in America."[14] The prospect of Birdwell spending Hughes's money on clothing prompted Lee Murrin to respond, "It might be bad to get Jane's clothes now because the picture might not open until Fall."[15] Undaunted (and optimistic), Birdwell's people assured Murrin "that the clothes being purchased were so substantial and moderate in the style that even if such a delay occurred her wardrobe would be in fashion and good taste."[16] Birdwell proceeded with the purchase, but Jane's wardrobe continued to be a point of contention. Via Lee Murrin, Hughes ordered $500 worth of purchases to be returned to Saks Fifth Avenue. As the clothes had already been altered to fit Jane, they could not be returned, and Birdwell's people continued to insist that unless "the picture is not released for another year, the clothes will be smart and ok."[17]

As the two parties continued to haggle over Jane's wardrobe, Hughes still did not release *The Outlaw*. The situation became even more complicated when Twentieth Century-Fox grew weary of the delays and decided to pull out of the distribution deal. Additionally, the studio began demanding over $35,000 reimbursement for the money it had expended so far in promoting *The Outlaw*. This was especially galling to Birdwell, who complained that the press material Fox had generated "is jammed with old-fashioned stunts, stunts I would have been ashamed to use 20 years ago," and that copy provided to the studio had been rewritten "into such a vomity style that [it is] completely unusable."[18] Even worse, press people at Fox had altered the images of Jane supplied by Birdwell's team. The press agent further groused, "They have changed the shape of the girl's breast, painted additions on to her shirt in various places and in general have ruined the product we are selling, namely Jane Russell as God made her."[19] Going forward, Birdwell wouldn't need to worry about outside interference. Howard Hughes had decided to release *The Outlaw* himself and Birdwell's office would have full control of the publicity.

The Chicago premiere never materialized. As 1942 was nearing an end, Hughes decided that a road show of *The Outlaw* would be the way to go, preceded by a live sketch with Jane and Jack, emceed by radio announcer George McCall. The two young actors were subjected to a grueling rehearsal schedule with Jules Furthman that went on for what seemed like an eternity to Jane. She later recalled reaching her breaking point. "How long can you rehearse one scene? So finally I said, 'We gotta stop this we're going nuts!'" She then described doing the unthinkable—confronting Howard Hughes. "With Howard, you never knew exactly which office he was in, so finally I found out which office he was in that day. And I went down and I picked up pebbles and threw them up on the window, and he stuck his head out. And I said, 'I wanna talk to you! We've gotta stop doing this, come and look at it!'" She continued, "I was yelling at him, so he came down and looked at [the sketch], and had a few suggestions. So, we got to do it another two weeks!"[20]

As the two young actors continued the intense rehearsal schedule with Jules Furthman, a railroad baggage car worth of scenery for the sketch was being constructed, including an impractically large tree that Hughes insisted on. Ultimately, Hughes continued to hold back on releasing *The Outlaw* but insisted on proceeding with testing out the live sketch before the end of the year. Even though pulling it together was straining the resources of those involved, Hughes wouldn't relent on forging ahead with Jane and Jack's stage debut. This mystified George McCall, who noted to Birdwell, "Cannot understand his hurry however he dropped something this morning that may be a clue. He said Russell was getting impatient. While this means little, I know that the Music Corporation, now her agents, have been raising Hell with Hughes and presume his haste to get some action may be occasioned by this."[21]

Levis Green had indeed moved over to the Music Corporation of America (MCA) agency and taken Jane with him. MCA had started in the 1920s as a booking agency for musicians, but by the late 1930s had become the largest talent agency in the world, representing clients in all fields of entertainment. This expansion had occurred largely because of Lew Wasserman, who would be a behemoth of the industry for decades to come. "I was still with Levis," Jane later recalled, "but now under MCA. Lew Wasserman brought muscle."[22] This may not have been a big-screen debut, but a test run of the sketch seemed to appease Jane and MCA for the moment.

There was some difficulty finding a theater willing to book an elaborate ten-minute sketch that didn't precede the movie it was promoting. Finally, the Rialto Theater in Tucson, Arizona, was secured for a three-day engagement in which Jack, Jane, and George McCall would appear in multiple performances per day in between screenings of *Road to Morocco*.[23] Writer Helen Morgan (not to be confused with the torch singer of the same name) and photographer John Florea of *Life* magazine accompanied the troupe to document the momentous occasion, which was almost cancelled due to issues shipping the set pieces. Ultimately, the sets did arrive in Tucson in time for the performance, "with the exception of the tree," George McCall relayed to Birdwell, "which never did get there. However, this was no handicap as it isn't necessary anyway."[24]

On November 30, 1942, Jane Russell finally made her acting debut—in a short sketch on a stage in Tucson. The results were not encouraging. As George McCall reported to Birdwell: "The sketch did not play well. There are many reasons for this. It has no finish. Production is inadequate and Russell, for some reason or other, does not look good on stage. All the qualities apparent in photographs are lost in the theater." He continued, "The costume designed for Russell will have to be changed. It is most unbecoming and is anything but

Excited crowds await entrance into San Francisco's Geary Theatre during a limited run of *The Outlaw* in 1943.

glamorous."[25] The local paper seemed to agree with McCall's overall assessment: "Screen history may not have been made by yesterday's event; only time and the unpredictable public can tell whether Miss Russell will prove another Jean Harlow. . . . Miss Russell, lovely enough to qualify as any photographer's dream girl—or for that matter, any man's dream girl, will probably do all right for herself in the glamour capital and with the movie public, but Buetal [*sic*] carried off the acting honors for the first performance."[26]

When he was notified of the poor performance, Hughes considered replacing Furthman and rebuilding the sets, but as he had become more and more preoccupied with wartime defense contracts, his time was spread thin and decisions about *The Outlaw* were not forthcoming. As McCall reported, "I do not know how this will progress as Hughes must look at it step by step and as yet hasn't looked at the first step."[27] Despite reports that *The Outlaw* would be roadshowed over the Christmas holidays, Hughes once again held it back.

At the end of December Angelo Rossi, mayor of San Francisco, wrote a gushing letter to Hughes practically begging him to premiere *The Outlaw* there. Rossi declared that in addition to the city's citizens recalling "the merit

and distinction of your previous films," San Francisco would like to "pay particular homage to the two unknown American youths, Jane Russell and Jack
Buetel, who have been lifted from obscurity to fame." He continued to lay it
on thick: "San Francisco salutes your courage in finding unknowns to portray such important roles" and "would welcome the opportunity of opening
its doors and its hearts to America's two new Cinderella children." Just to
make sure he covered all his bases, Rossi concluded, "San Francisco would
also like to honor you personally for the great contributions you are making
to the war effort through the genius of your aerodynamic skill."[28] The letter
seems to have done the trick; *The Outlaw* was scheduled to hold its premiere
at the Geary Theatre, which the mayor proudly announced by taking out ads
featuring elegant fonts in the local newspapers.[29] *The Outlaw* would have an
extended run at the Geary, with Jack and Jane appearing in the sketch serving
as a prologue to the film and supposedly containing a scene that had been cut
from the movie.

With the premiere set for January 29, Russell Birdwell & Associates
jumped into action to promote the film around the city. They dusted off the
tagline "The picture that couldn't be stopped!" devised a year prior, and
changed the promotional materials to proclaim Jane Russell as 1943's (as
opposed to 1942's) most exciting new screen star. They also resurrected one
of the Kodachrome Hurrell shots for oversized posters to be printed for the
premiere and subsequent run. After nearly two years of waiting, Birdwell was
more than ready to cap off the campaign. When he got Mayor Rossi to proclaim the arrival of Jack and Jane as "Cinderella Day" in San Francisco,
Louella Parsons couldn't help but comment, "You've got to hand it to Russell
Birdwell for thinking up the unusual."[30]

In true Howard Hughes/*Outlaw* fashion, on the morning of the premiere
it was announced that the event would be delayed a full week—for undis-
closed reasons.[31] The city was assured the show would go on, and when
Hughes arrived in San Francisco with his protégés a week later, it was finally
confirmed; *The Outlaw* would at last be seen. The moviegoing public may
have been delighted, but Jane was mortified by what greeted her on the ride
from the train station to the Fairmont Hotel. One of the Hurrell Kodachrome
images had been altered so that it appeared as if her blouse had been torn,
partially exposing her breasts, and her skirt was pulled up to her thigh. There
was no denying how provocative the photo, which had been printed on large
six-sheet posters plastered around the city and blown up as a massive billboard outside the Geary Theatre, was. "A half-hour before the train reached

the station," Geraldine later remembered, "I saw the huge billboards on every side, with Daughter spilled on a hay pile, guns in both hands and little or nothing on. I was ready to shriek."[32]

Jane's cousin Pat had accompanied her on the trip, with Aunt Ernestine close on their heels. "By the time I got there," Ernestine recalled, "Jane was beside herself, screaming up and down like a wildcat over the way they had pictured her on the billboards. I'd seen them in route to the hotel and felt like screaming with her. Instead, I listened to Jane in her wrath."[33] At a loss what to do, Ernestine sought out Howard Hughes to air the family grievances over how Jane was being portrayed. "It was our first meeting," she remembered, "but I saw no point pulling my punches. I gave him our blunt views on the sensationalism. He gave me a straightforward look. 'Well you know, Mrs. Henry, I can't make a Shirley Temple out of her.'"[34] With that, the ice was broken and Ernestine was able to have an honest conversation with Hughes that enabled her to see his perspective. Aunt Ernie relayed the conversation to Jane. "I found him a very nice man with a lot of problems here that you and I can't even begin to guess at. His judgment may differ from ours, but he honestly thinks this is the way to sell his picture. And it *is* his picture, his time, his energy, his millions of dollars. I wouldn't be too angry with him just because he doesn't see things the way we do."[35] Jane could only shrug her shoulders. "He'd gotten her on his side too!"[36] For Jane it was a lesson in learning to navigate her comfort zone. Maybe she could say no to the Hollywood wolves and photographers, but Howard Hughes was another animal altogether. "She enjoyed making pictures, but she did not like the way that they overemphasized the publicity on the bust-line at that time," Pat Henry later noted. "She would have preferred to not have that, but it goes with the territory and she just accepted it."[37]

The big night finally came on February 5 as *The Outlaw* had its gala premiere at the Geary Theatre. Crowds gathered around the theater for the festivities, which included the live skit with Jane and Jack. The decision was made that the sketch, now running around twenty minutes in length, was to serve as an epilogue, so the pair would be brought out onstage after their triumphant film debut. As the packed house settled in for the 121-minute western opus, it dawned on Jane and Jack that they had never actually seen the film. Not wanting to watch it from the wings and without a single seat available, the pair snuck up to the balcony and sat on the stairs of one of the aisles. When an usher ordered them to move, they managed to convince him that they were the same people up there on the screen and were allowed to stay.

Jane was required to promote *The Outlaw* on and off throughout most of the 1940s. Here she is pictured with Louella Parsons during a radio broadcast to hype the film.

Reviews of the evening were mixed. The film was largely received as kind of boring, but interestingly weird. *Variety* commented that *The Outlaw*'s "slowness is not so much a matter of length as a lack of tempo in individual scenes," adding, "Sex seldom rears its beautiful head in simon-pure prairie dramas, but since this is an unorthodox, almost burlesque, version of the tried and true desert themes, anything can and often does happen."[38] The *San*

Francisco Examiner pointed out that Hughes's "inexperience as a solo director is manifest in the film's slow pace and its laborious emphasis on ludicrously incredible details of romance and melodrama. Yet his willingness to take a chance does build up a few unusual and forcible effects."[39] Louella Parsons threw in her two cents: "Everyone will have to make up his own mind about *The Outlaw*. It is not a great film, but it is interesting and unusual, and you had better not miss it if you want to be able to take part in the many discussions it is sure to launch." Parsons was kind in her comments about Jane. "Jane is young and exciting and, while naturally she shows her lack of experience she does extremely well for a girl who had no previous dramatic training."[40] Reactions to the sketch were less generous, with *Variety* reporting, "Jane Russell and Jack Buetel both suffered bad cases of first-night nerves when caught in sketch and weren't aided by slow-paced staging."[41] Another reviewer was a little more blunt, referring to the skit as "painfully amateurish."[42]

No matter what the critics thought, Russell Birdwell had done his job well and interest in *The Outlaw* was high enough to sustain packed crowds at the Geary and later at the Tivoli Theatre for a solid seven-week run. By February 18, a local newspaper was reporting that over forty-six thousand people had viewed the film.[43] Halfway through, the lackluster skit seems to have been abandoned. Instead comedian and Warner Bros. mainstay Frank McHugh was brought in to perform with the duo. Jack and Jane would now be serving as "straight men" for McHugh during the live performances, which took place three times a day.

When Jane wasn't at the theater, she was stationed at the hotel, per Howard Hughes. "She was at liberty to go any place in the hotel, but she wasn't, under any circumstances, to leave the hotel," Geraldine later recalled. "You might call her a prisoner in the Vatican."[44] Pat Henry not only kept Jane company during the San Francisco run, she also served as a gatekeeper to deter curious onlookers. Pat proved to be too good at her job when she barred Howard Hughes from entering Jane's room. He called Jane out into the hallway, commenting, "Good Lord, does she do this with everyone?"[45]

The moviegoing public of San Francisco had welcomed Howard Hughes and *The Outlaw* with open arms, and by the end of its run the film had brought in $140,000.[46] Overall, the screenings seemed to be going off without a hitch, but controversy still managed to surround the film during the limited release. Two weeks into the San Francisco run, parents, school officials, and church groups made enough noise about the oversized posters of Jane around town that the city attorney felt pressured to consider filing warrants citing the

posters for violating the city's police codes. However, there was some confu-sion as to whom the warrants should be issued—the sign company, the Geary Theatre, or Howard Hughes.[47] The two companies responsible for the adver-tisements were alarmed enough that they agreed to take down the billboards. This slight controversy didn't satisfy Russell Birdwell's thirst for publicity, so he took out full-page ads in the *San Francisco Chronicle* and *Variety* pro-claiming, "'The Outlaw' Proves Sex Has Not Been Rationed." He extolled the virtues of Howard Hughes, who had fought the valiant fight against the cen-sorship boards, "which would have scissored the very scenes and situations which today are giving contented looks to thousands." He also encouraged theatergoers to see the film for Jane because "a million soldiers can't be wrong"—the number of military members he claimed had written in asking for a photo of her.[48]

It was only after the end of the San Francisco run that the PCA really seems to have taken notice of *The Outlaw*'s release. This was in part due to the San Francisco Motion Picture Council, a citizen watchdog group that wrote directly to Will Hays to express concerns that "a very disgusting portrayal of the feminine star was displayed throughout the San Francisco bay region, on large billboards." The letter went on to proclaim, "What the members of the San Francisco Motion Picture Council would like to know is—why was such a picture allowed to pass your Board of Censorship?"[49] Taking a closer look at the matter, it finally dawned on the PCA that the print screened in San Francisco may not have been the one given the certificate of approval. In June 1943 a special screening was arranged for Howard Hughes and Francis Harmon of the PCA in which one of seven existing prints of *The Outlaw* was projected. Satisfied that the projected print was the one approved by the Legion of Decency and the New York Censor Board, Hughes and Harmon drove to a storage facility where the specific print was tagged, sealed, and stored in the bonded warehouse, awaiting wide release. To drive the gravity of the situation home, Harmon advised Hughes that the approved print had to be the one released lest "enemies of the industry would attempt to pin the increase in juvenile delinquency, which already exists, to this picture and would attempt to draw unwarranted conclusions from such release to the detriment of Mr. Hughes and of the industry."[50] With the matter of the print seemingly taken care of, the PCA had assurance regarding the advertising when they received word from Russell Birdwell that, at least for the Los Angeles release, "there would be no objectionable advertising matter put out."[51] With all censorship issues apparently settled and a successful soft run

in San Francisco on the books, Howard Hughes was finally ready for *The Outlaw* to be released widely.

Except he didn't release it.

During the San Francisco run, Hughes had been able to dedicate some of his time to the film, but his main preoccupations were military defense contracts, including the development of the H-4 Hercules aircraft (aka Spruce Goose). *The Outlaw* remained in storage until a full year after World War II ended while Hughes focused his attention elsewhere. He did admit that military obligations were not his only motivation. "The longer I wait, the more valuable the picture will be," Hughes told Noah Dietrich. "I'm building up the public's desire to see *The Outlaw*."[52] Even though it was Hughes's own decision to withhold the film, he was more than happy for the public to believe the PCA and state censorship boards were the culprits in keeping Jane Russell off the big screen. This belief was prevalent enough that when a group of "6 Reconnaissance Boys" from "somewhere in Luxembourg" wrote the PCA imploring it to allow *The Outlaw* to be screened overseas, Joseph Breen felt compelled to respond.[53] "The picture has been approved by this office," Breen notified the concerned soldiers, "and the question of the distribution is a matter solely for Mr. Howard Hughes, who is its owner and producer."[54]

In early 1946 Hughes finally decided to release *The Outlaw* with United Artists as the distributor. Even though the publicity for the film, which was focused on Jane, had been rolling out for a full five years, Hughes and Birdwell were just getting started.

The plan of attack for the 1946 release of *The Outlaw* focused on a print advertising blitz highlighting the censorship "battles" over the film along with the reintroduction of Jane Russell. One ad, laid out in comic book form, presented the timeline of *The Outlaw* odyssey, bizarrely claiming that Hughes had finished and premiered the film in 1944. Apparently accuracy wasn't deemed necessary if the copy was good. One frame from the comic ad used for newspapers, portraying a sultry cartoon version of Jane, was accompanied by the question "What are the two great reasons for Jane Russell's rise to stardom? She's daring and exciting." Another newspaper ad actually referenced the film itself when promoting "The lady known as Rio . . . and the man she made notorious!"[55] Alliterative taglines were splashed on posters near images of Jane, proclaiming her "tall . . . terrific . . . and trouble!" or "mean . . . moody . . . magnificent!," while always noting that *The Outlaw* was Howard Hughes's "daring production."

Jack Buetel and Jane christen a promotional blimp in 1946. THE OUTLAW was emblazoned in neon on one side, and JANE RUSSELL on the other.

Hughes and Birdwell struck outrage gold when noted pinup artist Zoë Mozert was hired to give a refresh to the provocative image of Jane that had been used for the San Francisco posters. Jane modeled for Mozert, who recreated the lounging hay pose in oil on canvas. The result proved to be no less controversial than the photographs. Mozert, a San Fernando Valley resident who had been rising to prominence for her racy calendar girl paintings, was neither surprised nor concerned by the reaction to her rendering of Jane. "It's the sexiest painting I've ever done," she said at the time. "I suppose there's bound to be some fuss among the women's organizations. But they don't know how good that is for business."[56] Mozert's painting was reproduced in color for a full-page magazine ad, accompanied by arguably the most memorable line from the campaign: "How would you like to tussle with Russell?" The *American Weekly*, a syndicated publication that accompanied Hearst newspapers, ran this particular ad, but enough magazines refused to tussle with Russell for fear of backlash that the line was removed from the ads, replaced with "Exactly how it was filmed! Not a scene cut!," a less exciting alternative despite the exclamation points. The advertising was also taken to the skies: Hughes commissioned a blimp with Jane's name spelled out in neon, and a skywriter reportedly wrote "The Outlaw" above the city of Pasadena followed by two circles with dots in the middle.

The ads proved too much even for the film industry. Darryl Zanuck, president of film production at Twentieth Century-Fox, felt compelled to write to Joseph Breen, "When an ad like this appears in the paper after the conference we had the other day, I have a hell of a job keeping my boys in line. The whole campaign on this picture is a disgrace to the industry and I am on the verge of publicly attacking Howard Hughes with a blast in the newspapers."[57] Around the same time Zanuck was expressing his outrage, Archbishop John J. Cantwell of Los Angeles declared the film "morally offensive," noting, "We take occasion to advise our Catholic people and all right thinking members of the community that they may not, with a free conscience, attend a current much-advertised motion picture which has been condemned by the Legion of Decency and of its very nature is morally offensive to Christian and American womanhood."[58]

As crowds lined up around the block in cities where the film had been released, the Motion Picture Association of America (MPAA; the name by which the MPPDA was now known) condemned Hughes, accusing him of openly violating the bylaws of the organization, of which Hughes was a member, and defying decisions made by the group in regards to advertising for *The Outlaw*. A hearing conducted by the board of the MPAA was set to be held for Hughes to answer for his actions unless all advertisements were withdrawn.[59] Hughes responded, "I think it is about time people quit trying to tell the American public what it can see, read or listen to."[60] Then he filed a $5 million lawsuit against the MPAA and withdrew his membership from the organization. In his lawsuit Hughes claimed, "The entire 'Hays office,' in its very essential fundamentals is a group boycott in restraint of trade and in absolute violation of the antitrust laws of this county."[61] The money Hughes was seeking would cover perceived damages incurred by the censorship-induced delays, and he also requested a restraining order, preventing the MPAA and PCA from revoking their certificate of approval.[62] Since Hughes had of his own accord submitted the film and some of the advertising to the PCA for review, the judge ruled against him, noting that by seeking approval from the Production Code Administration under the Motion Picture Association of America, Hughes had confirmed the validity of the process. In September 1946 Joseph Breen moved forward with revoking *The Outlaw*'s certificate of approval.

The 1946 censorship battles took a surreal turn on July 7, when Howard Hughes crashed a plane into a Beverly Hills neighborhood. He had been test-flying an experimental army photographic aircraft that began failing shortly after takeoff on its maiden flight. Hughes tried to maneuver the plane onto the golf course of the Los Angeles Country Club but fell short, and it careened toward a group of houses at North Linden and Whittier Drives, ultimately ripping off the roof of one two-story house and crashing directly into another, with collateral damage done to two others. Miraculously no one was killed, but Hughes suffered a laundry list of devastating injuries and was initially given a fifty-fifty chance of survival. By the following day he was "resting and talking rationally."[63] Jane felt compelled to visit her boss and was allowed behind the police-guarded door at Good Samaritan Hospital. Hughes's condition seesawed in the ensuing days until he was finally stabilized enough to be released.

Joseph Breen had been monitoring Hughes's condition and on September 5 sent a cryptic wire to Francis Harmon at the MPAA in New York: "From very reliable source I learn that party is living in private home in Beverly Hills and transacting some business everyday. His mind is said to be clear and functioning well but his general condition not good chiefly because of failure of body burns properly to heal."[64] Two days later Breen sent Hughes the letter notifying him that *The Outlaw*'s certificate of approval was being revoked. If Breen thought a catastrophic plane crash was going to distract Hughes from the PCA's actions, he had once again underestimated his foe. On September 11 Hughes made his first public appearance after the crash by flying a plane to New York to confer with attorneys about actions to take against the MPAA and PCA. Though Hughes would make a full recovery, he would become addicted to pain killers and his behavior would grow more erratic as the years wore on.

In light of continued battles and controversies, *The Outlaw* had a limited release in 1946 but enjoyed long lines and decent box office. With RKO as a distributor, the film finally rolled out nationally in 1950. Worldwide distribution soon followed, though the prints of the film do not seem to have been immune to various degrees of editing and censorship, so runtimes vary. In every country the advertisements for the film prominently promoted Jane as the star attraction. In Mexico ads featuring Jane were plastered on the walls in Mexico City, Mazatlán, and Juárez. In Panama billboards were not permitted, so flyers were tacked to trees instead. Paris posted ads in the subways, and London displayed them in the rail stations. In Sydney a sporting goods store capitalized on Jane's *Outlaw* fame with an archery window display that encouraged shoppers to "develop Jane Russell health with archery."[65] In Manila one store attracted customers by having local girls pose as Rio on bales of hay in the shop's windows.

It had taken almost a decade, but *The Outlaw* was finally out.

Over the years the notoriety surrounding *The Outlaw* has far overshadowed the actual film which, as one reviewer admitted, could not be called "a bore. It has the perverse fascination of the freakish."[66] This is a sound summation of the film, which alternates between being amusing, unintentionally hilarious, confusing, and boring. There's no denying that the picture looks good thanks to the capable eye of cinematographer Gregg Toland. Walter Huston and Thomas Mitchell give respectable performances under the circumstances. However, Jack Buetel and Jane Russell suffered from having Hughes as their director and both are frequently stiff, no doubt the result of receiving direction along the lines of "Don't raise an eyebrow" or "Don't move your shoulder." By contrast, the early location scenes that remain (along with the hayloft meeting between Billy and Rio) give some indication of how much better the pair would have performed had Howard Hawks remained. At the same time, a Hawks's *Outlaw* would likely have been a very competent western as opposed to the existing bizarre opus from the mind of Howard Hughes, featuring a musical score handled by Academy Award winner Victor Young that is a curious combination of Tchaikovsky, Mexican traditionals, and music cues akin to a *Looney Tunes* short.

Hughes's fascination with breasts is obvious, as the necklines of Jane's tops get progressively lower as the film proceeds, not to mention the countless scenes highlighting her anatomy: she furiously rides a horse, is bound and gagged with her arms above her head, falls in a stream, and bends over at every opportunity. Geoffrey Shurlock of the PCA would later note, "Hughes corrupted the whole world on this mammary gland business. He started the exploitation of big breasts. He started the cinematic avalanche of breasts."[67]

While Hughes paid an extraordinary amount of attention to Jane's bosom, the male characters in the film are relatively unmoved by Rio. Billy the Kid and Doc Holliday never treat Rio particularly well, and both value a horse much more than her. Noted French critic André Bazin would point out, "Even the misogyny apparent in the American crime film some years earlier is a far cry from the cynicism of *The Outlaw*."[68] While trying to avenge her brother's death, Rio is raped by Billy and is later forced to take care of the wounded outlaw, which she does by famously keeping him warm in bed with her naked body. "One cannot reproach her for renouncing vengeance after making love," Bazin wrote. "She will henceforth love with as much fervor and fidelity as she once sought vengeance."[69]

Despite the constant emphasis on Jane's bosom, at the unexpected core of *The Outlaw* is the homoerotic triangle that emerges between Billy, Doc, and Pat Garrett. This aspect was so obvious that even in 1946, one reviewer summed up the plot as concerning "the rivalry of three men—two desperadoes and a former one turned Sheriff—not for the favors of the girl, as you might imagine, but for the 'friendship' of each other."[70] Or, as Bazin noted, "They constitute a Spartan group in which women have no emotional role."[71]

Although *The Outlaw* has had countless detractors over the years, it's not without its fans. André Bazin was among them; he called it "one of the most erotic films ever made and one of the most sensational scripts ever filmed by Hollywood."[72] He was particularly taken with the character of Rio, whom he viewed as multifaceted, not fitting the Hollywood western archetype of the virtuous woman or the prostitute with a heart of gold. "Those who were disappointed by the film," he insisted, "are either insincere or lacking in perception."[73] Historian Troy Howarth put it more simply: "It's grand entertainment. There's something so wonderfully demented about it, that makes it unlike any other film of its type from this timeframe."[74]

Joseph Breen would never get *The Outlaw* completely out of his system. When *Look* magazine ran a series of articles about Howard Hughes in 1954, Breen felt compelled to write to the West Coast editor to dispel the growing mythology surrounding the Production Code Administration versus *The Outlaw*. "This office never demanded 136 cuts from *The Outlaw*," Breen wrote. "All of the material set forth in this paragraph [of *Look* magazine], and in the one which follows — as far as this office is concerned — is utterly false. It is pure fabrication."[75]

Of the film and her performance, Jane grumbled, "I thought the picture was ghastly and that I looked like a wooden dummy. I don't know how I ever got another part. All that fuss over my, well, physicality was very embarrassing."[76] Looking back on the controversy and notoriety, Jane said, "I honestly feel sorry if *The Outlaw* publicity campaign was responsible for the young girl who decided that the only way to make it in show business was to shove out their bosom or take their clothes off altogether."[77]

9

Mrs. Robert Waterfield

After seven weeks of performing in San Francisco between screenings of *The Outlaw*, Jane Russell was tired—tired of being away from home, tired of playing straight woman to a comedian, tired of the endless publicity focusing on her breasts. Tired of missing Robert Waterfield.

In the midst of her late 1942 fling with John Payne, the UCLA football season started and Waterfield visited Jane, asking her to accompany his mother to the games. Despite his stone-faced demeanor and roving eye, Waterfield had been genuinely heartbroken when Jane called off the engagement and was having trouble moving on. Whether Jane wanted to admit it or not, she hadn't gotten him out of her system either. Jane adored Frances Waterfield, and the feeling was mutual, so she agreed to spend every Saturday driving Robert's mother from the Valley to the Memorial Coliseum, south of downtown Los Angeles. After the games Robert would drive his mother home and Jane would go to meet John Payne.

One Sunday Jane was hungover from a night on the town and feeling homesick for her pre-*Outlaw* life. She called Frances, who invited her over for dinner. Jane hesitated, but then agreed, over the protestations of John Payne, who suspected Jane still carried a torch for Robert Waterfield. Overcome by emotions, she began crying when she arrived. When the trio sat down for dinner, neither Jane nor Robert spoke or ate. "Oh, for heaven's sake," Frances groused at the table, "you two get the hell out of here—you're ruining my good dinner."[1] The pair went out to a swing in the garden and sat in silence. "We both knew I was home for good," Jane later recalled.[2]

The break hadn't changed the dynamic of their relationship, however. Waterfield continued to detest Jane's film career, and all the bosomy publicity didn't help. During the San Francisco run he came up once to visit, but he felt uncomfortable and the couple got into one of their frequent battles. He didn't even spend the night in San Francisco with her, but they did keep in touch via telephone for the remainder of *The Outlaw*'s inaugural run.

As the San Francisco engagement was coming to a close, Jane started hearing rumblings that Howard Hughes wanted to take *The Outlaw* on the road for a national tour. The thought of this was more than Jane could bear. At this point, all she wanted was to go back home and get married— assuming her prospective groom was agreeable. One person who was anxious for this to happen was Lew Wasserman at MCA. Eager to get Jane out of the paltry contract with Howard Hughes, he encouraged her to go back to Los Angeles and tie the knot. He even offered to loan Jane his car so she and Waterfield could elope to Las Vegas in style. Jane got ready to head home, but was too loyal to walk out on Hughes without warning him. She attempted to see him personally, but when he wasn't available, she notified one of his people of her intention. Contrary to what Wasserman may have had in mind, Jane wasn't concerned with getting a better deal; she just needed a break from the Hollywood grind. She wanted to quit. Hughes's people had Jane sign what was essentially a loyalty oath, promising not to make films with anyone else. This dashed Lew Wasserman's dreams of getting Jane a fat contract elsewhere, but she didn't care. All she wanted was to ride into the sunset with Robert Waterfield.

After their reconciliation, he had wanted to wait at least a year before they married. "Robert was still in his senior year at UCLA," Geraldine reasoned. "He was to graduate in June. Being frightfully proud, he didn't want to live on Jane's salary."[3] Jane wasn't having it. As far as she was concerned, it was now or never. Everyone who had known the couple during their tumultuous four-year relationship figured they would get married. It was just a matter of when, though the where was less in dispute. "He'll never stand still for an elaborate wedding, not *that* one," Geraldine would say.[4] Jane knew this as well, so when she pushed him to take the plunge, there was no doubt that they would elope to Las Vegas.

The day before Easter in 1943, Jane went to the Waterfield home at 7 in the morning. Seeing her at the back door, Frances inquired why she was there so early. "We are going to be married if I can get this big lug up!"[5] She got the big lug up and they headed out of town. With them was George Robotham, one of Waterfield's teammates who would later have a career as a Hollywood stuntman, and his girlfriend Jean Willes, who would go on to have a respectable career as an actress. The pair would serve as witnesses. On the way to Vegas, Jean and Jane slept in the backseat while George and Robert sat up front. "It couldn't have been less romantic," Jane remembered.[6] When the group arrived in town, they stopped at a chapel, and Robert sent Jane in to check it out. The

Robert Waterfield and Jane at La Posada shortly before they eloped in the spring of 1943.

chapel was filled with flowers for the Easter services that would be taking place the next day. Jane, wearing a powder-blue crepe dress, decided the blooms were there for her too. Without even going back out to confer with her future husband, Jane cornered the Methodist minister inside the chapel.

"Will you marry me?" Jane asked point blank.

"When?"

"Right now."

"Where's the groom?" came the puzzled response.

"Out in the car."

"Well, if you'll fetch him in, I think we can manage it."[7]

Jane retrieved her bridegroom and witnesses from the car, and on April 24, 1943, the Reverend Harold Broughton married Jane Russell and Robert Waterfield.[8] Jane was just shy of her twenty-second birthday.

After the nuptials, Jane phoned her mom, who was participating in an Easter play as Mary Magdalene. Called to the phone in full costume, she put her ear to the receiver to hear Jane simply say, "Mother, we're married." "Good," came Mary Magdalene's response. "When will you be back?" When Ernestine asked her sister if she approved of the news, she responded with a twinkle in her eye, "Ever take a good look at Bob's shoulders, Ernie? I was very glad to shift the responsibility from mine to his."[9] Geraldine maintained she was pleased by the pairing. "Waterfield was handpicked by the Lord for that girl," she would later say. "He loves and understands her and she respects him for it. They're both strong-willed characters but he's the head of that house, and to be the head of Jane's house is no small job."[10]

For the time being that house would be the home of Frances Waterfield. Two days after the wedding, as Jane was moving into the Waterfield residence, Robert was reportedly back in class.[11] When asked how she hoped to achieve a balance between her personal life and her career, Jane responded, "Everyone is telling me that I can't combine marriage and a career. I think I can. And if I can't, I'll take marriage. That seems more substantial."[12]

It wasn't long before Jane had the opportunity to test her ability to juggle marriage and career. Less than a month after the wedding, Robert reported to Fort MacArthur for induction into the army's candidate school. In early June 1943, before he was even able to graduate from UCLA, he was slated to be shipped off to Fort Benning, Georgia, for infantry training.[13] After reporting to Fort Benning, Waterfield called Jane as often as he could, complaining about how miserable he was. Jane was anxious to join him, but with Jack Buetel reporting for service in the navy, there were the persistent rumors that Howard Hughes was still considering an *Outlaw* road show featuring Jane making solo appearances.[14] Jane, deciding not to stick around long enough to find out, booked a train ticket to Georgia. However, before she could leave, Hughes caught wind of her intention and sent notification that she was being put on suspension without pay. Undaunted, Jane made the cross-country trip on a wartime packed train and arrived in Columbus, Georgia, the nearest city to Fort Benning.

Lodging was scarce, with many wives relocating to be near their enlisted husbands, but Jane was able to rent a room in a house. Not ideal, but it would have to do. With Waterfield drawing a salary of only $21 a month, Jane needed to find work, but she wasn't exactly qualified to do much of anything. Finally she convinced a beauty shop operator to allow her to do glamour makeovers. "I had a private booth and for a dollar I'd give a complete Hollywood makeup—Jane Westmore, I called myself. But as I had to split the dollar with the management I couldn't make much out of it."[15] Additionally, the humid Georgia summer caused her handiwork to melt off the faces of clients almost instantaneously, so that job dried up after a couple of weeks.

Waterfield was allowed to come to Columbus only one night a week, so Jane often traveled to the Harmony Church military base to spend the evenings with her husband, who would cry tears of frustration. When cousin Pat Henry rolled into town, Jane's spirits improved considerably, even if her surroundings didn't. Pat found work selling war bonds and Jane soon joined her. "I shared a furnished room with a gang of cockroaches and sold bonds for $15 a week," Jane explained. "The room cost $10 a week, so I had five bucks to eat on and pay for my bus trips out to camp to see Robert. But it was lots more fun than fighting with women's clubs," she quipped, refencing some of the blowback she had received from various groups regarding *The Outlaw* publicity campaign.[16]

Going under her married name, Jane was basically anonymous in Georgia for the first two months she was there. The press finally caught wind that *the* Jane Russell was living as a war bride in Columbus, and the Army Signal Corps sent a photographer to her place to take photos of her keeping house. At first Jane was irritated by this invasion of her privacy, but when a two-bedroom duplex suddenly became available to rent, "it certainly taught me the value of the red carpet treatment."[17] At the time, Jane and Pat bore a strong resemblance to each other, so Pat would often appease autograph hunters who mistook her for Jane. Both women found this hysterically funny.

Waterfield finished his training in September 1943, but was retained at Fort Benning to play football and basketball for the 176th Infantry teams, with the assumption he would be shipped overseas at some point. Even though Jane frequently threw out lines like "I'd just as soon be a good wife as a good actress," the months in Georgia were causing her to rethink her attitude about her film career.[18] She knew MCA was still eager for her to sue Howard Hughes and break her contract, but she wasn't sure what her next

Jane lays one on Robert Waterfield for the benefit of the camera at Fort Benning.
(Los Angeles Herald Examiner Collection/Los Angeles Public Library)

career move should be. Not knowing who to turn to, she wired her mother asking for guidance. Geraldine wrote back, quoting the Bible: "He that sweareth to his own hurt, and changeth not, he shall never be moved."[19] It was Geraldine's way of saying Jane needed to honor her existing agreement with Hughes, even if it didn't seem like the best option. Jane took the advice to heart and wrote a letter to Hughes referencing the same quote. He responded almost immediately, saying he wanted to see her in person.

When Waterfield was granted ten days' leave, the couple was eager to go back home for a spell. He flew back on an army plane, while Jane took a commercial flight, an arduous journey in those days. After numerous delays, largely due to getting bumped off her flights, Jane made it to Santa Fe, where she was able to get star treatment on a TWA plane owned by Hughes. After happily reuniting with family and friends, Jane finally went to see Howard in his office. "I was glad to see him," she later wrote, "but when I started toward him he backed around behind his desk. I had to chase him around the desk to finally give him a huge bear hug. He simply didn't know what to make of me."[20] Jane wasn't ready to give up on her film career, but with Waterfield's overseas deployment looming, she also wanted to spend as much time with him as possible, even if that meant going back to Georgia. Hughes so approved of and appreciated Jane's loyalty to himself that he agreed to lift the suspension while letting her go back to Columbus. Not only would she get to be near her husband, she would be collecting her weekly paycheck without having to actually work.[21] Jane had made a commitment to Hughes and honored it despite all his eccentricities, and he was more than happy to reward her for that.

In no rush to leave Los Angeles, Jane stayed behind for an extra month after Robert left, but finally rejoined him in Georgia. With the financial pressures eased by the weekly check from Howard Hughes, and with Pat Henry back in California training in the Women in the Air Force (WAF) program, Jane was mainly biding her time. In mid-1944 Robert injured his knee on the football field and was sent to a hospital in Atlanta for treatment. He and Jane held their breath as they waited to find out if he would be reassigned to a desk job or sent home. The injury turned out to be bad enough that he received an honorable discharge. After a year away from Los Angeles, the Waterfields would finally be able to start their married life, spared the agony of an overseas deployment.

The couple moved back into Frances Waterfield's house, where they had briefly lived before the move to Georgia. Robert was able to pick up where he had left off, and his return to UCLA was a triumphant one, with the *Los Angeles Times* proclaiming, "Football stock at UCLA soared sky high yesterday when Bob Waterfield returned to the Westwood campus."[22] He continued his studies toward earning a degree in physical education and his knee finally healed enough to allow him to return to the football field. Robert was finally coming into his own.

Jane, on the other hand, was languishing at Frances Waterfield's home. Howard Hughes had yet to make any decisions about the future of Jane's

The movie star wraps the football player's knee. His injury got him an early discharge.

career, and she was growing restless. "Instead of clipping press notices I clip hedges," she said at the time. "It's probably good for my health and figure but I'm getting kind of tired of being a corn-fed character. I want to be an actress."[23] To make matters worse, Geraldine had finally reached her breaking point with La Posada. With two sons in active military service and a third about to join the Merchant Marines, caring for the ranch was too much to handle and she decided to sell it. However, after experiencing a vivid vision of a house in an orchard on the southern end of the property, she decided the Lord's plan was for her to keep two of the seven acres and eventually rebuild. So she sold five acres, including the parcel with the house, and spent the remainder of the war living alternately with Ernestine in Fontana and her mother in Glendale.

As she languished in the Valley, Jane tried to laugh it off and make the best of the situation. "Howard has been paying me for four years," she told a local gossip columnist. "I started at $50 a week and now it's $250. That's nice for doing nothing except living with my husband and mother-in-law on a ranch in the valley."[24] Jane was adjusting to domestic life as best she could, although she still avoided the kitchen. Robert's "mother is a good cook," she said, "but I hate cooking."[25]

Married life had done nothing to temper the tempestuous nature of their relationship. Geraldine recalled once telephoning the Waterfield home and being unable to hear Frances on the other end of the line due to the loud arguing in the background. "Wait a minute and I'll close this door," Frances yelled into the receiver. "They are killing each other." When Geraldine chastised her daughter for this behavior, the response was "Mother, did it ever occur to you that we might *like* to fight?"[26]

As Jane grew increasingly restless, she tried to find the silver lining of having no film work. "The best part of making no pictures," she said, "is that people are now beginning to forget what I look like. I mean people on the street. I go to all my husband's football games, and no one bothers me." She summed up unenthusiastically, "I guess that's nice."[27]

Jane's prospects finally started looking better when Hughes agreed to loan her out to producer Hunt Stromberg for an independent drama called *Young Widow*. Based on a 1942 novel of the same name by Clarissa Fairchild Cushman, the story focused on Joan, a young woman coming to terms with the death of her husband, and then coming into her own as a laboratory assistant in Baltimore. Stromberg had optioned the book as soon as it was published, and by the time the script landed on Hughes's desk, Joan had been turned into a newspaperwoman and a war widow. Countless producers had reportedly tried to utilize Jane's services in the preceding months and years, but to no avail. However, this script impressed Howard Hughes. "This is the best woman's role in 10 years," he enthused to Stromberg. "Jane is yours."[28] In late 1944 word started getting out that Jane would finally be making a follow-up to the still infrequently seen *The Outlaw*.

Production on *Young Widow* was not as chaotic as *The Outlaw*, but it wasn't without its bumps. When Louis Hayward was cast as the male lead, the trades reported that his wife, Ida Lupino, would play the young widow, not Jane, who would instead star in Stromberg's other property, *Dishonored Lady* (later made with Hedy Lamarr). When Lupino and Stromberg butted heads over the script, Jane was back in.[29] After several delays, *Young Widow* finally started production in the spring of 1945 at the General Services studios on Romaine and Las Palmas, right up the street from Hughes's office. In what must have felt like déjà vu to Jane, William Dieterle was to be the director on the film but pulled out early on after a disagreement with Stromberg.[30] Next was André De Toth, who lasted less than a week before leaving, reportedly due to strep throat.[31] Edwin Marin was the third director assigned to the picture and the one to see it through, but he was as meticulous a director as Howard Hughes, focusing on such minute details that Jane felt she was once again giving a wooden performance. In the midst of production she had to be treated for appendix trouble, but soon returned to finish the film.[32]

By this time Jane had been in the public eye for five years, promoted primarily for her physical assets. Rather than capitalizing on that aspect, Stromberg sought to do the opposite, dressing Jane in modest costumes like tailored suits. "The role is highly dramatic," he said, "and relies entirely on acting and not at all on anatomy."[33] Jane echoed those sentiments: "I can't look dramatic in a sweater."[34] Stromberg's press agents were not amused, telling the producer, "Let us not kid ourselves, in these suits it ain't so good."[35] Some concessions were made, and a bathing suit scene was added. The prospect of Jane Russell in swimwear proved tempting to some industry people. "Fred MacMurray came to the set this morning," Jane told a visiting journalist. "He said he thought today was the day we were going to shoot the swimming pool scene. I don't know when we're going to get to that scene. They don't seem to be able to find a bathing suit they like on me. They keep testing me in a new one every night."[36]

Even though the film was completed in the summer of 1945, it did not start hitting theaters until February of the following year. As Hughes was still determined that *The Outlaw* be Jane's film debut, there was some confusion as to when United Artists could start rolling out either film, so the *Young Widow*'s release was spread out in various cities over the course of the year. When it did come out, the overall reviews were lukewarm, and those focusing on Jane's performance were rather brutal. "Beautiful, she is totally lacking in interpretive ability," said one reviewer, while another wrote Jane was "frequently embarrassing as an actress, particularly in a dramatic role, such as the present, and once in while the character is sympathetic. If Miss Russell has any forte, those bitter downturned corners of her mouth and sinister eyes indicate it's as a heavy."[37]

As a film with World War II as a backdrop, *Young Widow* had the potential to be an interesting character study of American women suffering from the psychological effects of the war, along the lines of the superior *The Best Years of Our Lives*. Instead, the film is uneven, melodramatic at times, and its leading lady, at this point in her career, was in over her head, unable to carry a dramatic picture. On the bright side, Penny Singleton and Marie Wilson are

Jane and co-star Louis Hayward get ready to shoot a scene for the Hunt Stromberg production *Young Widow*.

wholly likable and believable as Jane's roommates, and in Lee Garmes, Jane once again worked with one of Hollywood's best cinematographers. Poster art for the film deceptively featured Jane either in a bathing suit or a negligee (with artwork resembling Rosalind Russell more than Jane), and a 1952 re-release bizarrely retitled it *The Naughty Widow* in an attempt to sell tickets. None of it helped put across the underwhelming film. Another review, which

Jane would quote the rest of her life in wholehearted agreement, said something along the lines of "If the young widow had only died when her husband did, this picture need never have been made."[38]

When Jane finished production in mid-1945, the future of her film career was once again thrown into doubt when Robert Waterfield signed a professional football contract with the Cleveland Rams. After leading UCLA to its first Rose Bowl appearance in 1943, Waterfield had actually been drafted by the Rams, but his war service had intervened. Since returning to Los Angeles, he had fully recovered from the knee injury and gained national attention during the East-West Shrine Game, a post-season college football all-star game in which he led the West Coast team to victory and was named most outstanding offensive player. When he graduated from UCLA, the Rams swept in to sign him. General manager Chile Walsh declined to publicly reveal the terms of the contract but did note, "The fact that Waterfield is married to Jane Russell did not make signing him any easier."[39] The sum, lavish at the time, was $7,500 for the season.[40] Even though Robert was his usual stone-faced self about the deal, he was pleased and had no issues signing the contract.

Once again Jane would follow her husband out of town, though neither relished the thought of a winter in Cleveland. The situation proved even more grim when they moved into the St. Regis Hotel on Euclid Street, which once upon a time had luxury accommodations suitable for William Rockefeller, but had since been converted into small efficiency apartments with Murphy beds. The unit was a far cry from the roomy suburban homes they had grown up in, but they made the best of the situation, and their tiny space became a frequent gathering spot for Waterfield's teammates and their wives. Their living accommodations may have not been glamorous, but their story certainly was. The pairing of movie star and professional football player was great copy and the public ate it up. *Life* magazine found the power couple so irresistible it ran a pictorial spread showing Jane and Robert at Cleveland's Municipal Stadium as well as at the cramped apartment on Euclid Street.[41]

Their sacrificed comfort and the Rams' investment proved to be prudent. On the field, Robert launched his pro football career in spectacular fashion, leading the Rams to their first championship title since the team's formation in 1936. The indisputable star of the final championship game against the Washington Redskins, he was named MVP for the season, the first rookie ever to earn that honor. For most of the season, Jane had been on the sidelines cheering her husband on. By the time the championship game was played, in mid-December of 1945, Jane was still supportive, but she was lis-

The Waterfields during a lighter moment at home, circa 1946.

tening to the games on the radio at Frances Waterfield's home. Homesick and not wanting to spend Christmas in Cleveland, Jane had opted to come back to Los Angeles early. After the championship game, Robert stuck around long enough to sign a three-year $20,000 per season contract with the Rams and then got in his car and drove home.[42] With the war behind them, Robert excelling in pro football, and Jane possibly on the verge of another shot at a film career, the reunited couple enjoyed what Jane later recalled as "perhaps the best Christmas we ever had."[43]

Less than a month after the championship game, Jane and Robert received a late Christmas present when Dan Reeves, president of the Rams, announced the team would be relocating to Los Angeles. Despite the winning season, attendance had been consistently low at the games, and the formation of the rival Cleveland Browns the previous year didn't help. "The reason I'm moving to Los Angeles," Reeves explained at the time, "is that I believe it will become the greatest professional football town in the country."[44] The reasons mattered little to Jane and Robert. The next football season would be spent practically in their backyard and they were thrilled. The move would make supporting her husband from the sidelines easier and Jane was happy to do that. However, the past two and half years had made Jane realize that she was not cut out for a life of sheer domesticity. Mrs. Waterfield was ready to be Jane Russell again.

10

Kick-starting a Career

By the time Howard Hughes was ready to release *The Outlaw* in 1946, Jane Russell was ready to go back on the road for him. Although she was happily wed to Robert Waterfield, married life had nonetheless made her realize that perhaps she did want a career after all. However, before she resumed the personal appearances that accompanied screenings of *The Outlaw*, she demanded that her boss make some adjustments to the stage show. The poorly reviewed sketch initially devised when the film premiered in 1943 had been abandoned and replaced with the Frank McHugh routine, which wasn't much better. Now a few years wiser, Jane refused to play straight woman and instead demanded that she be allowed to sing onstage.

Fearful that Jane wasn't capable of carrying a tune well enough to hold an audience, Hughes turned to Jane's friend Portia Nelson. Jane had met Portia on the set of *Young Widow* when the latter was working as a secretary for the film's second director, André De Toth. The pair hit it off immediately, becoming lifelong friends. Portia would go on to have a successful career as a singer/songwriter/actress, including a memorable role as Sister Berthe in *The Sound of Music*. Upon hearing Portia sing, Jane had encouraged her to pursue a music career, practically demanding it, and Portia was always grateful to her for this. When Hughes cornered Portia and asked if Jane could sing, the answer was an emphatic "Yes!" Still skeptical, Hughes was determined to find a way to incorporate Jane's singing without the entire show hinging on it. Through Preston Sturges, Hughes found a comedian named Jimmy Connally, who did a bit with his wife in which he would goof around on the piano, barely allowing her to sing. Hughes felt this was safe, and begrudgingly, Jane made the compromise. Connally was booked to accompany her for an eight-week run of *The Outlaw* at the Oriental Theatre in Chicago.

Jane arrived in the Windy City on March 14, 1946, with Portia Nelson along for moral support. At that time the Oriental Theatre was still primarily a vaudeville venue, with film screenings peppered in between acts. Jane

Jane with bandleader Kay Kyser, who helped launch her radio and recording career.

would be making nine brief appearances a day along with other live performers on the bill. It did not take long for the theater manager to send Jimmy
Connally packing, opting instead to let Jane sing on her own. Portia, who had
encouraged Jane to take this plunge, was a nervous wreck, but Jane took it all
in stride, working with the manager to make song selections. Though not
formally trained, Jane loved to sing and welcomed the opportunity to do so.
When the time came, Jane was having a ball but the reviews of her act were
brutal. "La Russell coming on in the middle of the bill isn't doing herself a
whole lot of good with her current p.a. [personal appearance] outside of giving the crowd a figure to ogle at," wrote a reviewer for the *Billboard*. "Comes
on in skin-tight gown to do two torch numbers both of which ditties suffer
from her apathetic handling. Crowd gave her hefty but short mitt, indicating
they had enough."[1] The reviewer seems to have misread the audience. During
The Outlaw's eight-week run with Jane making personal appearances, crowds
packed the theater, generating a record $78,400 the opening week and hold-
ing strong for the remainder of the engagement.[2] The box office numbers,
however, did nothing to change the reviews. The *Billboard* viewed Jane's act a

second time and stuck to its original appraisal, noting she "tried to sing a couple of songs. The audience could have felt rewarded by a sight of the famed Russell figure, but it certainly could not have received any entertainment from her singing."[3]

The reviews were not of much concern to Jane, nor to Kay Kyser, the popular bandleader who booked Jane on his NBC radio show *Kollege of Musical Knowledge* in early 1947. Kyser had tried to get Jane on his show back in 1942, but Russell Birdwell had blocked it.[4] Now that five full years had passed, Hughes seemed to be loosening the reins ever so slightly. Kyser was impressed enough with Jane's rendition of "On the Wrong Side of You" during her first appearance that he brought her back a couple of months later for an extended run on the weekly show to sing and banter with Kyser and comedian Ish Kabibble. Kyser also gave Jane her first recording opportunity when she cut a 78 rpm record of "As Long as I Live" with Kyser and his band. "Miss Russell acquits herself credibly," wrote one reviewer of the recording. "Her voice comes from deep in her chest (sultry) and her enunciation distinct. Where she fails perceptibly is in her ability to project any real feeling." The reviewer went on to give Jane the benefit of the doubt, however, noting, "There are plenty of gals around who sound worse. Add to the fact that this was her first recording date and she must have been nervous. . . . It is worth noting, but the way, that Kyser has, if not always an ear, an eye for girl singers."[5]

In between the Kay Kyser appearances, booking agent Lou Walters signed Jane for her first non-*Outlaw* live gig. She would be spending a week in Florida at the Latin Quarter, a popular Miami nightclub that Walters happened to have founded. Jane would be receiving an impressive $15,000 for the run. Robert Waterfield was in between football seasons so he accompanied Jane to Miami as she looked forward to expanding her résumé. Jane was unsure of her ability to pull off a full set on her own, but the money was too good to turn down. Jane was having a drink in the bar of her hotel, where a beauty contest happened to be taking place on the outside patio. As a lark, the Ritz Brothers, who were in town for their own engagement and staying at the same hotel, encouraged Jane to award the beauty contest winner, so she did. That night, Jane made her first appearance at the Latin Quarter with a set that opened with "Pennies from Heaven" and continued with "The Wrong Kind of Love," "Poppa Don't Preach to Me," "That's the Beginning of the End," and "Everything's Moving Too Fast." According to one report, she "handed a surprise to customers who came to look instead of listen. She wore a modest black satin gown with a high neck, much more concealing than revealing."[6]

The critical response was more favorable than before, with the *Billboard,* very unimpressed with her performance in the Chicago engagement, now noting, "She has the ability to lend intimate room charm to a large spot and her easy, casual manner would do credit to a more seasoned performer. This was Miss Russell's first night club appearance and she clicked."[7] Jane remembered the show as being "not great, but fine."[8] By the second night she had traded in the high-necked gown for a strapless white number and was again called upon to present an award, this time to the winner of a local regatta.[9]

As far as Jane could tell, the engagement went well enough. However, when it was time for club co-owner E. M. Loew to pay up, it seems he was suffering from buyer's remorse—he refused to fork over the $15,000. Regarding Jane as more of a sideshow curiosity than a legitimate performer, Loew stated Jane was "a visual attraction" with "no acting ability" who had jeopardized her potential to draw a crowd with her impromptu appearance at the beauty contest and her choice of wardrobe. When Jane presented at the beauty contest, wearing a simple sundress, "she looked less inviting than a tired working girl, one whose weekly earnings were $15 instead of $15,000."[10] Further, Loew claimed, the high-necked dress she wore on opening night "created a poor impression . . . and dissipated the previous effect and impression built up in the general public's mind as to the personal charm and physical beauty of the defendant."[11] In case the point was lost on anyone, when the complaint went to arbitration, Loew said the high-necked dress had dispelled "a legend concerning the irresistible charms of Miss Russell, with a particular emphasis applied to her bosom."[12] Jane was unaware of any such provisions dictating her wanderings or her wardrobe and was never told there was an issue with her singing. As the public battle got nasty, mainly due to Loew's comments, Jane offered to take a reduced rate of $12,500 just to make it all go away. She was still capable of joking about the incident, quipping, "So, I'm bust am I?"[13] Ultimately, arbitrators settled the dispute, siding with Jane and awarding her the full $15,000. Despite this less than optimal outing, Jane followed up the Miami shows with a brief vaudeville engagement at San Francisco's Golden Gate Theater.[14]

The year 1947 marked the end of the first contract Jane had signed with Howard Hughes when she had been selected for *The Outlaw.* She didn't have much to show for her film career under Hughes except two movies and an avalanche of publicity photos, but Jane's loyalty to him remained strong. "He is always considerate, and I would much rather be signed to him than at a big studio, where I could walk across the lot and bosses probably wouldn't even know me," she told Hedda Hopper at the time. "If I need $5, I'm certain he would always be willing to let me have it."[15] Asked by Hopper how often Jane conferred with her enigmatic boss, she revealed, "O, about once every two years." During those infrequent conferences, "he asks me if I'm happy and if everything's going along all right. And I say 'Fine.' And he says, 'Fine.' And two years later, maybe sooner, I talk to him again—almost always on the telephone."[16]

To initiate the contract negotiations, Hughes summoned Jane to his home on Christmas Eve. Jane protested because of her holiday family plans, but he insisted. Not wanting to cross the boss, Jane acquiesced and drove to his home, which she later remembered as cavernous, dark, and drafty. She met with Hughes briefly, giving him hell for living in such a cold space, both literally and figuratively. It was only later that she realized December 24 was Hughes's birthday. He had insisted on discussing her contract in person on that date because he didn't want to be alone.

Jane signed the second deal with Hughes, though this time, the term would be for four years rather than seven, and instead of yearly salary increases via options, she received a significant raise at the outset.[17] Jane would be paid forty weeks out of the year, whether she was working or not. Of the twelve unpaid layoff weeks, Jane was unfazed. "The thing is that I don't want to dedicate all my time to pictures, and it takes all your time when you're working," she confessed. "I sleep 10 hours a night, and when you have to get up at 6 o'clock in the morning, and don't finish at the studio until nearly 7 in the evening there is no time to spare."[18] She also revealed why she had been appearing on stage and radio with greater frequency. "I have my own stage and radio rights under my new contract, and so I can choose my own time for those activities." Now all she needed was to be cast in another film, though she was longing for a different type of role. "I don't like these lovely lady parts with the hero practically kneeling at your feet," she said. "I'd like to do comedy roles like the ones Jean Arthur has had or those smoothies Irene Dunne does. I'm sure I can do it."[19] As it turned out, a golden film opportunity was about to be placed firmly in her lap.

The Paleface, produced by Paramount Pictures and starring Bob Hope, would be a Technicolor tale of a hapless Old West dentist who inadvertently gets caught up in a covert federal operation led by Calamity Jane. Directed by Norman Z. McLeod, the film would have a healthy budget of over $2 million, with Hope earmarked to receive $135,000 of it.[20] Barbara Stanwyck had briefly been considered to fill the no-nonsense role of Calamity Jane opposite Hope's bumbling Painless Potter, but her expected price tag of $149,000 made

Jane and Bob Hope confer with director Norman Z. McLeod on the set of *The Paleface*. Jane adored Bob Hope and credited the film with saving her career.

producer Robert L. Welch flinch.[21] What he needed was a marquee actress who could play straight woman to Hope while not breaking the bank. Jane, while not a critical success, was still a viable box office draw, and she garnered press attention. Plus she could be hired for less than many other name actresses at the time. When Levis Green contacted Jane to meet him and Welch at Paramount Pictures posthaste, she took him literally. "I arrived in a pair of wild African print shorts with a skirt that matched the top, buttoned at the waist only," she later wrote, "black sandals, and my hair flying. Robert had bought me a new black Cadillac convertible for Christmas, and I had the top down."[22] Green was mortified by her appearance, but still took her into Welch's office. The producer saw something of his Calamity Jane in Jane Russell and agreed to cast her. Now that *The Outlaw* had been released (kind of), Howard Hughes had less cause for keeping Jane off the silver screen. The deal was struck and Jane would finally have the opportunity to appear in a major studio production. When Bob Hope was notified that Jane would be his co-star, he responded, "That's like punishing a rabbit by putting him in a lettuce patch."[23]

Originally, the producers hoped to get Jane for $50,000 total, but the final deal was she would receive $10,000 a week for a guaranteed minimum of ten weeks.[24] In mid-July 1947 Jane reported to the Paramount lot for fittings of her *Paleface* costumes, which cost around $4,500 in total. They included a buckskin jacket and pants set as well as another set comprised of just a corset and pantaloons.[25] She would be photographed in both outfits for publicity photos but—unsurprisingly—it was the image of Jane wielding guns while wearing only undergarments that made its way onto the posters for the film.

Jane wasn't thrilled at being bound in a corset but was otherwise ecstatic about the assignment, viewing it as a chance to play a role in which she could be an active participant. "In both my previous films I was just like a dummy," she commented. "I always stood in one place, or sat in one place nearly motionless as possible. The other characters did things. I had nothing to do. In 'Paleface' it's just the opposite. I'm in action all the time. Right in the first few minutes I shoot three men in a bathhouse."[26] Not only was Calamity Jane a better role than Rio in *The Outlaw* or Joan in *Young Widow*, the production went smoothly. There were no delays, no changes to the Frank Tashlin/Edmund Hartmann screenplay, and only one director. Jane reported to work at 9:00 in the morning on July 29, and finished exactly ten weeks later on October 1. Years later, looking back on the experience of making *The Paleface*, Jane would often comment, "I thought I'd died and gone to heaven when I made *Paleface*.... I probably would have died if I hadn't made this picture, career wise."[27]

She also thoroughly enjoyed working with Bob Hope, whom she had previously met at a party in 1940 before she had been signed for *The Outlaw*. "He's delightful to work with," she'd later say. "There's as much comedy going on off the screen as there is on."[28] She added, "Everything's relaxed except his chocolate eyes, which never stop darting, never missing a thing."[29] The feeling was mutual for Hope, who affectionately nicknamed her Lumpy, a tongue-in-cheek nod to Jane's fabled figure, which she took in stride. *The Paleface* marked the beginning of a long professional relationship and personal friendship between the pair. Over the years Jane and Hope would perform together on stage, radio, and television. Just days after wrapping *The Paleface*, Jane joined Hope on his radio show to perform a parody of *The Outlaw*.[30]

For her performance in *The Paleface*, Jane didn't need to look further than her own front door for inspiration. "I just made up my mind that I was going to be a female Bob Waterfield," she would later say, "because all the lines were flat and dry." When a reviewer later commented that Jane had a wooden face throughout the picture, she was delighted. "We use to call Robert 'Stoneface' so I knew I'd made it."[31] Asked later on if Hope was surprised by her comedic timing, Jane shot back quickly, "I think he was happy about it!"[32]

The Paleface was well received by both critics and the general public, which flocked to theaters. *Variety* commented of Jane's performance, "She makes an able sparring partner for the Hope antics, and is a sharp eyeful in Technicolor."[33] Another reviewer seconded this assessment, commenting that the producers "have found what to do with Jane Russell. As Calamity Jane, frontier markswoman whose laconic speech and forbidding mien make demands on thespian grace, she fulfills a destiny that has been hitherto obscured by her exterior and more noticeable talents."[34]

Despite being Hope's straight woman, Jane's comedic timing is on full display in *The Paleface,* and it's evident what she was capable of on-screen when given a tight script, a capable director, and a stable shooting schedule. The experience was also a revelation for Jane, who until that point had thought multiple directors and countless takes were the norm for film productions. The film still rewards watching decades later: Jane and Hope shine together, the comedy largely holds up, and the film's climatic chase scene is impressive. However, the stereotypical and insensitive Hollywood treatment of Native Americans is extremely problematic for modern-day viewers, giving the film an uncomfortable undertone. The film's prominent "Indian" actor is actually Espera Oscar de Corti, an Italian American who made a career as the self-invented Native American Iron Eyes Cody.

Composer Victor Young scored *The Paleface.* His work in this case proved much more effective than his music for *The Outlaw.* While the film would not garner Young one of his many Oscar nominations, the song "Buttons and Bows," composed by Jay Livingston and Ray Evans, would go on to win the Academy Award for Best Music (Song). The charming tune would be recorded by many artists over the years, including Dinah Shore, who had a number one hit with her rendition. In the film Hope serenades Jane with the song. However, when awards season rolled around, Jane later explained, "Funnily enough, on the Academy Awards that year, they asked me to sing 'Buttons and Bows.' Now, I didn't know all the words to it. And if anybody was ever paying attention . . . I'd change part of the first eight [bars] and into the second, and put the second up into the first. I saw the writers after the show, and they were the ones that knew that's what had happened!" Jane's flub appears to have gone unnoticed, with *Picturegoer* noting, "When it was announced that Jane Russell, the one and only, was going to sing 'Buttons and Bows,' . . .

Jane poses with Ray Evans and Jay Livingston backstage at the 1948 Academy Awards ceremony. (Copyright © Academy of Motion Picture Arts and Sciences, from the Academy Awards show photographs of the Margaret Herrick Library, Academy of Motion Picture Arts and Sciences)

nobody knew she could sing as well!"[35] One person surprised by Jane's performance was Robert Waterfield, who had attended the awards show with his wife. As one publication noted, "Bob was so surprised and delighted that when Jane got back to her seat he couldn't help breaking out of character—he jostled knees halfway down the row of seats to meet and kiss her."[36]

The shooting of *The Paleface* may have been a breeze, but it took Paramount a year to release it in theaters. While she waited for the film to hit screens, Jane went back into the recording studio, where she cut eight tunes, released by Columbia Records as a set of four 78 records in a deluxe album featuring a sultry image of a negligee-clad Jane on the cover. In the liner notes of the set, titled "Let's Put out the Lights," Jane's years of publicity-laden notoriety were acknowledged, but now there were promises of singing that was "soft, intimate, and incredibly close to your shoulder. In one album, she shoots Oomph, It, Purr and Ping all to pieces, and establishes herself as considerably more than a merely decorative performer."[37] The recordings, which featured orchestra accompaniment directed by Lou Bring, include "Do It Again" (George Gershwin and Buddy DeSylva), "Love for Sale" (Cole Porter), and "A Hundred Years from Today" (music by none other than Victor Young). *Variety* mildly praised the album. "While technically, all that can be said about the Russell voice is that it's pleasant and manages to carry a melody well, what makes the album is the production and packaging applied by the recorder."[38] Jane then spent a chunk of 1948 on the road, performing in vaudeville houses, and even sang a few tunes at the thirty-third National Orange Show in San Bernardino, California, not too far away from Aunt Ernie's farm.[39]

As *The Paleface* was starting to hit theaters, Jane found out her next assignment wasn't too far removed from the last. Instead of a stone-faced Calamity Jane, she would be portraying a stone-faced Belle Starr in the independent production *Montana Belle,* another western. Based on an M. Coates Webster story of the same name and adapted by hardboiled novelist Horace McCoy, this heavily fictionalized account of the real-life Starr centers on her teaming up with the notorious Dalton gang, a collaboration that's complicated when she becomes business partners with a saloon owner played by George Brent. The film was to be produced by Howard Welsch, formerly of Universal Pictures, for his Fidelity Pictures company and released by Republic Pictures. Ann Sheridan's name had been tossed around as a possible Belle Starr, but it was soon announced that the other girl with "oomph" would be filling the role.[40]

After Jane's experience at Paramount with Bob Hope, *Montana Belle* was a bit of a letdown. She later described it as a "dreadful picture."[41] However, she did enjoy working with veteran director Allan Dwan, who afforded Jane the opportunity to sing on camera for the first time. In a way this came about through Jane's own suggestion. Her character, by day the gruff outlaw Belle Starr, by night assumes the identity of Montana, a more feminine and blonde-wigged alter ego who works in the saloon. Jane was so confused as to why Starr would be working at the saloon that she asked Dwan, "What am I doing in this place? Why do I have this saloon? . . . Would she sing?" Dwan perked up at this suggestion. "Can you sing?" he asked.[42] Jane jumped at the chance to sing on-screen and contacted Portia Nelson for an original song. Nelson obliged with "The Gilded Lily," co-written by Margaret Martinez. Whatever misgivings Jane may have had about *Montana Belle,* she clearly enjoyed performing "The Gilded Lily," which is a fun, saucy number, along with the more sentimental traditional ballad "My Sweetheart's the Man in the Moon," which she performs later in the film. Overall, *Montana Belle* is an underwhelming and forgettable film, and while Jane's musical numbers are enjoyable enough, she and George Brent don't exactly ignite the screen. Her Belle Starr is far less effective than her Calamity Jane. Fortunately, if she had any qualms about *Montana Belle* being a lackluster follow-up to *The Paleface*, she need not have worried.

During the first half of 1948, Howard Hughes had obtained a controlling interest in RKO Pictures and was now in charge of the studio. In what would later be described by historian Betty Lasky as a "systematic seven-year rape of RKO," Hughes almost immediately made devastating personnel cuts and derailed productions, while at the same time he planned to star Jane in bigger-budget productions, even if it were at the expense of RKO.[43] Hughes may have been running the studio, but Jane would remain the property of the Hughes Tool Company and be loaned out to other studios, including RKO. Given this turn of events and the impending general release of *The Outlaw* (1946 had been a limited release), Hughes feared the mid-budget *Montana Belle* would, as associate Noah Dietrich put it, "lower Jane's value as an attraction."[44] Dietrich, now on the RKO board of directors, was dispatched to meet with producer Howard Welsch and strike a deal to get *Montana Belle* away from Fidelity and Republic and moved over to RKO. Dietrich would later claim negotiations dragged on so long that he witnessed the life cycle of the pigeons that roosted outside his hotel window. Ultimately, a deal was struck; Hughes purchased the film for $600,000, giving him the freedom to release it through RKO when he felt the timing was right.[45]

As it turned out, Hughes would sit on *Montana Belle* for three full years after purchasing it, finally releasing it in the fall of 1952. The reviews were tepid, with *Variety* noting of Jane's performance, "Insofar as the star's acting prowess is concerned in this entry, it's safe to say that her more recent efforts are much better."[46] Promotion of the film seems to have been a low priority—Jane's stand-in was sent to the San Francisco opening to plug the film by walking up and down Market Street wearing jeans and wielding handcuffs and a cap pistol.[47] In Cheyenne, Wyoming, a theater manager tried to drum up *Montana Belle* business at a nearby army base by distributing his own handbills featuring Jane and seared with the words, "Bold! Brazen! Blazing!," a takeoff on the notorious publicity from *The Outlaw*.[48]

Jane's next film would be a complete change of pace, as Hughes made good on his plans to loan her from his own company to the studio he was in charge of. RKO would have to shell out $100,000 to borrow Jane for *It's Only Money*, a farcical comedy co-starring Frank Sinatra and Groucho Marx, who "jumped at the offer" when approached by Hughes.[49] The story, directed by cinema veteran Irving Cummings in what would turn out to be his last film, presents Sinatra as a hapless bank teller who unexpectedly wins big on the horse races but hides his winnings for fear of being accused of a recently discovered bank embezzlement. Jane plays his long-suffering girlfriend/neighbor/co-worker, and Groucho is the restaurant waiter they turn to for advice.

Four writers would be credited for contributing to this inoffensive and underwhelming film, which began shooting at RKO toward the end of 1948. Jane remembered the production as being "not very happy," primarily because Sinatra's life was in turmoil, as he had recently broken up with his wife Nancy and was discreetly seeing Ava Gardner, who often came to the set.[50] Groucho wrote of Jane, "I was pleasantly surprised by Jane. After all the publicity she's had, I expected her to walk on the set wearing a low cut dress and a set of the Breen office rules. Instead, I found a rather shy, quiet creature, very sweet and very beautiful."[51] As for Sinatra, the legendarily caustic comedian would note, "Sinatra's up-and-down career was mostly down during this period. He nevertheless maintained the temperament of a great star. You never know when you might need it again."[52] Groucho may have found Jane to be on the demure side, but during production she also demonstrated what a forceful personality she could have. As her longtime stand-in Carmen Nisbet (Carmen Nisbet Cabeen after her marriage) relayed, "All through the shooting of *The Paleface,* Jane kept at me to get my hair cut short. I told her I liked it long. Then while we were making *It's Only Money,* she started the campaign all over again. I wouldn't give in. But finally, while they were setting up the last shot, Jane grabbed me, merrily pinned me down and with her own little scissors trimmed my hair on one side of my head." The stand-in had no choice but to visit the studio hairdresser and have the other side cut short as well. "But I'm not mad," she continued. "Jane was right—I guess I do look better this way."[53]

If there was one positive outcome of the shoot, it was that Jane was able to sing on-screen again. Even better, the number, "Kisses and Tears" by Jule Styne and Sammy Cahn, was a duet with Frank Sinatra, though on-screen they would be singing to each other on either side of a shared apartment wall. When the two recorded the song, Jane's pleasant but less-than-powerful voice was overshadowed by the formidable Sinatra, so the crooner reportedly had to stand as far away from the mic as possible while Jane stood closer.[54] Still, Jane welcomed another opportunity to show off her musical talents on film, and Howard Hughes was now convinced that she was more than

Longtime stand-in Carmen Nisbet Cabeen and Jane on the set of *The Paleface*. The two would remain close friends and spiritual partners for the rest of their lives.

capable of carrying a tune. Going forward, he no longer had qualms about Jane's singing.

Hughes may have approved of Jane's vocals, but he was not enamored with *It's Only Money*. The film had respectable previews and a decent amount of coverage in the movie magazines, but Hughes decided to shelve it. This was due in part to his continued desire to keep Jane's reputation as an actress somewhat untarnished as he moved toward the general release of *The Outlaw* in 1950. Also, as Hughes had previously been romantically linked to Ava Gardner, he was not a fan of Frank Sinatra and had no problem sticking him on the shelf. Jane and Frank probably would not have minded if the film never saw the light of day, but Groucho felt otherwise. At the time he was still getting his footing as a solo act after decades of performing with his brothers, so he was anxious for the film to be released. After it had been buried for two years, he even took it upon himself to draft a letter to Howard Hughes. "I wonder if you could spare a few moments to release a picture that was made some years ago involving Jane Russell, Frank Sinatra and your correspondent. The name of the picture, if memory serves, is 'It's Only Money.'"[55]

It's not clear if Groucho's pleading had any effect on Hughes, but eleven months later, the picture was finally released, though some changes had been made, specifically the title and billing of the stars. As Groucho wrote succinctly to Leo Rosten, who received the story credit for the film, "'It's Only Money' is now called 'Double Dynamite' as a tribute to Jane Russell's you know what and will open around Christmas at the Paramount in New York."[56] Along those lines, Groucho would later joke that the film had four co-stars. In addition to the title change, Hughes demonstrated his dislike of Sinatra by bumping him from top billing to third. Jane was listed first and the poster art featured her in a low-cut blouse with Marx leering at her. Sinatra was nowhere to be seen on the advertising, other than his third-billed name.

Jane may have initially welcomed the opportunity to be in a light comedy, but in the finished film she lacks any sort of chemistry with Sinatra and has trouble being convincing as his earnest, simpering girlfriend. Her most effective scene is with Don McGuire in which she's out to dinner with him and quite drunk. "I do hope they leave all this scene in," Carmen Nisbet proclaimed, "because Jane plays it to the hilt—including a priceless moment when she is literally cross-eyed."[57] When the film was finally released, reviews were neutral, with many commenting disappointedly on Jane's modest clothing. Ultimately the film did nothing to advance the careers of the three principal players.

Years later Groucho, who has a bathtub scene in the film, commented that with *Double Dynamite* "my acting career almost went down the drain."[58] As Jane summed up hers and Sinatra's roles: "He was playing a dumb little guy and I was playing a dumber little girl and it was a stupid picture, but we sang in it."[59]

11

House in the Clouds

After Jane signed her second contract with Howard Hughes, she and Robert finally felt financially secure enough to move out of Frances Waterfield's home. The designer in Jane was itching to build a house rather than purchase an existing one, but the question was—where? After the end of the war, Geraldine turned her attention to the acreage of the ranch she had retained after selling La Posada. She was delighted when all four of her sons expressed an interest in building homes on the land. Over the next few years, the Russell family compound would gradually spring up as the Russell boys formed families of their own and built homes of varying styles. Nothing would have pleased Geraldine more than handing over a parcel of land to Jane and Robert to build on the compound, but he refused. "He wasn't going to get suckered up in that rat's nest of a family," Jane later recalled.[1]

With the compound officially off the table, Jane decided she wanted a home with a view. She began surveying available vacant hillside lots throughout the Valley, but Robert, who was averse to change, kept rejecting them. Claiming she had looked at about 90 percent of the two thousand available lots, Jane began to despair. Finally she found the absolute perfect site in the Sherman Oaks neighborhood—a hill that had been partially leveled off by a previous property owner who had never followed through with construction. Comprising four lots designated as 14888 Round Valley Drive, the acreage was located south of Ventura Boulevard, rested in between Beverly Glen and Sepulveda Boulevards, and backed up against eighty acres of undeveloped land that would one day become the city-owned Deervale-Stone Canyon Park. The parcel, with its breathtaking views of the San Fernando Valley, was undeniably perfect, and Robert Waterfield conceded defeat.

Jane immediately envisioned a pool on the leveled area and a two-story house that would hug the remaining hill on the south side of the property, with a long, winding driveway leading up to the bottom floor. To help make these design dreams a reality, Jane hired Kemper Nomland Jr. to draw up the

Jane relaxes by the pool at her "house in the clouds," a Mid-Century Modern residence in Sherman Oaks she helped design.

plans. Nomland, who, with his father designed Case Study House #10 in Pasadena that same year, was no stranger to the Russell clan. "I chose Kemper as our architect," Jane said at the time, "because I've known him all my life. His father built homes for Mother and my grandparents, and I knew he was honest."[2] Nomland Sr. had indeed designed La Posada, so his son was well aware what he was getting himself into when planning a home for the head-strong Jane. "We questioned Kemp and we argued with him about construction and design and in the end he always compromised because after all, we were the people who were going to live in the house."[3] Whereas La Posada had been heavily influenced by the Spanish Revival style popular in the 1930s, this new home would bear many marks of Mid-Century Modern, a style that Nomland had embraced. Jane was impressed that he "combined a knowledge of solid old-fashioned construction and an education in modern design. That's the exact combination Bob and I wanted in our house, something built of stone and wood like a 17th century English manor house with all the glass and openness of contemporary homes."[4]

There were two main points of contention between Jane and Nomland: Jane wanted wood beams on the ceiling of the large living room to give the impression of warmth, something the architect deemed completely unnecessary. "I don't care whether we need them to hold up the roof or not," Jane argued. "I want beams!"[5] She got them. The other request challenged the architect's design prowess—Jane wanted to be able to access any room in the house from the front entrance, rather than have to walk through the living room to reach the other rooms. "Look Jane," Nomland told her, half joking. "I don't know how I can do that unless we built a front hall up through the middle of the house like an elevator shaft."[6] This sounded fine to Jane, and the result was a front entrance on the ground level off the carport, naturally lit by a skylight, with a winding redwood staircase leading up to the main "tunnel" that led to the various rooms of the house. The curved staircase was adorned with tropical plants and a stone Buddha that had once been inside the Clover Club, a defunct Sunset Strip hangout. This downstairs area contained a kitchen/bar for entertaining at pool parties, and swimmers also had two dressing rooms to utilize, each featuring murals Jane had painted herself. Jane had dabbled in art over the years and continued to do so, favoring painting and sculpture.

The main living/dining room on the upper level, with its beamed ceiling, was enormous and could comfortably accommodate a gathering of one hundred guests. It was well furnished and multileveled, which broke up the enormity of the space. The dining area was one step up from the rest of the room, and the fireplace was two steps down, which provided an inviting sitting area. Jane worked with three interior decorators to furnish the house, including Harriet Robings Shellenberger, a popular local designer and frequent collaborator of architect Paul Revere Williams.[7] The decor had a heavy Chinese influence that Jane insisted was "not Chinese modern. It's modern decorated with emphasis on old Chinese."[8] For furniture, Jane went with the higher-end Baker Company and also sought out replicas of "old Chinese designs," as she put it. She also revealed, "For a personal touch I created my own dinnerware—large, square plates of pouf umber with gold dripping around the edges." She clarified, "Pouf umber is what I call the color you get when you mix raw umber and burned umber together. Some people call it mud, but I like it so much that my whole living room is done in it."[9] The main room also contained a "music corner" featuring a baby grand piano. "This is a house that looks as though I should go dripping through it in gold lamé and a long cigarette holder," Jane said. "But I don't. It's blue jeans for me."[10]

The Waterfields continued to have different tastes and interests but, as Jane explained, "Considering such contrasts, it's surprising that Robert and I didn't have any big disagreements when we built our very modern house. He

131

When designing the home, Jane included a den Robert Waterfield could retreat to, though she often used it to read scripts.

offered no suggestions at all, but I knew he wanted a den, so the architect and I had a good sized one built in the house for him."[11] As a result, one of the first rooms off the main hub was the den, where Robert could slink off and be surrounded by his football trophies and hunting rifles. Here Jane would sometimes hole up to read scripts, but it was more often used as a place of seclusion where Robert could watch television. The only room not connected to the main hub was the master bedroom, where Jane could hunker down for the night, sleeping like a bear in hibernation. Whereas the walls of the den and main room were wood, the bedroom featured a lavender textured wallpaper framing Waterfield's childhood bed, which they had become so accustomed to they decided to keep. A huge fan of music, particularly jazz, Jane installed an expensive sound system in the bedroom so she could play records from her collection. The kitchen, which featured Chinese-inspired wallpaper, contained one gigantic cabinet that served as a pantry as well as storage for all cooking utensils. The single storage space was a feature Jane devised herself; she deemed it more efficient than multiple cabinets throughout the area. Not that she had any plans to personally cook. Robert handled that task. As Jane explained, "Robert does all the cooking. I detest cooking, but since he gets a big bang out of tossing off a meal he makes no complaints. He's very expert on meats, sauces and salads—all typical he-man meals."[12]

The original plans called for a five-room residence at a cost of approximately $10,500, not including the price of the land.[13] Determined to create the perfect home that she hoped would one day include children, Jane was hyper-involved in the construction, visiting the site as often as she could. Robert may have been initially skeptical about leaving his childhood home, but once the house was completed, he fell in love with it. "Jane wanted a house in the clouds," he said. "On the level. I don't know how she did it, but that's the kind of house we live in. And it's darn well constructed, too."[14] When the couple was interviewed on the popular Edward R. Murrow show *Person to Person* in 1956, it was broadcast from the house in the clouds.

Now that they finally had a place of their own, Jane and Robert truly began settling into their marriage, establishing roles and boundaries. In addition to cooking, Robert handled the couple's finances, which Jane claimed was due to her complete inability to manage money. "I just haven't a head for money, I guess," she admitted, "and I refuse to think about it." Jane's financial failings also prompted Robert to provide his wife with much of her wardrobe. She explained, "Because of my habit of coming home with a new table or the like when I go out to buy a dress, Robert sometimes comes home with a new dress for me when he goes out for a shave and a haircut. He has bought me a barbecue dress, sweaters, and other wearing apparel. His taste is surprisingly good. As he had come to learn, I am not one of the ten best dressed women in America; maybe he's fighting to keep me from being one of the ten worst! . . . He thinks I should spend a bit more time on wardrobe details."[15]

Jane shows off the bedroom of the Sherman Oaks home. She deliberately designed the room to be dark to ensure she could get her full nine to ten hours of sleep every night.

Because of their disparate interests Jane and Robert often engaged in activities separately. Jane favored the arts, and loved traveling to New York to attend Broadway shows. When Robert wasn't on the road with the Rams, he preferred to stay close to home, favoring local fishing and hunting excursions. Jane had little to no interest in football, but was always supportive of Robert's exploits on the field. "I love to go to the Ram games," she said, "but I wouldn't walk across the street to see any other team play. I like to watch the Rams because of Bob and because I know many of the players, their personalities and their problems. That's what makes the Rams' games so much fun for me."[16] Jane became knowledgeable about football by default and often marveled at how Robert's teammates could steer any conversation to the sport: "If you happen to mention that you'd like to go to some place like Bemidji, Minnesota, where I was born, for a real North Woods vacation, you've launched a conversation that'll last the rest of the evening. One of Bob's giant friends will exclaim, 'Minnesota? Wonderful place. Gosh will you ever forget that Minnesota-Illinois game when Minnesota stopped Red Grange?' . . . No kidding, I've listened to so much football tales I can personally replay any big game of the last ten years."[17] Jane took a sensible view of their relationship. "It's a good thing that opposites attract. Robert and I have so little in common when it comes to hobbies, so it's sort of to each his own."[18]

Jane and Robert had both found success in high-profile careers, but each would always maintain close relationships with friends they had made in high school. Robert was particularly guarded about who he spent time with, often resistant to socializing with Jane's friends from the film industry. However, Jane's two-time co-star Vincent Price decided to take on the challenge of befriending Robert Waterfield. After many failed attempts at using his charm on the football hero, who would respond with little more than monosyllabic answers, Price finally snapped, snarling at Waterfield, "I want you to know that I don't know anything about football—and I loathe it!" A string of pent-up insults followed. Robert found the frustrated outburst hilarious and endearing, and got along fine with Price from that moment forward. "Bob likes honesty in people," Jane explained. "It's a passion with him. He'll talk football all night with someone who knows what he's talking about. He hates to yak with people who are just trying to make an impression."[19]

Jane always got along well with cast and crew members, but she also tended to favor close friends from Van Nuys High School. "I made lousy grades in school," she would say, "but I made good friends."[20] One member of the Van Nuys High gang described Jane as a "lame brain," explaining, "She's really vague. Forgets everything. But she's got the biggest heart in Hollywood. She's so sweet about everything. Even though she's vague, we consider her sort of a pillar."[21] Since Robert was usually unavailable to travel with Jane for out-of-town personal appearances, she would often treat these friends to trips, bringing one along as a travel companion. Her friends always got a kick out of accompanying their movie star friend. "We call Jane the Queen," one noted. "It got started back in Atlantic City when Jane was doing personal appearances for *The Outlaw*. Jane would take 11 people to dinner at the swankiest hotel and sign Boss Howard Hughes' name to the check. Were we impressed."[22] Even though Jane's gang dated back to high school, they weren't exactly in Robert's good graces. As columnist Hedda Hopper wrote, "The gang refers to Jane's husband as the Great Stoneface. And, as is so often the case, not much love is lost between Bob Waterfield and his wife's girl friends. Jane has two Dobermans, Blitz and Trinker. The girls suspect that Bob has trained them to be a little unfriendly."[23]

With Jane's home life finally starting to develop a rhythm of sorts, Jane worked on perfecting methods of ensuring she would be getting her nine to

Jane displays her extensive record collection and Seeburg console library record player. She was an avid music enthusiast with a particular love of jazz.

ten hours of sleep every night, which she considered vital for functioning. "Few things peeve me, provided I've had enough sleep the night before," she explained. "All I want is nine hours—but I don't mean eight and a half! We Russells can always sleep. If we don't sleep, we can't even think, let alone get around and look normal." At home, "I sleep like a bear in a hole—the room dark, the bed and pillow soft—none of this new orthopedic hard mattress stuff for me." When traveling "that nine hours business figures into all of my appointments. For instance, in New York, when I wanted to take in some of the hot music spots on 52nd Street, I always figured backwards from the time I had my appointment the next day. Supposing I had to make a personal appearance at 10 A.M., I'd count backwards and thus find out I could be out as late as 1:00 A.M. the night before and still get my sleep." Jane's insistence on getting her nine hours spilled over into air travel as well. She refused to take overnight flights, claiming she was incapable of sleeping on a plane; yet as soon as she boarded, "I put plugs in my ears, wrap myself up in a blanket and curl up like an old snake from take-off till get-there."[24]

Sometimes Jane's quest for sleep would backfire. During a personal appearance tour with Bob Hope "I stayed in a hotel right across the street from the theater because I couldn't be bothered trying to find a cab. I wanted to sleep as long as possible and if I ran to bed after the last show—we were doing something like eight shows a day—I could get my nine hours sleep a night. I always slept in a long flannel nightgown. And I would throw my fur coat over it, run across the street, and then zip into my beads when I got over there, getting on stage just as Bob was announcing me."[25] This arrangement seemed to work fine—until it didn't. One morning she overslept and didn't have time to change. Instead she barreled onstage in the nightgown and fur, ignoring the audience while she told Hope, "I'm not ready. Keep on talking while I go back and get made up."[26] The audience ate it up, thinking it was part of the show, and Hope, without missing a beat, successfully stalled for time. "Nothing throws him," Jane later recalled. "He can absolutely handle anything."[27] When Jane reappeared onstage, she acted as if nothing had happened.

As the 1940s wound down, Jane was finally settling down domestically, though the future of her career still seemed to be in flux. The second Hughes contract was inked and his controlling interest in RKO seemed to point to more film opportunities for Jane. However, Hughes was so unpredictable there was no way for Jane to guess what was going to happen. She continued to fill her time with stage work, and in April 1949 booked another run at the Oriental Theatre in Chicago. Now that she had more stage experience under her belt, the reviews were kinder. *Variety* noted, "Jane Russell has acquired plenty of poise since her last trip around. . . . Her voice is good and she packs the same s.a. [sex appeal] as her figure."[28] She would occupy a good chunk of the summer with live engagements in Atlantic City and Hartford.

As the seasons changed, Jane had the opportunity to go abroad for the first time when she was booked for a two-week engagement at the Princess Theatre in London. Jane grabbed one of her high school pals and hopped on a Pan American flight, arriving in Paris for a short stay before heading to England for the September 26 debut.[29] It seems *The Outlaw* publicity machine was still doing its job; opening night was a sellout, with over fourteen hundred people packing the house to see Jane. The evening was a smashing success and Jane received an ovation. *Variety* reported, "She won over a restive audience with her first number."[30]

Jane's act was part of a vaudeville lineup, so her set, which included musical accompaniment by Frank Weir and his orchestra, lasted only a half hour. Jane performed popular hits of the day, including a duet of "Tea for Two," with Weir and a rendition of the song from *The Paleface* that earned her the nickname the Button and Bows Girl. Onstage Jane had an easy rapport with the audience, at times sitting on the orchestra steps as she crooned into a hand-held mic. She was even able to poke fun at herself as she referenced her early publicity and spoke of the film she made, "which my mother wouldn't let me see."[31]

On returning from her first trip abroad, Jane had much to reflect on in looking back at the past decade. She hadn't aggressively sought a film career, and yet she had become an international star. Because of Howard Hughes, and in spite of him, Jane was still a name film actress at the end of 1949. The avalanche of publicity for *The Outlaw* had launched her career, but it was so over the top that it became something she needed to transcend. Amazingly, she was able to do that, possibly in part because she took such a pragmatic view of her career. "As I look back on all that happened to me," she said at the time, "I think I was like an ostrich about the whole thing. It was as though it was all happening to someone else. It wasn't a matter of my having to live up to anything when I started out in the business. I didn't have anything to live up to. I didn't have any acting experience. But that didn't bother me because I had never thought of having any kind of a career to begin with anyway."[32] While her film career seemed to be on more stable ground, pending the whims of Howard Hughes, Jane was still insistent that she was not obsessed with her standing in Hollywood, claiming, "I have no great urge to be a star. I do enjoy my work more and I might be disappointed now if someone told me I could never be in pictures again, but I'd pull through."[33] There was no danger of Jane disappearing from film screens, however. In fact, she was about to enter the most prolific period of her career.

12

Mitch

At the end of 1949 Jane seemed to be focusing more attention on music than film, but the 1950s would end up being a major turning point for her acting career. For her first major production on the RKO lot, Jane was cast in a film, tentatively titled *Smiler with a Gun* but ultimately released as *His Kind of Woman*, opposite Robert Mitchum. In early 1949 Mitchum had served a fifty-day jail sentence for marijuana possession. Most movie moguls would have viewed the incident as nothing short of a career-ending scandal, but to Howard Hughes it screamed publicity. Hughes secured celebrity attorney Jerry Giesler for Mitchum and rushed two of the actor's pictures onto the screen in order to capitalize on the case. Hughes's gamble paid off, and even though Mitch went to jail (Geisler got the charge reduced to a misdemeanor), he would emerge as the biggest star on the RKO lot. The entire incident would cause Mitchum to develop a deep appreciation and sense of loyalty to Hughes. Given Mitchum's tough-guy screen persona and status at the studio, it was almost a foregone conclusion that Hughes would eventually team him with Jane Russell.

In *His Kind of Woman*, Mitchum plays a down-on-his-luck gambler who is offered a mysterious proposition by an unknown party: $50,000 to go down to Mexico and await further orders. As it turns out, an underworld boss (Raymond Burr) who had been deported to Italy is footing the bill, planning to steal Mitchum's identity to regain access to the United States. In Mexico Mitchum falls for Lenore Brent (Russell), a nightclub singer trying to remake her own identity by hitching herself to an eccentric film star (Vincent Price). The film was directed by John Farrow, whom Mitchum would later describe as "a sadist," though Jane was kinder in her assessment: "He was very nice to us, but he would be nasty to some of the other kids." She added that Farrow was "needling all the time. If you needled him back, it was ok. But if you didn't think you could do that—other people were terrified."[1]

Jane arrived on the RKO lot in late March 1950 and completed her scenes less than two months later.[2] As far as everyone could tell, it was a smooth

Robert Mitchum and Jane on the set of *His Kind of Woman,* where the pair met and became life-long friends. (RKO Radio Pictures photographs of the Margaret Herrick Library, Academy of Motion Picture Arts and Sciences)

shoot, and Farrow believed he was handing over a completed film. After viewing Farrow's cut, Howard Hughes thought otherwise and ordered retakes of some scenes. It had taken the mogul months to get around to viewing the film, so shooting resumed nearly six months after principal production had wrapped. After finishing five days of retakes with a new director, Robert Stevenson, Jane and the rest of the cast may have thought they were done, but that was hardly the case. Hughes had decided the climax of the film was anti-climactic, and yet another director, Robert Fleischer, was called in to fix it. At the time Fleischer was under suspension for refusing to direct a subpar script a studio exec had tried to assign him. Hughes assured Fleischer that revising the end of *His Kind of Woman* would only take ten to fourteen days. Plus, Fleischer's participation would get the suspension lifted. The director thought it all sounded too good to be true, but relented and got to work on retakes along with devising additional scenes with screenwriter Earl Felton and Hughes. Under the influence of Howard Hughes, the ending of the film, which likely needed only some beefing up, instead ballooned out of control. "More. He had to have more," Fleischer later wrote of working with Hughes on the picture. "Howard was getting hooked on the thing like an addict. The more we gave him, the more he wanted. How about Vincent Price, the principal comic relief in the picture, organizing a rescue party? Why not? How could we leave Jane Russell out of this merriment? No way."[3]

In May 1951, a full year after Farrow had completed *His Kind of Woman,* Jane reported to the set to be directed by Fleischer. Jane, in fact, got off easy with the reshoots. She was barely in the climatic scenes, instead getting locked in a closet by Vincent Price's character before he heads out to where the action is. Price and Mitchum, on the other hand, were subjected to a seemingly never-ending shooting schedule. A massive yacht set was constructed and built on to continually as new scenes were written. The shoot, which would not be completed until August 1951, dragged on for so long that Price threw a party to celebrate his one-year anniversary on the film. Mitchum's spirits sank lower and lower until he finally snapped, drowning his frustrations in alcohol. The revisions reportedly added well over $750,000 to the budget. In the eleventh hour, Hughes decided to replace Lee Van Cleef, who had originally been cast as antagonist Ferraro, with Raymond Burr, a decision that required considerable retakes. The shoot was so frenetic that advertising for the film, including a double-page color ad in *Life* magazine, started showing up nearly two weeks before the retakes with Burr were even complete.[4]

Remarkably, after the interminable delays, *His Kind of Woman* was released mere weeks after production finally wrapped. The resulting movie is a respectable crime/drama with strong film noir leanings that three-quarters of the way in devolves into a fever dream, intercutting torture scenes with slapstick comedy. The changes in tone in the rewritten climax are jarring, leaving the viewer wondering what could have possibly been transpiring off-screen to produce such a bizarre movie. Vincent Price's role was beefed up considerably for the third act, and while he is delightful as the hammy actor Mark Cardigan, it often feels as if he jumped off the reel of a different film and came crashing into *His Kind of Woman.* Jane later said, "When they did the retakes on *His Kind of Woman,* Vinnie got to play a character for the first time. A really zany nut. And he enjoyed it immensely."[5] When the film was released in September 1951, reviewers were underwhelmed. The consensus was that Jane had been given nothing to do. *His Kind of Woman* would go on to lose $825,000, the approximate cost of the rewrites.[6] Years later when interviewing Jane and Mitchum, historian Robert Osborne asked, "If we

Mitch and Jane are swarmed by fans after a stage appearance at the Orpheum Theatre in Los Angeles to promote *His Kind of Woman*. (Los Angeles Herald Examiner Collection/Los Angeles Public Library)

knew Howard Hughes as you both were able to know him, would we be as fascinated by him as we are today?" Neither hesitated to respond in the affirmative.[7]

In retrospect, Jane actually fares well in *His Kind of Woman*, far better than in the two previous films she made under the thumb of Howard Hughes.

She looks absolutely stunning in a form-fitting wardrobe designed by Howard Greer at a cost to the studio of $4,500.[8] Her introduction in the film, singing a lively tune called "Five Little Miles from San Berdoo" accompanied by a piano and guitar duo, is memorable, as is Mitchum's reaction when he first lays eyes on her during the scene. For her second number, "You'll Know," she's given the full A-picture treatment, and is flawlessly photographed. She even had the opportunity to record both songs, which were released as a record in Britain. If *The Paleface* demonstrated Jane's comedic talents, then *His Kind of Woman* established her as a bona fide movie star, projecting a level of on-screen glamour the public hadn't yet seen. Much like *The Outlaw*, the delightfully bizarre end result that is *His Kind of Woman* is one that only the incomprehensible mind of Howard Hughes could produce.

When the publicity campaign for *His Kind of Woman* launched, Hughes proved he hadn't lost his ability to attract controversy when promoting a Jane Russell movie. For the film's key art, Hughes turned to artist and designer Mario Zamparelli, a personal favorite Hughes had employed for years, using him to design "logos, movie posters, casinos and airplane interiors for Hughes operations including Trans World Airlines, Hughes Airwest, Hughes Helicopters and RKO Studios."[9] From 1958 to 1976 Zamparelli would serve as Hughes's chief executive designer.[10] For *His Kind of Woman*, the artist created an oil painting of Jane in a low-cut strapless gown leaning over a reclining Robert Mitchum. Compared to the artwork of Jane used on the posters for the 1943 premiere of *The Outlaw* in San Francisco, Zamparelli's rendering was positively tame. British officials, however, scandalized by the amount of Jane's visible skin, ordered six inches of neckline added to the art before they would allow billboards to go up around London. One journalist described the result as "giving Jane the appearance of wearing a bodice so high it practically chokes her."[11] Zamparelli was outraged, and not shy about letting his ire be known, calling the censorship "an inexcusable liberty. I worked five weeks on that portrait. And they ruined it in five minutes."[12] Launching into a tirade for the benefit of an American columnist, Zamparelli railed, "I painted her as she is. And what is painting, after all, but an expression of real life?" He continued angrily, "When you have Jane Russell in front of you—wearing a low-necked dress with nothing under it—certain sensations come forth. And I, as an artist, put those sensations, via a brush on canvas. Why not cover up the Venus de Milo? Or any other classic nudes? What makes me so mad is the way they accept fine art and ban what they call 'commercial' art. I say there is no distinction."[13] To add insult to injury, the censorship issue in Britain was not the first one to spring up regarding this particular piece of art. "In the original painting her dress was a lot lower," the artist admitted. "Almost everything showed. But the [Breen] office made me lift the neckline . . . inch by inch. It was excruciating pain to my artistic soul." Zamparelli concluded dramatically, "Then England goes and, without my authority, covers her up even more. They actually censored the censored version!"[14]

No matter what the censors might do or say, Hughes heartily approved of the artwork, so much, in fact, that he decided to blow it up three stories tall and erect it at the busy intersection of Wilshire and Fairfax in Los Angeles. The oversized advertisement weighed thirty tons and measured thirty-five by forty-five-feet. The *Los Angeles Times* reported that "an antique and gilt replica of the frame around an old masterpiece in the New York Metropolitan Museum of Art will provide a setting."[15] The colossal billboard would be unveiled as part of a glitzy industry gala planned to roll out in three phases: a cocktail party behind the billboard, the unveiling, and a buffet dinner and dance with Tony Martin and an orchestra providing mood music. The painting was moved into place in the middle of the night, so as not to disrupt traffic, and prepped for the unveiling.[16] Then, at the eleventh hour, the gala was abruptly cancelled. Neighbors had complained that the massive painting would be a dangerous distraction to drivers, and studio execs feared that in excess of five thousand people might show up to the unveiling, rather than merely the five hundred invited guests. Plans to tour the giant billboard around the country were scrapped and the painting was quietly removed without fanfare. The artwork would be used, unaltered, on the American poster art and in magazine ads.

Starting with *His Kind of Woman*, the RKO lot became a familiar and comfortable place for Jane. She appreciated working at the smallish studio as opposed to a behemoth like MGM. "It was like being at your home away from home really," she later said. "We all knew each other very well."[17] She was given a star dressing room on the lot, which she had painted pale pink, and her wants and needs were attended to (for *His Kind of Woman*, the studio paid for the Burdick sunlamp Jane requested so she could get a tan in between takes).[18]

Jane was also given a top-notch behind-the-scenes group to work with. Recognizing a good thing when she saw it, Jane would gradually come to develop a personal crew that was earmarked for her pictures, even when she was loaned out to a different studio. Her preferred team included hairstylist Stephanie McGraw, wardrobe mistress Mary Tate, makeup artist Layne "Shotgun" Britton, stand-in Carmen Nisbet, and cinematographer Harry J.

Wild. "I can't stand to be fussed over much," she would say. "My first make-up man was Ernie Westmore, and I absolutely adored him but he took three hours to put on my make-up in the morning, and I made up my mind I was never going to go through that again. So from then on I made up myself. I had Shotgun Britton as a make-up man and he was there to tell me what was wrong, or what I needed. . . . Little by little I found people that worked quickly and efficiently, and also had a sense of humor. I finally found an entire crew."[19] This group became so synchronized that the members practically had Jane's routine down to a science: "I could get to the studio at 8 and be on the set at 9. Other people were spending two and half or three hours in the morning. I had no patience for that."[20] At most studios, having a dedicated crew would have been highly unusual, but Jane had an unusual boss. "It was Howard Hughes," Jane would later say. "If it hadn't been him, I probably could never have done that."[21]

RKO also assigned Jane a publicist. Edith Lynch was at first apprehensive about her new client, but her fears were allayed upon meeting Jane, whom she found "shy, impatient, and loud—a roaring mouse. But with all that bluster, she couldn't quite hide the humor and kindness in her—an earthiness and wisdom that fascinated everyone; she was a really funny gal." Lynch, who would work for Jane for well over a decade and become a lifelong friend, described her as "a confusing mess of opposing traits: honest, empathetic, bright, loud, impatient, lazy (by her own admission), shy, sympathetic, bossy, disorganized, and creative."[22]

Between the end of principal photography and the beginning of retakes on *His Kind of Woman*, Jane was assigned to her next picture, *Macao*. Another crime drama, the film would again star Jane opposite Robert Mitchum, though this time around the script would be tailor-made for the pair. Figuring the two biggest stars on the RKO lot were likely to be teamed up for the production, writer/producer Stanley Rubin drafted *Macao* specifically for a Russell-Mitchum pairing, though this was news to Jane. "I had no idea that he was writing anything for me," she admitted. "I heard later that he had written it with me in mind."[23] The character of Julie Benson would be a no-nonsense, quick-witted, guys' gal, a role Jane was comfortable playing. Set to direct the picture was Josef von Sternberg, a veteran filmmaker whose visually stylized movies in the 1930s with his muse, Marlene Dietrich, had been the pinnacle of his long career. Now staring down the end of his time in Hollywood, von Sternberg was basically fulfilling a two-picture deal with Howard Hughes by directing *Macao*.

Set in Macao, a China-adjacent Portuguese colony, the film follows an expatriate drifter (Mitchum) who is mistaken for an undercover detective by both local authorities and a crime lord after his wallet and identification are pickpocketed by an embittered and equally drifting nightclub singer (Russell). A romance develops between the two, but is complicated by the gambling kingpin (Brad Dexter) who employs Russell, his jealous girlfriend (Gloria Grahame), and the actual undercover detective (William Bendix) who is posing as a traveling salesman.

The exotic locale and colorful characters should have lent themselves well to von Sternberg's aesthetic, but the shoot turned out to be an extremely unhappy one. Von Sternberg's autocratic style did not mesh well with Mitchum and Russell, who resented what they saw as a divide and conquer approach. "Joe was really something," Mitchum later recalled. "He told me, 'We both know this is a piece of shit and we're saddled with Jane Russell. You and I know she has as much talent as this cigarette case.'"[24] Mitchum, who had become fast friends with Jane while filming *His Kind of Woman*, wasn't having it. "Mr. von Sternberg," he replied, "Miss Russell survives, so she must have something. Lots of ladies have big tits."[25] Relations went downhill from there. Von Sternberg forbade food or drink on the set, so Mitchum responded by laying out a picnic between takes or preparing a greasy deli lunch on a lectern the director used for his script. Mitchum recalled, "I used to tell the crew, 'Why don't you quit? Fuck him and the boat that brought him. Let's all go home.'"[26] The crew didn't go, but everyone did follow Mitchum's lead, not allotting much respect to the director, whose heyday was long behind him. "He was very short," Mitchum said. "He wore suede trousers and scarves. He used to stand on a box. And our cameraman, Harry J. Wild, when he lost patience, would throw down his hat and kick it. Once, he kicked the apple box and von Sternberg fell off backwards. I think von Sternberg sort of lost heart at that point." Jane would often recount how, after the picnic stunt, von Sternberg confronted Mitchum, yelling, "Do you want to get fired?" To which Mitchum responded, "No, you'll get fired."[27]

Von Sternberg did not get fired, and the film was finished on October 19, 1950.[28] After the film received underwhelming feedback at preview screenings, retakes were deemed necessary, but they would not be done by the original director. Reshoots and additional scenes were shot by Robert Stevenson, Mel Ferrer and, predominantly, Nicholas Ray. Filming recommenced in February 1951 and dragged on through August, meaning Jane and Mitchum worked on *His Kind of Woman* and *Macao* simultaneously. Mitchum also contributed to the film off-screen, assisting Ray with some of the rewrites. In a dual interview with Jane in 1996, Mitchum said, "Jane and Nick Ray came up to me with a big sort of legal pad and several pencils, and said—" "Write it!" interjected Jane. Mitchum continued, "So I go in the dressing room and write in the morning, and they'd get a secretary to type it up, and then we'd shoot in the afternoon." "The best scenes are the ones he wrote," Jane said, referring to Mitchum.[29] For Jane, the set without von Sternberg was much more pleasurable; she later commented, "It was a lot of fun making *Macao.* Especially watching one director go and another one come in. And I loved working with Mitch and everyone on the thing, except the director."[30] Nicholas Ray and Harry J. Wild attempted to mimic von Sternberg's on-screen aesthetic in the new scenes, but to von Sternberg the tampering was a slap in the face. He barely mentioned the film in his memoirs, written years later, saying only, "After *Jet Pilot* I made one more film in accordance with the contract I had foolishly accepted. This was made under the supervision of six different men in charge. It was called *Macao,* and instead of fingers in that pie, half a dozen clowns immersed various parts of their anatomy in it."[31]

Another point of contention for von Sternberg was Jane's wardrobe in *Macao.* Jane's and Gloria Grahame's costumes were assigned to designer Michael Woulfe, who had been under contract to RKO since 1949. When Woulfe signed the deal with the studio, executive Sid Rogell warned him, "It's a whole different ballgame now that Howard Hughes owns the studio. You better make the clothes look sexy!" As Woulfe later noted, "Nostradamus himself couldn't have made a more accurate prediction about the future."[32] Woulfe suspected that Hughes would be more hands-on in *Macao* than he had been in the previous non–Jane Russell films he had worked on. His suspicions proved correct. Hughes, via a telephone call, gave the designer explicit instructions on how he wanted Jane dressed. According to Woulfe, Hughes wanted Jane's wardrobe, "whenever possible, to be low-necked (and by that I mean as low as the law allows) so that the customers can get a look at the part of Russell which they pay to see."[33] As Woulfe recalled, "'Operation Sexy' commenced immediately. I tossed out any sketches that didn't display Jane's magnificent breasts in all their glory. I tried to invent new ways to make the cleavage more enticing. Generations of costume and clothing designers before me took on this challenge. Sadly, no new and miraculous techniques had been discovered."[34] Woulfe followed Hughes's instructions to a tee, although in the process "I ignored my finer instincts of taste and did my job as requested."[35] When von Sternberg was later brought on to direct the

Jane, clad in the gold metal mesh gown from *Macao,* looks over the sketch for the dress with designer Michael Woulfe. This was one of the rare times Howard Hughes allowed Jane to wear a high-necked frock on-screen. (Michael Woulfe Papers of the Margaret Herrick Library, Academy of Motion Picture Arts and Sciences)

picture and saw Woulfe's sketches, he was apoplectic, raging against the costume designer for being, as Woulfe later recounted, "too involved with her 'tits and ass.'"[36] Von Sternberg, planning to create a "new" Jane Russell, accused the designer of deliberately thwarting this scheme. Howard Hughes had spent a decade carefully crafting Jane's sex goddess image, paying as much attention to her at times as he did the Spruce Goose, so Woulfe marveled at von Sternberg's attempt to "take her hard-earned image and toss it aside like a moldy piece of bread."[37]

Against his better judgment (and under threat of being taken off the picture by the vice president of production), Woulfe acquiesced, and with the new costume sketches, "Jane's image was now scrubbed clean of all that nasty sexiness that helped make her a star."[38] As a result Woulfe was caught in the middle of a battle between Hughes and von Sternberg over Jane's costumes. According to Woulfe, the director would scream at him in person, and Hughes would deride him via memo. In one piece of correspondence, Hughes complained, "I think Russell's wardrobe as displayed in this test is Christ awful. It is unrevealing, unbecoming, and just generally terrible."[39] It was a fight von Sternberg was destined to lose, and Jane's sexy on-screen image remained intact. In the process, the director managed to further alienate his cast and crew, particularly after an especially heated encounter in which von Sternberg punched Woulfe in the arm, ripping his sweater. Jane and Mitchum had become friendly with Woulfe and, according to the costume designer, defended his honor by refusing to report to work until von Sternberg apologized. A begrudging apology was offered to placate the two stars, and a replacement sweater was sent to Woulfe. *Macao* would be the last film von Sternberg made in Hollywood.

Despite the tug-of-war over the designs, Jane's wardrobe in *Macao* is spectacular. "She looked fabulous in the outfits," Woulfe later recalled. "All her charms were intact."[40] Two of Woulfe's designs, a halter dress and sweater/skirt combo, were turned into dress patterns that could be mail-ordered for 50 cents. Adhering to Howard Hughes's quest to present Jane's breasts as defying gravity, Woulfe modified a store-bought cashmere sweater with an understructure.[41] There would be no unsightly bra seams in *Macao*. The show-stopping costume of the film was a gold evening gown made of metal mesh that weighed twenty-one pounds and cost $550 (roughly equivalent to $6,000 in 2020) to make.[42] Jane needed three people to help her get into the dress, and when the cameras were rolling, she had to be careful how she moved since the metal made a clinking sound easily picked up by the microphones. "It certainly is heavy," she said at the time. "I feel like crawling instead of slinking around in it. I would hate to go to a party in it."[43] Although the gold mesh dress was high-necked, Howard Hughes was enthusiastic about it "because it is so startling." However, upon seeing the tests of the garment, he became incredibly concerned with every last detail of how Jane's famed bosom appeared in it, drafting a nearly eight-hundred-word memo expressing these perceived issues.

> The fit of the dress around her breasts is not good and gives the impression, God forbid, that her breasts are padded or artificial. They just don't appear to be in natural contour. It looks as if she is wearing a brassiere of some very stiff material which does not take the natural contour of her breasts.
>
> Particularly around the nipple, it looks as though some kind of stiff material underneath the dress is forming an artificial and unnatural contour.
>
> I am not recommending that she go without a brassiere, as I know this is a very necessary piece of equipment for Russell. But I thought, if we could find a half-brassiere made of very thin material so that the natural contour of her breasts will show through the dress, it will be a great deal more effective.
>
> In addition to the brassiere situation, it may be that the dress will have to be retailored around the breasts in order that it will more naturally form to the proper contour.
>
> Now, it would be extremely valuable if the brassiere, or the dress, incorporated some kind of a point at the nipple because I know this does not ever occur naturally in the case of Jane Russell. Her breasts always appear to be round, or flat, at that point so something artificial here would be extremely desirable if it could be incorporated without destroying the contour of the rest of her breasts.
>
> My objection to the present set-up is that her breasts do not appear realistic in any way. The over-all shape is just not realistic and at the nipple instead of one point which would be very desirable and natural, there appears to be something under the dress which makes several small projections, almost as if there were a couple of buttons on the brassiere or under the dress at this point.
>
> One realistic point indicating the nipple, if it could be incorporated realistically into the brassiere and show through the dress, would be very fine. The trouble with the setup now is that where the nipple is supposed to be there is more than one projection and it looks very unnatural. Also, the balance of her breasts from the nipple around to her body appears to be conical and somehow mechanically contrived and not natural.

This is difficult to explain, but if you will run the film I think you will see what I mean.

What we really need is a brassiere of a very thin material which will form to the natural contour of her breasts and, if possible, which is only a half-brassiere, that is to say which supports the lower half of her breasts only.

The brassiere should hold her breasts upward but should be so thin that it takes the natural shape of her breasts instead of forming it into an unnatural shape. Then, if something could be embodied in the dress itself at the point of the nipple to give it just one realistic point there (which Russell does not have) and if this could be accomplished without putting anything into the dress which will disturb the contour except right at the point of the nipple, this would be the ideal solution.

You understand that all the comment immediately above is with respect to the dress made of metallic cloth.[44]

It's not clear if Jane was ever aware just how much attention Howard Hughes paid to her nipples.

One of the more interesting garments designed by Woulfe for *Macao* wasn't worn by Jane. As he later said, "In the film, Gloria [Grahame] played a croupier in a gambling den. Some of her costumes were fun. I created a gown with long sleeves that ended in gloved fingers. The fingers were finely embroidered in gold, and there was an ominous feeling when she spread her hands and gather[ed] all the chips from the table—like tentacles removing the riches from their owners."[45] The unique gown did little to assuage Grahame's resentment at being cast in a supporting role with little to do. When her soon-to-be-ex-husband, Nicholas Ray, took over directing duties, Grahame supposedly joked that she would forego alimony if he removed her from the film.[46]

Macao started hitting theaters in March 1952, with von Sternberg receiving the sole directing credit, though he probably would have preferred that his name be removed from it altogether. As *Variety* noted, the film contains "the cliched elements of adventure, romance, and intrigue . . . yet all it adds up to is a routine formula pic."[47] While the film is formulaic and uneven, it's not without its virtues. The set designs are striking, particularly the gambling den, featuring baskets tied to strings being moved up and down to transport money, and the climatic chase scene is memorable; it takes place on a boat dock where the characters weave in and out of hanging fishing nets. William

Jane and Mitch share a playful moment at the Shadow Mountain Resort & Club in Palm Desert, California.

Bendix does a lot with the little his character is given and, as in *His Kind of Woman*, Russell and Mitchum are sizzling on-screen. And Jane got to sing again. *Macao* would end up losing $700,000 though, as in their previous pairing, the additional scenes and retakes added a lot to the budget.[48] Despite the losses, Jane was now considered an A-picture star; she received, $165,000 for her services.[49]

After making two pictures together, Jane and Robert Mitchum developed a lifelong friendship. Jane always spoke glowingly about "Mitch" and marveled at his writing talents, which she felt he should have utilized more. She was also impressed with his ability to digest a script with ease. "He was a wonderful guy," she would later say. "He had a memory that wouldn't stop. He could read a script through maybe twice and know it, know the whole thing. He had one of those photographic minds, and he was lots of fun."[50] Jane would also note, "I think we did have good chemistry for film because he was my type of guy. Robert Mitchum and I were really very close and good friends."[51] Mitchum was equally fond of Jane, whom he nicknamed Hard John because, as Jane explained, "I remind him of the meanest woman he ever knew and he's always calling me 'The Original Hard John,' a ha-ard man to shave."[52]

Was there more to Jane and Mitchum's relationship than friendship? Jane would later fess up to frequently developing crushes on her co-stars, but with Mitchum, there did seem to be something more than a mere passing infatuation. In interviews in the years after Mitchum's death in 1997, Jane sometimes made comments that could be open to a romantic interpretation of their relationship. Once, asked, "What did you love about working with him?," Jane was quick to respond, "I loved Robert Mitchum!"[53] A later exchange between Jane and actress Terry Moore was more revealing:

JANE: Mitch and I were very natural together.
MOORE: You were like brother and sister, you were so close.
JANE: No, it wasn't quite like that.
MOORE: Really?
JANE: We had the hots for each other.

Jane continued:

Well, we were very, very close, and—Oh, Howard. I can remember sitting in his car, it was right down the driveway from my house. He had come there and I was to go and talk with him. He was going to tell me that he understood that I wanted to divorce Robert, and Mitch and I would get married. I said, "No way, that's ridiculous!" He thought Mitch was going to divorce Dorothy and he would put us together. I said, "Don't you know that it's perfectly ok to love two people. It doesn't mean you divorce somebody and go with the other one."

Asked who was a better kisser, Robert Mitchum or Richard Egan, with whom Jane would later co-star, she replied, "I never kissed Richard Egan, except in the picture."[54]

In her 1985 autobiography, Jane referenced the first time she strayed during her marriage to Robert Waterfield. In 1957, while working on *The Fuzzy Pink Nightgown*, Jane threw a party in her dressing room for some of the cast and crew.

One of my old loves, whom I'll call Lance, telephoned, and I invited him over. He was separated from his wife and feeling blue. One by one the kids from the picture left and pretty soon the two of us were sitting there alone, quite loaded, and talking about old times, swearing our undying love. Neither of us wanted or needed the whole physical act. We'd sidestepped that for years. . . . It had been a truly beautiful relationship. Yet, because we were drunk, I'm sure, we did the one thing I'd sworn I would never do. We went to bed.[55]

Was "Lance" Robert Mitchum? Jane never confirmed this publicly, so one can only speculate based on the scattered comments she made over the years. Whatever their relationship off-screen may have been, their onscreen chemistry was undeniable. Asked why she thought they paired so well on film, Jane replied, "We looked like we deserved each other."[56]

13

Wing-Ding Tonight

Jane barely had a moment to catch her breath before Howard Hughes assigned her to her next film, another crime drama in which she would be playing a nightclub singer for the third consecutive time. Jane reported for hair and makeup tests on *The Miami Story* in December 1950, but by the time production actually began the following April, the title had been changed to *The Las Vegas Story*. Robert Stevenson, who had shot retakes with Jane on *His Kind of Woman* and *Macao*, was to direct the entire picture, and Victor Mature was cast as Jane's leading man. She would once again be acting opposite her pal Vincent Price, along with Brad Dexter, whom she had worked with on *Macao*. Cinematographer Harry J. Wild was also assigned to the film because, as Jane explained, Howard Hughes "liked the way Harry photographed me. He was very particular about that. So, he had Harry under contract."[1] Michael Woulfe was enlisted to design Jane's costumes and began working on the film, but he was abruptly pulled off and replaced with Howard Greer, who had created Jane's gowns for *His Kind of Woman*. Years later Woulfe was still bitter at the missed opportunity to work with Jane again, and he claimed that three of his designs were used, uncredited.[2]

In *The Las Vegas Story* Jane plays Linda Rollins, a former Las Vegas nightclub singer who is forced to confront the past she's been trying to forget when her inveterate gambler of a husband (Vincent Price) insists on spending a few days in her old stomping ground. There she encounters Dave Andrews (Mature), a former flame she abandoned while he was overseas during the war. The developing love triangle is further complicated by an insurance company detective (Dexter) who tails Linda to ensure that an expensive necklace in her possession is not mishandled. Jane would once again have the opportunity to sing on-screen, though most of the musical duties were handled by popular singer/songwriter Hoagy Carmichael, cast as the pianist at the casino where Jane's character once worked.

Filming on *The Las Vegas Story* went smoothly, with much of the production shooting on location in Las Vegas. The film wrapped at the RKO studios in late June.[3] Post-production didn't seem to have suffered from as much interference from Howard Hughes as Jane's previous two films, but *The Las Vegas Story* would not be released until early 1952. True to form, the film would have its share of Hughes-induced controversy—which, for once, didn't involve Jane. In the midst of production, Paul Jarrico, the screenwriter on *The Las Vegas Story,* was called by the House Un-American Activities Committee (HUAC) to testify about communist sympathizers working in the film industry. When he defiantly invoked his Fifth Amendment rights, Hughes fired him and stripped him of his writing credit on the film. Hughes then filed a lawsuit against Jarrico in order to ensure he would not have to pay for the writer's services or give him the writing credit. This marked the first legal action taken by a film studio against a subpoenaed witness who refused to cooperate with HUAC. Not one to back down, Jarrico sued RKO for violating the rules of the Screen Writers Guild. Caught up in the hysteria of the McCarthy-era witch hunts, Jarrico lost the court case and was blacklisted from working in Hollywood.[4]

Cut from the same cloth as *His Kind of Woman* and *Macao, The Las Vegas Story* is far less engaging than its predecessors and at times is very slow-paced. It does pick up at the end for an impressively filmed chase involving a helicopter but, as *Variety* noted of the climactic scene, "It's 10 minutes of exciting footage that enlivens an otherwise rather dull 87 minutes."[5] Still, *The Las Vegas Story* is not without its bright spots. Jane looks gorgeous in Howard Greer's designs, and she clearly enjoyed her scenes with Vincent Price and Hoagy Carmichael, though she and Victor Mature don't ignite the screen as brightly as she and Mitchum did. If nothing else, the extensive footage of 1950s Las Vegas, including a lot of neon signage, might be the film's greatest virtue, with the Flamingo Hotel standing in as the movie's fictional Hotel Fabulous. When it came time for the film's premiere, there was little question that the cast would be returning to Vegas.

As 1951 rolled along, Jane was busier than she'd ever been, with no signs of slowing down. In terms of her career, she may have been more fulfilled than at any point in the past decade, but that didn't stop her from feeling there was a large gap in her life. Her brothers had been starting families, so the Russell compound was bustling. Jane was getting desperate to contribute her own addition to the ever-growing brood. She and Robert Waterfield had been married for eight years, and for Jane it was almost unthinkable they had been wed so long without having kids. Even though Jane would not be able to have biological children as a result of the botched abortion in 1942, there was never any question in her mind that she and Robert Waterfield would have a large family, even if it meant they would have to adopt. Robert was cool on the idea, but Jane remained undeterred.

She started publicly expressing her desire to adopt, and her comments were picked up by the Associated Press and splashed all over newspapers around the county.[6] In response, Jane received a letter from a woman whose pregnant daughter planned to put the baby up for adoption. Were the Waterfields interested? Jane anxiously read the letter to Robert, fearful he would reject the opportunity. "Do whatever you want" was his reply, and that was enough for her.[7] On June 21, Jane was at the Sportsmen's Lodge in Studio City celebrating her thirtieth birthday when she received news that the baby had been born. It was a girl. Since Jane was finishing up *The Las Vegas Story* and still tied up with reshoots on *His Kind of Woman* and *Macao*, Frances Waterfield was dispatched out of state to pick up the baby. Jane and a reluctant Robert Waterfield met Frances and the baby at the airport. They named the little girl Tracy. Much to Jane's delight, and perhaps surprising himself, Robert immediately took to fatherhood, assisting Jane with late-night feedings and even attempting to change the baby, though the result looked more like a sarong than a diaper.

Motherhood did not have an impact on Jane's career, nor did it affect demand for her services. Clark Gable had wanted to borrow Jane for *Lone Star*, a big-budget MGM western directed by Vincent Sherman. Howard Hughes refused to loan her out, and the part went to Ava Gardner instead. Jane claimed the missed opportunity didn't bother her. "I would like to do a picture with Gable sometime," she said. "But not *Lone Star*. There's nothing for a girl in it. The plot concerns two men." Jane added, "The person most disappointed because I didn't do *Lone Star* was my husband. Robert has always figured Gable as his kind of guy—a guy who likes to fish and hunt. He wanted to meet Gable and make a hunting date."[8]

Hughes may have had qualms about Jane going to MGM and co-starring with "the King of Hollywood," but he was agreeable to a return to the Paramount lot and a reunion with Bob Hope for *Son of Paleface*. A sequel to the 1948 hit, the film would again be produced by Robert L. Welch, who also co-wrote the screenplay with Frank Tashlin and Joseph Quillan. Tashlin would also be assuming directorial duties. Set thirty or so years after the events of the first film, *Son of Paleface* follows the mishaps of Peter "Junior"

Jane returned to the Paramount lot in 1951 for *Son of Paleface,* which co-starred singing cowboy Roy Rogers in addition to Bob Hope.

Potter (Hope), a recent Harvard grad who heads west to retrieve his inheritance from the town of Sawbuck Pass, where his father, the now deceased Paleface Potter, once resided. He quickly discovers that dear old Dad died in debt to practically every resident in town and that the chest of gold he expected to cart away is empty. Shades of *Montana Belle,* the film has Jane

Jane visits pal Bob Hope on the set of *Road to Bali,* which included a brief cameo by Jane.

playing a gold bandit nicknamed The Torch who moonlights as a saloon owner/performer known as Mike or California Rose. She becomes the object of Hope's affections as he concocts a plan to marry her and pay off the debt with her fortune. Hope's character inadvertently gets caught up in a covert plot to catch The Torch led by a government agent disguised as a singing cowboy (Roy Rogers).

While officially a sequel, *Son of Paleface* barely builds off of its predecessor, so the film can stand alone. Jane's character has no relation to Calamity

Jane from the previous film, and her *Paleface* character is never actually referred to by name. Successful elements of the original film were heightened for the sequel: slapstick comedy, sight gags, and musical numbers. Since Jane and Roy Rogers's alter egos in the film are singers, there are plenty of songs, including a reprisal of "Buttons and Bows," which the three leads sing as a trio. Jay Livingston and Ray Evans, who penned the Oscar-winning song, were brought back to compose three more tunes: "California Rose," "What a Dirty Shame," and "Wing-Ding Tonight." Two additional songs were by Jack Brooks: "Four Legged Friend," which gave Roy Rogers the opportunity to pay tribute to his beloved horse Trigger, and "Am I in Love?" performed as a charming duet by Jane and Hope. The pair later recorded a two-sided 78 rpm record of "Am I in Love?" and "Wing-Ding Tonight."

Jane was ecstatic to be working with Bob Hope again; she didn't mind being his straight woman, and she always felt confident acting opposite him. She also enjoyed sharing a set with Roy Rogers, whom she was already acquainted with, and was probably relieved that she was a big enough star to receive billing over Trigger. Jane welcomed the opportunity to make another picture on the Paramount lot, though this time around she would be bringing her RKO crew, including cinematographer Harry J. Wild. As on the set of *The Paleface*, filming of the sequel went smoothly, and Jane got a kick out of a scene in which she bathes in the same barrel Paulette Goddard used in the film *Unconquered*. *Son of Paleface* would go on to be a smashing success at the box office.

After enduring a decade under the thumb of Howard Hughes, Jane finally seemed to have a viable career in Hollywood. With a house in the clouds, a marriage on somewhat stable ground, and an infant daughter, she seemed to have it all. However, she still longed to have the large and noisy household she herself had experienced growing up. Little could she know that her quest for an extended family would bring international attention and, for once, controversy that wasn't caused by Howard Hughes.

14

International Uproar

The year 1951 had been one of the busiest of Jane's life. As it started winding down, she received an invitation to go to England to appear at the sixth annual Royal Film Command Performance, a gala charity event benefiting the Cinema Trade Benevolent Fund. The high-profile event consisted of a movie premiere followed by an all-star stage show. The performers would also be formally presented to members of the British royal family.

When Hughes found out about the invitation, he called upon designer Michael Woulfe to "see that she is properly dressed" for the occasion.[1] Woulfe would design two dresses for Jane: one for the formal receiving line and the other for the stage performance. Determined to stand out when meeting the royals, Jane had Woulfe design a mink-trimmed red velvet gown with a matching hood. For the dress she would wear on-stage, Jane wanted satin, but Woulfe insisted on crepe, declaring it "softer, more appropriate." Jane was adamant and refused to budge, prompting Woulfe to declare, "All right. You want to look like a galloping whore, I'll use green satin and I'll get a pot of philodendron and hang it on your ass! That ought to look good to you!" Jane, who was a difficult person to insult, replied, with a trace of a smile, "But I don't like philodendron, Michael."[2] Woulfe designed the green satin gown.

Since football season was in full swing, it wasn't possible for Robert to even consider accompanying his wife. Instead Jane decided to take Geraldine, who wouldn't be in the receiving line but would still need suitable clothing. Jane managed to find two free hours in between scenes at the studio to meet Geraldine at Nancy's of Hollywood, the clothing shop where she had been a model a decade earlier. Apprised of the important customers, the store manager assigned four salespeople to Geraldine and promptly started bringing out gowns. As Geraldine later recalled, "They took one look at me, and Daughter rushed me across the street to get a foundation garment. Back we dashed and the dress parade continued."[3] Once a serviceable dress was found, the hats were brought out, but this proved to be a less successful endeavor.

Jane in Paris in late 1951. The French press was enamored with Jane and tailed her relentlessly during her visit.

"They put hats on, and Daughter took them off. I felt just like a stuffed bunny."[4] Before the hat conundrum could be solved, Jane's two hours were up. "We will get your hats in Paris," she whispered to her mother before disappearing from the store. A bit shell-shocked, Geraldine stopped off at the beauty parlor on her way home, asking the stylist, "Is there anything you could do to me in a few minutes? I'm off to see the Queen."[5]

Jane and her mother flew to Europe in late October, which gave them enough time for a brief stay in France. Geraldine had never been to Paris before and was delighted to have the opportunity, but after spending an afternoon in a high-end fashion salon, she later admitted, "In my heart I was glad I had my little gown from Nancy's U.S.A."[6] The press photographers in Paris were unrelenting. Jane tried to be accommodating, but when an especially persistent pair of photogs began following her and Geraldine as they walked down the street, she'd had enough. Geraldine, unnerved, recalled, "I didn't know what we should do, but Daughter allowed them to get very close behind us and then, turning sharply, she exclaimed, 'Shame!' They must have understood, for they both turned on their heels and walked away."[7] Jane had a good reason for not wanting a lot of press attention on her trip. In addition to the Command Performance, she had business of a more personal nature to attend to.

Jane's older brother had died before she was born, but there was a part of her that always mourned the loss. She didn't have a choice in being the oldest sibling growing up, but with Tracy it could be different. Jane wanted to adopt a son older than her infant daughter. In the United States she had been told there was a two-year waiting list, a delay she was not willing to endure. Since she was going to be in Europe anyway, Jane figured she would investigate adopting a child outside the United States and, as she later admitted, "I used the red carpet and I got into a lot of orphanages that were very difficult to get into in those days."[8] A friend was able get Jane inside a local orphanage during lunchtime, where she observed long rows of tables filled with children staring into their tin plates with zero emotion. For Jane, who had grown up around loud, happy, rowdy kids, the scene was heartbreaking. "These children had no personality," she later remembered, "and I suddenly realized it was because no one had ever loved them. They didn't know how to love or even to hate back."[9] Jane was further depressed to learn that none of the children in the orphanage were actually available for adoption, having been placed there by family members who never visited, but at the same time would not allow them to be adopted out. The experience left an indelible mark on her.

After only four days in Paris, Jane and Geraldine moved on to Nice, where they would be meeting Jane's old pal Pat Dawson, who was now living in the area with her husband. The couple had a place in the village of Èze, which was remote enough that Jane was able to get a break from the press. While Geraldine relaxed in Èze, Jane traveled to Italy to visit an orphanage in Genoa. Since she was not Catholic, she was able to see only one child, who turned out to not be available for adoption. Discouraged but not defeated, she spent a few days in Èze, then she and Geraldine moved on to Great Britain. At the airport in London, Jane announced to the waiting press that she was interested in adopting a British baby, specifically a blond, green-eyed boy around fifteen months old.[10] Shortly after landing, the pair sent a wire to Jane's brother Tom reading, "Have arrived in London. God save the King." He responded with, "God *help* the King! Mother will save him."[11]

Before Jane could focus her attention on expanding her family, she first needed to prepare to meet the queen of England. Rehearsals began for the Command Performance, which was being produced by actor-turned-executive Ben Lyon. Jane hosted a cocktail party in her hotel suite for the press. Lyon arrived so late, after everyone else had left, that Jane already had her hair in pin curls and was barefoot. Some photographers had remained at the hotel, however, and insisted on getting a shot of actress and producer. "Well, Daughter had never been stuck in her life," Geraldine later explained, "so she grabbed a hat, pulled it well down over the pin curls, then proceeded to drape on my veil, and out she went, saying, 'The shot is from the knees up.' Everyone laughed at the ridiculous combination of hat, veil and bare feet."[12]

Jane did manage to break away for a short trip, hopping a TWA flight to Frankfurt, where she visited another orphanage and met a boy she ached to adopt. This time she was told it would take a special act of Congress to allow immigrant children into the United States. "I knew nothing about getting a special act of Congress," Jane later remembered, "but I said I'd try."[13] By the time she returned to London, Jane's desire to find a child to adopt was appearing on the front pages of British newspapers right next to stories about Winston Churchill's reelection as prime minister. As had happened in the United States, she started receiving letters from people looking to find a home for their children. However, since the British Adoption Act of 1950 had made it illegal for a non-British person to adopt a British child, Jane could not take any of these offers seriously.

One afternoon Jane and Geraldine were in their hotel room at the Savoy when they received an unexpected phone call from a young Irish woman named Hannah Florence "Florrie" Kavanagh. She was calling from the lobby of the hotel, there with her fifteen-month-old son, Thomas. She explained that she had seen the recent articles and was willing to surrender Thomas, hoping the actress could give her son a better life than she ever could. When Geraldine explained that Jane was not allowed by law to adopt an English baby, Kavanagh was quick to reply that Thomas was Irish, not English. "Bring him up," Jane responded.

Mother and child came up to Jane's hotel room and the blue-eyed, golden-haired Thomas was placed on the bed. As far as Jane was concerned he was perfect, except for one thing: fearing complications down the line, she was vehemently opposed to adopting a child whose parents were known. Florrie, twenty-six, explained that she and her husband Michael had barely been making ends meet caring for their two older children, and the birth of Thomas had added to this strain. Earlier in the year Florrie had suffered a nervous breakdown and spent three months recovering at the Springfield Mental Home in England.[14] Though she was much better, her husband still feared for her health. "She told me a dreadfully sad story," Jane said at the time, "and pleaded with me to take the baby to America and let it have some of the good things of life."[15] Jane would later write, "I think she thought she was sending him to heaven."[16] During the meeting Geraldine did all the talking. For once, Jane was tongue-tied. Finally she spoke up, telling the nervous mother she would consider it and get back in touch. As Jane relayed, "At first, I said 'No — impossible.' But the poor girl seemed so desperate that I finally gave in. She has two children and is very hard up. So, what could I do?"[17]

After Florrie left, Jane and Geraldine prayed, both claiming to have received a message from the Lord telling them all barriers would be broken down. Jane decided to take Thomas Kavanagh back to the US with her for a three-month "holiday," after which she would figure out what to do with the child. Getting clearance to take him out of the country was going to take weeks, so Jane and Geraldine would be leaving on their scheduled flight without him. Friends would bring Thomas overseas in time for Christmas.

The next day, November 5, 1951, the Command Performance was held at the Odeon Leicester Square. The event would host the world premiere of the film *Where No Vultures Fly*, followed by the live performance featuring the invited film stars. A receiving line kicked off the charity gala: Jane, Lizabeth Scott, Van Johnson, Burt Lancaster, Fred MacMurray, Dan Duryea, Zachary Scott, Orson Welles, and Peter Lawford were presented to Queen Elizabeth (later known as the Queen Mother), Princess Margaret, and the Duchess of Kent.[18] The queen had prepared remarks for each personality, so when she got to Jane, she commented on how much she had enjoyed Jane's pictures with Bob Hope.

Over the years Jane had been often maligned for her lack of clothing sense, but at the Command Performance she was radiant in Michael Woulfe's creation. "The most brilliant gown among the film actresses who were presented tonight," wrote one reporter, "was worn by Jane Russell. It was a heavy

Dan Duryea and Jane arriving at the Odeon Theatre for the premiere of *Where No Vultures Fly*, part of the Royal Command Performance. Jane's gown, which was red velvet trimmed in mink, was designed by RKO's Michael Woulfe for the occasion.

scarlet off-the-shoulder crinoline gown edged with mink. She also wore a velvet hood and carried a muff of mink."[19] For the live performance following the film screening, Jane changed into her green satin gown. Geraldine described this portion of the evening as "sort of a variety show, very silly but lots of fun."[20] The evening capped off with a grand party, though at that point Jane was starting to feel sick with a sore throat.

When Jane awoke the next morning, she was seriously ill. Two doctors came to the hotel and diagnosed her with strep throat. She was ordered to remain in bed for the remainder of the day until it was time to go to the airport for the flight home. But then she received an unexpected phone call. Bayeux Baker, a friend of Jane's who was working abroad as a foreign service officer, and Gordon White, a British publicist, had managed to get all of Thomas Kavanagh's paperwork cleared and had obtained a passport from Irish officials. If Jane could get down to the Irish legation to sign all the papers, she would be cleared to take Thomas home with her that very day. Geraldine would need to pack up all of Jane's things for the plane ride, including the two Michael Woulfe gowns, which had been packed in boxes that reminded her of coffins. "My head was swimming," Geraldine later recalled. "Those awful coffins, and those dresses had to go back in them, and drawer after drawer of bags, purses, costumes, jewelry! Every ten minutes, I'd run to the window and take a long deep breath to keep going."[21]

The Kavanaghs were taken aback by the sudden turn of events but agreed to put Thomas on the plane with Jane and Geraldine. Everyone convened at the airport, where Jane was allowed to board the plane first because, as a TWA official noted, she was "prostrate with grief at the thought of taking the child away from the mother. We had to take her aboard the plane before the other passengers."[22] A tearful Florrie handed Thomas over to Geraldine, who boarded the plane and sat across the aisle from Jane. An astute reporter, skimming the passenger manifest, put two and two together when he saw "Thomas Kavanagh (infant)" traveling to 13541 Leadwell, the same address as Geraldine.[23] When Florrie Kavanagh entered the plane unexpectedly to say one last good-bye to her son, the reporter followed her. Jane, Florrie, Geraldine, and Thomas all burst out crying with the reporter observing. Jane promised to take good care of the boy, and Florrie departed with the reporter in tow. Geraldine managed to calm the boy down for the long flight, while Jane kept her distance because of her illness. As she got off the plane, Florrie informed reporters, "I have always loved her pictures. Now I know she is a real person."[24] The next day Thomas's five-year-old sister was quoted as saying, "Mummy cried all night, but I didn't because she said he would be coming back."[25]

By the time the trio landed in New York, word of Jane taking the baby had traveled across the ocean, and a large group of reporters was waiting at Idlewild Airport. It was pouring rain, so a man on the flight draped his coat over Geraldine and Thomas, then led them into a waiting room. Howard Hughes

Geraldine Jacobi and Jane put on a good face for photographers after arriving at Idlewild Airport with Thomas Kavanagh.

had also been notified, so he dispatched RKO representatives to meet them. There were so many reporters and photographers waiting for Jane that the RKO reps decided their best move was to give the press their story. After taking a breath and composing themselves, Jane and Geraldine took Thomas out to the waiting media and were all smiles as they posed for photographers. "I'll take care of the baby until I find a home for him," Jane told reporters. "I feel that it's not in the best interests of the child or myself to adopt him when the parents know about the boy's whereabouts."[26] Questioned about the ethical implications of taking the child, Jane defended herself. "Well, the baby was handed to me, and when someone hands you a baby, kiddo, you don't just drop it."[27] The story made the front pages of newspapers all around the country.

After meeting with the press, Geraldine blew through an airport shop and purchased a new wardrobe for Thomas while Jane bathed him in the cloakroom. In an attempt to divert the press, Jane sent Geraldine and Thomas to Denver, where her brother Tom was living. Jane would go on to Los Angeles where, hopefully, the cameras would follow her instead of the baby. Plus, as she told her mother, Jane needed to get "straight home and get this affair straightened out with Bob."[28] The events of the preceding two days had been such a whirlwind that Jane hadn't had time to contact her husband. Jane had telephoned him the day Florrie Kavanagh had visited the Savoy—but hadn't mentioned the possibility of a new addition to the family. Before Jane had a chance to get back home, however, the press had already given the news to a blindsided Robert Waterfield. Asked about the baby Jane was bringing back from London, Robert admitted that it was "news to me. Jane didn't mention the baby when I talked to her by phone Sunday night. But if it's true, that's fine with me."[29]

Jane's attempt to thwart members of the press proved futile when they located Tom Russell's Denver residence and proceeded to let themselves in the house to snap a photo of Geraldine and baby Thomas. "You have to hand it to the press, the way they ferret things out," Geraldine admitted. "A regular F.B.I.!"[30] After that incident, Geraldine received a wire from her daughter reading, "Change your flight and your name." Geraldine wired back, "Mrs. Goldberg arriving tonight."[31] Rather than picking up the pair at the airport herself, Jane asked her brother Jamie to do it. The Rams had played a home game that day, and by the time Geraldine's plane touched ground, the game was over, so Jamie drove her and the baby straight to the Red Barn, a restaurant on Van Nuys Boulevard where some of the players dined after games. When Geraldine and Thomas arrived, the players gathered around the car as Robert got a first look at his new son. The baby took to Robert immediately. Waterfield, who was already in good spirits after having led his team to a first-place tie with the Chicago Bears for the NFL National Conference, picked up the boy and joked, "He knows if I like him he gets to stay."[32] Jane later remembered this first meeting with the players being at their home, not a restaurant, but the result was the same. Any notions Jane had of finding a family to adopt Thomas disappeared the second Robert connected with the child. Thomas Kavanagh had found a home—if the British Parliament would allow it.

The incident had generated so much international press that British officials, had they been inclined to, found it difficult to turn a blind eye. And not everyone was so inclined. Michael and Florrie Kavanagh were both originally from Ireland, but Thomas had been born after the couple relocated to London, so Britain arguably had some jurisdiction over the boy. Marcus Lipton, a member of Parliament, was particularly vexed by the chain of events and expressed his outrage publicly, demanding that the House of Commons investigate Jane's actions. "We don't want to export babies to Hollywood or anywhere else."[33] Jane would later dismiss Lipton's actions: "That was just a member of Parliament who wanted everybody to know he was on the ball."[34]

Lipton went on record saying the situation was "rather irregular."[35] In fact, Jane taking an Irish baby to the United States was far from irregular. The adoption laws in Ireland were ambiguous, resulting in what one historian has referred to as the "effortless acquisition" of Irish children by wealthy Americans.[36] During the two preceding years, a cottage industry of sorts had developed, with hundreds of Irish children, many of them illegitimate, being shipped to the United States, sometimes in exchange for money. The practice was so prevalent that the *New York Times* had even reported on six Irish children who traveled together to New York to meet anxious adopting adults.[37] The only unusual circumstances in Jane's case were the speed with which the Éire passport and US travel visa had been obtained and the press coverage the story received.

On the US side, officials had not deemed the incident problematic because the number of British immigrants who had entered the country that year was well below the cap. However, once Parliament became involved, with Lipton doggedly demanding an investigation, the Federal Bureau of Investigation felt compelled to open a case file on Jane and look into the incident. Ultimately, the agency seemed to follow a policy of appeasing Marcus Lipton without actually putting Jane's adoption of the baby at risk. After an initial assessment, a recommendation was made that "any statements furnished voluntarily by Miss Russell and her mother not be witnessed by or in the presence of Bureau Agents inasmuch as those statements may be used by the British authorities for possible prosecutive action."[38] Clyde Tolson, the second ranking official at the FBI, suggested handing the affair over to the State Department and Immigration and Naturalization Service (INS). FBI director J. Edgar Hoover agreed with the directive, personally passing the investigation to the commissioner of the INS.[39]

Publicly, Jane claimed to welcome the inquiry, definitively stating, "It is all perfectly legal. . . . If all I wanted to do was steal a baby from England, I had fifty letters from people in England offering me children—begging me to take them back to the United States."[40] Geraldine was overwhelmed by the experience, especially when INS conducted formal interviews with her and Jane:

> R.K.O. sent their lawyer with us. When we were all seated, and the stenographer was taking transcript, I could see by the questions that they were being framed to hang us. I asked the enquirer if I might talk to him privately, off the record. He consented, and the room was

cleared. I told him exactly the truth, what we had been told and how we had acted on it.

He asked if any money had passed between the Kavanaghs and ourselves. We answered, "None whatsoever."

It seemed that one report was that we had kidnapped the boy. Another report was that we had bought the boy for a sum. When we had finished our private discussion, he recalled the other official, and then the investigation continued. This time a different set of questions was asked, and they were quite satisfied with the answers.[41]

Following the interview with the federal government, RKO determined it was all more than the studio wanted to deal with. Jane was called to the studio front office where lawyers advised her to return the child to London. Robert Waterfield was inclined to agree. He was quickly becoming attached to Thomas, but once Parliament started shrieking foul, he panicked, telling Jane, "My God, send him back."[42] Jane refused to back down. As far as she was concerned, the Lord had sent her a clear message; these were the barriers that would be broken down.

Being officially investigated was certainly unwelcome, but Jane got off easy compared to the Kavanaghs. Not only were they castigated by neighbors for giving Thomas up, at the urging of Marcus Lipton, the British House of Commons began its own investigation. The couple was charged in April 1952 with "unlawfully permitting the care and possession of the infant to be transferred."[43] Jane was not charged, prompting a resentful Michael Kavanagh to lash out publicly: "It looks as though Miss Russell is keeping in the background while we take our medicine. I only hope we receive some communication from someone over there before the case comes up."[44]

Jane paid for a barrister to defend the Kavanaghs in court. They pled guilty, but were discharged conditionally for one year, the equivalent of probation. It seems the magistrate presiding over the case was not immune to the charms of Jane Russell. "I have had the opportunity to see some of the letters written by Miss Russell to the child's parents, and if they are any reflection on Miss Russell, then she must be a very very nice woman."[45] Still, lest the case inspire copycats, the magistrate felt compelled to explain, "I am bound to say that if this law is broken again by anyone else, I think it extremely unlikely that the law will take the same view I have taken today."[46] Even the prosecutors seemed satisfied with the court's decision, noting, "There is no allegation for any moral turpitude against anyone, either against Miss Russell for adopting the child, or who is in the process of adopting it, to either of the defendants."[47] Jane was also happy with the result, which was delivered in April 1952. "I am delighted that the Kavanaghs were freed of all blame," Jane told reporters. "My husband and I shall continue to give Tommy the best home and care we know how. As soon as we are assured we can adopt him legally, we shall do so."[48]

Despite the blowback from their action, the Kavanaghs stoutly defended their decision. Florrie had spent time living in Springtime Camp, a decommissioned US naval camp that had later become home to some of England's poorest residents. She knew abject poverty and therefore maintained the belief that sending Thomas away was the best choice. At one point she even considered giving up her other two children, though that does not seem to have come to pass. "I'd think I was being a very selfish person by hanging on to them just because I have had the trouble of bringing them into the world—or on the grounds of mother love," she said in the midst of the media circus. "I love them all—that is the only reason I can part with them." She continued, "I always wanted to make something of my own life. I didn't have the chance. That is why I want my children to get a break . . . and that is why I can give them up."[49] Her husband agreed, stating simply, "We haven't really the right to hold them back."[50]

At first Jane had maintained her stance that she was not going to adopt Thomas but would instead find a home for him after the three-month "holiday" was up. She even went so far at one point as to say she had some friends who might be interested in taking him: "I can't tell you their names even if they're in movies. They're very substantial families."[51] Geraldine backed up her daughter, saying, "Thomas is the guest of the Waterfields and that's all I can say. No decision has been made."[52] In the midst of all the uncertainty, Thomas celebrated his first Christmas in Sherman Oaks where, according to Geraldine, "He got a carload of presents. He got sweaters and caps and socks in every color, toys that pushed and pulled and everything." She also noted, "His parents called from London on Christmas Day. Jane sent them a lot of gifts too."[53] After Thomas had lived with the Waterfields for a couple of months, it had become clear how the couple felt about the boy. "Tommy is part of her family now and she's crazy about him," an unnamed friend explained. "But she wants to wait until the fuss about this has died down before she does anything and she hasn't made any decision as to what she will do."[54] When the three-month holiday was up, it turned out that the temporary visa RKO claimed Thomas had come to the States on was actually a per-

In 1968 Jane brought Thomas to London to meet Florrie Kavanagh, his birth mother.

manent resident visa. By Christmas of the following year, the Waterfields had formally adopted the child, and in March 1955 Thomas Kavanagh Waterfield officially became a US citizen.[55]

Despite Jane's qualms about adopting a child whose parents were known, and against the advice of friends and adoption professionals, Jane did maintain periodic contact with Florrie Kavanagh. While filming a movie in England in 1954, Jane met with her, showing her photos of Thomas, which his birth mother was delighted to see. Florrie never wavered in the belief that she had made the correct decision. "Jane Russell," she said in 1955, "is a truly wonderful person. She's the only mother Tommy knows. I'm glad I did it."[56] Jane was always honest with Tommy about his past. He later noted, "There were never any secrets with her and she was happy to give me whatever information she could about my birth mother. That side of things was always pretty open and I've known for as long as I can remember."[57] In 1968 Jane even flew Tommy to England to meet Florrie in person, though he later admitted, "I think looking back I was too young to really realize or appreciate how much it meant. I remember we all had dinner, and it was very pleasant, but it's only as I've gotten older that I've realized how much Hannah [Florrie] did for me."[58]

After giving up her son, life for Hannah Florence Kavanagh continued to be challenging. She suffered a drug overdose in 1968 but survived.[59] In 1980 she was found murdered in a burned-out flat. Sixty-plus years after the international indent, Thomas journeyed to Derry (officially Londonderry), the Irish city where his birth mother had been raised. There he was able to connect with blood relatives and gain a greater appreciation of what his birth parents had done. "I can only imagine the deep emotions she felt and what she went through and she did that because she wanted a better life for her son," he said. "I'm not a mother but I have a son and I can't imagine what it must have felt for her to give her little boy up, but she did it with the best intentions."[60]

The experience had been a trying one for everyone involved. Ultimately, Jane found not only her son but, in due course, her life's calling. For now, however, she and Robert were occupied adjusting to their expanding family, managing their evolving careers, and navigating their disparate personalities.

15

What Happened in Vegas

The new decade was proving to be momentous for Jane Russell and Robert Waterfield. Not only were they now parents to two young children, Waterfield had reached the zenith of his career, helping lead the Rams to their first NFL championship since moving to Los Angeles. Jane's career had also kicked into high gear as she became a staple on the RKO lot. On the surface, it seemed the movie star and the football player were on top of the world.

At the beginning of 1952, *The Las Vegas Story* was finally ready to be released, and a gala premiere was scheduled for mid-February in Las Vegas. Parental obligations were of little concern to RKO; Jane was expected to appear at the premiere, which would be held at both the Huntridge and Fremont Theaters, preceded by a televised parade down Fremont Street. Jane arrived in Las Vegas on Sunday, February 10, along with publicist Edith Lynch, who would be coordinating Jane's full itinerary. Since the triumphant football season was over, Robert Waterfield decided to accompany Jane to the premiere and drove up a day later.

On February 11 Jane presented a set of World Book Encyclopedias to a school for children with disabilities. Mickey Goodwin, a student at the school, was selected for the photo op.[1] Next Jane, along with *The Las Vegas Story* actors Brad Dexter and Gordon Oliver, appeared at a Lions' Club meeting at the Last Frontier Hotel, followed by a show at the Nellis Air Force Base.[2] Back at the Hotel Flamingo, where she was staying, Jane looked forward to a reunion with her husband. However, Robert Waterfield had caravanned up with Rams coaches Hamp Pool and John Sanders, teammate Don Paul, Rams' radio announcer Bob Kelley, and Schlitz beer representative Ozzie Lang, together with all their wives. When he got to Vegas, Robert was more concerned with socializing with his Rams cohorts than spending time with his wife, something she resented bitterly, causing her to feel sorry for herself.[3] The stage was set for a rocky evening.

Later that night Jane and Robert went to the El Rancho Vegas Hotel with the group to see comedian Ben Blue perform. Jane proved too good a target for Blue, who cracked a few jokes about her famous figure. By this time Jane had learned to roll her eyes when confronted by such publicity and wise-cracks. "After all these years," Jane said at the time, "I'm getting hardened to such remarks."[4] Waterfield, however, took exception. He had been married for nearly a decade to a woman whose career had been launched on publicity regarding her breasts, who had been named Miss Anatomy by the Harvard Anthropology Club as recently as 1950, and whose bosom had been described by the press with every possible adjective and euphemism. That night the comedian's remarks drove Waterfield over the edge. The football player became visibly enraged. Hotel employees witnessed Jane put "a restraining hand on her husband's arm and stage-whisper sharply, 'Now stop it! Please Bob, don't make any trouble!'"[5]

When Blue became aware of Waterfield's reaction to the set, he tried to smooth things over. Some newspaper accounts reported Waterfield following Blue into the hotel lobby and shaking the comedian by the lapels, but the incident was probably a bit less sensational. "Bob is a wonderful fellow and I made a stupid mistake," Blue said of the evening's events. "It was all in fun but he took it wrong. After the show I went over to his table and apologized. Jane accepted my apology but Bob wouldn't. He didn't threaten to hit me. Even a shove from Bob Waterfield would probably kill me."[6] Jane tried to downplay the incident. "This has all been greatly exaggerated. We've been friends of Ben's for years. His remarks were—ah—personal and we didn't think them funny, but we just got up and left after the show."[7]

That wasn't quite true. Before they left their table, Jane too reached a boiling point—with her husband. She ran her fork down his face, leaving four scratches. As Jane later revealed:

He didn't do anything, but tears of humiliation formed in his eyes. Everyone watched in silence. When we got home [to the hotel] he went to the mirror and looked at his face. I came up behind him and said, "Honey, I'm so sorry." He just turned and slapped me. I fell back, but stupid me, I didn't stay there. I was mad as hell. He had never slapped me before. I said, "Oh, I'm sure you can hit harder than that," so he did. I got up as many times as I could and finally, when the room was spinning, I said, "You poor fool, you don't have any idea what you've just done." He left without a word.[8]

176

A heavily made-up Jane appears onstage at the Fremont Theater for the premiere of *The Las Vegas Story,* despite the swollen jaw and black eye delivered by Robert Waterfield during a dispute the previous night. (Los Angeles Herald Examiner Collection/Los Angeles Public Library)

The next morning the left side of Jane's face was severely bruised and swollen. She called Robert, who had spent the night in Bob Kelley's room, telling him to come over and view his handiwork. He got only as far as the door of the hotel room before snarling, "Well, you'd better stay here. You can get a divorce in ten weeks in this state."[9] With that, he left and almost immediately drove back to Los Angeles with Bob Kelley.

177

Jane called Edith Lynch to her room and relayed what had happened. Lynch assessed the damage and then called RKO publicity chief Perry Lieber, who was in town to oversee everything. It was the day of the *Las Vegas Story* premiere and RKO was flying out a press corps to cover the full day of festivities leading up to the main event.[10] There was never a thought of canceling Jane's personal appearances. By the time Dr. Jack Cherry came to her room to examine Jane, the RKO publicity machine was churning and a story had been concocted: a sudden gust of wind had blown open a taxicab door, which hit Jane in the face. Despite the fact that Waterfield had come to Las Vegas specifically to escort Jane to the premiere, the media was notified that he had to get back to Los Angeles for some sort of business.

The press dutifully reported RKO's story about the car door, but it's doubtful anyone was really buying it. One reporter wrote, "From the limbo of the lost, the age-tested 'swinging door' explanation for a black eye was exhumed yesterday by actress Jane Russell."[11] No amount of makeup could hide the physical damage Waterfield had done to Jane's face, and the bruising and swelling was obviously done by more than a car door. Not only was the incident with Ben Blue's act at the El Rancho public knowledge, employees at the Desert Inn claimed to have seen the couple quarreling inside the hotel the previous night.[12] It didn't help that the press reported the incident inconsistently. Some newspapers said the car door incident had happened the previous night, while others said it had happened that day as Jane was getting in a cab to attend a Chamber of Commerce luncheon.[13] Yet another paper had Jane walking into her hotel door, but was unable to confirm it with Jane, who offered another line of defense by claiming to have been so drunk that she didn't remember what happened.[14] She was able to skip the Chamber of Commerce lunch, but had to go through with the parade as well as an onstage appearance for the premiere, her swollen face barely concealed. After the film was shown, Jane rushed back to the hotel, avoiding any post-premiere festivities.[15]

The next day, which happened to be Valentine's Day, Edith Lynch purchased a pair of sunglasses (charged to RKO) to conceal Jane's black eye.[16] Jane took the chartered plane back to L.A. with Vincent Price and the press corps RKO had flown out for the premiere. Jane later recalled that Price had been "very sweet during the parade, but on the plane on the way home with all the newsmen, he hollered, 'Come on with that wind story, we all know Waterfield hit you.' Big laugh."[17] Robert had been advised to meet his wife at the airport, which he did, also wearing sunglasses. Jane and Robert both put on their best magazine smiles as they faced the press and denied there was

Jane (wearing sunglasses to hide her black eye) and Robert Waterfield feign affection at the airport upon her return from Las Vegas. (Los Angeles Herald Examiner Collection/Los Angeles Public Library)

anything wrong with their marriage. "I don't know anything about black eyes," Robert grumbled. "This is ridiculous."[18] "It makes a good story, doesn't it?" Jane joked feebly.[19] The reporter for the *Los Angeles Examiner* seems to have been the only one to notice the four scratches on Robert's face made by Jane's fork. When they finished with the press, the two walked arm and arm away from the plane. Watching the Waterfields depart, Vincent Price could only sigh and proclaim, "Love, it's wonderful."[20]

When they got home, Robert took a good look at what he had done and promised he would never do it again. Jane chalked the entire incident up to the fact that they had both been drunk. She would later admit, "Robert Waterfield and I both drank from the time we were about eighteen years old. It was social drinking, and there came a time when I just couldn't handle it anymore and I ended up drunk and couldn't remember what happened the day before or the night before."[21] After the incident in Las Vegas, Jane stopped drinking for two and a half years but, as she later wrote, "it got very boring being the only sober person in the crowd, so eventually I went off the wagon."[22] Jane confessed to the incident, along with other examples of domestic violence, in her 1985 autobiography, but how prevalent was the abuse overall? Jan Lowell, who helped ghostwrite an early version of Jane's autobiography, said, "Honey, he beat the bejesus out of her. Apparently this is a football thing. She used to talk to the other football wives. They were all battered women. He beat her, she was a battered wife."[23] Curiously, despite detailing the Las Vegas occurrence in her book, when later asked point-blank in an on-camera interview if Waterfield had been violent, Jane looked away from the interviewer, almost embarrassed, and said, "No . . . not . . . no. It was just . . . it got impossible."[24]

It does not appear that Jane considered ending her marriage at the time; it could have jeopardized her hopes of adopting Thomas. Instead Jane forged ahead publicly as if nothing had happened. Remarkably, the very next day Jane (wearing, as one paper noted, "a 'black' eye that was turning to sunset hues") appeared in a Burbank courtroom with Robert and Tracy to finalize the adoption.[25] A few days later Jane appeared in court once again to serve as a character witness for a friend who was accused of fur theft. Covering that court appearance, a local newspaper was quick to note there was "not a sign of the black eye which cause such a furor at Las Vegas, Nev. movie premiere 10 days ago."[26] It seems the press and public quickly forgot what had happened in Vegas—by the end of the year, the *Los Angeles Times* would run a piece about the happy Waterfield household.

If Jane had spent much of 1951 in front of movie cameras, the opposite was true of 1952. During the first half of the year, her only film work was a cameo in the Bob Hope/Bing Crosby vehicle *Road to Bali*. Wearing her "Wing-Ding Tonight" costume from *Son of Paleface*, Jane's appearance was a sight gag, not requiring her to speak any lines, and it took only one day to shoot.[27] However, just because RKO wasn't assigning pictures or loaning her out, it didn't mean Jane wasn't working. That year saw a mini-avalanche of Jane Russell movies hitting the screen, and they needed to be promoted. In

Jane, still showing signs of a black eye and swollen jaw, appears in court with Robert Waterfield (*right*) to finalize the adoption of their daughter Tracy. (Los Angeles Herald Examiner Collection/Los Angeles Public Library)

addition to *Double Dynamite,* which Howard Hughes finally released during the final week of 1951, theatergoers were also able to see Jane in *The Las Vegas Story, Macao, Son of Paleface,* and *Montana Belle,* which Hughes had also pulled off the shelf. After only three Jane Russell films released in the entirety of the 1940s, Howard Hughes seemed to be making up for lost time.

Paramount took advantage of the lull in Jane's film activity to book her on an extensive personal appearance tour with Bob Hope to promote *Son of Paleface*, which took her on the road for much of the summer of 1952. As the year dragged on, no additional movie roles materialized. This may have been due to the fact that Howard Hughes's unorthodox management style had thrown RKO into turmoil; additionally, the mogul had grown weary of running a movie studio. Hughes figured if he could unload the studio quickly and for the right price, he would not have to endure any financial losses. In September 1952 Hughes sold his RKO stock to a Chicago-based syndicate that had zero experience in the film industry but did have a certified check for $1.25 million that served as a down payment. All contracts with RKO would be included in the sale, except for Jane's. For the four years Hughes had been running RKO, Jane had remained the property of the Hughes Tool Company.

During the second half of the year, there had been some rumors that Jane would be teamed up with Victor Mature a second time in an RKO production called *Split Second*. The noir thriller would be actor Dick Powell's directorial debut, but while he did end up at the helm, the actors were Alexis Smith and Stephen McNally rather than Jane and Victor Mature.

If Jane was at all worried by the lack of film roles, she needn't have been. The year 1952 had started with a weird mix of marital strife and increased parental responsibility but would end with Jane landing the most memorable role of her career—opposite an up-and-coming blonde on the Twentieth Century-Fox lot.

16

Blondes

In March 1952 Twentieth Century-Fox purchased the rights to produce a film adaptation of the Broadway musical *Gentlemen Prefer Blondes*. The story, which follows the international exploits of a gold-digging, platinum-haired flapper named Lorelei Lee, had originally appeared in 1925 as a best-selling novel by Anita Loos; it was then adapted as a stage play and a 1928 silent film (now considered "lost"). Nearly twenty-five years after first introducing the world to Lorelei Lee, Loos resurrected her fabled character for another run on Broadway, but this time opted to transform the story into a musical. Loos collaborated with Joseph Fields on the book, while Jule Styne and Leo Robin were brought on to contribute music and lyrics, respectively. When the show debuted at the Ziegfeld Theatre in December 1949, it was an instant hit, what the *New York Times* called "a vastly enjoyable song-and-dance antic put on with humorous perfection."[1] The show would run just shy of two years, logging 740 performances. It was only a matter of time before Hollywood came knocking.

When the deal was inked with Fox, the studio obtained the rights to all previous theatrical and cinematic incarnations of *Gentlemen Prefer Blondes* for $150,000, which was divided among Loos, Fields, Styne, and Robin.[2] The stage role of Lorelei Lee had been a breakout part for Carol Channing, but it was unlikely Fox would consider a New York stage actress for the film. After all, the studio had their own resident blonde, Betty Grable, under contract. Columnist Hedda Hopper went so far as to announce that Grable would indeed be assuming the role of Lee, with Ginger Rogers possibly signing on in the secondary role of Dorothy Shaw.[3] But Fox had another blonde under contract who had been exceeding the studio's low expectations of her by resonating strongly with audiences. Studio head Darryl F. Zanuck had finally started to see potential in this up-and-comer, but he still hadn't quite figured out what to do with Marilyn Monroe. She had recently worked with Howard Hawks in the comedy *Monkey Business* starring Cary Grant and Ginger Rogers, and the director immediately spotted Monroe's natural gifts as a comedienne. The studio, however, had been slow on the uptake, most recently casting her as a psychotic babysitter (*Don't Bother to Knock*), a murderous femme fatale (*Niagara*) and, in a bit part, a Victorian streetwalker (*O. Henry's Full House*). According to Hawks, Zanuck asked for advice on forwarding Monroe's career, to which he responded, "Darryl, you're making realism with a very unreal girl. She's a completely storybook character. And you're trying to make real movies." Further pressed, Hawks offered, "Well, you've got a great story over here, *Gentlemen Prefer Blondes*." Zanuck was completely unconvinced that Monroe could pull off a musical, but Hawks persisted, insisting, "I know goddamn well she could."[4]

Still, even Hawks suspected that Monroe had her limits. When Zanuck started pushing him to direct the film, Hawks was emphatic in his qualified acceptance: "I'll do it if I can get somebody to back her up, somebody to *hold* her up." "Like who?" asked Zanuck. "Jane Russell," was Hawks's instant response.[5] Zanuck's skepticism over the whole concept increased; he could not fathom Howard Hughes loaning him the Hughes Tool Company's prized possession. Hawks, never a man to mince words, told the mogul, "Darryl, you're really not too smart. You're just in your own little circle and you don't know anything going on outside. I found Russell . . . and you say I can't get her? Get her on the phone." It was a phone call Jane had been waiting to receive for almost twelve years. All Hawks had to say was "Janie, I got a story for you," and she replied, "Fine, when do we start?"[6] Hawks warned her that the role of Dorothy Shaw could possibly be overshadowed by whoever played Lorelei Lee, but it didn't matter to Jane. After the false start on *The Outlaw*, she would finally have the opportunity to be directed by Howard Hawks—and in a big-budget Technicolor musical, no less.

Howard Hughes was in the process of taking RKO off his plate and, not having anything lined up for Jane, was amenable to the loan-out. However, Jane's services would come with some provisions, along with a healthy price tag of $175,000.[7] Per the usual for Jane, Hughes stipulated that Harry J. Wild handle cinematography duties on the film, and that she be allowed to bring over her whole hair, makeup, and wardrobe crew. Additionally, brunette Jane would be getting top billing above the title on *Gentlemen Prefer Blondes*. "I'd been around a long time!" Jane later joked when asked about the billing. "I was an old broad."[8] With Jane secured for the film, Monroe was officially assigned the role of Lorelei Lee in mid-June, and filming was set for November 1952.

Now that two women with famously curvy figures had been cast as the leads, it seemed ill advised to keep the story set during the Jazz Age, a period synonymous with flat-chested flappers. Additionally, the role of Dorothy Shaw, Lorelei's close friend, needed to be beefed up to align with Jane's billing and paycheck. Screenwriter Charles Lederer was brought in to update the time period of the film and elevate Jane's role. Ultimately, it was a major overhaul of the source material because, as Lederer said, "I had to make it up from scratch because there wasn't any story. . . . What amazed me was that the musical had no book to speak of, and you realized that it was actually a success as a revue rather than a musical story of a book."[9] Of the dozen and a half songs written for the stage musical (but not necessarily used), only three made it into the film: "Bye, Bye Baby," "Diamonds Are a Girl's Best Friend," and "I'm Just a Little Girl from Little Rock." The latter was revamped and turned into the duet, "We're Just Two Little Girls from Little Rock." Two additional songs, "Ain't There Anyone Here for Love?" and "When Love Goes Wrong," would show up in the screen version, courtesy of Harold Adamson and Hoagy Carmichael.

Howard Hawks was a director who possessed a great deal of confidence in his own abilities, but he was still capable of identifying his limitations. Having no background in musical theater, Hawks was adamant that someone experienced handle the filming of the musical numbers. Jack Cole, a high-strung imp of a man bursting with talent, was brought on to turn Jane and Marilyn into camera-ready dancing showgirls. Jane had regularly been singing on-screen, but had little experience with dancing. The closest she had come to choreographed musical numbers were "The Gilded Lily" in *Montana Belle* and "Wing-Ding Tonight" in *Son of Paleface.* Even then she had kind of sleepwalked her way through the limited choreography. Monroe's turn as a showgirl in *Ladies of the Chorus,* which had afforded her two solo numbers, "Anyone Can See I Love You," and "Ev'ry Baby Needs a Da-Da Daddy," didn't amount to much more experience than Jane's. Cole had no delusions of making either woman the next Eleanor Powell or Ginger Rogers, so the numbers were designed with modest choreography. It would still take a great deal of effort to make the dance numbers seem effortless in the final film.

Intense rehearsals started on October 10, 1952, a little over a month before filming was supposed to begin. For the rest of her life, Jane would always reserve the highest praise for Jack Cole, saying, "When I first met Marilyn, we were rehearsing the dancing, and neither one of us were dancers. Jack Cole would be very tough on his own dancers but he was the patience of Job with us. He was so dear and sweet and he would do it over and over until we were doing it without even thinking because that was the only way we could do it."[10] Cole was equally fond of Jane. "Jane Russell is a very likable, easygoing, California lady, no vanities at all."[11] For the month of rehearsals, Jane exhibited just the slightest amount of vanity, remembering, "I never dressed up but always wore lips and lashes. Marilyn looked like she'd just crawled out of bed—no make-up, tangled hair, and blue jeans."[12]

Assisting Cole was Gwen Verdon, who would become a Broadway legend in her own right. Verdon's son Jim Henaghan Jr. later said, "Marilyn and Jane Russell were the stars but neither one could dance. Both had trouble moving to music and Mom was given the job of changing that; in watching the movie one sees that she was more successful with Marilyn." He continued, "All through her life my mom would not sit still for attacks on Marilyn's lack of will. She always remained very fond of her. Ms. Russell fell into that category also; she worked very hard [but] her problem was she didn't move in a sexy manner."[13] Verdon would later theorize why Jane may have had more issues adapting to the dance moves, noting that a dancer needs to warm up "in order to keep in shape, to straighten out jumbled muscles and keep ourselves generally resilient. Otherwise, we simply couldn't go into our routines in the show and accomplish what we wish to do. But every warm-up movement is a standard one: no athletics. In fact, athletic girls—a girl such as Jane Russell, whom I once coached, had an awfully hard time trying to dance. Muscles too well developed."[14] According to Jane, the differences between her and Marilyn's dance styles was deliberate. "You see, when we first started working on the musical numbers, Jack didn't know me too well," she explained. "Most of the numbers called for both Marilyn and myself to do identical steps and sing the very same lyrics. However, as he became familiar with both of our reactions and deliveries, he started improvising, until now we can both be doing the same number yet we both look different. He had Marilyn doing the ultra feminine gestures. . . . He has me doing the more boyish outdoor type of movements."[15]

The completed script for the film was submitted to the Production Code Administration for approval in October 1952. Overall, Lederer's work passed muster, though Joseph Breen deemed the lines "Those girls couldn't drown. Something about them tells me they couldn't sink" as "completely unacceptable." As a result, only the former line was retained. Well aware of who would be starring in the film, Breen was quick to note: "At the outset, we direct your particular attention to the need for the greatest possible care in the selection and photography of dresses and costumes for your women. The Production Code makes it mandatory that the intimate parts of the body—specifically the breasts of women—be fully covered at all times. Any compromise with the regulation will compel us to withhold approval of your picture."[16]

The task of designing PCA-appropriate costumes for *Gentlemen Prefer Blondes* was given to designer William Travilla, who had worked with Marilyn on *Don't Bother to Knock,* and would go onto create many of Monroe's iconic looks, including the pleated halter subway dress in *The Seven Year Itch.* An initial array of costume changes was fabricated, and tests of Jane and Marilyn filmed. As Jane later recalled, "Billy Travilla put me in tight belts and full skirts. It was going to be totally different from the way Marilyn dressed." When Zanuck saw Jane in these initial designs, Jane explained, "he said I looked like a guy in drag."[17] Jack Cole elaborated on the disastrous costume tests:

> We did double tests for clothes, just walking, the two of them. . . . Well, Jane was being Jane—you know, like an iceman in drag—and as soon as the camera would go on, Marilyn would . . . well, I said to her, "Darling, Jane Russell is Jane Russell, so don't walk in front of her." She just unconsciously would cross in front of her. We looked at the rushes, and it was a disaster for Jane. Mr. Zanuck requested that the film be destroyed and that Jane never see it. Then Jane got a whole new wardrobe because, next to Monroe, Jane looked like what I said she looked like . . . a very good looking, sexy iceman, but an iceman.[18]

In addition to the issues with Jane's costumes, Travilla had a serious misfire with Monroe's outfit for the showstopping "Diamonds Are a Girl's Best Friend" number. Presumably ignoring the warnings from the Production Code Administration, Travilla designed a costume that consisted of black net, strategically placed "diamonds" and, as Cole described, "a little horse's tail coming out of her ass with a little diamond horsefly on the tail."[19] According to Jane, "When Zanuck saw it, he shrieked, 'GET THAT OFF THE SCREEN!' He was just livid. He absolutely wouldn't let her wear that costume."[20] Instead Monroe would wear a strapless pink satin evening gown, which became one of the most recognizable costumes of her career. After this disastrous first run, Travilla scrapped the wardrobe and, as Jane later explained, "Poor Billy Travilla went back to the drawing board. He and I sat down and we had a talk. I told him all the problems Michael [Woulfe] and I went through. We knew what I could wear and what I couldn't, and never a full skirt. I said I have a short body and long legs and I need this and that and

Husband Robert Waterfield and Jane share a serious moment on the set of *Gentlemen Prefer Blondes.*

the other. And so he did it and from then on the clothes were fabulous."[21] Since the film was being shot in saturated Technicolor, the costumes for the stars used a wide color palate, which was fine by Howard Hawks. "You got color that really came out and hit you," he later said. "There was no sense in trying to dodge it." As he had previously explained to Darryl Zanuck, "The girls were unreal; the story was unreal; the sets, the whole premise of the thing was unreal. We were working with complete fantasy."[22]

As it turned out, it wouldn't take much to make Marilyn and Jane stand out from each other. They had polar-opposite personalities that actually complemented each other and translated well on-screen. Jane may have been at a different studio, but she was still her no-nonsense yet personable self, sticking to her routine of rolling in an hour before her call time and relying on her crew to make sure she was ready. This was the opposite of Monroe, who would get to the studio at the crack of dawn to have her makeup done by Allan "Whitey" Snyder. While Jane was open and could strike up a conversation with pretty much anyone, Marilyn was much more reserved. Looking back on her time working with Monroe, Jane said, "She was very shy. . . . She loved Whitey, her make-up man. She was a very loyal, sweet gal. And she was a great deal more intellectual than most people think. She was always reading."[23] Jane later demonstrated these differences in personality recounting an episode on set when Tommy Noonan, who played Marilyn's love interest, was asked what it was like to be kissed by Monroe on-screen: "He said, 'I felt like I was being swallowed whole.' Well, she overheard that, and she burst into tears and went running into the dressing room and closed the door. It took forever to get her out. Now that's ridiculous! You know, I would just say, 'You'd be so lucky, honey!'"[24]

Fox's treatment of the two stars of the film was very different. Fox rolled out the red carpet for Jane, treating her like a visiting queen on the lot. Thinking this was hilarious, Jane and her makeup guy Shotgun Britton played a practical joke on the cast and crew: "He would be out on the set and I would stick my head out [of the dressing room] and say *Shot!* And he'd say, 'I'm coming madam! I'm coming madam!' And he'd come running across. The others were looking at this and going, 'God, she must be a real bitch. What's she like?' And he'd come in and close the door, and we'd both laugh, scream, and hug each other."[25] Marilyn, on the other hand, had to fight even to get a dressing room. Years later, she said, "I remember when I got the part in *Gentlemen Prefer Blondes*. Jane Russell—she was the brunette in it and I was the blonde—she got $200,000 for it and I got my $500 a week, but that to me was, you know, considerable." She continued, "The only thing was I couldn't get a dressing room. I said finally—I really got to this kind of level—I said, 'Look, after all, I am the blonde and it is *Gentlemen Prefer Blondes!*' Because still they always kept saying 'Remember, you're not a star.' I said, 'Well, whatever I am, I *am* the blonde!'"[26] Marilyn got her dressing room.

After over a month of rehearsals, filming on *Gentlemen Prefer Blondes* finally began on November 17, 1952.[27] Members of the press would have loved a Russell versus Monroe feud, even if it was manufactured for their

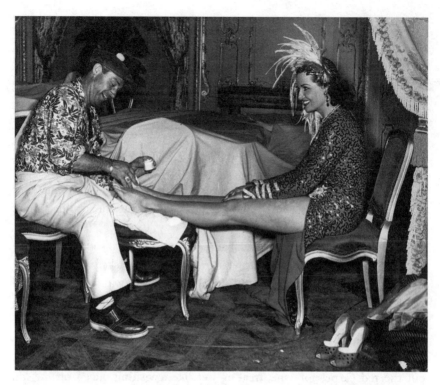

Layne "Shotgun" Britton tends to Jane's feet on the set of *Gentlemen Prefer Blondes.* Jane adored Shotgun, who was her makeup artist on most of her films.

sake, but neither woman was having it. Ego-fueled jealously was never Jane's style, and Monroe was still too early on in her career to exhibit much temperament. Plus the women genuinely liked each other. Jane was impressed with Marilyn's work ethic and desire to excel. She later stated, "Marilyn worked very hard. I would go home after a day's work, and I was exhausted! I wanted to go home and spend it with my family, and eat dinner, and relax for a few hours. She'd go and work with her coach until midnight sometimes. And then turn around and come back the next morning. I don't know how she did it."[28] Marilyn was never averse to hard work, although she later developed a notorious reputation for tardiness. This trait did pop up early on during *Gentlemen Prefer Blondes.* After showing up an hour late for rehearsal one day, she was told by Jack Cole, gently but firmly, "Marilyn, don't ever come late for me."[29] Monroe never made him wait again.

After filming began, Monroe did start arriving late to the set. Hoping to curtail this behavior before it got out of hand, Whitey Snyder went to Shotgun

Britton for help. Shotgun, in turn, went to Jane, who later remembered, "At the beginning, she was afraid to go on the set even. Whitey told Shotgun, 'She's all ready, she's been in way before Jane. But, she's just nervous about going out on the set, and that's why she's starting to be late.' So, I went by her dressing room and said 'C'mon Blondl, let's go, we've got ten minutes.' She'd say 'Oh, ok!' And she'd get up and we'd trot along down." Jane employed this method for the remainder of the shoot and Marilyn was always on time. In between takes Jane would sometimes sketch Monroe to help pass the time. In the last interview Marilyn ever gave, which appeared in *Life* magazine two days before her death, the subject of *Gentlemen Prefer Blondes* came up. Jane, she said, "was quite wonderful to me."[30]

Marilyn's upbringing as a lonely waif was the opposite of Jane's, but they had run in similar circles during different phases of their lives and had many acquaintances in common, which possibly contributed to their camaraderie during the filming. James Dougherty, Marilyn's first husband, had gone to high school with Jane (Marilyn had also briefly attended Van Nuys High), and he had worked with Robert Mitchum at the Lockheed manufacturing facility. Both Marilyn and Jane had modeled for Tom Kelley and would be forever linked to the photographer: Jane for being "discovered" through one of his photos, and Marilyn for the nude images that sparked a firestorm of publicity when used on the 1952 Golden Dreams calendar (and later in the first issue of *Playboy*). At the time of filming, Marilyn was dating baseball legend Joe DiMaggio and was interested in hearing Jane's perspective on marrying an athlete. Marilyn exhibited as much interest in sports as Jane did, noting of their romantic partners, "Only, they play different kinds of ball, don't they?"[31] Las Vegas seems to have been a distant memory for Jane, as she enthusiastically endorsed nuptials with the Yankee Clipper, though years later, looking back, Jane would comment about athletes, "The most egotistical people in the world. And my husband liked her husband [Joe DiMaggio]. When they'd meet, they'd talk stats all night and Marilyn would fall asleep on the couch."[32]

During production Jane adopted Marilyn as a kind of kid sister, exhibiting a tremendous amount of empathy for Monroe, who was experiencing the same type of amped-up sex symbol publicity Jane had been enduring for over a decade. "I know what Marilyn is going through because I had the same kind of provocative excitement as an impetus to my career," Jane said at the time. Wanting to impart the wisdom of Howard Hawks she had received back in 1940, Jane passed along the same advice, commenting, "She has to learn how

Actor Max Willenz and Jane stand outside her dressing room as she gets ready to imitate Marilyn Monroe in *Gentlemen Prefer Blondes*.

to say 'No' to things. However, I've found that Marilyn is capable of taking care of herself in most matters and far more so than most people give her credit for."[33] Sensing Monroe's inner turmoil, Jane even invited her co-star to attend a session of a Hollywood Christian group that she had recently become involved in. Monroe did attend, but decided it wasn't for her. "Jane tried to covert me to her religion," Marilyn said, "and I tried to interest her in Freud."[34]

Jane may have had an easy time working with Marilyn, but the road was bumpier for Howard Hawks on the other side of the camera. Monroe suffered from crippling insecurities and self-doubts. Monroe's acting coach Natasha Lytess was constantly on set, and Marilyn used Lytess as a crutch, looking to the coach for approval after every take. This proved too much for Hawks, who tried banning Lytess from the set, only to have to allow her back due to Monroe's protestations. Hawks also had a hard time effectively communicating with his blonde star, but this was where his gut feeling about Jane paid off. "It wasn't easy, that film," Hawks said later. "But it wasn't difficult because I had Jane there. And Jane would do for her . . . I'd hear them talking, Marilyn would whisper, 'What did he tell me?' Jane wouldn't say, 'He's told you six times already,' she'd tell her to do it again."[35]

Jane took it all in stride; she was having a great time. After a decade-long hit-or-miss career, Jane knew a golden opportunity had landed in her lap and she was going to make the most of it. "I've really enjoyed making 'Blondes,'" she said at the time. "For the first time I get to play *me*. I'm not some sleepy siren or gangster's foil, I just am what I am." She appreciated that the script had been retooled "with the idea of letting me appear on the screen as I really appear in private life with my friends."[36] The result is arguably the strongest performance of Jane's career and certainly the most memorable. Jane hoped *Gentlemen Prefer Blondes* would be a springboard for similar roles. "I hope this new idea comes off," she said. "There has been a gradual breaking away from the strictly glamour formula. Those pictures with Bob Hope, I think, began establishing me in audiences' minds as a comedienne. 'Blondes' should complete that change."[37]

For Jane, working with Howard Hawks was everything she had hoped it would be; he was "a perfect gentleman, just like always."[38] Many others who interacted with Hawks over the years found his stern facade off-putting, but this was never the case for Jane, who "found him a very warm man."[39] This probably had something to do with Jane's ability to get along with people and also because Hawks's personality was similar to her father's. "In both cases," she later noted of her relationships with Hawks and her father, "I learned to read them, to know when they liked or disliked something."[40] Even though Jane's cinematographer had been foisted on Hawks, the director found Harry J. Wild's short temper hysterically funny. Assistant director Paul Helmick later recalled, "Harry Wild would jump up and down on his felt hat, he'd get so mad. Howard got more laughs out of him than anyone."[41]

The comedic talents of Jane Russell and Marilyn Monroe are on full display in *Gentlemen Prefer Blondes*, which is greatly aided by their chemistry and genuine fondness for each other. There is also no denying that both women did indeed exude a great deal of sex appeal on-screen. This amused Hawks to no end, who recalled that the on-screen persona of each woman was the polar opposite of what she was like in person. "We made the movie and I used to laugh," the director later recalled. "Here are these two sex queens. Now, nobody would ever take Marilyn out, nobody paid attention to her. She sat with no clothes on the set and everybody just walked right by her. And some pretty little extra'd go by and everybody'd whistle. And she couldn't get anybody to take her out. And Jane Russell had never known anything but one man . . . the beginning of high school, and she married him and lived there. She was like an old shoe, you know? I never thought of either of them as having any sex."[42] Yet once the cameras were rolling, Hawks couldn't deny the overwhelming presence both women had. "But Lord," he admitted later, "well, now the whole *thing* was sexy. For God's sake, all I'd do was make a scene of the two of them walking down towards the camera and people'd want to attack them."[43]

Marilyn may have been given the film's most notable number, "Diamonds Are a Girl's Best Friend," but Jane also had her own solo song, which has become a surefire crowd-pleaser. "Ain't There Anyone Here for Love?," one of the additional numbers penned by Harold Adamson and Hoagy Carmichael, seemed to be tailor-made for Jane. Performed in the gymnasium of a cruise ship, the song has Jane moving among members of an Olympic team who are more concerned with their exercise regiments than her. Dressed only in flesh-colored swim trucks, the athletes move through choreography that includes slow-motion wrestling and the formation of a rear-end-lined promenade for Jane to bounce through, which gives the whole number not-so-subtle homo-erotic undertones. The scene, cut for television airings in the United States and theatrical screenings in Britain, later gave Jane status as a gay icon. The filming of the number also provided one of the few unscripted moments in the film. At the end of the number, Jane crouches down next to a pool, allowing the athletes to jump over her to dive in. When the scene was shot, she was accidentally knocked into the water. As Jane later explained, "It wasn't planned. They let the poor dancer go that did it. That was on a Friday, and we had to wait all weekend and come back and shoot the thing on Monday without my going into the pool. Which is ridiculous, because I was sure they were going to use the one in the pool, and they did."[44] Jane was also thrilled to be sharing the screen with her brother Jamie, who appears as one of the dancing athletes in this number as well as in "Bye, Bye Baby" earlier in the film.

Jane and Marilyn have a private conversation shortly before being immortalized in cement at Grauman's Chinese Theatre in Hollywood.

As an added bonus, Jane was given the opportunity to perform an abbreviated reprise of "Diamonds Are a Girl's Best Friend" doing her best Marilyn Monroe impersonation. When asked if she was offended by Jane's imitation, Monroe reportedly said, "Why should this bother me? I know Jane wouldn't do anything that would hurt me."[45]

Jane finished working on the film on February 10, 1953, and it was ready for release by July.[46] For publicity leading up to the film's release, both women recorded their songs in a studio; the result was released on vinyl by MGM. Jane and Marilyn were also invited to perform the time-honored ritual of sinking their hands and feet into cement in the courtyard of Grauman's Chinese Theatre on Hollywood Boulevard. Marilyn jokingly suggested they memorialize the parts of their anatomy each was most known for: Jane by bending over into the wet cement, and Marilyn by sitting in it.[47] Also rejected was Marilyn's request to dot the *i* in her name with a diamond. A rhinestone was used instead, although it was soon stolen. True to form, Jane made no attempt to present any illusions about herself. "Always one for personal comfort," she later wrote, "I was wearing my usual big shoes, so no aspiring actress will have any trouble whatsoever getting her feet into my footprints!"[48]

Following the filming of *Gentlemen Prefer Blondes*, Marilyn and Jane were always friendly to each other, but never became any closer as friends than they had been on set. Jane later commented, "We were very friendly on the picture, but I don't think anyone got that close to Marilyn and stayed that close. She seemed to change her friends according to which group she was with."[49] When Marilyn broke up with Joe DiMaggio in 1954, Jane found out via William Travilla, who was working with Jane on a film at the time. Jane felt compelled to reach out to her, writing a ten-page letter addressed to "Dear Little One." "I've never written such a letter—But I love you very dearly & I don't want you to be unhappy ever." She signed it, "Old Jane."[50] The following year, when Marilyn was living in New York, Jane was in town promoting a film and fund-raising for adoption advocacy. Marilyn reached out to Jane via a secretary to offer assistance. During that same period, James Haspiel, a teenager who along with six other youths had become friendly with Monroe, recalled being tasked with delivering a note from Marilyn to the hotel Jane was staying at.[51]

One day in August 1962 Jane was enjoying a day at the beach with a group of girlfriends, all commiserating about problems in their life while at the same time laughing about them. It occurred to Jane how nice it would be if Marilyn could be there with them. The next day Jane's former co-star was found dead in her Brentwood home. She was only thirty-six. Jane would often wonder if things might have been different had she tried harder to reach out.

Gentlemen Prefer Blondes was a smash hit and the eighth-highest-grossing film of 1953. Jane would always hold the film in high regard. "Dorothy from 'Gentlemen' was my favorite role since it combined comedy with my love of music," Jane said thirty-five years after the film's release. "There's also an earthiness about Dorothy that is very much like me."[52]

A curious footnote to *Gentlemen Prefer Blondes* was the amount of time it took for Howard Hughes to get his money from Fox for Jane's services; a delay for which he was completely at fault. At no point before or during filming was a formal contract signed by the two parties, and payment was never requested. As the release date drew near, Harry J. McIntyre in the studio's publicity department started to panic. "Do you think we would be reasonably safe in advertising," wrote McIntyre to a studio lawyer, "that we could dub the voice of Miss Russell [for international release], authorize the use of her image in a television trailer, and otherwise use her name and portrait for the normal advertising of this picture?"[53] When the studio did not get an answer from Hughes, Fox took a leap of faith and used Jane's likeness to promote the film. The studio continued its attempts to get an answer from Hughes, but to no avail. Finally, nearly five years after *Gentlemen Prefer Blondes* had started production, Hughes demanded $265,000, claiming the filming had lasted longer than he had agreed to. Even though Fox had been trying to pay him for half a decade, Hughes had the gall to include accrued interest in the amount. Just to make the whole thing go away and to finally get Jane off the books, the studio agreed to pay $205,000 instead of the original $175,000.[54] By not allowing Fox to pay him, Howard Hughes had made an additional $30,000 off Jane Russell.

17

A Woman of Faith

Jane Russell was always one to speak her mind, seldom giving a thought or care to what public perceptions of her might be. She had been introduced to the world as a smoldering sexpot, but this was a persona manufactured by Howard Hughes and Russell Birdwell. As Jane's career progressed, Hughes sought to maintain this on-screen illusion, and Jane usually obliged when she was in front of the camera. Still, she usually managed to infuse her earthy personality into many of the characters she played. The person she was in real life, however, may have surprised many who knew Jane only through her film roles. This was especially true when it came to Jane's deep-rooted Christian faith, which was something she always wore proudly on her sleeve.

Geraldine had always had a deep faith, but her beliefs were amplified after the death of her first child. "I guess that's what turned her to real religion," Jane said. "Until then, she'd always said, 'I've got such wonderful plans—*and God, you go ahead and bless them.*' After Billy's death, Mother began to say, 'Lord, what would you like *me* to do?' The result was that we five little Russells were raised by the Bible. We never went to any particular church, but never a day passed that we didn't have a family worship together. We'd read a few verses from the Bible and most always pray together."[1] Geraldine also opened up her home to complete strangers on Saturday mornings to conduct Bible study, sometimes going so far as to advertise the services in the local newspaper.[2] Geraldine's background in acting and oration served her well in this capacity, prompting Jane to say, "My mother, I think, was the best Bible teacher that ever walked."[3] She elaborated, "She had a wonderful, very practical way of describing everything in the Bible and making it very real, very now, today. It wasn't something you just did on Sunday and the rest of the week you lived your life."[4] In later years, Jane would look back fondly on her mother's methods of instilling faith into her life. "Mom used to ring a bell, we had seven acres, and so she'd ring a bell every day. And my brothers and I, and whoever we were playing with, would come and sit

A demure portrait of Jane at her home in the mid-1950s. Her on-screen sex symbol persona was always at odds with her spiritual real-life self.

around under the fig tree in our jeans and we'd have a Bible study. And she would stand up there and act it all out, and she was just fabulous. Slowly all my friends ended up at Mother's back door."[5]

Geraldine's influence on her daughter was strong, and Jane's faith was ingrained at a very young age. "I can remember giving my heart to the Lord when I was six years old," Jane later claimed. "On my way home from school, and it was a neighbor lady. And then she called my mother, and told my mother who was thrilled. I was perfectly willing, but she was the first person to say, 'Would you like to give your heart to Jesus?' I said 'Yes!'"[6] This incident remained meaningful to Jane for the rest of her life. "Everybody should have that kind of a day and remember it, just like they do their wedding day."[7]

Jane's faith remained strong until adolescence, but started to waver when she began hanging around with, as Jane described, a "crowd that wasn't goody goody. The ones that did things first—smoked, necked, ran around in cars. We were rebellious. Black sheep, I guess."[8] During this period, Geraldine leaned hard on her faith, noting, "I kept praying she'd drop them. They were destroying everything I'd tried to teach my daughter." Ultimately, Geraldine decided to embrace the group rather than fight it. "It was all or nothing at all," she later remembered. "At first I rebelled. 'Lord, do I have to take that awful gang?' I'd ask myself. 'But the answer came, 'All or none."[9] This approach worked better than Geraldine expected. Maxine West, one of Jane's high school girlfriends, commented, "We found we could go to Mother Russell when we were afraid to go anywhere else. She never condemned us, and before we were through we'd be praying with her."[10]

Jane would later note that her faithless period lasted "for about three years. I got to the end of the teens, and I knew more than my mother or anybody in town. The Lord gave me just enough rope to go out there and hang myself. And then I came home to Mom. She said, 'You know Daughter, the Lord puts the white railing along the side of the highway going up the mountain to keep you from going over. They're not there to restrict you. They're there to protect you.'"[11] It was during this period that Jane terminated her unwanted pregnancy, a procedure that, due to the lack of safe options, almost killed her. As far as Jane was concerned, the incident proved that straying away from the Lord meant peril. Her faith would not waver to that extent again.

After selling La Posada and moving to the adjacent two-acre orchard, Geraldine continued to hold Bible studies, which usually took place under a large chestnut tree. When the rains came, Geraldine moved the meetings into her small house; she dubbed the gatherings Kitchen Chapel. The space was so cramped that attendees started requesting a bigger location. Geraldine decided to offer up some of her property so a chapel could be built. She later wrote of the 1949 construction:

Before I could turn around, they were at it. Daughter phoned Ken, and he came in from the desert in his trailer. They laid the forms. The boys poured cement, and the girls put on the roof. Everyone brought a bucket of paint or a pail of nails and up it went. The fastest thing built you ever saw! We held our first meeting by candlelight with no walls—just the floor and the roof; and we sang and sang every chorus and hymn we knew. My, it was fun! Between the things we wanted to do, and the things the building inspectors would permit, the chapel turned out to be very unique and individual. At the end of the year, we had to push the north wall out to enlarge it to twice its size. Then we felt a need for a recreation room, so we built "The Eagle's Nest." God is the Great Eagle, and we are eaglets learning to fly. This room has a huge fireplace and large glass windows. We hold baby showers, wedding receptions, Bible study and potluck suppers in "The Eagle's Nest."[12]

Jane often attended her mother's sessions, noting, "These people come here because they get the same thing out of it that I do—that God is up there taking care of me and if I do right by Him, He'll do right by me."[13] In addition to the gatherings at Geraldine's, Jane also helped start the Hollywood Christian Group. As she explained, "We would meet in different people's houses. And we would have different speakers, they were usually Protestant, but we would have different speakers come and talk. Because a lot of the kids in Hollywood had come from someplace else and felt strange going to the local church, but they didn't feel strange in coming to someone's house that they knew. And that's how that started."[14] Among the attendees were Roy Rogers and his wife Dale Evans. Jane didn't restrict her faith to these gatherings, and she was not shy about letting her faith be known on film sets. Jane's stand-in Carmen Nisbet Cabeen became her prayer partner during film shoots. As Carmen later explained, "We used to be in the dressing room, and when the door was closed, then everybody knew that Jane and Carmen were in the dressing room praying. Once in a while, one of the crew men would come by and knock on the side of the trailer and say, 'Say one for me!' So we would."[15]

This spiritual devotion was shared by Jane's brothers and their growing families, but was not something Robert Waterfield appears to have subscribed to. The Russell clan expanded their contributions beyond the Eagle's Nest by helping to build the Chapel in the Canyon in the Canoga Park neighborhood. Jane helped design the chapel, located at 9012 Topanga Canyon, while brothers Tommy and Jamie served as contractors.[16] Described as requiring no offerings and having no locked door, the Chapel in the Canyon invited Geraldine to teach classes that Dale Evans, with great fondness, later recalled attending.[17] Jamie Russell also crossed his faith with filmmaking, hoping to counter what he viewed as Hollywood's "wishy-washy, milk toast

Jane checks in on brother Jamie as he edits his religious film *A Son Is Born*. (George Brich, Valley Times Collection/Los Angeles Public Library)

treatment of religious films." The result, produced by Chapel Films, was a 105-minute feature titled *A Son Is Born,* which was filmed on weekends and holidays over the course of four years. Jamie explained the extended production time: "With the exception of three professional actors, the cast and crew are all amateurs. The picture cost under $10,000 and took so long to make because we periodically ran out of money." Jamie wrote, directed, edited, and acted in the feature, and called upon brothers Tom and Ken to assist.[18] It's not clear if Jane provided anything more than moral support.

Jane was so quick to throw out a Bible verse that when she started working on her memoir in the 1980s, her then husband John Peoples commented to ghostwriter Jan Lowell, "Please don't let her walk on water."[19] Throughout the years, Jane never belonged to a specific church or subscribed to a particular denomination. "I don't think about it as religion, even," she said. "I just feel that it was the way I was brought up—to believe in the Bible and to believe that God is love."[20] Asked to expand on her spiritual outlook, Jane responded, "Just practicing the Golden Rule. You can't get anything better than that. I believe in turning the other cheek not so much because of the other fellow or being 'big' about things, but just because it makes me feel better inside. Sure, I feel like getting even sometimes—who doesn't? I'm no goody-goody. But then you have to sit down and realize that most people who do mean things do them because they're sick with fear. And so they lash out at other people. When you think about it that way, you feel sorry for them."[21]

Jane matter-of-factly admitted to speaking in tongues, a phenomenon referred to as glossolalia. She would later describe being overcome at one church while receiving a "spirit baptism." As she later remembered, "At this one particular church, it was charismatic, if you will, or whatever. They were seeking the baptism. So Pat [Henry] and I sat down and sought the baptism, and we both got it that day."[22] Jane and Geraldine would claim that the message they received about the adoption barriers while praying in a London hotel room came via this method. When Jane first started working on her autobiography with Jan and Bob Lowell, she set up a session so the couple could personally witness glossolalia. Jan Lowell later relayed:

The most important thing to Jane, as far as I could see, was her relationship with God, really serious. She once asked us if we knew anything about Pentecostal. I said, "Yeah, you talk in tongues, period, that's all I know." She never asked what my religion was, she didn't care. She said, "All right, I am going to get the gang down here and we're going to have a meeting," of whatever the hell they called their group, "and you and Bob will sit in on the talking in tongues thing." There were four other women; one in particular, Carmen, I think it was, she came down from a different state to be there, was the woman who did the actual talking in tongues. We all sat on the floor, all these women and my husband, holding hands, while Carmen went into this trance and started talking what sounded like gobbledygook and then she would say, "Anybody want to ask a question?" She would then answer the question. So I went over to her and I asked her some question about my daughter and she went into this trance, came out with the gobbledygook, and then she told me things about my daughter that made my hair stand on end. I wrote it down and you know, my daughter has it to this day—because she was so right about my daughter's personality that really it was stunning, and I thought, "Wow, there is something to this talking in tongues."[23]

Gerry Cornez, who worked as executive director of Jane's charitable organization starting in the 1970s, had a similar experience when Jane invited him to her house: "I walked into the house and there she was sort of kneeling on the floor. They had this gigantic hassock, it was a big round thing in the middle of the living room, and she and three of her friends were there and their eyes were closed and they were talking in tongues. I didn't even know what that was. I really still don't quite know what it is."[24]

In addition to her faith, Jane also came to be a strong believer in astrology, which experienced a surge of popularity in the 1970s. Jan Lowell said that when she and her husband Bob met Jane,

she wanted to know when I was born and I said, "I'm a Leo." She said, "You can't be a Leo, I hate Leos, I never get along with Leos." I said, "Well, Bob is a Virgo, he makes up for it. But I am an eight-month baby, I was supposed to be born in September, which would have made me a Virgo, but I was born a month too soon." So she said, "What date, what time, where?" I told her. Two days later, she said, "I talked to Suzanne [White, author of astrology books] and she said you were born on the cusp, early in the morning, and you really are a Virgo and not a Leo." I said, "I'm glad you solved that problem for me!"[25]

Gerry Cornez had similar experiences, noting, "She would say things to me like, 'Oh my God, you're a Leo? No wonder why. That explains everything. Bob Waterfield was a Leo.' She would say things like that without ever explaining them."[26]

Jane spoke often about her faith in the Lord, which the media found intriguing and would sometimes run features on. For as much time and money as Howard Hughes put into promoting Jane's bustline, he never seemed to try to muzzle her when it came to discussing her spirituality. Had Jane been at one of the larger studios, which often would carefully craft complete personas for their contracted actors, she may not have had the freedom to express this aspect of her life. As was often the case with Howard Hughes, he was an impossible-to-predict wildcard. He was certainly aware of Jane's spirituality, and while he did nothing to curb her public acknowledgments of these beliefs, he also made no attempt to temper the exploitation of her anatomy on the screen.

Jane had been mortified by the publicity images surrounding *The Outlaw*, and she resented that they followed her for the rest of her life, but she was perfectly fine with the actual roles she played in her films. To the naysayers who had a hard time reconciling the screen siren with the Bible-quoting Valley girl, Jane responded, "Unless all play-acting is to be banned or at least terribly restricted, my sort of role is as important and admissible as any." She continued, "To present 'The Passion Play' you must have a Judas, and no one indicts the man who accepts this part. To tell a story of a woman who makes questionable use of her beauty, you must have someone to portray that woman."[27] No matter what others thought, Jane never had trouble compartmentalizing her sexy film roles and her spiritual personal life. However, while she was usually game for anything requested of her on-screen, Jane did have her limits—as Howard Hughes was about to find out.

18

J. R. in 3D

Howard Hughes had unloaded his controlling RKO stock to an inexperienced Chicago-based syndicate in September 1952. Five chaotic months later, he regained control of the studio by purchasing back the stock at a profit of $998,000.[1] Again at the helm, he green-lit the production of five films, all to be shot in 3D. The 3D method had become a recent industry craze following the successful release of the first 3D color feature, *Bwana Devil,* a few months earlier. The opportunity to tout "J.R. in 3D" was one too good to pass up, so *The French Line* was included as a starring vehicle for Jane.

Seemingly inspired by the cruise liner setting of *Gentlemen Prefer Blondes, The French Line* would also be a Technicolor musical set on a ship. Written by the wife and husband team of Mary Loos (niece of Anita) and Richard Sale, *The French Line* had Jane playing a Texas oil heiress who hides her identity on a transatlantic voyage in order to find a man who loves *her* and not her millions. Veteran director Lloyd Bacon was brought in to run things, but Howard Hughes would still be keeping a close eye on the picture. As usual, he was hyper-concerned with Jane's appearance, particularly how the assets of his greatest asset would appear in 3D. Production commenced on May 25, 1953, even though Jane's leading man had yet to be decided.[2] A week and a half later, Mexican-born Gilbert Roland was hired to play a suave Frenchman, and he rounded out the main cast, which included Mary McCarty and Arthur Hunnicutt.

Designer Howard Greer, who had worked with Jane on *His Kind of Woman* and *The Las Vegas Story,* was again assigned to her on *The French Line.* Michael Woulfe was also brought on to handle outfits for some of the other actors, as well as an entire line for a fashion show sequence. Woulfe, who considered Greer his nemesis, wasn't thrilled, noting, "And now with the crap news about his assignment to do Jane's clothes on *The French Line,* I was relegated to creating the wardrobe for the supporting cast."[3] Woulfe's fortunes changed a few weeks into production. Due to Greer's ill health and Howard Hughes's whims,

Jane attends an event with costume designer Michael Woulfe.

Woulfe took over Jane's designs on the film as well. "You're younger and accus-tomed to his [Hughes's] way of doing films," Greer reportedly told Woulfe as he was leaving. "You seem to be able to put up with the nonsense."[4] Almost imme-diately after taking over, Woulfe started to get hounded by Hughes about Jane's clothes. For a scene on a shuffleboard court, Hughes insisted Jane be seen in a swimsuit. ("But seriously," inquired Woulfe, "who would wear a swimsuit while playing shuffleboard?")[5] Woulfe was instructed to design more than a dozen swimsuits and then photograph Jane in them, both dry and wet. "It surprised me that Hughes wanted to see them wet since no scene called for Jane to be in the pool," he later mused. "I wondered if he just liked to ogle women with wet, clinging swimsuits that offered an enticing glimpse of their nipples."[6] After repeated requests from Hughes to lower the bustline, which caused production delays, the swimsuit was finally approved.

With that hurdle cleared, Woulfe moved on to his next Howard Hughes challenge. This time he needed to convince the mogul to sign off on a cos-tume that both Jane and Mary McCarty would be wearing in their duet "Any Gal from Texas": matching strapless red-sequined leotards with cowboy hats and gun holsters. Hughes needed some convincing to allow Jane to sport a holster, but he finally relented. He was also hesitant to have Jane dressed identically to another actress (apparently because she wasn't Marilyn Monroe) for a musical number, but he also finally agreed to that. The duet with McCarty convinced Hughes that Jane needed a solo showstopper, so he put in a request for an additional song to be written for her. Giving little thought to the budget, Hughes demanded that a second fashion show be added to the film that would lead into Jane's new musical number. Woulfe was able to cut corners for the added fashion sequence by retooling existing costumes, including the croupier gown he had designed for Gloria Grahame in *Macao*. For Jane, however, another costume would need to be designed from scratch. Little could Woulfe know that this last outfit would put him square in the middle of a battle royale between Jane and Howard Hughes.

The additional song, "Looking for Trouble," written by Josef Myrow, Ralph Blane, and Robert Wells, would be the climax of the film and feature Jane doing a pseudo-striptease. Hughes wanted a spectacular but skimpy costume for the sequence. Woulfe had just finished *Son of Sinbad* (not released until 1955), for which he had designed a revealing two-piece costume for belly dancer Nejla Ateş. The bikini had been making waves in France, so Hughes envisioned a costume for Jane that would be a cross between a bikini and Ateş's outfit. Woulfe protested bitterly, later explaining, "Putting this costume on Jane would be a disaster, especially since Hughes was already in the middle of a battle with the censors about the skimpy attire and sexually suggestive dance routines in *Son of Sinbad*. But unlike other studio heads, he seemed to have no fear of clashing with the censors. Besides, he was probably already indulging in a fevered fantasy of Jane Russell dancing up a storm in the brief, glittering, titillating bikini."[7] When Jane found out what was being planned for her, she threw a fit. "What's wrong with him?" she exclaimed to Woulfe. "I think he's going crazy!"[8] Still, Jane relented and showed up for fittings of the costume, which took a long time to construct; it was so small that only one person could work on it at a time, hand-sewing on each jewel. "It would have taken half the time to finish this long tedious job if four hands could have worked on it simultaneously," Woulfe later recalled.[9] When it came time to show up on set wearing the barely-there outfit, it was too much for Jane. As she later recalled, "Nobody in America wore a bikini in those days. It was only the naughty girls in the south of France. When I tested it, even the camera crew went 'Oh no!' So I took the bikini off and went to the beach."[10]

Jane had rarely (if ever) shown any sort of temperament on a movie set, but Howard Hughes had finally pushed her too far. In late July 1953 Jane left rehearsal early, claiming she had been ordered home by her doctor due to illness.[11] Instead of going home, Jane headed to Ocean House, an exclusive luxury hotel in Santa Monica, built by William Randolph Hearst, that originally had been the private residence of Marion Davies. Jane was officially on strike, and refused to come back until the bikini was scrapped. Hughes couldn't understand what the problem was, but rather than talking to Jane personally, he continued to use Michael Woulfe as an intermediary. While attempting to appease both Hughes and Jane, who had each dug in their heels over the bikini, Woulfe developed a duodenal ulcer. Woulfe's doctor commented, "You'd be surprised how many patients I have with the same ailment, all in the employment of Howard Hughes."[12]

The studio convinced Jane to have photos taken in the costume for Hughes to see, so Woulfe, along with wardrobe assistant Mary Tate and stills photographer Ernest Bachrach, were dispatched to Santa Monica with the bikini. "When we entered her room," Woulfe later remembered, "we found her visibly upset, almost in tears. Photo sessions are usually fun, but this unpleasant task at hand squashed any attempt at levity."[13] The group decided that Jane would make the costume look as uncomplimentary as possible in the images. According to Woulfe, "Jane posed in the costume, contorting her body to show how unflattering it looked on her. She twisted and rolls of fat suddenly appeared around her middle. She stood erect, putting out her chest, and half of her bosom was exposed. These photos would surely demonstrate that the costume was horribly wrong for Jane."[14]

Howard Hughes loved the photos.

Jane remained on strike for a total of eight days, causing the entire production to go idle, at a cost of over $28,000.[15] She returned to the studio with Woulfe in order to sit in on the telephone call with her boss from the office of associate Walter Kane. At one point during the call, Woulfe exited the office so Jane and Hughes could discuss the matter in private. "If I was forced to choose who would win the argument," Woulfe later recalled, "my money was on Hughes."[16] Instead, Jane emerged from the office triumphantly exclaiming, "The costume is out!"[17] Jane had gone headlong into battle with Howard Hughes—and won.

Jane was still amenable to performing "Looking for Trouble," but Woulfe now had a seemingly impossible task in front of him. "We knew Hughes wanted something sensational that he could exploit to gain publicity for the film," he remembered. "Jane was willing to wear the costume as long as it covered her

Howard Hughes wanted Jane to wear a bejeweled bikini in *The French Line,* but she refused. This one-piece with teardrop cutouts was the compromise.

discreetly. Could we combine 'outrageous' with 'somewhat modest'?"[18] It was Jane who came up with the solution; she suggested adding cutouts to a one-piece garment to give the illusion that she was wearing less clothing. Woulfe obliged, constructing a one-piece leotard of black silk satin with three large teardrop-shaped cutouts in the front, each lined in rhinestones. The costume was Russell-approved but still needed to pass muster with Hughes, who wanted it to be extremely low cut without any sort of built-in foundation. He continued to believe that Jane's breasts defied gravity. Woulfe knew the costume was too skimpy for Jane to be able to dance around without falling out of it, so the studio's engineering department was brought on to help with the task of adding some sort of underwire that would be undetected by Hughes. "The man who was assigned to the boob enhancement task did the moulding and shaping directly on Jane's dummy," Woulfe said. "I don't know whether he used trigonometry, algebra, possibly a sextant, or just common sense, but he did a hell of a job."[19] The musical number was filmed, and production on *The French Line* finally wrapped on August 20.[20] Hughes's fight with his biggest star was seemingly over, but the war with Joseph Breen and the Production Code Administration was just beginning.

The script for *The French Line* was submitted to the PCA in March 1953 and, after some adjustments, was approved the following month. Knowing full well who he was dealing with, Joseph Breen was quick to point out "that our final judgement will be based on the finished picture."[21] When the final cut of the film was submitted in November, the PCA noted at least ten unacceptable Jane Russell "breast shots," including the "Looking for Trouble" number, which had "many troublesome elements."[22] These elements included a number of close-up shots of Jane taken at a higher angle, which Hughes no doubt hoped would cause Jane's breasts to jump out in 3D while she, according to the song's lyrics, "popped all the corn in Nebraska." The PCA also took exception to a monologue in the middle of the song in which she describes what kind of man she's looking for: "Seventeen to seventy will do. It ain't the age, it's the attitude!" The suggestive camera angles, matched with the monologue and the costume, were too much for the PCA. *The French Line* would not be getting a certificate of approval.

This meant little to Hughes, who booked the premiere for the end of December in St. Louis, where it was sure to rankle the city's large population of Catholics. Hughes knew exactly what he was doing as all hell broke loose at the PCA and in St. Louis. Jack Vizzard, an employee of the PCA, was sent to Missouri to discuss the situation with Archbishop (later Cardinal) Ritter. Vizzard later recounted what happened next:

> The Archbishop, who had been pondering by himself, finally spoke up. "I've been thinking," he said, "of forbidding all Catholics under my jurisdiction from attending the movie, under pain of mortal sin. What do you think?"
>
> He stood there, calm and alert, turned half sideways, waiting intently for my reply. I weighed the question cautiously. This was a severe censure, the most powerful in the episcopal arsenal. St. Louis was a heavily Catholic city, and the imputation would probably saturate deep into the population. But a spirit of independence was creeping into the air. What if the proclamation were ignored? There was a famous axiom that applied in these circumstances. It states, "Never slap a king in the face, unless you're sure you are going to knock him off his throne."
>
> But gamble or no gamble, the die would have to be cast. I concurred in the thinking of the Archbishop. "I think it's a very good idea," I said.

"Very well then," he accepted. "If you think it's a good idea, I'll do it. You *do* think it's a good idea?"

"Yes."

He nodded, "I'll publish it Sunday," he said.

An odd sensation coursed through me. In those days, the values represented by the action were still alive to me, even though slightly raveled. I felt strangely responsible. From this point on, should some Catholic go to hell as a result of my back-room manipulations, I would not be uninvolved. The thought that there might be an enormous disproportion here had to be suppressed. That the eternal fate of a human being should have to be connected to Jane Russell's mammaries, no matter how heroic, was a bit much.[23]

Hughes moved ahead with the premiere, set for December 29, 1953. If he thought the archdiocese and his old foe Joseph Breen were his main adversaries, he was wrong. As it turned out, Jane was not through battling him over *The French Line*. Unlike *The Outlaw*, which Jane had viewed for the first time during the premiere, she was able to screen *The French Line* ahead of time—and she wasn't happy. "It wasn't the dance so much as the camera angles," she later said. "Anyone who knows the picture business knows that you never know how anything will look until you see the film. Where there are usually long shots of a dance of this type, there are close-ups!"[24] What Jane found particularly galling was that "Looking for Trouble" had been tacked onto the end of the film without any context. "It was never made clear in the story that the millionairess did the naughty number to get even with her fellah, to make him mad," Jane said. "I begged them to put in one short scene to show some motive for it. They all looked at me like I was bananas. I'd already held up shooting for two weeks. Finally, a scene was shot. No film was in the camera, I'm sure, for I never saw it, nor did anyone else."[25] Jane would always maintain that she had no objections to the song or the costume. "I did the whole number tongue in cheek, and I saw nothing wrong with it whatsoever, if there'd only been a motive."[26]

For the second time on one picture, Jane put her foot down with Hughes. Her contract was up in February, and she was feeling less loyal than usual. She refused to go to St. Louis and publicly decried Hughes's decision to release the film without a certificate of approval from the PCA. "I thoroughly agree with the Breen Office," she said to the press. "It's the public's safeguard and the actor's too. I certainly don't want to be associated with any picture that's denied a seal." She continued, "I fought and beefed and argued over scenes in that picture. I have no more say-so over what finally appears on the screen than I did in *The Outlaw*. I hope and pray the studio will see the light and make the cuts requested."[27] In a final dig at her boss, Jane added, "I had nothing to say about such things before. But now I won't be drawn into the affair. My contract is up in February, and this experience will color the possibility of my re-signing."[28]

Despite the controversy (or perhaps because of it), *The French Line* opened to long lines in St. Louis. Members of the police department's "morality squad" were dispatched to the Fox Theatre where the film was showing, threatening to shut it down if the movie was deemed obscene. While two scenes were found to be objectionable, no actions were taken to yank the film out of the theater. For a population that had lived through the horrors of World War II, moralistic reactions to films like *The French Line* were starting to seem absurd. As the uproar in St. Louis raged on, movie pioneer Samuel Goldwyn commented, "We must realize that in the almost quarter of a century since the code's adoption, the world has moved on. But the code had stood still. Today there is a far greater maturity among audiences."[29]

For Howard Hughes, it was all publicity to be exploited. Posters for the film featured taglines like "J.R. In 3D! It'll knock both your eyes out!," "That Picture! That Dance!—you've heard so much about!," and "Need We Say More?" Perry Lieber at RKO sent out press packages proclaiming that the controversial costume weighed "only seven ounces," and claiming that the press had been banned from the set during a song set in a bubble bath because it called for Jane to expose herself "down to Mr. Breen's frown."[30]

When the film started hitting theaters in early 1954, it continued to stir up controversy. The Protestant Motion Picture Council condemned the film on behalf of "48,000,000 American Protestants," and screenings were banned at a theater in Memphis.[31] Satisfied that he had won this latest battle against Breen, Hughes did eventually allow cuts to be made, and *The French Line* received a PCA certificate of approval in March 1955. The biggest casualty of this "approved" cut is the "Looking for Trouble" number; it was retained, minus the monologue, but presented in an extreme long shot, which does indeed dilute the effectiveness of the dance. Overall, *The French Line* is rather dull and pales in comparison to *Gentlemen Prefer Blondes*. It's uneven and the songs aren't particularly memorable or always necessary. For example, it's not clear why a fashion designer (McCarty), who maintains sophisticated airs for her clients, would perform a campy duet with an oil heiress in the middle of one of her fashion shows. Jane was correct in her assessment that "Looking for Trouble" comes out of nowhere and makes absolutely no sense within the context of the film. However, on its own, the uncensored "Looking for Trouble," is incredibly entertaining and one of Jane's most memorable moments on film. Unfortunately, it's the censored version of the song that is usually included in television airings and rental copies of *The French Line*. Of incidental note to viewers is the first film appearance of Kim Novak, who was cast as one of the models in the earlier of the two fashion show sequences.

In her thirteen years with Howard Hughes, Jane had endured her fair share of unwanted hype and controversy, but the stir around *The French Line* was too much. As she later wrote, "Well, the shit hit the fan again. Censors screamed. Howard couldn't get a seal of approval. Even my old friend Dr. Evans of the Hollywood Presbyterian Church said, 'That girl's no Christian.' I was sick."[32] Enough was enough and Jane finally confronted her boss. She later revealed, "I remember telling Howard after that, that I never wanted to be in another picture that was having trouble with the Breen Office. And he said, 'I promise you, you never will. But if you tell anybody, I won't admit it.' Now, that's how stubborn he was."[33]

With the expiration date on Jane's contract looming, Howard Hughes wasted little time getting her assigned to another film after production wrapped on *The French Line*. Jane was leery about doing *The Big Rainbow*, a film about deep-sea treasure hunters that would feature extensive underwater cinematography. She felt the story was flimsy, and in many scenes the actors' faces would be obscured by diving equipment. Harry Tatelman, the producer on the film, was friends with Jane and offered to let her collaborate with the screenwriter on shaping her role in what would ultimately be released as *Underwater!* Having this type of input appealed to Jane, so she agreed and reported to the studio on October 17, 1953, for hair and makeup tests.[34] This turned out to be news to actress Lori Nelson, who was under contract to Universal Pictures but thought she was going to be the film's star. "The only loan-out I had at Universal was to RKO for 'Underwater,'" Nelson recounted. "Howard Hughes wanted me for the lead and he paid Universal a fortune. However, Jane Russell owed them a picture. They didn't have a vehicle for her so they gave her my role and built in a little part for me."[35]

Jane's involvement was also news to director John Sturges, who was under the impression he would be filming a B-picture off the coast of Catalina Island that essentially starred an Aqua-Lung (aka SCUBA diving equipment), still a novelty to many moviegoers. When he found out that the picture had been elevated in status and was set to film in Hawaii, Sturges called his agent to complain. The agent responded, "Let me see if I've got this right, John. Instead of unknowns, Hughes wants to give you his star? Instead of low-budget, he wants to give you a big-budget? Instead of faking it someplace, he wants you to go to the right place?" Without waiting for a reply, the agent snapped, "Don't ever call and bother me again!" and hung up.[36]

Gilbert Roland would be appearing opposite Jane once again, though this time he would not be her love interest. Jane's loan-out from the Hughes Tool Company would be taking a $200,000 chunk out of the budget, so her romantic lead would need to be a relative (and inexpensive) unknown. Jane sat in on the onerous process of reviewing film reels and screen tests for the perfect leading man and became fixated on Richard Egan, who had appeared in a handful of supporting parts, primarily for Universal. Hearing of Jane's involvement in the casting decision, Egan "called Jane Russell the night before our first story conference for 'Underwater' to thank her for being instrumental in getting the role for me. She was carefully cryptic about accepting my thanks. She actually sounded embarrassed."[37]

Egan was initially surprised by how demure Jane seemed, but when he met her in person, he found out otherwise. Within two hours the dark-haired Egan found himself in the chair of studio hairstylist Larry Germain because Jane had decided his character would look better with sun-bleached locks. This attempt turned Egan's hair a putrid orange so it was immediately dyed back. But Jane didn't give up—a week later she convinced Egan to go to a different stylist, who managed to produce both orange and green results. The actor then endured another session in Germain's chair, which resulted in a bleached-burned scalp. Egan flew into a rage as Jane cowered in a corner. "The master sergeant had, in an instant, changed to a frightened recruit," he later commented of Jane's response. Eventually, the desired result of dark hair with blond tips was achieved. "To be horribly honest, which I hate to do," Egan admitted, "the sun streaked hair looked very good. But I didn't mention it, and neither did Jane."[38]

The hair-bleaching incident set the tone for Jane's relationship with Richard Egan, which found them constantly engaged in good-natured sparring. "We were fighting from day one," Jane said. "Other people thought we were serious, but we weren't at all. We both adored each other, but we battled back and forth all the time."[39] Jane and Egan became great friends, and he remained one of her favorite co-stars. Egan described Jane as "sensitive, boisterous and unpredictable, impatient and growling, warm and vital, sneering at flattery but in love with the whole wide world."[40]

Production on *Underwater!* was set up off the coast of Hawaii's Kona district in November 1953, with additional scenes scheduled to be shot in Honolulu.[41] Sturges and Harry J. Wild took a crew to Kona that included Pat Dean Smith, Frank Donahue, and Jack Ackerman, who would be acting as underwater stunt doubles for Jane, Gilbert Roland, and Richard Egan. However, Roland and Young were cast after the Hawaii production began, adding an extra layer of difficulty to the location shoot. "Hughes was enough to drive you nuts," Sturges said. "In his inimitable fashion, he let me sit over there [in Hawaii]. He would not make up his mind who the leading men were. So I got as close to the divers as I dared without letting you see their faces."[42] Jane was supposed to arrive in Honolulu at the beginning of December, but inclement weather caused the shooting in Kona to be severely delayed. After about a month in Kona, the thirty-person crew returned to the mainland without Jane ever having set foot on the islands.[43] Instead the principals shot primarily on the RKO lot, where a giant water tank had been constructed. Some limited local location shooting took place on Balboa Island and at Sequit Point on what is now called Leo Carrillo State Park.[44]

Michael Woulfe was brought on again to design Jane's wardrobe, which included numerous bathing suits. Some two-piece suits were made, but as they were more modest than the bikinis the naughty French girls were wearing, Jane was agreeable. In one scene Jane was supposed to wear a nightgown while having a late-night heart-to-heart with her husband (Egan). Woulfe knew he was up to the task. "I had been so brainwashed by Hughes," Woulfe later noted, "that if a scene called for Jane in a nightgown, bingo: The nightgown must be sexy, satiny, clinging, and curvy."[45] However, Jane, feeling more empowered than at any point in her career, overruled Hughes on the nightgown design. "Michael, I want to wear a high-necked, long-sleeved nightgown in the scene," she declared. "This is not negotiable!" Woulfe was skeptical, but didn't argue. "Even with all the costume madness she endured during the production of *The French Line*," he said, "I never saw a threatening look in Jane's eyes. But I sure as hell did now."[46] Woulfe obliged, and then braced himself for the inevitable phone call from Hughes—but it never came. Inexplicably, the demure nightgown remained in the final cut without any objections from Hughes.

Underwater! was originally slated to be shot in 3D, but that proved too difficult to achieve in the underwater footage. Instead the film would mark the RKO debut of the Superscope widescreen process, which was the studio's answer to other deluxe formats such as Cinemascope and Cinerama, designed to lure viewers away from television sets and into movie theaters. Superscope was one selling point of the film, but as with her other pictures for Howard Hughes, Jane herself would be the focal point of the marketing campaign. Posters and advertisements of Jane in a red swimsuit dominated the artwork, including taglines like "Skin Diver Action . . . Aqua Lung Thrills" and "Jane Russell as You've Never Seen Her." The artwork, created by Mario Zamparelli, soon caused some mild controversy because of the bustline depicted, but not for the usual reasons. Once the posters and advertisements started circulating, Lyn Jones, a twenty-one-year-old model from New York, filed a $100,000 mental-anguish lawsuit against RKO claiming a painting of Jane's head had been placed over a painting of her body on the ads. She said she had posed for the cover of *Collier's,* which did indeed feature artwork almost identical to Zamparelli's. The artist denied it, stating that the bodies of four different Hollywood models were used to create a composite body, which Jane's likeness was then added to.[47] When the lawsuit came before a judge, no decision was made and it looked like the case was heading to trial. Then, a little over two weeks later, Jones abruptly dropped the suit, stating it was all a big mistake, while RKO held firm that there was no settlement.[48] Jones may not have received any money, but she did receive a healthy amount of press coverage, including an illustrated write-up in *Life* magazine, featuring a photo of her in a bikini. As for Jane, she had no comment on any of it.

When *Underwater!* was finally ready for release in early 1955, RKO pulled out all the stops for the premiere, which was literally held underwater. Hughes flew around two hundred members of the press to Florida to attend the premiere, which was held in a submerged "theater" in Silver Springs. This natural wonder and tourist attraction had often been used on film shoots, including *Creature from the Black Lagoon,* and was deemed a perfect spot for the unusual event. A fifteen-by-twenty-foot screen, coated in aluminum dust to increase reflection and mounted in a steel frame, was submerged in twenty feet of water. A projection booth made of glass was suspended below a boat and pointed at the screen. Participants needed to wear SCUBA gear and swim down to the benches anchored at the floor of the springs in order to watch the film. Jane, Lori Nelson, and Richard Eagan attended the premiere and were good sports, donning swimsuits, fins, and Aqua-Lungs, and submerging themselves in the water. Most viewers reportedly lasted only five to ten minutes underwater before rising back to the surface. Gilbert Roland, who was not a fan of water, opted out and skipped the premiere altogether. Those guests who preferred not to get wet were invited to view the film

Jane and Richard Egan decked out in SCUBA gear for the literal underwater premiere of *Underwater!* in Silver Springs, Florida.

through the portholes of submarines. Others chose to get a glimpse of the setup via glass-bottom boats. The stunt reportedly cost RKO $80,000.[49]

In addition to members of the press, other actors attended the premiere, including Debbie Reynolds, Barbara Darrow, and Jayne Mansfield. Over the years Hollywood lore has arisen around Mansfield's appearance: (1) her agent surreptitiously got her onto one of the chartered planes to Florida; (2) during the premiere a strap of her red bikini broke when she jumped into the water, exposing her own ample bosom to the crowd of media covering the event; and (3) Jane Russell became so enraged by the attention the other Jayne was getting, she stormed off in a huff. Mansfield's presence was certainly noted in press coverage, but if her top really flew off, it doesn't appear to have been covered in mainstream media. The most that seemed to have been written about Mansfield's appearance was "Jayne Mansfield, wearing a Bikini suit and diving mask, several times was mistaken for Jane Russell."[50] Jane's alleged fit of temperament is also dubious; it would certainly have been out of character and writer Bob Thomas, who attended the event, later said, "Ah yes. That was indeed a dizzying episode of Hollywood madness. Jane Russell, sweet lady that she is, wasn't at all peeved that Jayne hogged the spotlight."[51] If it seemed that Jayne "hogged the spotlight" at the event, the actual write-ups remained loyal to the studio that hosted the event. Of Mansfield's appearance, Edith Lynch would say, "We've always believed that Jayne Mansfield, then a newcomer at Fox, was first boosted by RKO. She had brought a bathing suit that Jane R. would have never dared wear. One look around after her arrival, Jane asked, 'Who's the blonde tomato?' Never one to articulate, she gets it all said in one sentence."[52]

When *Underwater!* opened in New York, RKO continued to pull out all the stops. A swimsuit-clad Jane floated high above Times Square after a five-story billboard was wrapped around the building that housed the Mayfair Theatre. Unfortunately, the film turned out to be less exciting than the posters or exclamation point in the title suggest. *New York Times* film critic Bosley Crowther commented, "Seldom has anything so trifling as this story of delving for treasure beneath the seas been dished up as feature entertainment." He concluded, "The presentation of Miss Russell is like one of those fountain pens that is guaranteed to write underwater. It is novel but impractical. Miss Russell does nothing underwater that she hasn't done better above."[53] Jane's decision to play her character as a Cuban hasn't aged particularly well, though it's doubtful her inconsistent accent and bronzed skin, obtained while sunbathing on the roof of an RKO building, were ever well received. As was the case with *The Outlaw*, the advertising outshone the actual film.

Underwater! did, however, end up being a significant film for Jane Russell, but not because of her performance or the advertising. As it turned out, *Underwater!* would be the last film Jane Russell ever made for Howard Hughes.

19

WAIF

After Jane and Robert formally adopted Thomas Kavanagh, the media circus died down and they were poised to move on as a family. However, the entire incident continued to rankle Jane, and she remained especially haunted by the visits she had made to European orphanages at the end of 1951. At a German orphanage she had been told that approving the international placement of a boy she wanted to adopt would take congressional approval. She had been compelled to leave the German boy behind, but after the adoption of Thomas was finalized, she decided to turn her attention to lobbying Washington for change. "Rather than obtain a special act of Congress for one child, I vowed then and there to at least try to get our country's doors open for homeless children."[1]

In addition to tackling legislation, Jane was also interested in forming some sort of organization that could play a role in facilitating international adoption. Not knowing how to do this, she turned to her lawyer Samuel S. Zagon, who helped her set up the International Adoption Association (IAA), a nonprofit corporation. Figuring this was just a movie star whim, Zagon, according to Jane, "said 'I think it is very nice, and I think it is very charitable of you, and I will certainly help if I can,' and then he figuratively patted me on the head in a 'go away little girl' manner."[2] Jane was quick to add, "He has gotten himself into more problems as a result of our first meeting than he ever dreamed of, I'm sure."[3]

Jane became president of the IAA and turned to her Hollywood friends to establish a board of governors and group of supporters that included Irene Dunne, ZaSu Pitts, Frances Marion, Adela Rogers St. Johns, Loretta Young, Colleen Townsend, June Allyson, Dick Powell, Dale Evans, Roy Rogers, Bob and Dolores Hope, and Vincent Price. Initially the group hoped to determine how many children could be admitted into the country if some sort of formalized international adoption program were set up. Instead it was the ongoing war in Korea that soon provided the opportunity to promote legislative

Jane and an unidentified woman sit in the courtyard of the Turnabout Theater with Forman Brown, proprietor of the theater, in preparation for a WAIF benefit to be held there. (Yale Puppeteers & Turnabout Theatre Collection/Los Angeles Public Library)

change. Like World War II, the Korean War had produced a large number of orphaned children. Some US military personnel expressed an interest in assuming custody of Korean-born children, but were prohibited from adopting, largely due to immigration quotas. Emergency legislation was proposed in 1953 that would authorize five hundred foreign-born children under the age of six to enter the country and be adopted by American military personnel. This may not have been exactly what Jane had in mind, but it was a start. In May 1953 she got her feet wet in political lobbying by flying to Washington, DC, to speak to congressional members at a luncheon and advocate for the bill's passage, which finally happened that July.

Jane was anxious for the IAA to play a meaningful role in international adoption and believed the best way to do this was to piggyback on an existing organization already doing the work she was interested in. The problem was she didn't know if these types of organizations even existed. As Jane recounted, "I wrote letters to various and sundry organizations to find out if there were any existing organizations doing inter country adoption—and I either received vague replies or none at all."[4] Jane even contacted former First Lady Eleanor Roosevelt, who was supportive but didn't have any suggestions. Jane was finally steered to the Ford Foundation, a philanthropic organization founded by Henry Ford and his son Edsel that focused on human welfare. Joseph McDaniel Jr., secretary of the Ford Foundation, responded to Jane immediately, suggesting she contact International Social Service (ISS), an international nongovernmental organization that, for nearly thirty years, had been specializing in the welfare of children faced with "complex social problems as a result of migration."[5] McDaniel wrote a letter of introduction to William T. Kirk, general director of International Social Service, and on May 12, 1953, Jane wrote her own letter to Kirk, noting, "We are not lobbyists for any particular bill, but are simply American citizens trying to get as many children as possible out of institutions and into qualified homes."[6] Within days Jane received a response from Kirk: "I have just returned from Switzerland, where we have had a world conference of our offices, and one of the main topics was intercountry adoption. . . . At present we do not have sufficient funds. . . . We are swamped with the casework already at hand. . . . But, can you come to New York and talk?"[7]

Jane's timing could not have been better. In August 1953 Congress passed the Refugee Relief Act, which included the approval of four thousand nonquota immigrant visas for eligible orphaned children. In the months leading up to the passage of the act, Jane worked tirelessly, contacting members of the House and Senate to support the legislation. She noted, "The more I look at the overall picture, the more I am convinced that our job is not only to coordinate existing adoption channels but also to develop a public relations effort geared to educating citizens of the world by every means available, including screen, television, radio, newspapers, and magazine articles."[8] To enact this

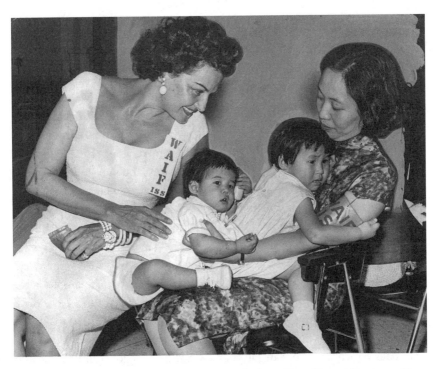

Jane with two orphans newly arrived in Los Angeles from Hong Kong. Also pictured is Mrs. G. Lee, who accompanied the two girls and forty-seven other children on the long plane ride in June 1962. (Art Worden, Los Angeles Herald Examiner Collection/Los Angeles Public Library)

publicity campaign in favor of the Refugee Relief Act, Jane turned to none other than Russell Birdwell, the same man who had implemented the "mean, moody, magnificent" marketing campaign for *The Outlaw* a decade before. Jane may have resented Birdwell packaging her like a can of tomatoes, but she was more than happy to utilize his talents to promote this cause.

With the passage of the Refugee Relief Act, the doors had been opened for international adoption, and it became clear to Jane that the biggest contribution she could make would be in the areas of public education and fundraising. In September 1954 the International Adoption Association was absorbed by International Social Service, and Jane, along with Samuel Zagon, was elected to the board of ISS. In place of the IAA, a new division called WAIF was formed to serve as the fund-raising arm of ISS. Funds raised by WAIF would go directly to ISS and, according to Jane, be "used for salaries and expenses of workers in International Social Service's twenty foreign offices who handle all the details of locating the children and processing the necessary adoption papers."[9] Jane Russell had become an official player in a global organization, headquartered in Geneva. WAIF would operate out of Los Angeles.

WAIF turned out to be an ideal way for Jane to use her movie star status and industry connections to benefit a cause she so vehemently championed. Over the years WAIF hosted countless fund-raising galas, including the annual star-studded Imperial Ball, held at various locations around Los Angeles including the Beverly Hilton, the Ambassador Hotel, and the Hollywood Palladium (where Princess Margaret and her husband Lord Snowdon were honored guests in 1965). Gerry Cornez, who would serve as WAIF's executive director starting in the 1970s, remembered learning about these events as a child. "When I was a kid," he said, "I sort of knew about it [WAIF] because I would read about it in fan magazines. I would always see about the WAIF Ball, 'Oh, look at all these stars.' I had no idea what WAIF was or what it meant, but there was a ball and I wanted to be a famous actor, so therefore this is gonna be my life and I better get used to it. Little did I know that I'd be running that ball from the kitchen!"[10] In addition to the Los Angeles office, Jane helped establish successful chapters in Palm Springs, Palmdale, San Francisco, San Diego, New York, Chicago, Honolulu, Seattle, and Portland.

Jane also used Howard Hughes to benefit WAIF, though he was probably none the wiser. "When Perry [Lieber] wanted me to make a personal appearance," Jane said, "I would say 'Okay, but I get a round trip ticket anywhere I want to go, no questions asked.' We'd go and do the thing and then I'd go to Washington and nag Senators and Congressmen and we got laws changed, and all kinds of things. Every time we had a fundraiser, or anything, the Hughes office would take a whole table or two tables, or something. In a way, without Howard Hughes, we never would have gotten WAIF going. I don't think he even knew about it!"[11] Throughout the years Jane dedicated a portion of her earnings to WAIF, and would often convince the studios she worked at to match her salary dollar for dollar as a donation to WAIF.[12]

Jane also encouraged her fans to support WAIF. Those who wrote to her requesting an autographed photo would receive, along with the photo, a letter stating, "In return for this photo, I ask that you send a few dollars to WAIF—it would really help. If you can send more, it would help tremendously. Contributions of $20 or more will make you a national member of WAIF—then you'll *really* be a member of my fan club!"[13] WAIF would operate under ISS for twenty-four years, and then independently for another

Robert Waterfield and Jane view artist Margaret Keane's *Tomorrow Forever,* on display during a WAIF function in 1963. (Los Angeles Herald Examiner Collection/Los Angeles Public Library)

twenty-three. For over four decades Jane used every method at her disposal to benefit WAIF. Her screen image had often been at odds with her real personality, but Jane was able to see the movie star persona as a means to an end, the promotion of WAIF. "One thing I would say about Jane," Gerry Cornez reflected, "is because she became a star so young, anything she wanted in life was a phone call away. So she could get to Eleanor Roosevelt and she could get to the Ford Foundation and she could do all of these things. She could go back to Los Angeles and get people like Bob and Dolores Hope and Roy Rogers and Dale Evans—both sets of those people were adoptive parents—to get involved and to run benefits and to show up and to get people like Frank Sinatra."[14] In an attempt to encapsulate her on-screen/off-screen qualities, writer Jim Henaghan wrote, "By any standard, Jane Russell is an enigmatic figure, because very few know her completely. To the movie fan, she is a legend. To actors and actresses, she's a good person to work with. To her children, she's 'Mama' for real—and to the lonely kids of the world, she's hope."[15]

Jane greets Franklin D. Murphy, chancellor of UCLA, and his wife, Judith Harris Murphy, at the 1967 WAIF Imperial Ball, held at the Beverly Hilton Hotel. The ball was one of WAIF's hallmark fund-raising events. (Los Angeles Herald Examiner Collection/ Los Angeles Public Library)

In addition to fund-raising and meeting with politicians, Jane would often personally welcome children to the United States as they were beginning their new lives. "One of the most touching experiences in this world," Jane said, "is to meet a plane with from five to twenty children arriving in the United States from Greece, Germany, Italy, or Korea, Japan, or Hong Kong. The parents are there to claim them, happy and anxious."[16] One flight from Hong Kong containing forty-nine children was met not only by Jane but by Attorney General Robert Kennedy. Jane also traveled around the world, meeting with the ISS social workers who handled the adoption caseloads. She was surprised to learn that "to qualify for this work, one must have a science degree plus two years' of graduate study in social work. And yet, like so many employed in the field of services, they receive little more than adequate income. They have to be dedicated people—and they are."[17]

Over the years WAIF has often been referenced as an acronym standing for Women's Adoption International Fund or World Adoption International

Fund. Jane preferred to refer to it as just plain WAIF, an organization meant to assist the homeless waifs of the world. "Some publicist decided that acronyms were 'in,'" said Gerry Cornez, "so he devised one and, unfortunately, we were never able to shake it."[18]

Jane would often cite Marilyn Monroe to exemplify what a "waif" meant to her; she firmly believed that Marilyn's lack of a stable home base growing up caused so many of the anxieties and insecurities that plagued her as an adult. Jane did acknowledge that, ideally, children should remain in their native countries, but when in-county adoption proved impossible, "immigration to another country where the resources and child welfare systems would allow them to find the families they needed, would be best."[19] In short, Jane's approach was for WAIF to seek "families for children and not children for families. For the child is the client; the child is the one in need."[20] Jane would further elaborate on this philosophy: "Months of careful work have been given toward effecting these unions and the rewards are gratifying, knowing that childless homes are brightened but, more important that abandoned and orphaned children have been given their rightful heritage—the security of loving parents and homes."[21]

During WAIF's first seven years, ninety-five hundred children were placed in adoptive homes.[22] By the time the organization ceased operation in 2000, that number had grown fourfold. "During the time that WAIF existed," Cornez stated, "which was like forty-five years, forty thousand kids found families. I used to call Jane the godmother of all these kids."[23]

20

Russ-Field

As Jane stared down the end of her contract with Howard Hughes, she was starting to envision a future without him. She was unimpressed with most of the films Hughes had put her in, and was sick of his modes of publicity. However, there was still a part of her that remained loyal to her longtime boss. The *French Line* bikini incident had been a tipping point for Jane, but even then, she was still open to maintaining a working relationship with Hughes, noting, "I'll sign with Howard again, but for one picture a year only."[1] However, after viewing the final cut of *The French Line* and getting caught in the middle of the backlash over the film's release, Jane had finally been pushed over the edge. When February rolled around, she did not renew her contract with the Hughes Tool Company, though negotiations remained open. "I'm just not ever again going to be put in the position of having to make a picture as questionable as 'French Line,'" she said. "I hated it from the beginning, but it was never as shocking as the camera angles that made the finished product."[2] Two months before making this proclamation, Jane had already taken a step toward independence by forming a production company with Robert Waterfield called the Russ-Field Corporation.

Waterfield had retired at the end of the 1952 football season, wryly stating, "I'm old . . . and tired."[3] For his last home game in December 1952, sixty thousand fans packed into the Los Angeles Coliseum to pay their respects to the man whom the *Los Angeles Times* called "one of the greatest football players of all time."[4] The Rams retired his jersey number, seven, during the day's festivities, and he was inducted into the local Helms Hall Major Football Hall of Fame.[5] Despite being married to an internationally known movie star with a dominating personality, Robert Waterfield had managed to stand apart and carve out a name for himself. Now that his playing days were behind him, he was going to turn his attention to the film industry and go into business with his wife. Waterfield wasn't a complete stranger to movie sets. In the early 1940s he had briefly worked as a stunt double for actor Michael O'Shea. More

228

Jane and Robert Waterfield share a serious moment during their Russ-Field period.

recently he had appeared as "the man who throws thunder with his hands!" in *Jungle Manhunt,* an installment in the Johnny Weissmuller Jungle Jim series. He had also played himself in *Crazylegs,* a biopic about Rams team-mate Elroy Hirsch. Now he would be focusing his energies on the business side of production.

Even before filming ended on *Underwater!* in February 1954, reports started showing up that Russ-Field's first film would be a screen adaptation of the musical *Guys and Dolls,* produced by Bill Goetz and starring Jane and Clark Gable.[6] There were also rumors that Dick Powell was hoping to direct Jane, Robert Mitchum, and John Wayne in a film called *The Long Wire.*[7] Instead Jane and Robert signed a six-picture distribution deal with United Artists, which included a provision that Jane would star in three of the six films. For its first picture, Russ-Field purchased the rights to an unpublished manuscript titled "The Way of an Eagle" written by Margaret Obegi, a San Fernando Valley friend who wrote it with Jane in mind. Hunting for a suit-able co-star, Jane set her sights on Jeff Chandler after seeing the Brooklyn-born actor's portrayal of the Apache leader Cochise in the film *Broken Arrow.* Chandler was under contract to Universal-International at the time, so the studio used the impending loan-out as leverage to get Jane to do a picture for it. Chandler was already lined up to star in *Foxfire*, a Technicolor melodrama that June Allyson had been slated for but had recently dropped out of. Jane agreed to star in *Foxfire*, which was produced by Aaron Rosenberg and made as a loan-out from the Russ-Field Corporation. Production was scheduled for June 1954.

Foxfire was an adaptation of Anya Seton's novel of the same name. Known for her extensively researched historical novels, Seton had been inspired to write *Foxfire* after visiting a remote Arizona mining town whose glory days were long in the past. The screenplay, written by future Pulitzer Prize winner Ketti Frings, was a loose adaptation of the source material. The Great Depression setting was updated to a modern one, and this adaptation would be oozing with Hollywood stylings. In the film, Amanda Lawrence (Jane) is a New York socialite who impulsively marries Dart (Chandler), a brooding mining operations manager in a small Arizona town. Amanda finds herself navigating a relationship with a moody man she barely knows while adapting to life in a small town whose residents exhibit their fair share of prejudice against the local Native Americans, including her husband, who is half Apache.

Directed by Joseph Pevney and co-starring noir favorite Dan Duryea, *Foxfire* was shot on location in both Oatman and Kingman, Arizona, as well as the Apple Valley Inn, a once-trendy resort. Jane was able to bring her usual hair and makeup crew with her, but this time Harry J. Wild would not be photographing her. Instead she would have the opportunity to work with legendary Oscar-winning cinematographer William H. Daniels, whose long career included over twenty films with Greta Garbo. Jane would also be working with a new costume designer. Bill Thomas would go on to win an Academy Award for *Spartacus*, but for *Foxfire* he designed a simple but extremely eye-catching wardrobe for Jane, taking full advantage of the Technicolor process by incorporating bold hues into his creations. For once Jane's costumes were not being scrutinized by Howard Hughes, much to the relief of Jane and her designer. "A woman is much more exciting when she's covered," Thomas said while working on *Foxfire*. "Jane Russell knows this too. She was delighted when we talked about covered-up dresses for this new picture. She said she'd been trying for that for years." He continued, "I've left her arms bare, but the necklines are cut up to the throat. There's one evening dress with narrow straps over the shoulders, but nothing strapless. I don't like strapless on anyone."[8] Even though Jane wasn't with her whole RKO family, she enjoyed the film, later calling it "a good one . . . Joe Pevney churned it out in a few weeks."[9]

Costume designer Bill Thomas and Jane look over sketches for *Foxfire.*

Foxfire, although one of Jane's lesser-known films, is one of the most interesting of her career. She infused a great deal of her own character and personality into the role of Amanda, but it's an earnest performance, setting it apart from comedic roles like the dry Calamity Jane in *The Paleface* or the sarcastic Dorothy Shaw in *Gentlemen Prefer Blondes.* The film's exploration of interracial relationships and prejudice against Native Americans is unusual for the time, as is its (Production Code–approved) handling of the subject of miscarriage. The relationship between Amanda and Dart has its moments of music-swelling Hollywood passion, but it is also complicated and frequently unhappy. As was typical of the time, non–Native American actors were cast, including the bizarre decision to have Austrian-born Celia Lovsky portray an Indian princess living on an Apache reservation. This "brown face" casting extended to Jeff Chandler, who desperately wanted to avoid becoming type-cast in Native American roles, but who welcomed the part in *Foxfire,* which had more depth than his previous characters. The film also gave Chandler the opportunity to sing the movie's theme song, for which he also wrote the lyr-ics. The accompanying music was composed by Henry Mancini, who was in the midst of a prolific run at Universal-International. *Foxfire* proved to be notable in that it was the last American film made with the three-strip Technicolor process, "which is why I still looked great when I watched it on TV," Jane joked later on.[10] For a story set in a decaying town, the film is gor-geous, largely due to the color and costume designs. "It's amazing," film his-torian Kat Ellinger commented, "how much glamour Hollywood can really, really squeeze into this desert mining town."[11]

While Jane was making *Foxfire,* she was also in pre-production on Russ-Field's first film. The proposed *Way of the Eagle* with Jeff Chandler never got off the ground after Jane lost the lone copy of the manuscript, so Russ-Field's inaugural production would instead be *Gentlemen Marry Brunettes.*[12] Jane had been cool to making this pseudo-sequel to *Gentlemen Prefer Blondes,* but United Artists thought it was a slam dunk and insisted on it as part of the dis-tribution deal. Anita Loos had written the sequel to her hit novel, but for this film, only the title would be retained. Mary Loos and Richard Sale, who penned *The French Line,* handled the screenplay, which turned out to be a complete departure from the source material, featuring all new characters. Instead of the beloved Lorelei Lee and Dorothy Shaw, *Gentlemen Marry Brunettes* focuses on the Jones Sisters (portrayed by Jane and Jeanne Crain), New York showgirls who are lured to Paris by an agent who hopes they will be as big a draw as their sister-act mother and aunt had been decades before. Richard Sale would direct the film, and Robert Waterfield would receive his first on-screen producing credit. Filmed in color and in the CinemaScope widescreen process, the movie would be shot on location in Paris and Monte Carlo with interiors at the Shepperton Studios outside of London. It seemed no expense was being spared for the production—until Alan Young and Scott Brady were cast as the romantic leads. "I was frantic," Jane later wrote. "Both guys are dear and I had loved Scott like a brother since we worked

Jane and Jeanne Crain in costume for the "I Wanna Be Loved by You" number in *Gentlemen Marry Brunettes.* The costume had originally been designed for Marilyn Monroe to wear while performing "Diamonds Are a Girl's Best Friend," but was ultimately rejected as too risqué.

together in *Montana Belle,* but how were we going to sell enough tickets to cover that very expensive budget?"[13] Alan Young later joked, "Jane was the big budget; I sure wasn't!"[14]

In an attempt to strike gold twice, Jack Cole was once again brought on to do the choreography, with Gwen Verdon assisting. *Blondes* alum William Travilla designed the costumes. For Jane and Jeanne's rendition of "I Wanna

Be Loved by You," he resurrected a frock originally designed for Marilyn Monroe to wear while performing "Diamonds Are a Girl's Best Friend." That costume had been rejected, deemed too risqué when *Gentlemen Prefer Blondes* was being filmed, but Travilla added massive amounts of feathers, which apparently made the bejeweled net outfits modest enough. Jane was apprehensive about the scope of the film, noting, "I felt that a big expensive production was being hung on my shoulders, and they just weren't broad enough."[15] She also fretted about leaving Thomas and Tracy behind for the shoot, projected to last several months. Given the media circus that had surrounded Jane the last time she was in Europe, she felt it best to leave them at home with Robert. To make matters worse, Jane was able to secure a work permit only for her stand-in Carmen Nisbet, so the rest of the regular crew would not be working with her.[16] On September 8, 1954, she boarded a TWA flight with Carmen and flew to Paris.[17]

The shoot was scheduled to last three and a half months, which turned out to be unbearable for Jane. It didn't help that the Parisian press was less enamored with Jane than with her French-speaking co-star Jeanne Crain. "I guess I didn't let them be their charming selves with me," Jane said with typical candor, "but when it comes to hand-kissing, it always leaves me a little on my left foot. I'm strictly from the San Fernando Valley, shall we say."[18] After a month Jane became so achingly homesick that when Robert arrived for a visit, "I knocked him to the floor and raped him," Jane later wrote. "Then I threw my arms around him and cried like a baby."[19] Waterfield was supposed to stay for a month, but Jane was so despondent that he extended the visit even though he "didn't have anything to do and was bored to death," said Jane. "But he stayed on because he knew it helped me."[20] The shoot dragged on, and when Jane discovered she would not have enough time to go back to Los Angeles for Christmas, she was beside herself. She vented her frustrations in a letter from London to columnist Hedda Hopper, whom she addressed as "Dear Mother." "This picture Gentlemen Marry—is going on forever. I burst a blood vessel the day they told me—'no home for Xmas.' My old man is with me—but I'm sure he'll go home to have X-mas with our poor children. I'll probably head for the Alps & bury my head in a jar of hot buttered rum & self pity. Jeanne Crain is luckier—Her old man has gone home to collect all four children & bring them back. I can't bring my son to this city."

Jane continued on a lighter note: "On one side of us we have Jean Simmons & Stewart Granger making a picture, 'Deadlock,' & on the other side none of the crew wear hats anymore—it's too much trouble taking them off. They have four Sirs in the picture Sir Laurence Olivier, Sir Cedric Hardwick [*sic*], Sir Ralph Richardson, & John Gielgud. But I've got news for them—their crew all sneak over onto our set to watch us shake the beads." She signed off, "See you next year,—love, Old Jane."[21]

While working in Paris, Jane visited famed fashion designer Christian Dior, who had recently been touting a "flat chested look." The press delighted in reporting that with Jane, Dior was up against his biggest challenge. "Do not worry," the designer's aide promised, "Miss Russell presents us with no problems we cannot overcome." After the fitting, reporters were equally delighted to run headlines proclaiming, "Christian Dior Fails to Debosom Our Jane."[22] When filming moved over to London, Jane was once again invited to the Royal Command Performance where she, along with Rudy Vallee and Shelley Winters, was presented to Queen Elizabeth II.

When the film was finally released in October 1955, it was met with a lukewarm reception by both critics and audiences. The *New York Times* called it "an aimless, uninspired charade that is saved from being a complete dud by a clutch of sturdy standard tunes and a quick Cook's Tour of Paris and the Riviera. The brunettes look good, too, but one wonders how they ever got involved in this witless adventure."[23] Despite the production value, the film is uneven and drawn out, and the decision for Jane to play the wide-eyed Lorelei-like role was a huge misfire. Much of the film is set outside to take advantage of Paris, but many of these scenes come off as extraneous and seemingly included for no other reason than to justify the location shoot. The "sturdy standard tunes" referenced in the *Times* review consisted of multiple Rodgers and Hart songs like "Have You Met Miss Jones?" and "My Funny Valentine," along with other past hits like "I Wanna Be Loved by You" and "Ain't Misbehavin'." These musical numbers are also hit or miss. For example, "Ain't Misbehavin'," which features Jane and Jeanne in an oversized cooking pot surrounded by blackface (and bodied) natives, has not aged well.

The film isn't completely without its virtues. The flashback scenes with Jane and Jeanne portraying the flapper sister act are high energy and fun, and Jane is a hoot when taking on the role of the Jones Sisters' elderly mother. Rudy Vallee, playing himself, is a highlight, as is the Christian Dior wardrobe featured in a scene where the sisters are lavished with gifts and clothes. The scenes where the sisters pass up one job after another due to French costume requirements (or lack thereof) bring a smile, as does Jane and Jeanne's fan-dance version of the song "Daddy." It's not a great film, but it's enjoyable enough; it suffers mainly because of its title. *Gentlemen Marry Brunettes* deceptively sets the viewer up to watch a sequel to *Gentlemen Prefer Blondes,* but then doesn't deliver. The film "needed Marilyn," Jane later mused. "No doubt about it."[24]

As Jane spent her lonely Christmas in Europe, counting the days until production was over, Howard Hughes was preparing to deliver a belated holiday gift. Jane had failed to renew her contract with Hughes in February, but the mogul had not given up on staying in business with one of his favorite stars. Even though he was on the verge of selling RKO and getting out of the motion picture business altogether, he had maintained negotiations with Jane's agents throughout 1954. "Howard couldn't bring himself to part with her," Noah Dietrich said, "even though he was phasing out his motion picture production. After all, he had made her a star, and he didn't want other producers to be cashing in on what he created."[25] Now that Jane had her production company and marquee name, she no longer needed Howard Hughes. The only reasons she really had for signing another contract with him were sheer loyalty to her boss and some sort of amazing incentive, too good to pass up.

The deal that Hughes ultimately came up with was an astoundingly good one for Jane. She was to make six pictures for Hughes over the course of five years, or be loaned out to another studio at Hughes's discretion. She would be allowed to make an additional eight pictures outside of the Hughes agreement, though they would need to be "Class 'A' feature length motion pictures," with one of them specified as "*The Ten Commandments,* to be produced by Cecil B. DeMille, or a feature length motion picture of similar quality and magnitude."[26] Film shoots would be limited to sixteen weeks, lest additional monetary compensation accrue, and her work days would be from 9:00 a.m. to 6:00 p.m., with some exceptions. The cherry on top of the deal was that Jane would get paid $1 million for the five years of work, or $166,666.67 per picture. Instead of being paid per film, she would receive $961.54 per week for twenty years.[27] In other words, she would work for five years, but get paid another fifteen for doing nothing. Noah Dietrich found the deal questionable, but Hughes explained his rationale to Dietrich: "I'm paying her a million dollars for five pictures—two hundred thousand per picture for a star of her caliber is not bad at all. But by paying her over a twenty-year period, . . . I'm really paying her only half a million, because I can invest the money and get back a half-million in interest."[28] As Jane said simply, "He wanted to make the deal attractive enough so I would sign. And he succeeded."[29]

Lew Wasserman at MCA had been trying to get Jane to leave Howard Hughes for over a decade, since 1943, when he first encouraged her to break

Jane hugs Tracy and Thomas at Idlewild in January 1955, in between flying from the *Gentlemen Marry Brunettes* shoot in Europe to the *Underwater!* premiere in Florida.

her contract while on suspension. When he got a look at the deal Hughes was proposing, he asked Jane, "Are you sleeping with this guy?"[30] Other than one instance when Jane had spent the night in Hughes's guest room, and he had made a failed attempt to re-create the bed-warming scene in *The Outlaw,* Jane and Howard's relationship had been strictly platonic. They had always maintained a mutual respect for each other, though Jane wasn't shy about speaking her mind. "I often hollered at Howard," she wrote, "and I think in a funny kind of way I scared him. Jim Bacon, the columnist on the *Los Angeles Herald Examiner,* told me Howard had once confided to him, 'That woman terrified me.'"[31] Jane had also been extremely loyal to Hughes, which is something he valued immensely. Looking back on the twenty-year deal, Jane commented, "I know he did it because I finished out that first lousy contract."[32] Wasserman couldn't see any reason for Jane not to agree to the deal, so on December 29, 1954, Jane entered into her third and final contract with Howard Hughes. Almost immediately, Twentieth Century-Fox agreed to take three of the six pictures in the deal.[33]

Production on *Gentlemen Marry Brunettes* wrapped shortly after the New Year. Jane was desperate to leave London and get back home to her children. Instead Howard Hughes gave her a momentary reason to regret signing with him again. The *Underwater!* premiere in Silver Springs, Florida, was scheduled for January 10 and there wasn't time for Jane to cross the country twice. When Perry Lieber at RKO notified Jane that she was needed in Florida, she shrieked "No!" but Hughes was adamant: no Jane—no premiere. Lieber agreed to fly Tracy and Thomas, along with Frances Waterfield and a friend, to New York to meet Jane's incoming flight, which left London on January 6.[34] The children were thrilled to see their mother, especially Thomas, who clung to Jane throughout the night. The next day Jane and the kids spent the day with Vincent Price, who was recovering from a disastrous four-performance run of the play *Black-Eyed Susan.* He probably welcomed the distraction of taking Jane and the kids in a horse-drawn carriage around Central Park. Early the next morning, Jane snuck out of the hotel to take a plane down to Florida for the *Underwater!* premiere, and almost as quickly flew back to New York, where Frances and the kids were waiting. Thomas refused to speak to Jane, thinking he had been abandoned. He gradually warmed up to his mother again, and the stutter he had developed during her absence eventually disappeared. After returning home, Jane fell ill with the flu and went to Palm Springs to recuperate.[35]

Jane's reunion with the family was short-lived, as she got ready to go back to work. Her first picture under the new deal would be *The Tall Men,* a big-budget CinemaScope western for Twentieth Century-Fox starring Clark Gable and directed by Raoul Walsh. The story line focused on a longhorn cattle run from Texas to Montana in the post–Civil War era, with a love triangle thrown in for good measure. The script called for more heads of cattle

Jane adored Clark Gable, her co-star on *The Tall Men*. Here the two take a break while on location in Durango, Mexico.

than could be procured, so production would take place in the countryside outside of Durango, Mexico, where a sufficient amount of steers could be gathered for the film. Once again Jane would need to be on location for a long stretch of time. She wasn't happy about the location shoot, but was thrilled to be working with both Gable and Walsh. Jane and Gable hit it off immediately. She would often refer to him as "the biggest tease who ever walked."[36] Gable had just become engaged to Kay Williams and was in high spirits. On set he took to referring to Jane as "Grandma," the nickname his character uses for hers in the script. Despite their twenty-year age difference, the pair also got along well on-screen. "He was fifty-four and very aware of the passing of time," Jane later said. "Did we have chemistry? I think so—I adored him, respected him, and so did the audience."[37] The passage of time had not diminished Gable's stature as the King of Hollywood, so he would receive top billing over Jane, a rare occurrence for her 1950s films.

Jane was especially happy to be working with Raoul Walsh. Others may have found the director's gruff exterior off-putting, but not Jane. "I adored him," she would often say. "I called him Father."[38] Jane sent Walsh telegrams on

Father's Day every year and would stay in touch with the man she called "gruff and wonderful and soft as sugar inside" until his death in 1980.[39] Walsh was equally impressed with Jane, later writing, "Jane was her usual tall graceful self. Her hair was black as a raven's wing, accentuated by black earrings contrasting with those famous white hands of hers." He also noted, "Jane Russell endeared herself to every Durango citizen under the age of ten to twelve by hiring all the ice-cream carts in town and leading the happy owners into the largest mixed-school yard. Watching her one day, Carlos [a local resident assisting on the production] said, 'That one has a heart as big as the world.' Like every male around, he was in love with Jane and made no effort to hide how he felt."[40]

Robert Waterfield had not accompanied Jane on the shoot. The marriage had gradually been becoming more strained, and a few weeks into production he called Jane unexpectedly, asking if she wanted a divorce. She didn't. A few days later he arrived on set and although he was distant at first, he eventually warmed up. Robert had expressed little interest in *Gentlemen Marry Brunettes,* but an outdoor opus with Clark Gable and Raoul Walsh was more his pace. Gable enjoyed poking fun at Waterfield by loudly asking Jane about John Payne whenever Robert was in earshot. Nonetheless, before the end of the shoot, Robert had lined up Gable and Walsh for Russ-Feld's next proposed production, *Last Man on the Wagon Mound.* It would be another year before production commenced on the film, which would be a joint venture between Russ-Field and Gable's production company GABCO. It was released at the end of 1956 as *The King and Four Queens,* co-starring Eleanor Parker, Jo Van Fleet, Barbara Nichols, and Jean Willes, who had been a witness at Jane and Robert's wedding in 1943.

Released in the fall of 1955, *The Tall Men* would end up being one of Gable's bigger hits of the 1950s, and one of Jane's bigger-budget productions. Co-starring Robert Ryan and Cameron Mitchell, and featuring a sweeping score by Victor Young, *The Tall Men* is a visually arresting film that shows off the widescreen CinemaScope process to its full advantage. Jane worked with William Travilla a third time, and his designs managed to be appropriately low on glamour but still incredible complimentary to Jane. In her overall filmography, *The Tall Men* is a highlight.

Jane finished work on *The Tall Men* in June 1955, and barely had time to catch her breath before reporting to Columbia Pictures for *Hot Blood,* opposite Cornel Wilde. Originally titled *No Return* and later *Tambourine, Hot Blood* was the brainchild of director Nicholas Ray and had been in development at RKO since 1952. Ray's first wife, Jean Evans, had conducted extensive firsthand research on a Romani gypsy community in New York's Lower East Side, which Ray had found captivating. Drawing from Evans's research, Ray sought to direct a film that would accurately reflect the lives and customs of the Romani people. He hired Walter Newman to write the screenplay; Newman produced a sober script with a downbeat ending. Ray was enthusiastic about the script, as was Jane, and he wanted to cast her opposite Marlon Brando. However, when Brando's availability seemed increasingly unlikely, Robert Mitchum was considered. Ultimately, development came to a complete standstill when RKO executives started regarding the project as too "arthouse."[41] Producer Howard Welsch eventually bought the rights back from RKO and, at Jane's request, brought on co-producer Harry Tatelman, who had originally wanted Nicholas Ray for *Underwater!* In 1955 a deal was struck with Columbia, which wanted the production to start in July of that year. However, the three-year lag had made a detrimental impact on the film. Ray and Jane were still attached, but Jane had been so consumed with Russ-Field and back-to-back-to-back film productions that she was unable to muster enthusiasm for much of anything. Ray had just finished *Rebel without a Cause* with James Dean and was still heavily involved in post-production on that film. "The tragedy and the flaws of the film," Ray said of *Hot Blood*, "can be attributed to my overestimation of my own capacities and my underestimation of my involvement in *Rebel Without a Cause*."[42]

Hot Blood had an additional hurdle to overcome when Columbia executives requested extensive rewrites, which Walter Newman was unwilling to execute. Jesse Lasky Jr. was hired instead and even did some additional firsthand research by interviewing the king of the Gypsies in Los Angeles. However, now that the production schedule had been launched into hyperdrive, much of the authenticity Ray hoped to bring to the story fell by the wayside in the rush to get the script approved and the cameras rolling. This was compounded when the decision was made to film not in New York City but on the studio back lot, setting the film in a nondescript urban location that looks suspiciously like suburban Los Angeles, thanks to a couple of scenes shot on Lankershim Boulevard in North Hollywood.

Jane had been wanting to work with Ray ever since he had done the reshoots on *Macao,* but she was so exhausted that this production was one of the few times she exhibited move star temperament. *Hot Blood* "was my first picture with Nick Ray—an old friend." she later said. "I was in such a nasty mood from no rest that we almost lost our friendship."[43] Ray had had a great working relationship with his young cast on *Rebel without a Cause* and hoped

Jane and director Nicholas Ray on the set of *Hot Blood.* Jane had wanted to work with Ray ever since doing reshoots with him on *Macao,* but she was too exhausted during this production to actually enjoy it.

to get his *Hot Blood* actors together to go over the script in similar fashion. Jane wasn't having it. "Nick wanted to 'get together and talk,'" she said, "and I was going, 'Oh Nick, will you just give me the damn script!' He'd want me to come in early and look at the sets, but I just wasn't up to it, and it was disappointing for him."[44] Consolations for Jane were her reunion with her hair and makeup crew and the fact that her brothers Jamie and Wally both had credited parts in the film. However, she found the conditions at Columbia disagreeable. "Columbia was a dreadful lot," she remembered. "The others were kind of civilized, with a little park in the middle or something, and the dressing rooms were nice. Over there the dressing rooms were dreadful. I've heard of a secret passageway that Harry Cohn used to use. I could believe it at that studio, the way it was built; like an old haunted house."[45]

Hot Blood may not have been the film Nicholas Ray had in mind, but it's still enjoyable. Ray June's CinemaScope cinematography is gorgeous and takes advantage of the rich color palette of the film. Even though Jane was exhausted, she still looks radiant and has good chemistry with Cornel Wilde. They play a couple navigating an arranged marriage that started out as a con job on Jane's part, but turned into the real thing. Nick Ray was quick to identify the failings of *Hot Blood,* but was also able to point out its virtues. "The stuff that takes place in the gypsy headquarters," he later said of the film, "the trial and the marriage, should go to the Library of Congress, because that's the way it was and there is no other record of it in our film history."[46]

After finishing *Hot Blood,* Jane was allotted a break from film production, or at least film production that required her to be in front of the camera. For their first non-Jane film, the Waterfields had settled on a script based on the short story "The Most Dangerous Game." The production, titled *Run for the Sun,* saw Harry Tatelman once again co-producing, with Richard Widmark and Jane Greer starring. The production went on location to Acapulco in the late fall of 1955, and Jane tagged along, finally having a break in between movies. While cast and crew, including Robert Waterfield, toiled away in the jungle, Jane slept in and lounged by the pool. The breakneck pace she had been maintaining for the past year had taken a toll on her physically and mentally, so the time in Acapulco gave her a much-needed rest before she was to report for her next film job, which was just around the corner.

Twentieth Century-Fox had purchased the rights to the 1951 William Bradford Huie novel *The Revolt of Mamie Stover,* and was getting ready to start shooting at the end of 1955. Huie's book follows the trajectory of Mamie Stover, a Hollywood hopeful from Mississippi who is used and abused by a film producer who ships her off to work for Honolulu's leading madam shortly before the attack on Pearl Harbor. Instead of being beaten down, Mamie becomes the brothel's star attraction and highest earner, which enables her to became an unrepentant real estate war profiteer and ultimately the madam of the brothel. The story would need to be severely sanitized to qualify for a certificate of approval from the Production Code Administration, but Mamie Stover would still be a plum role. Susan Hayward, Lana Turner, and Marilyn Monroe had all been considered for the title role as well as Jane.[47] Ultimately, Fox decided to make *The Revolt of Mamie Stover* the second picture in the Howard Hughes deal and borrowed Jane for $225,000.[48]

Much to Jane's delight, Raoul "Father" Walsh was brought on to direct and Richard Egan to co-star. She looked forward to tackling the dramatic role. "Taking the Mamie Stover part was quite a consideration. If we can do it the way we want to, the movie will have a great deal of dramatic quality, considerably more than anything I've done so far. Our screenplay, like the novel, is the story of a girl who makes the wrong decisions. It's a very emotional part and I'm looking forward to starting work."[49] The film would be shot on location in Honolulu, with a re-creation of the attack on Pearl Harbor serving as a major set piece. The locals welcomed the cast and crew with open arms; approximately four hundred extras were employed at a rate of $11 per day, plus lunch, for the Pearl Harbor evacuation scene.[50]

Jane arrived on Oahu on November 29, and even though the time off in between *Hot Blood* and *Mamie Stover* had been brief, she was rested and in high spirits during the shoot. "Just call me Flaming Mamie!" she wrote to Hedda Hopper from the islands in early December. "That's what the crew and even the natives around here call me. I guess you know by now that for the first time in my life I've dyed my hair red to match the long-haired wig I wear in part of the film. . . . I think it looks great but Robert will probably floor me when he sees it!"[51] Jane was clearly in a good mood. "It's beautiful, wonderful, and the greatest here."[52] The Asian design aesthetics on the islands appealed to Jane, so she "went shopping every minute I can sneak away."[53] She also took advantage of being in Honolulu to promote WAIF. "Some of the gals in the WAIF Auxiliary in L.A. gave me names and addresses of friends here to contact and I hope before I leave, to start an Auxiliary here," Jane wrote to Hedda Hopper. "So many of our requests come from the Islands for the orphans of Japan and Korea. I really think this should be a good place for WAIF to get established."[54] When WAIF celebrated its Silver Jubilee in the early 1980s, the Hawaiian chapter was still going strong.

As much as Jane enjoyed the shoot and loved working in Hawaii, she was still hell-bent on getting back home in time for Christmas. "The light had been a little spotty," she wrote of the shoot, "and we haven't moved quite as easy as expected, but Raoul Walsh assures me we're on schedule. Every time a cloud passes over the sun, I get jittery. I missed being home for Christmas

Richard Egan and Jane rehearse a scene from *The Revolt of Mamie Stover*.

last year (spent that one in London) so I've just got to get home this year."[55] Much to Jane's relief, production in Hawaii finished before Christmas. Jane flew back to Los Angeles on December 22.

In order to appease the PCA, screenwriter Sydney Boehm, who also received a writing credit on *The Tall Men*, had to make some major

245

adjustments to Huie's original novel. Instead of being beaten and scarred by a Hollywood producer and shipped into Hawaiian sex trafficking, the film version of Mamie is escorted out of San Francisco by the authorities, presumably for violating vice laws. In the film the brothel is transformed into the Bungalow dance hall, where lonely men pay for dances and drinks—and nothing more (except maybe a game of gin rummy). When Bertha Parchman, proprietor of the Bungalow (played flawlessly by the incomparable Agnes Moorehead), lays down the rules of her respectable joint, it's so heavy-handed that it feels as if a member of the PCA could have been standing just out of frame, ready to disapprove at any moment. Huie's Mamie takes full advantage of increased demand and decreased restrictions on prostitution during the war, enabling her to develop strong connections with her biggest customer, the US military. Her revolt comes when she defies the harsh rules, known as the "Thirteen Articles," imposed on prostitutes by local authorities. In the film these rules are instituted by the Bungalow, so Mamie's "revolt" is less impressive. The book Mamie gets her house on the hill and a military husband, whereas on film she needs to repent by giving away her money and going back to Missouri. The film is so watered down that Bosley Crowther opened his *New York Times* review, "If you must know why Mamie Stover had to leave San Francisco, you'll have to ask someone other than this reviewer, who did not get the answer from the film. . . . The suggestion was that Mamie was quite a wicked dame. But all we saw of her thereafter led us to conclude unhappily that she was not only peculiarly righteous but also insufferably dull."[56] Later asked if she wished the film had been more gritty and realistic, Jane responded, "No, I probably wouldn't have done it."[57]

Assessing William Bradford Huie's body of work, writer Jonathan Yardley would describe him as "a man who believed in equal opportunity for everybody long before that became the social and political received wisdom, but also a man who believed that only a part of humankind—a small part, in all likelihood—is capable of seizing that opportunity and making the most of it."[58] It seems Huie meant Mamie Stover to fall into this latter category as someone to be lauded for her ingenuity and resourcefulness. This is not how Jane saw the character. Asked if Mamie was "bad," Jane would respond in the affirmative. "She's all for money. . . . She ruins her life."[59] To the question of whether Mamie's decision to exploit prostitution to her own advantage was an admirable action of independence, Jane answered, "I asked the writer, 'Would you like your daughter to be a prostitute?' And he said, 'Oh I think that might be one of the most interesting jobs a woman could have.' And I thought, 'You jackass. I'm certainly glad you're not my father.' Does that answer your question, honey?"[60]

What the film lacks in overall excitement, it makes up for visually. *The Revolt of Mamie Stover* may not be the best film in Jane Russell's filmography, but it's certainly one of the most aesthetically pleasing. The beauty of Oahu is on full display in Technicolor and in CinemaScope, with the locations incorporated more seamlessly than in *Gentlemen Marry Brunettes*. With her flaming red hair, Jane is positively stunning in William Travilla's standout costumes, including a hula skirt–inspired evening gown. Egan's character, a writer who cheats on his upper-crust girlfriend (Joan Leslie in her last feature film) while harshly judging Mamie, grows tiresome, but Agnes Moorehead as the madam (but not really a madam) is a delight. The best scenes in the film are the ones between Russell and Moorehead, two hardheaded business-women with a grudging respect for each other. An entire film of the two of them running the Bungalow is an enticing thought.

As Jane closed out 1955 in Los Angeles, she was also wrapping up a cha-otically busy but prolific period of her career. For someone who had only three films released in the entirety of the 1940s, Jane gave audiences the opportunity to see her star in fourteen during the first six years of the next decade. With Russ-Field up and running and the Hughes deal in place, Jane seemed poised to continue a film career as one of Hollywood's best-known movie stars. However, less than two years after making *The Revolt of Mamie Stover,* Jane would make only one more film—and then disappear from movie theaters for the remainder of the decade.

21

Do Lord

In September 1953 Jane agreed to make an appearance at a fundraiser for Hollywood's St. Stephen's Episcopal Church, which was celebrating fifty years of service to the community.[1] Also slated to appear were vocalists Connie Haines, Beryl Davis (who attended the church), and Della Russell and her husband, crooner Andy Russell. All were scheduled to sing except Jane, who was basically there to be introduced as the star of *Gentlemen Prefer Blondes* and draw a crowd, something she was not exactly thrilled about. Connie Haines had been part of the Hollywood Christian Group, so Jane was already acquainted with her. As Connie rehearsed in one of the basement rooms, Jane interrupted her. "Connie, what am I going to do, just stand there with egg on my face?"[2] Haines suggested that she, Jane, Beryl Davis, and Della Russell sing an old church spiritual together, such as "Do Lord." Della Russell was hesitant, explaining she had grown up Catholic and had never sung those types of songs. Davis, who had been born and raised in England and was unfamiliar with American spirituals, also begged off. Jane responded to both women's protests, "You're going to learn one right now!"[3]

And they did.

As it turned out, the women's voices blended so well that they enthusiastically went ahead and performed "Do Lord" for the audience at St. Stephen's and received a standing ovation. By chance, an A&R rep with Coral Records, a subsidiary of Decca, was in the crowd and liked what he heard. Less than a month later, the women were in a recording studio cutting a seven-inch single of "Do Lord," arranged and accompanied by composer Lyn Murray. During the first recording session, the signing quartet did take after take, but the song just wasn't coming together. Connie Haines described what happened next:

Jane beckoned the musicians.
"Who, me?"

The drummer acted as if he were being singled out for execution. "All of you."

Jane's was the command of a first sergeant. "It's pray time!"

The members of the band came forward to us hesitatingly. We reached out our hands, guiding them into a circle. We [four] girls closed our eyes and bowed our heads. The musicians followed suit. I peeked and caught a few roaming eyes and winks.[4]

The perfect take was soon achieved, and in the presence of Bing Crosby, who had happened to stop by. In January 1954 Coral released a single titled *Make a Joyful Noise unto the Lord* that had a twangy, upbeat version of "Do Lord" on one side and a combination of "I've Got the Joy," "Summertime in My Heart," and "Oil in My Lamp" on the other. The single sold surprisingly well, with a portion of the profits donated to the Youth for Christ Movement. The women soon went back to the studio to record "I'm Really Livin'," another single with a compilation of "Talkin' about the Lord," "Ev'ry Day with Jesus," and "Forgive Me Lord" on the flipside. Before long they started receiving offers for radio, television, and personal appearances. Without even trying, Jane had launched another career.

Based on the strength of the first single, the quartet became an official entity under the management of Russ-Field. The corporation paid overhead costs and then distributed royalties evenly among the four women, each of whom donated her cut to the charity of her choice.[5] After a while, a portion of the profits would come off the top for WAIF before being divided. The women prided themselves on their various spiritual backgrounds; Beryl the Episcopalian, Della the Catholic, Connie the Presbyterian, Jane the nondenominational Christian. They officially dubbed themselves the Four Girls but, according to Connie Haines, "'Bosoms and Bibles' was the phrase that was hung on us."[6] This may have been unsettling to Connie, Beryl, and Della, but it was old hat to Jane. As Haines explained, "We shed tears over it and said a few prayers as well. We were serious and totally dedicated. Finally, Jane concluded, 'We may as well have a sense of humor about this and just hope that they spell our names right.'"[7] Jane was equally dismissive of those who decried the Four Girls' upbeat pop arrangements of spiritual hymns. "Real church people don't have an awesome fear of God," she said. "Rather, it's a warm friendly feeling for Him. Our songs are joyful and happy."[8]

Shortly after the women recorded their second single, Della divorced Andy Russell and then dropped out of the singing group. Actress Rhonda

The Four Girls—Connie Haines (*sitting*), Rhonda Fleming, Beryl Davis, and Jane—get ready to perform during National Music Week in May 1954. (Bill R. Watson, Los Angeles Herald Examiner Collection/Los Angeles Public Library)

Fleming, a Mormon, stepped in to take Della's place and the Four Girls cut another single, "Jacob's Ladder," backed with "Give Me That Old Time Religion." Coral Records also engaged Jane for some solo recordings, which included the song "Forevermore" with Johnny Desmond (who had sung the title song to *Gentlemen Marry Brunettes*), and a spoken-word record that had updated versions of "Little Red Riding Hood" and "Cinderella" written by

Robert Waterfield and Jane arrive with their son Buck at the Los Angeles Superior Court in November 1956 to formalize the adoption. (Los Angeles Herald Examiner Collection/ Los Angeles Public Library)

Steve Allen. Coral also released an instrumental album titled *My Love for Jane* featuring a photo of her on the cover as a sales gimmick. Fleming's participation was occasional, based on her film schedule, but Jane, Connie, and Beryl would perform together for decades to come, even recording a full-length album for Capitol Records called *The Magic of Believing*.

In April 1956 the Four Girls were rehearsing for an appearance on the live variety show *Shower of Stars* when Jane received a phone call. After a brief conversation, she hung up and turned to her friends. "I've just had a baby."[9]

After adopting Thomas and Tracy, Jane had often expressed a desire to adopt two more children. At the beginning of the year, a doctor had notified Jane of a baby due in April who would be available for adoption. Robert Waterfield was initially hesitant, but finally relented. The baby, a boy they named Robert John, was officially adopted by the couple in November 1956. Robert's Rams teammates usually referred to him by his nickname, Waterbuckets, so the baby was always referred to as Buck, never Robert. Buck would be the last child to join the Waterfield clan, and would become especially close to his dad.

In between shooting films, recording and performing spiritual hymns, and attending to a family, Jane was also involved with the production of the Russ-Field films she was not appearing in. In their spare time Jane and Robert would read countless scripts, which felt like a chore rather than a pleasure. There remained an underlying tension to their relationship, but after living a largely separate existence during Robert's football career, Jane enjoyed the couple's working on a "united effort."[10] Searching for a second Russ-Field vehicle for Jane to star in, they briefly set their sights on Elinor Pryor's novel *The Big Play*, hiring Jesse Lasky Jr. to adapt it. When that project stalled, they instead turned their attention to another novel: *The Fuzzy Pink Nightgown* by Sylvia Tate.

The novel's Laurel Gold is a hard-nosed movie star who has made a career as filmdom's ultimate sex symbol. Two days before Christmas, she is kidnapped by two men who hope to collect $50,000 ransom (an offensively low amount to Laurel), but misjudge the personality of their hostage. The kidnappers also suffer from the poor timing; they snatch the actress as she is on her way to the premiere of her film *The Kidnapped Bride*. Fearing Laurel's disappearance will be perceived as a cheap publicity stunt, her studio hesitates to report her absence, and Laurel herself is worried it will do harm to her career if word gets out. The Hollywood satire seemed like a perfect part for Jane to sink her teeth into, so Russ-Field purchased the rights and hired screenwriter Richard Alan Simmons, who had penned the script for *The King and Four Queens*. Academy Award winner Norman Taurog was brought on to direct, and William Travilla would be designing Jane's wardrobe for a fifth and final time.

Initially, Keenan Wynn and Ray Danton were cast as the amateur kidnappers, with Danton serving as the primary love interest. However, after viewing the initial rushes, Robert Waterfield felt Danton, who was a full ten years younger than Jane, looked it on-screen.[11] A replacement would need to be found. Taurog had directed multiple Martin & Lewis features, and knowing Dean Martin was looking to branch out beyond his partnership with Jerry Lewis, wanted him for the role. Instead Jane decided to cast Ralph Meeker, whom she had seen on Broadway in *Picnic*. Jane later believed Martin was so unhappy by Jane's selection of Meeker over him that he purposely never had her on his television program. Taurog wanted to shoot *Fuzzy Pink Nightgown* as full-blown comedy in Technicolor, whereas Jane, with "the mystery and romance of it in mind," wanted it shot in black and white.[12]

Because of these conflicting visions, the end result is an uneven film that can't decide if it's a romantic comedy or a drama. Jane was inclined to agree that the film did a poor job of blending its disparate elements. "It should have been one way or the other," she later wrote, "but as it turned out it was neither. That was one time the star should have had nothing to say" about the direction the film should take.[13] When the film was released in late 1957, the *New York Times* commented, "An ordinary piece of feminine night clothing is a pretty flimsy excuse for putting together a long, long movie."[14] Even though the *Fuzzy Pink Nightgown* didn't turn out as Jane envisioned, she still enjoyed playing Laurel Stevens (changed from Gold for the film), and regarded the film as a personal favorite besides *Gentlemen Prefer Blondes*. "That picture, and *Gentlemen Prefer Blondes,* are the closest to the real me. I felt the most natural doing them." Looking back at the character of Laurel, Jane would say, "She was a movie star, but she's very down to earth, very practical, no nonsense, and 'get right to the point.'"[15] Jane's early scenes as the brash blonde-wigged movie star are effective and fun, particularly her scenes with her assistant, played by Una Merkel. Ultimately, it's Jane's performance that makes the film watchable.

It was during the filming of *Fuzzy Pink Nightgown* that Jane had the tryst with the man she later referred to as "Lance" in her autobiography. It took place in her dressing room late on a Saturday night after the cast and crew had left. When Waterfield awoke at 3:00 in the morning to find that his wife had never made it home, he became worried and drove down to the studio. Finding his wife and Lance in her dressing room, fully clothed but thoroughly intoxicated, he went into a rage. Jane left, "scared as hell," managing to make it home even though she was drunk. When she walked into the house,

I was numb as I entered our dressing room. Robert grabbed the front of my shirt, pushed me up against the wardrobe doors, and said, "Did you go to bed with him? Did you?" When he raised his other hand, I said, "Go ahead, hit me. It'll cost you thousands of dollars if we can't shoot." I was scared but calm. He simply dropped both hands and left the room. I crawled into my nightgown and into the bed, my head swimming.

When I woke up, I was so hung over I couldn't move. Robert came in and sat on the side of the bed. I said, "Robert, I'm so terribly sorry." I was destroyed that I'd broken my word. Sitting me up, he put his arms around me and said, "Honey, we're just going to forget this ever happened, okay?" I couldn't believe it. I was so grateful I could have died. Huge tears welled up in my eyes, and we clung to each other.[16]

Jane's relief was short-lived. Despite saying they would forget the incident, Waterfield did not forget, nor did he forgive. For the next two and a half years, he was distant and made sure Jane knew how he felt. Robert had engaged in his own extramarital affairs, including one while Jane was stuck in Europe for Christmas during the making of *Gentlemen Marry Brunettes*. However, when Jane confronted him about his own infidelities in the midst of the extended freeze out, Waterfield grabbed a Bible and swore he had always been faithful. Jane felt she had no choice but to believe him. Instead she sought whatever distraction she could find though, as it turned out, this would not come through film work. Hughes, continuing to phase out his involvement in the film industry, was no longer actively looking for movies to star her in. With the Waterfield marriage in limbo, Russ-Field's activities came to a grinding halt as well. Also, Jane was approaching her late thirties, not a valued age for lead actresses in Hollywood. The 1950s had been an extremely prolific period of Jane's film career, but *Fuzzy Pink Nightgown* was the last film she made for the rest of the decade.

A welcome distraction soon presented itself when Jane was invited by radio deejay (and later longtime honorary mayor of Hollywood) Johnny Grant to travel to Japan and Korea on a USO tour called Operation Starlift. Jane jumped at the chance to fly far away from her troubled marriage. Before departing she would need to notify Howard Hughes in writing that she was leaving Los Angeles, per her contract.[17] Even though Howard Hughes wasn't as actively involved in her career as he had once been, he still wanted to maintain some semblance of control for the five years she was obligated to him. With that bit of business out of the way, Jane grabbed Edith Lynch and flew to their first stop, Tokyo, via Hawaii. When she arrived in Japan, Jane was delighted to meet a member of the armed forces and his daughter, who had been adopted through the aid of WAIF. The Japanese media presence amounted practically to a mob scene at a scheduled press conference as reporters clamored to get their first look at Jane. When she got to Korea to perform for the GIs, the reaction was just as enthusiastic. "The fellows over there were just great," she said. "For our first show they stood in line from 2 to 8 p.m."[18] Johnny Grant noted that the GIs must have spent a small fortune on film photographing Jane.

Johnny Grant and Jane in Korea during the Operation Starlift USO tour.

As usual, WAIF was never far from Jane's thoughts, so she organized a fundraiser in Japan for the organization. She took advantage of the trip to visit an orphanage in Seoul that WAIF had previously worked with to place children. Edith Lynch accompanied Jane and was so moved by both the children and Jane's dedication that she became heavily involved with WAIF from then on. In Korea, Jane was escorted to a bunker outpost where she could view Jane Russell Hill—twin peaks of a mountain range so named in her honor by the soldiers. Maintaining her sense of humor, Jane played along and peered through an army scope to get a good look at her geographic namesake.

When Jane returned from Asia, the climate was still icy at home, and Jane began to see a therapist to cope. In the fall of 1957 she received an unexpected offer for a four-week engagement at the Sands Hotel in Las Vegas. Dean Martin, who had been performing in the Copa Room at the hotel, had to pull out unexpectedly to film *The Young Lions,* so manager Jack Entratter was relieved to have Jane step in on relatively short notice. Jane made her Las Vegas debut in October 1957 in an act that spoofed her career as a Hollywood sex symbol. During her forty-minute set, Jane wore slinky gowns that showed off her famed frame, and also briefly donned the cape from *The French Line's* "Looking for Trouble" number; was carried onto the stage, lounging on a bed, by four tuxedoed men; did a duet with brother Wally, who was planted in the audience; and bumped and grinded her way through songs like "Be Happy with the Yacht You Got" and "The Gilded Lily." Jack Benny and Scott Brady sat stage-side for opening night, but former co-stars Jack Buetel, Robert Mitchum, and George Brent all sent their regrets.[19] Even though Robert Waterfield was still punishing Jane for her earlier indiscretion, he accompanied her to Las Vegas for the opening. However, when Lance called the night of the opening, Waterfield became so enraged that he stuck around stage-side just long enough to be seen watching her act before heading home in a huff.

As 1957 turned into 1958, rumors floated that Howard Hughes had purchased the rights to the novel *Pale Moon* as a starring vehicle for Jane, but nothing materialized. She continued to navigate icy waters with Robert while the couple tried to provide as stable an environment for their children as they were capable of. She also started leaning more toward personal appearances as a replacement for film work. In August of that year she performed at the Illinois State Fair, receiving $6,000 for the appearance.[20] Jane also received an offer to perform on the SS *Leilani* cruise liner heading for Hawaii. Jane readily accepted after the ship's PR department agreed to let her host a cocktail party benefitting WAIF on one of the docked ocean liners in Honolulu. Another perk was that she was able to bring her mother and her children, except Buck, who was too young to come, so he stayed home with Robert. Esther Williams was on board, similarly using the opportunity to get away from strained romantic relationships, and she also had brought her mom and kids along. Jane and the family spent time in Oahu in Maui, where she visited Jack Ackerman, Richard Egan's swimming double in *Underwater!* She also spent time promoting WAIF and assisting with organizing the benefit. When it was time to go home, Esther Williams opted to fly home rather than fulfill her obligation to the cruise line. Jane would also have liked to return home quickly, but wouldn't dream of reneging on the deal. She was too much of a professional.

Back in Los Angeles in September 1958, she began planning for a two-week engagement at the Latin Quarter nightclub in New York where she would be receiving $6,500 per week, starting October 24.[21] The show had been booked by E. M. Loew, owner of the club of the same name in Miami who had sued Jane years before. Despite Loew's derogatory public comments at the time, Jane had remained under the impression that booking agent Lou

Jane and Esther Williams play shuffleboard with unidentified crew members on the SS *Leilani*. (Image courtesy of the Roy Windham Archive)

Walters had been the one to file suit. When Loew expressed his surprise that Jane would perform at one of his venues, she realized her mistake but still went through with the engagement. For the nightclub act, Jane was backed up by a pianist, a bongo player, and three male dancers dressed in black. Reviewers applauded the production value of the show but were less enthusiastic about her voice, noting, "She doesn't have the strength to project sufficiently and in trying to get up the necessary volume, sometimes the color goes out of the pipes."[22] The reviews made no difference to Jane. She had always loved performing live and would continue to book nightclub engagements for the rest of her life.

Robert Waterfield eventually ended his siege against Jane, and they returned to their "normal" lives. However, the underlying tension that had always existed in their relationship continued to build—it would soon reach a fever pitch. Their joint business venture was also coming to an end. Russ-Field had produced four of the six pictures the company owed United Artists, two of which (those Jane was not in) had made money. United Artists didn't seem particularly interested in pursuing the last two films and neither were Jane and Robert. The Russ-Field Corporation was officially dissolved in July 1960.[23]

Jane had spent a good part of the 1950s as the queen of the RKO lot, commanding top billing and a six-figure salary. By the end of the decade, the film industry was changing as the power grip the studios had began to dissolve. Content was also changing as audiences continued to become more sophisticated, and the outdated Production Code seemed more and more absurd. It wasn't clear what role (if any) Jane would play in the evolving industry. As she navigated what the 1960s would mean for her professionally, she would also finally be forced to take a hard look at her personal circumstances and decide once and for all if she could continue to build a life with Robert Waterfield.

22

On the Stage and Small Screen

In between film shoots, Jane had made periodic forays onto the small screen. She participated as herself on *What's My Line?*, *Person to Person*, and *This Is Your Life*, and sang, often as a member of the Four Girls, on *The Ed Sullivan Show* and *Shower of Stars*. In the late 1950s, Jane briefly tested television as a venue for acting. Her first TV appearance in an acting role was on *Colgate Theater*, an anthology program. The episode, titled "Macreedy's Woman," was produced by Dick Powell's Four Star Productions and Russ-Field, with the hope that the episode might serve as a pilot for a stand-alone series. Jane described the show, set in San Francisco, as "a story about a woman night club operator who does detective work on the side."[1] Asked why the show had not been picked up for series, Jane shrugged and sighed, "It wasn't a western."[2] Powell likewise lamented, "We've got so many good things beyond Westerns on the shelf."[3] If the episode is any indication of quality, sustaining it as a long-term series would have been a stretch, but at least it gave Jane another excuse to sing in front of the cameras while spectacularly dressed.

For her next small-screen acting job, Jane played it safe and went the western route, appearing on *Desilu Playhouse*'s "Ballad for a Badman." In the episode Jane plays a song-and-dance lady performing with a traveling caravan in the Old West. "I'm a bad girl with a good heart and I try to save my sisters from a life of sin."[4] Interestingly, her costume for the episode was the red-sequined one-piece outfit designed by Michael Woulfe that she had worn a few years earlier for the "Any Gal from Texas" number in *The French Line*. She enjoyed making the episode, playing opposite Jack Haley and Mischa Auer, remarking, "It was the same as making a movie, only shorter which makes it nice. It just took ten days."[5] Of the transition many screen stars were making to television, Jane commented, "This whole Hollywood movie and TV business is just like summer stock now. You go and do the best you can. No one worries about losing face. No one has a face to lose anymore."[6] Jane had enjoyed shooting the prerecorded episode, but shied away from doing scripted live television. "Like a lot of other movie-trained actresses, I was taught to learn lines quickly and then forget them quickly. I'd like to do a live dramatic show but I worry about lines. The thought of 40,000,000 people watching the show would throw me."[7]

Jane would also do an episode of *Death Valley Days* as well as a couple of episodes of *The Red Skelton Hour,* but otherwise stuck to unscripted guest appearances. This suited Jane fine; she claimed she could never be talked into "doing a TV series. I'd go out of my mind playing the same role week after week."[8] As for a return to film, "Lately I've refused all offers," she said. "Unless something really special, something elegant comes along I won't consider motion pictures. I've had it."[9] As time wore on, however, she seemed more open to returning to movie theaters. "There are a couple of things I'd like to do in pictures but some of the scripts have been bad. And some of the producers didn't have the money. They want your name so they can get the money from the bank."[10]

This period saw a lot of veteran film actors not only transitioning to television but also trying their hand at theater, appearing in small stock productions. Jane received numerous offers, but always turned them down due, at least in part, to her fear of having to memorize and retain the lines of an entire script. Finally she was offered a play she really liked, along with a pitch from a very persuasive producer. *Janus,* a modern-day comedy written by Carolyn Green, was being produced by Ben Segal, who had focused on drawing marquee movie stars to increase business at his small-tent theaters. Jane agreed to appear in the show, which would be directed by Ella Gerber and staged at three intimate theaters in the round: Oakdale Theatre in Wallingford, Connecticut; Warwick Theatre in Warwick, Rhode Island; and Colonie Musical Theatre in Latham, New York. Agreeing to the play was a huge gamble for Jane, who admitted, "I'm scared stiff. There's a lot of dialogue for me in the play and I am wondering if I can remember it all. I've never given a sustained performance like this before. I'm worried about whether they'll be able to hear me all over the tent." She added, "I'm worried—well, let's put it this way, I'm just plain worried."[11] Hedda Hopper advised Jane against live theater but became even more adamant when she found out it was theater in the round. "Migosh Jane," she shrieked, "that's where the audience reaches out and plucks the daisies off your dress."[12] Ben Segal attempted to allay everyone's anxieties. "She'll come through like the wonderful trouper she is."[13]

Jane may have been nervous, but she looked forward to the challenge. "It's a new experience," she said, "and I hate doing the same things over and

Jack Haley and Jane in the "Ballad for a Badman" episode of *Desilu Playhouse.*

over again. I loathe being in any kind of rut."[14] When *Janus* opened in August 1959, the theater was packed with a crowd eager to see Jane Russell's stage debut. One reviewer noted, "She appeared to be a bit nervous at the start of the play, but eventually warmed up to her part."[15] Another reviewer wrote that Jane could indeed act, but "the performance fell well below the mark of perfection one would expect of a professional actress. However, considering the fact that Monday night was Miss Russell's very first time on a live stage, and the first role she's ever had which required much acting, she did better than I'd expect."[16] After getting past that first performance, Jane was elated. She wrote to Hedda Hopper, "You were right. They really can pick the daisies off your dress in theatre in the round. Having a ball and love it now that we really opened last night." She continued, "This will fracture you—Oakdale Theatre Ben Segal wants me back next year to maybe do a musical. Guess the full house stunned him too."[17]

As Jane was testing out other avenues of acting, Robert Waterfield had returned to his first love—football. In 1958 he signed on as an assistant coach for the Los Angeles Rams. Less than two years later, he signed a five-year contract as head coach. Even though Robert was back in his element, he was much less equipped for coaching than he had been as a player. As one writer noted, "It was hard to be a good coach. Some people seemed to have what it took and some didn't. It was as if Waterfield didn't know how to do the little important things right, the things that united a team rather than letting it drift apart. Just because of the way he was and what he did and didn't do, he built a barrier between himself and his players and they responded with mistrust and by calling him 'Stoneface.'"[18] Despite the difficulties Waterfield would experience as a coach, his return to the game had a positive effect. He and Jane were able to settle back into the familiar routine of working separately but coming together for a cocktail at the end of the day to catch up. For the moment there was peace in the Waterfield home. Jane could still muster enough interest in football to attend Rams home games, and would occasionally accompany her husband on the road, though this is when the marriage would resume unraveling. When Jane traveled with the team for away games, she and Waterfield were often seen fighting in public. Deacon Jones, a defensive end on the team, later recalled an uncomfortable indecent in which a drunken Jane practically passed out at his feet while the team disembarked a plane.[19]

Jane continued to book personal appearances and engage in work for WAIF, which took her both around the US and internationally to Mexico City, Buenos Aires, and Cairo, among others. Jane's time away enabled Robert to develop a new evening habit: hanging out with the Rams coaching crew at Pucci's Restaurant on Ventura Boulevard in the wine cellar, dubbed the Purple Foot Room. Jane quickly discovered that Robert had no intention of resuming their evening cocktail catch-ups, nor was she invited to join him at the restaurant. As the Robert-less evenings wore on, Jane grew increasingly lonely and desperate for adult companionship. The intense isolation led her to do something she'd sworn she never would—engage in an extramarital affair.

Jane had connected with a businessman, whom she referred to in her autobiography as Dan Darby, through mutual friends. The two quickly developed a strong rapport. Jane enjoyed his company and sympathetic ear, and started calling him in the evenings while Robert socialized in the Purple Foot Room. Initially the relationship with Darby was platonic, but that started to change when Jane went to Chicago in late 1961 to star in a production of *Skylark* at the Drury Lane Theatre. Jane and Darby spoke on the phone every night, much to the consternation of Edith Lynch, who had accompanied her. Darby also flew out to the Windy City to spend a weekend with her, though Jane claimed it was just a friendly visit, nothing more. From that point on, he started sending her a dozen lavender roses whenever she was out of town, because her hotel room in Chicago had been painted lavender. The flirtation eventually turned into a full-blown affair. When Jane went back to Chicago in January 1962 for a three-week stint at the Living Room nightclub, Darby flew out as well and the relationship intensified. In March 1962, when Jane was in Houston performing at the Cork Club, Darby called every night, which continued to rankle Edith Lynch. She finally confronted Jane about the affair, which led to a big enough argument that Lynch packed her bags and flew back to Los Angeles early.

Jane and Edith quickly mended their rift; that April the pair flew to Australia for a stint at the Chequers nightclub in Sydney. Being away from both Dan Darby and Robert Waterfield gave Jane time to ruminate over the preceding few months. As she sat in an Australian hotel room on her nineteenth wedding anniversary, she made a decision about her future: she wrote Robert a tearful letter saying it was time to end the marriage, but not alluding to another man. Then, she put on her makeup and evening gown and went onstage, "feeling more like Pagliacci than Jane Russell," she later wrote.[20] Before the letter reached him, Robert was contacted by Geraldine, who told him he needed to pay more attention to his wife. Robert, who seldom heard from his mother-in-law directly, was shaken to the core. When Jane returned from Australia, her family was there to meet her, but the children were ashen-faced—Robert had told them their mother might never come home.

After assuring the three children she wasn't leaving and putting them to bed, Jane confronted Robert and confessed to the affair. He insisted she call it off, which she did, but four weeks later she resumed the meetings with Dan.

Her marriage seemed like a lost cause, and she had decided she wanted to be with Dan. Robert, not ready to end the marriage, confronted Darby directly, but the boyfriend said the decision to end his relationship with Jane was hers to make. Jane and Robert had one final confrontation over the affair. Up to this point, Robert had managed to keep his temper in check, but he finally snapped when Jane asked for a trial separation. "He grabbed me by my shirt front," she later remembered, "and systematically banged my back into the full-length cupboards in the breakfast room and finally flung me into the wrought iron chair of the breakfast table, shouting, 'All you want to do is fuck around!'"[21] Stunned and in physical agony, Jane packed her bags, grabbed the kids, and spent the remainder of the summer at the couple's beach house in Malibu.

With the marriage seemingly over, a friend revealed that Waterfield had engaged in affairs of his own. While Jane was in London during the shooting of *Gentlemen Marry Brunettes*, Waterfield had carried on in the Malibu beach house with Russ-Field's secretary. Empowered with this information, Jane demanded a trial separation and that Robert move out of the Sherman Oaks house. Waterfield was humbled, and Jane took some satisfaction in that. "There was no more of his standing on a pedestal looking down on this terrible, rotten, fallen woman I was supposed to be."[22] Jane continued the relationship with Darby, but soon discovered she was not the only woman in his life, and that he had a history of trysts with married women. The relationship fizzled out. As Jane came to terms with this, Robert had also been forced to do some soul searching. The man who could never verbally express his love for his wife wrote her a letter, finally putting his feelings into words. It was enough for Jane, and the couple reconciled.

For the next three years, Jane and Robert's marriage flourished in a way it hadn't before, largely due to Robert's newfound attentiveness to his wife. They even started attending Sunday services together at the Bel Air Presbyterian Church. As another peace offering, Robert agreed to get rid of the beach house where his trysts with the secretary had taken place, and it was sold to actress Doris Day and her husband Marty Melcher.[23] In its place they purchased a vacation home in Newport Beach. Robert's football experience had become less pleasurable, and in November 1962 he resigned as head coach of the Rams. Even though Jane was still collecting her weekly check from Howard Hughes, it wasn't enough to sustain the household. Jane had been using the personal appearances as a way to escape her unhappy home life, but now she would need to do them for some extra income.

Beryl Davis, Connie Haines, and Jane perform onstage in 1963 wearing gowns designed for them by Mr. Blackwell.

Not wanting to be on the road alone, Jane convinced Connie Haines and Beryl Davis to reunite and they developed a nightclub act that somehow combined the Hollywood glamour of Richard Blackwell's (aka Mr. Blackwell) costume design with their spiritual message. Connie Haines was always impressed with Jane's abilities, noting, "Jane's background in films helped her help us with lighting. She even carried her own gelatins with her to transform into correct coloring some of the harsh and purple spotlights." She continued, "She sparred with the press beautifully, blocking the sex-oriented questions good-humoredly and bringing the interviews into spiritual focus."[24] The trio performed at the Riviera in Las Vegas as part of the long-running show *Louis Armstrong & All Stars*. The women's act was well received; *Variety* commented, "As a trio, the singers have a good sound, and their publicized $62,000 Blackwell wardrobe is a glittering plus."[25] Jane would have preferred not to be away from home, but she did love performing with Haines and Davis. "I don't consider this work," she said. "This is a ball. All three of us sing for fun when we go to each other's houses. Now we're getting paid for it."[26]

Jane finally returned to the big screen in 1964, though it would only be for a guest appearance as herself. Aaron Rosenberg, who had produced *Foxfire*, was prepping *Fate Is the Hunter* for Twentieth Century-Fox and looking for a big name for a small part in this CinemaScope aviation disaster film. Glenn Ford was set to star as an airline executive trying to determine the cause of a deadly crash by piecing together the events leading up to the incident. The large ensemble cast included Nancy Kwan, Rod Taylor, Suzanne Pleshette, Wally Cox, Dorothy Malone, and Mary Wickes, among others. The script called for a World War II flashback sequence at a USO camp, for which Rosenberg hoped to cast a name actress who had been around in the 1940s but hadn't lost her figure. Jane, as statuesque as ever, fit the bill perfectly. Still, she was not exactly clamoring to go back before the cameras. However, she had become close to Rosenberg and his wife Eleanor, who had assisted early on with WAIF, so Jane relented. "I'd never have come back if Aaron hadn't talked me into it," she said at the time. "But Aaron and his wife are our closest friends."[27]

Jane reported for work wearing the Blackwell evening gown she had worn performing with Connie Haines and Beryl Davis. Asked on the set if *Fate Is the Hunter* marked her return to motion pictures, Jane was quick to respond, "I really don't want to make pictures. The only things I have to do are three pictures I'm supposed to make for Howard Hughes."[28] Even though her role is small and her lip-synching leaves a lot to be desired, Jane is a welcome addition to *Fate Is the Hunter*. It's a compelling melodrama with a strong cast and impressive set design, particularly the site of the airplane crash and some spectacular views of the recently constructed LAX Theme Building.

The following year Jane went before the cameras again, this time in a co-starring capacity. Producer A. C. Lyles at Paramount Pictures was making a western called *Johnny Reno* starring Dana Andrews as a US marshal trying to maintain law and order in a town hell-bent on administering mob justice.

Jane on the set of *Fate Is the Hunter*, one of a handful of films she appeared in during the 1960s.

The script called for an older actress to play Nona Williams, Johnny Reno's world-weary, saloon-owning love interest. Lyles wanted Jane, so he appealed to her personally. "I had lunch with Jane," said Lyles, "and four hours later, she said 'I just can't say no.'"[29] Jane wasn't bursting with enthusiasm, but she retained an appreciation for the studio lot where she had made *The Paleface* and *Son of Paleface*. "I was never wild about working," she admitted, "but I did enjoy studio life. When you're working at a studio, it's like being part of a big family. Paramount was always my favorite studio, and I find that a great many people I knew before are still here."[30]

Nona, a strong-willed character with a checkered past and an eye-catching Edith Head wardrobe, was a decent enough role and suited Jane's personality well. Even though she was past her prime—according to Hollywood standards, at least—she was still given a scene in a bathtub and there's an excuse to have her dress ripped off at the shoulders. The sex appeal of Jane Russell had not diminished, though not everyone was fully convinced. A reviewer for *Films and Filming* wrote, "Unfortunately, sometimes one would rather not find out how former favorites have aged, and the years have been a little cruel to Jane Russell, though her brazen glamour is still in evidence. She is one of many players who could have done with firmer direction."[31] Overall, *Johnny Reno* is a serviceable western made watchable by a reliable cast that includes Lon Chaney Jr., John Agar, Lyle Bettger, and Richard Arlen. While not the strongest entry in Jane's filmography, it's enjoyable enough.

When the film was ready to be released, Lyles "called to tell her [Jane] that the picture, 'Johnny Reno' was fine. She said she had fun doing it. I told her to get ready for the next one, 'Waco' and darned if she wasn't rarin' to go."[32] *Waco,* another western directed by R. G. Springsteen, who had also directed *Johnny Reno,* focused on a gunslinger who is brought to a lawless town to try to restore order. Jane would again be playing the long-lost love of the title character, this time played by Howard Keel. Nona in *Johnny Reno* had straddled the right and wrong side of the law in the name of self-preservation, but Jill Stone in *Waco* is the straitlaced and righteous wife of a preacher (who has a very dark past). Even though Jane is able to seamlessly insert her no-nonsense personality into Jill, it's a less colorful role than Nona Williams and less memorable. Her Edith Head wardrobe is so appropriately modest that an image of Jane from *Johnny Reno* was used on the *Waco* poster instead. Like *Johnny Reno, Waco* has a respectable cast, including Brian Donlevy, Terry Moore, John Agar, Gene Evans, Richard Arlen, and DeForest Kelley, plus the added bonus of a theme song featuring a spoken-word performance by Lorne Greene of *Bonanza* fame. Both *Johnny Reno* and *Waco* were released in 1966.

Asked why she had decided to reappear on the big screen, Jane publicly blamed boredom for her return, claiming she had become a "hunting widow" by Waterfield's extended absences during gaming season. As she told columnist Sheilah Graham, "I didn't work for two years because I'd been on the road in nightclubs and hotels, and I was exhausted. But after two years of taking it easy I was bored to death."[33]

Perhaps boredom did play a role in Jane's returning to the work she claimed to never have been overly enthusiastic about. At the same time, work provided Jane with a distraction from her home life, as it had done in the past. The peace that had existed in the Waterfield home for the previous three years was coming to an end. Jane's marriage was about to unravel for good.

23

Endings, Beginnings, and Endings

Jane and Robert Waterfield had come close to splitting for good in 1962 after the blowup surrounding the revelation of each other's infidelities. They had managed to reconcile and the marriage even thrived for a while, but eventually the relationship continued its drawn-out demise. As Thomas became a teenager and butted heads with Robert, the tension in the household began to build again. Then Robert discovered the game of pool and started spending all his time at the Barrel, a cocktail bar on Van Nuys Boulevard. Jane didn't care for the folks Robert began hanging out with at the Barrel, and she bitterly resented that her husband had once again begun spending time away from home. The arguments returned with a vengeance, and Jane, who had abused alcohol on and off for many years, turned to the bottle with greater frequency to cope with a marriage whose days were numbered.

In the spring of 1966 Jane went up to Toronto to appear in a production of *Pal Joey*. The offer had come on short notice and she had little time to prepare. This was complicated even further by a revolving door of directors and choreographers. When the show opened, Jane had a hard time with her lines and kept accidentally singing Frank Sinatra's version of "Bewitched, Bothered, and Bewildered," which had been modified from the stage version, a standard practice for radio. The experience of stumbling in front of a live audience was deeply humiliating. Despite the *Pal Joey* mishaps, when she received an offer to return to the Drury Lane Theater in Chicago for a production of *Catch Me if You Can*, Jane jumped at the chance. Since the production was scheduled for July and August 1966, when school was out, Jane took Tracy and Buck, aged fifteen and ten, to Chicago with her. Thomas opted to stay at the Eagle's Nest with Geraldine. At one point while Jane was in Chicago, Robert came to town for a football coaching job. The reunion was unhappy and the couple fought constantly and drank heavily. Jane, miserable and hungover most of the time, muddled her way through the play while at the same time dreading the end of the production when she would need to go home.

Peter Savage and Jane discuss a scene in *Cauliflower Cupids* on location in the Riverdale neighborhood of New York. (Image courtesy of Paula Petrella, Peter Savage Film Enterprises)

Her manager Kevin Pines came to the rescue by lining up a movie for Jane that would be shooting in New York. "I never even knew they made movies in New York," came the response from the Hollywood movie star.[1] "It's called 'The Honorable Frauds,'" Jane reported during production, "and I play a wealthy dame who's lost all her money. We're all sitting around like

271

vultures waiting for a rich relative to die. We've got a big house with 18 rooms and 80 acres of gardens. We're going to be shooting here for three weeks."[2] *The Honorable Frauds* was an independent film written, co-directed, and starring Peter Savage, who had previously helped his friend Jake LaMotta write the memoir *Raging Bull.* Savage plays Johnny Stiletto, the head of a Mafia gang who is looking to retire from his life of crime, at the same time humorously trying to stop his pregnant daughter from having sex with her fiancé before she is married. Jane plays the haughty aunt of the groom-to-be who will approve the marriage only if Stiletto can convince an ailing rich relative to leave his fortune to her.

Jane's scenes were shot at a mansion in the Riverdale section of New York, and the atmosphere helped relieve the personal tension and anxiety she was experiencing over her imploding marriage. She didn't seem particularly perturbed even when the producers ran out money after the shoot was done, indefinitely delaying the release. Ultimately, the bank, which had a lien on the film, auctioned it off to the highest bidder at the end of 1967.[3] After some retooling, the film would finally be released as *Cauliflower Cupids* in 1970 and rereleased as *The Godfather and the Lady* a few years later, presumably to capitalize on the success of the two Francis Ford Coppola *Godfather* films. *Cauliflower Cupids* is a truly bizarre film. It has a very 1960s aesthetic and occasionally scenes are ramped up to Benny Hill–esque speeds for comic effect. Still, the film has its charms, with the Mafia gang portrayed by former boxers Jake LaMotta, Rocky Graziano, Willie Pep, Paddy DeMarco, Tony Zale, and Petey Scalzo. Despite the personal stress Jane was experiencing at the time, she looks absolutely stunning in the film, particularly in one scene where she sports a beehive hairdo and an electric-blue Grecian gown. She had looked somewhat worn out in the last two films made for Paramount, but she looks luminous in the independent *Cauliflower Cupids.*

After wrapping up filming in New York, Jane flew back to Los Angeles to face the inevitable. As she suspected, her relationship with Robert Waterfield continued to deteriorate at a rapid pace. Work provided Jane with another respite when she received an offer from actor Tom Laughlin to play a character part in an independent film he was making called *The Born Losers.* Laughlin had been trying for years to get *Billy Jack,* a screenplay about discrimination against Native Americans, off the ground, but with little luck. In 1966 the outlaw biker genre was launched with the release of Roger Corman's *The Wild Angels,* so Laughlin decided to insert his character Billy Jack, a half-

Navajo Green Beret veteran, into a biker film. The decision paid off, and Laughlin got enough financing to make the film, which he would also star in and direct (under a pseudonym). Getting the film released was another matter, so he needed a star name to get a distribution deal. For all of Jane's proclamations about not wanting to work, she always harbored a desire to do truly dramatic film roles. "I've lived a life," she said at the time. "Why can't I play those dramatic parts for some new director who can see the new me, instead of glamor parts? Glamor has bored me for years and years!"[4] Shelley Winters had advised Jane to take small character parts while keeping an eye out for choice starring roles, so Jane agreed to be in *The Born Losers*. Her two brief scenes as a rough-around-the-edges mother whose teenaged daughter is raped by a biker gang would be shot in a day and pay $1,000.

Even though Jane's screen time was brief, she took the job seriously. Delores Taylor, an executive producer on *The Born Losers* and Laughlin's wife, later recalled:

> I remember after she agreed to do the film that we had to go get her costumes. I mean, we didn't have a costume or a wardrobe department! So we met her at Frederick's of Hollywood. And I had the kids with me. As a matter of fact, I think they were there with me because I couldn't hire babysitters. And she met us there and she tried all kinds of things on. . . . She knew what the character needed and she tried different things on. And she was the one who actually chose the stuff that she wore on this.[5]

On the day Jane was to shoot her scenes, Laughlin was recovering from an appendectomy. He should have been convalescing but, fearful he would lose Jane if he rescheduled, he went to work. As he was directing one of her scenes, Jane caught him icing the incision area, clearly in agony. As Laughlin recalled, "She comes up and says, 'I don't work for stupid directors. I'm leaving the set.' And I just about vomited. You know, she caught me with the ice pack. She says, 'Oh, by the way. And if you're ever smart enough to get well, I'll come back and work for as many days as you want for free.' I couldn't believe the kindness and the generosity. So I did go and got it taken care of. And she came back and she worked. . . . She was just magnificent."[6]

For Jane's big dramatic moment, when she has a complete meltdown, Laughlin drew off her nerves to enhance her performance. As he explained,

This was her big scene, and we prepared and prepared. She was so nervous, and she was about to go. And I said, "OK, lunch." And I broke for lunch. The camera and everything was set! You know, everything was set. And she was so angry at me. After all she'd done for me! And we did our lunch. And I wouldn't talk to her. I ducked so she couldn't find me. . . . We came back and everything was set. We didn't have to set anything. Just flick on the lights and go. And boy, she just—a brilliant actress—used that and just ripped.[7]

The scene called for Jane to angrily push a pair of attorneys out the door, but she pushed them into the bedroom by mistake. Laughlin went with it, turning it into a slight comedic moment with Jane simultaneously crying and laughing hysterically. Jane's performance in that scene included "real tears," he said. "There's no glycerin in this folks!"[8] Decades later, Laughlin would refer to her as "the magnificent, wonderful, incredible Jane Russell. And what a magnificent, magnificent human being she is."[9]

The feeling was mutual. "If I could have worked with other directors like him," Jane said, "and done bigger parts like that one. I would have been happy."[10] *The Born Losers* was released by American International in July 1967 and became a huge moneymaker. Straddling the fading tenure of the Production Code and the introduction of the film ratings system, *The Born Losers* shocked some with its handling of violent subject matter, but impressed others with its contemporary approach. Unfortunately for Jane, the film did not lead to similar parts as she had hoped.

Back in Sherman Oaks, things were decidedly unhappy and barreling toward a complete break. The end finally came on Christmas Day 1966, when Jane and Robert got into a particularly nasty fight that ended with Jane smashing a dinner platter and collapsing into a sobbing heap in Thomas's room. Geraldine, who had spent Christmas at the Sherman Oaks home, witnessed everything and was shocked. She had endured the fallout from Jane's tumultuous relationship for years and had always sent her home to work it out with prayer. Now even Geraldine had to admit defeat. "Get up, Daughter," she said quietly to a weeping Jane. "Let's go home."[11] As Jane continued sobbing in her mother's bedroom, Robert showed up at his mother-in-law's house, but Geraldine turned him away. Jane flew to Hawaii for New Year's to clear her head. When she came back, she knew what she had to do. "I never in a million years thought I would ever divorce," she said later. "But it was a matter of sanity. There was absolutely no way out."[12]

Attorney Max Fink and Jane at the Los Angeles Superior Court during her divorce from Robert Waterfield.

Jane moved into the Eagle's Nest with Tracy. Buck, who idolized his dad, opted to stay at the Sherman Oaks home, and Thomas was undecided about where he wanted to go. When Jane went back to the Sherman Oaks residence to gather her belongings, she found a large black funeral wreath lying on her side of the bed. She thought this was hilarious, and in return left a pool cue with the seven and eight balls on Robert's side: seven for his Rams jersey number and eight, along with the stick, as a symbol of where he had spent most of his time toward the end of the marriage. He was equally amused. "It was the only funny part of our divorce," Jane later wrote.[13]

Jane filed for divorce in early February 1967, claiming she had "sustain[ed] and suffer[ed] extreme cruelty" at the hands of her husband, that Waterfield had inflicted bodily harm, and that he had been liquidating community assets in order to deprive her.[14] She also asserted that Robert had "maliciously induced" Thomas and Buck to stay with him, and spoke disparagingly of her to the boys in order to alienate them from her. Waterfield denied all allegations, asserting "that in truth and in fact, plaintiff's excessive drinking habits have created such a problem for the plaintiff that she has made it impossible for the true objective of matrimony to be attained."[15] Robert went on to claim that Jane "has concealed supplies of liquor in various parts of the residence of the parties in order that she may satisfy her drinking desires at various hours of the day," and that she "has consumed alcoholic beverages in the early hours of the morning to such an extent that she is incapable of caring for the minor children of the parties."[16] Jane could not help being amused by his claim that on Christmas, she "was under the influence to such an extent that she was incapable of cooking any meals for the family."[17] Given Jane's long-standing aversion to the kitchen, even the kids found this hilarious.

The divorce was ugly and would be drawn out over the next year and a half. When the couple had to appear in court, Robert sat next to Jane and muttered, "Well, this sure is a goddamn degrading and humiliating end you've brought us to."[18] Jane remained resolute, even as the *National Enquirer* tabloid ran a front-page headline screaming, "SHE WAS A DRUNK."[19] As the lawyers haggled and the battle raged on, sixteen-year-old Tracy, especially affected by the divorce, tried to commit suicide by taking an excessive amount of pills before class at Van Nuys High. She was unsuccessful but remained at high risk. This jolted Robert into cooling down somewhat, but the divorce continued to drag on until July 1968. In the end Robert kept the house in Sherman Oaks, which he had been hesitant to build but had grown to love. Jane would keep the Newport Beach house. The majority of the couple's assets, estimated at approximately $800,000, were divided equally, with Robert keeping an inheritance from his mother, who had passed away in 1963, along with some oil interests and an undeveloped lot in Malibu. Jane kept her weekly paycheck from Howard Hughes along with land on Woodman Avenue that was zoned for apartments. Jane got custody of Thomas and Tracy, moving into one of the houses on the Russell family compound, while Buck stayed with Robert.[20]

The relationship between Jane Russell and Robert Waterfield had lasted almost thirty years, but it had finally burned itself out. To those who were mystified that Jane could have stayed with him for so long, she explained, "Robert was sexy, dynamic, opinionated, extremely bright, witty, and as stubborn as they come. You either find that kind of man irresistible and exciting or you don't understand him and can't tolerate him for a moment."[21] Looking back at his parents' relationship, Buck Waterfield commented, "There was a real love-hate relationship between those two. They couldn't be away from each other, but they couldn't be together either."[22]

As Jane waited for her divorce to be final, she continued performing with Beryl Davis (Connie Haines had retired), and the pair did a brief engagement at a club on Ventura Boulevard called Bonnie & Clyde's.[23] In June 1968 she flew out to Niles, Illinois, just outside Chicago, to star opposite Tony Dow in a production of *Here Today* at the Mill Run Playhouse. Co-starring was Roger Barrett, a stage actor who also did commercial voice-over work and had enjoyed a brief appearance in the motion picture *Days of Wine and Roses*. In addition to sharing the same profession, Jane and Roger had similar tastes in art and music, and both felt deeply about their spiritual faith. Much to Jane's delight, Barrett had no interest in sports. In personality and temperament he bore more of a resemblance to Jane's old flame John Payne than Robert Waterfield. Barrett was a levelheaded, uncomplicated person who preferred to leave drama on the stage and out of his personal life.

The two embarked on a whirlwind romance almost immediately. Jane thrived in a relationship—so different from her marriage—rooted in mutual respect and trust, in which differences were worked out without arguments. For Jane, being with Roger was uncomplicated and sheer bliss. Two months after meeting in mid-June, they decided to get married. When she broke the news to the press, Jane said of her groom, "Roger has the most beautiful voice in the world, is 6'3," blue-eyed and has curly hair and lots of it. He's three months older than I am. He is a Baptist. I'm nothing, but everything."[24] As for their future plans, Jane gushed, "I hope we can live in New York, Los Angeles, and Chicago, where Roger does many of his voice-overs." She added, "Oh, I'm so happy, I can't stand it!"[25]

Even though it was short notice, Jane wanted to have a large wedding to make up for her Las Vegas elopement with Robert Waterfield in 1943. The service was set for 2 p.m. on August 25, 1968, at the Beverly Hills Community Presbyterian Church. The couple chose a Mexican theme and Jane wore a hot-pink gown designed by former fashion model Suzi Brewster that was made of a heavy silk with embroidery. Barrett wore a white suit. Jane's brothers were ushers, except for Wally who sang. Tracy was a bridesmaid. The guest list was large and included many of Jane's co-stars. Howard Hughes was invited, but did not come. Instead he sent a giant basket of flowers and a Spanish coffee table. After the ceremony, Della Russell (now Koenig after getting remarried) hosted a reception at her nearby home.

Jane and Roger Barrett are all smiles in the days leading up to their wedding. (Los Angeles Herald Examiner Collection/Los Angeles Public Library)

The couple immediately started making plans for the future. They hoped to continue doing plays together, including a road show production of *Hello, Dolly!* When Jane and Beryl received an offer to do a tour in England, Jane jumped at the chance. Roger, who had never been there before, would be joining her, along with Thomas, who had become a proficient drummer and would be playing in the act. Their first stop was London, and there Thomas was able to meet his birth mother, Florrie Kavanagh. Back in 1951 Jane had been hesitant to adopt a child whose birth parents were known, so the fact that she would make the effort for Thomas to meet Florrie reflected her self-confidence, which had served her well both personally and professionally over the years. After London, Jane and Beryl did a tour of Wales and England. Afterward Jane and Roger stayed on a bit longer, but his chronic back problems had been exasperated by his inability to find a chiropractor for an adjustment. After they returned to the States, his back pain persisted, but the doctor's fear about possible heart problems were allayed. Back in Van Nuys, the couple made plans for Christmas and looked forward to the *Hello, Dolly!* road show. They had decided that instead of flying from town to town and staying in motels, they would live and travel out of a motor home. For the first time in years, Jane was truly happy.

On the morning of November 18, 1968, Jane awoke to find Roger still in bed, which was unusual as he was an early riser. He was in agony because of his back, so Jane tried to relieve some of the pressure by pushing down on his spine. Afterward he sat on the edge of the bed, looking so drawn that Jane ran to the phone to call the doctor. Before she was able to finish the phone call, he screamed out in pain and fell backward on the bed. At the age of forty-seven, Roger Barrett was dead.

It was the same age Roy Russell had been when he passed away. A heart attack resulting from a blood clot was the cause of Roger's death. The funeral was less than three months after the wedding, with most of the same guests in attendance. Those who had received thank-you notes from Jane for wedding gifts now received a note of thanks for sympathy and support. Howard Hughes sent flowers to the mortuary and Jane's home. Jane was in a daze. Della Koenig convinced her to spend some time in Acapulco, which helped temporarily, but when she returned to Van Nuys for Christmas, she finally snapped. As the reality of her loss flooded over Jane, she once again turned to the bottle and fell into a deep, dark depression. Not wanting to be alone, she asked a friend to move in with her, but living in the house she had briefly shared with Roger was too much. She moved into the Newport Beach house, then lived on a boat she named *The Outlaw* for a while. Gradually the depression started to lift, though Jane would never fully recover from the death of Roger Barrett.

A little less than a year after Roger's death, Jane received an offer to make a cameo appearance in a film called *Darker Than Amber,* which would be

Jane can't keep her eyes off new husband Roger Barrett as Thomas looks on during a trip to London in 1968.

shooting off the coast of Miami. The film would star Rod Taylor as Travis McGee, the protagonist of a series of mystery/suspense novels written by John D. MacDonald. Jane would be playing Alabama Tigress, a widow who's been hosting a nonstop party on her yacht for over a year. The film was meant to launch a franchise based on the book series, but it failed at the box office, though the fight scenes inspired Bruce Lee to hire director Robert Clouse for *Enter the Dragon*. As for Jane's part, most of her footage as the Alabama

Tigress ended up on the cutting-room floor. *Darker Than Amber* was the last feature film Jane Russell would ever make.

It was a whimpering end to a career that had lasted almost thirty years. Her body of work had had some bright spots, but was often hampered by middling roles. Jane never generated the box office totals that someone like Marilyn Monroe did, but she was a respectable draw whose billing and salary were boosted immensely by her association with Howard Hughes. At the same time, being under the thumb of the eccentric multimillionaire was often why she got stuck with the glamour-girl parts she grew so weary of. "I want to act," she would say, "instead of standing up there half naked."[26] She was capable of putting her foot down with Hughes when it came to her publicity, though she did it sparingly. The battle she never did wage with Hughes was one for better roles, so she was not able to effectively make the transition to character parts as she got older.

The 1960s had been a roller coaster for Jane, who had seen two marriages and a film career come to an end. From the age of twenty-one, Jane had been a wife and a film star, but now she was neither. With the end of the Howard Hughes payments rapidly approaching, the new decade had brought Jane to a crossroads. The woman who had often said she was "born married" was now going to need to decide, on her own, what direction her life would take.

24

A Life Off-screen

As Jane struggled through her period of depression, she still managed the occasional television appearance and kept up her involvement with WAIF, which included making a public appearance at an all-star boxing match that benefited her beloved charity. After a year and a half of mourning, Jane decided she was well enough to officially reenter public life.

In the summer of 1970, she went to the Memorial Hall in Dayton, Ohio, to star opposite comedian Soupy Sales in the musical *High Button Shoes*. The local reviewer wasn't overly impressed with Sales, but said of his co-star, "We have no complaint about Jane Russell, the number-two star. Jane endures and she puts a song across visually even if the sound doesn't quite emerge from the diaphragm."[1] Her next engagement came the spring of 1971 as she revisited *Catch Me if You Can,* which was being staged at the Meadowbrook Dinner Theatre in Cedar Grove, New Jersey. By this time Jane had grown comfortable appearing in productions at small theaters. A run on Broadway, on the other hand, was an intimidating prospect she had avoided, often citing the time commitment as being out of sync with parental responsibilities. With Buck still living with his dad and Thomas and Tracy entering adulthood, however, Jane would have a harder time justifying turning down an opportunity to appear on the Great White Way if an offer presented itself. "In the past," she said, "I thought the worst thing that could happen to any person was being stuck in a hit play. You'd be in the show for years and separated from your family. Of course my children are now living away from home, and there's no problem of becoming homesick. It doesn't matter where I live."[2]

While Jane was doing *Catch Me if You Can,* a golden opportunity for a Broadway show finally came. *Company,* a groundbreaking and sophisticated musical comedy written by George Furth with songs by Stephen Sondheim, had opened in the spring of 1970 to much fanfare and multiple Tony nominations. In early 1971 producer Hal Prince was on the lookout for an older actress to replace Elaine Stritch in the role of Joanne. Stritch, a beloved

Broadway veteran who had earned a Tony nomination for her role in *Company*, was going to be leaving the Broadway production in order to join the national tour. Prince saw Jane being interviewed on *The Dick Cavett Show* and thought she might be a big enough personality to take on the role of the brassy and acerbic Joanne. Jane, who had seen *Company* with Stritch as Joanne, was intrigued, but she was also terrified at the thought of taking on the role, which included the showstopping number "The Ladies Who Lunch." Not wanting to feed Jane's anxiety, manager Kevin Pines failed to tell her that a scheduled meeting with Prince and Sondheim was actually an audition. On the way there Pines tried to prep Jane for the audition in a roundabout way and failed miserably. When they arrived, Jane was blindsided when asked to sing a song and run lines. She was ready to kill Pines, but managed to pull herself together and get through the audition with no preparation. She nailed it. The part of Joanne was hers.

Jane continued to appear in *Catch Me if You Can* while she was learning her role for *Company*. As the pressure started to build, Jane was finding it impossible to learn new lines. She also had a hard time wrapping her head around the intricacies of Sondheim's songs. She started to be fearful that when the show opened, it would be a repeat of the *Pal Joey* disaster years before. Her anxiety worsened, causing insomnia. To someone who always needed nine to ten hours of sleep, the situation became unbearable. On top of it all, she had started dating a clergyman named Paul Mills, but the relationship was fizzling out. For all the turmoil she had endured during her marriage to Robert Waterfield, she still believed that relationship had grounded her in some way. "She was so desperate to have someone who was her own," said Kevin Pines. "Without that, it seemed as if she had no base, no foundation."[3] Jane took to the bottle again, begged Pines to get her out of *Company*, and had a complete psychotic break. Not knowing what else to do, Kevin Pines had Jane locked up in the psychiatric ward of a hospital to get help. The experience was harrowing, but after a short stay, she got better. Pines had been able to cancel the *Company* contract without repercussions, but Jane decided she still wanted the part if Hal Prince still wanted her. He did.

When Jane explained her anxieties to Prince, he had her rehearse her routines alone before joining the rest of the cast. Ethel Martin, a dancer who had worked under Jack Cole, assisted Jane one-on-one until she started to become comfortable with the part. Even after Jane started rehearsing with the cast, however, she continued to have a hard time grasping the character of Joanne. Finally, Barbara Barrie, who was also in the show, explained to

Jane that the story was about "a group of people who don't know each other. And everybody's being terribly polite to everybody else. Joanne's a person who has no patience with idiots. She comes in and sort of takes over."[4] In other words, Joanne was a first cousin of Jane Russell. Armed with this perspective, Jane began to get a firmer hold on the part, though she was still nervous about the short rehearsal timeline. "At the moment it's all a blue haze," she said at the time. "I've been hot and cold on the whole idea ever since I said yes. I'm frightened, not that there is so much dialogue to learn. But the score is tricky and the lyrics so special. Hal Prince has been wonderful."[5] Still, she was excited for the opportunity to break out of the types of roles she felt she had always been trapped in. "That's the great thing about going into 'Company.' And I'm doing it because it is something I've never done before, a musical on Broadway. I'm playing a real woman and my anatomy is secondary."[6]

As Jane became more comfortable in the role of Joanne, she had a new hurdle to overcome: her wardrobe. Like many designers over the years, D. D. Ryan had a hard time figuring out how to dress Jane. Ryan tried putting her in a long wide skirt, a style that had always been problematic given Jane's long legs and body shape. She also wanted to dress Jane in opaque tights, which would have obscured one of her best features. When Jane tried on the first costume, "I looked like . . . Ernest Borgnine in drag."[7] A second dress wasn't much better, and Hal Prince agreed, so he gave Jane the green light to find something off the rack. Jane headed to Fifth Avenue and found what a reporter described as "one of those little-nothing, bias-cut, black crepe Pauline Trigère dresses that display the figure—but on a low-key basis."[8] Jane felt the design could benefit from sleeves and called Trigère directly to let her know. The designer, caught off guard by Jane's forthright call, managed to sputter out that she didn't think sleeves were a good idea. On opening night, Jane wore the dress—with sleeves.

Jane made her Broadway debut on May 13, 1971. According to one reviewer, "She's still a knockout looker whose first entrance is met by silent whistles from the men and envious sighs from the women in the audience." The reviewer continued, "Miss Russell brings the proper touch of warmth to the role of the thrice-married wise-cracking femme. Her one major scene with lead Larry Kert in a cocktail lounge and her vocal of 'The Ladies Who Lunch' are both standouts. She is an experienced singer with a pleasant, if not exceptional voice. She should become even better when she becomes more relaxed."[9] After everything she had endured the last few years, the evening

Jane as Joanne in the Broadway production of Stephen Sondheim's *Company*. (Photo by Martha Swope, ©Billy Rose Theatre Division, The New York Public Library for the Performing Arts)

was a triumph. The whole Russell clan came out to New York to support her. Even Robert Waterfield showed up, briefly prompting rumors of a reconciliation. Jane regarded the positive reviews as a high point of her professional career, which came on the eve of her fiftieth birthday. However, even this accomplishment couldn't overcome the boredom that set in after she had been doing the musical for three months. At the end of October, Jane opted to end her triumphant run on *Company*. Vivian Blaine stepped into the role of Joanne and Jane went back to Los Angeles.

She arrived back home just in time to put the finishing touches on her newest project—an eighty-unit apartment building in Van Nuys. She had received ownership of the lot on Woodman Avenue in the divorce and had finally moved forward with developing the land. Jane had long been interested in architecture and interior design. In addition to the Sherman Oaks home she had shared with Robert Waterfield, Jane had also helped design the Chapel in the Canyon in Canoga Park, and had also come up with an affordable and efficient floor plan for a family home she hoped to mass-market, although that idea never got off the ground.[10] "I've been studying houses all my life," she remarked, "and I've built several for myself. I've seen so many apartment buildings go wrong that I decided I couldn't do any worse in building one myself."[11] Rather than hiring an architect, Jane designed the complex with her brother Tom, who was the contractor on the job. A structural engineer was hired to make sure the project was up to code, and an architecture student named Eric Diesen, who was a friend of Jane's son Thomas, drew the elevations.

Jane chose a New Mexican motif for the complex at 7924 Woodman Avenue, and named it Taos West. "I like the idea of going back to our Spanish and Mexican origins in California buildings," she explained. "I especially like the New Mexico style of round poles, arches and adobe."[12] Once upon a time, Woodman Avenue, which was near the Russell compound, had been peppered with agricultural ranches. Now it had developed into a high-traffic Valley artery, lined with both commercial and apartment buildings. Jane took this into consideration when designing Taos West, choosing not to include windows on the front of the building. As she explained, "I like the walled front. Windows may look all right from the outside, but who wants to sit on a porch and look out at traffic on Woodman Avenue?"[13] Jane planned to occupy one of the units, so she designed something that personally appealed to her. The apartments were split-level with two bedrooms, two bathrooms, beamed ceilings, and an oversized patio. "The effect is private,"

Jane poses at the entrance of Taos West, a luxury apartment complex in Van Nuys she built and helped design. (Yoram Kahana/Shooting Star International)

she said. "I can get from the garage to my apartment without seeing anyone. It's like having your own townhouse."[14] Taos West opened to the public in late 1971, featuring a posted sign that read, "Jane Russell Presents Taos West Apartments—two bedrooms, $245—included all utilities, security."[15]

Company had proved to Jane that long runs on Broadway were not to her liking, but she still enjoyed performing in small doses. "Actually, I prefer stock to Broadway," she remarked. "For one thing, they pay more. On Broadway, they think a performer should work for the prestige. And stock engagements don't last as long. I like to do a show for a few weeks and then turn to something else. It's hard to do a long run in New York without getting bored or stale."[16] Weeks after opening Taos West, Jane headed up to Northern California to star in a production of *Mame* at the Circle Star Theatre in San Marcos. "'Mame' has been a great challenge to me," Jane said of her latest production. "I love the show and the score is divine. But I'm on my feet the whole time and with performing in the round, there's a lot of extra motion running up and down the aisles."[17] The audience responded wildly to Jane as Mame, and while Jane never received high marks for her voice, her presence was undeniable. "Jane Russell brought a certain sultriness to the part," wrote the *Oakland Tribune*, "a combination of her lusty voice and world manner. She is not a good singer and was off key most of the night, yet her featured numbers were moving. Her best asset is her full-bodied presence, a vigorous quality she has to put life into a part."[18] Jane enjoyed playing Mame enough that when the production closed on February 4, she immediately launched into rehearsals for an additional run in the Midwest. In March she returned to the Mill Run Playhouse in Niles, Illinois, where she had met Roger Barrett, to star in another two-week run of *Mame*.

The year 1973 also brought a new type of role to Jane's repertoire: commercial spokesperson. Manager Kevin Pines had struck a deal with the Playtex Corporation for Jane to film a series of commercials promoting the company's "18-hour bras," designed for the "full figured gals" of the world. It was a perfect partnership. The woman whose career had been launched on the size of her breasts was finally able to capitalize on her anatomy—on her own terms. Jerry Ansel, a prolific commercial director, would be shooting the ads. Ansel was no stranger to film stars, having previously worked with both Debbie Reynolds and Ida Lupino on commercials, so he and Jane got along great. They would work together for over a decade, making around two dozen Playtex commercials together, often shooting in New York, and once traveling to Acapulco for a shoot. For a generation that had been born too late to have seen Jane on the big screen during her heyday, the commercials were a memorable introduction. Gerry Cornez, WAIF's executive director from the 1970s through the 1990s, remembered one event in particular:

> Jane was propped up on the back of a convertible, like you would in the old days, and they were taking her picture and she was answering questions from reporters about WAIF and kids and stuff like that. There was a little boy there and he said, "Can I come up, can I have my picture taken with you?" I was standing right next to her so I remember this clearly. She said to him, "You don't need your picture with me, you don't know who I am," and he said, "Of course I do, you're the bra lady."[19]

While Jane was in New York filming the first round of Playtex commercials, writer Dotson Rader received the green light from *Esquire* to write a feature on her for the December issue. The resulting article was bizarre and at times extremely unflattering, with Kevin Pines painting Jane as currently one of the most in-demand stars, which was decidedly not true. The article, focusing almost exclusively on Jane's spirituality, presented her as proclaiming her beliefs in a bombastic and forceful manner. Rereading the article forty years later, Gerry Cornez reflected, "She was not a proselytizer. One knew (if they knew her) where she stood personally, but it didn't lead her friendships or work, either in entertainment or WAIF. She talked about it if asked or thought it might help someone, but didn't push."[20] The article also quoted her as deriding the nascent feminist movement: "Don't tell me the Women's Lib is fine and everything. I don't like their attitudes. All these liberals. They support homosexuality and lesbians, all the stuff against nature. It's unnatural bullshit. The Lord laid down the rules. Why the hell don't those gals follow them?"[21]

As Jane got older, she would embrace right-wing Christian talking points more and more, but her actions were often a maddening contradiction to her words. Of this passage, Cornez mused, "Remember the time in which this happened. As a Republican and religious stalwart, she would not publicly be pro-lib or pro-gay. *And* she was selling bras, not burning them. Kevin [Pines] and so many of those she adored in her work and personal life were gay, and she herself benefited by being a strong woman."[22] It is certainly true that Jane was a strong woman, and she often resisted assuming the "traditional" feminine role at home; yet she would always verbally take an anti-feminist stance.

Years after the *Esquire* article, she held firm on that belief. "I am definitely not a feminist, because I think there is a wonderful place for men and there's a wonderful place for women. And I see no reason at all why they should try to be the same." In practically the same breath she also acknowledged a belief in the equality of men and women but added, without elaborating, "Feminism is a great deal more than that. It's nonsense, most of it."[23]

As for her derogatory comments about gays and lesbians, Jane's words and actions never seemed to line up. In later years, largely due to *Gentlemen Prefer Blondes,* Jane would develop a large gay following. According to Yvonne Bracamontes, who was close friends with Jane in her final years, she didn't mind this status as a gay icon. "She would just love people for whoever they are," Bracamontes remembered. "I mean she even went to the Castro Theater in San Francisco. She just loved people for who they were and they loved her. They were her fans. She just loved them back. That's just Jane."[24] By the time Jane appeared at the Castro in 2004 for a screening of *Gentlemen Prefer Blondes,* the theater had long been an LGBT cultural center. Marc Huestis, who booked Jane for the event, was initially hesitant about having her appear, given her reputation as a right-wing Christian. When her agent at the time, Marvin Paige, repeatedly proclaimed, "I repeat, *do not* tell her if there are drag queens in the show," Huestis had additional cause for pause, as he had indeed booked Matthew Martin and Jordan L'Moore to perform as Jane and Marilyn.[25] But he took a leap of faith, so to speak, and forged ahead with having Jane appear. When she arrived for the screening and found out the floorshow would have female impersonators, Paige assured Jane she could stay in the green room during the performance. "If you put me in that darned green room, I'll knock your block off," came Jane's reply. "I want to see the floorshow. It sounds terrific."[26] The night was a smashing success, and Jane posed for photos with the drag versions of herself and Marilyn.

Yvonne Bracamontes is also quick to point out that Jane later became close friends with Ron Russell, a female impersonator and gay rights advocate who frequently performed as Jane. Gerry Cornez noted that if Jane actively discriminated against people based on their sexual orientation, it would have adversely affected many of her relationships. "So many of WAIF's volunteer leaders would have done an about-face if they suspected for a moment that Jane was anything like these [*Esquire*] quotes depict," he said. This included Judy Tobias, WAIF's national president who "worked side by side with Jane for forty years. She was Jewish, a devoted Democrat, the mother of a gay son, and a charter member of EMILY's List" (an organization whose mission is to elect pro-choice Democratic women to office).[27]

Jane's contradictory actions also extended to her beliefs about abortion. After her own harrowing experience in 1942, Jane always claimed to be staunchly anti-abortion, and indeed she spent the better part of her life advocating for the option of adoption. However, when a male acquaintance told Jane that his girl-friend, Pepper Aarvold, was pregnant, Jane offered some advice. As Pepper later remembered, her boyfriend "was not ready for a child and told me he never really thought much about having a family. I had two small children from my first marriage. While having dinner at our favorite restaurant, the Smoke House, he told me Jane had given him the name of a doctor just over the Mexican bor-der who had an excellent reputation among the people Jane knew and trusted. His name was Dr. Quinada and he would provide me with a safe abortion." Pepper opted to have the baby, but "raged to my boyfriend about Jane's hypoc-risy. I did that more than once. Why didn't she recommend adoption? Why, because of her religious beliefs, did she ever recommend abortion?"[28]

When the *Esquire* article was published, Jane was unhappy with the unflattering portrayal. So was International Social Service, which was still working with WAIF at the time. Gerry Cornez, then employed with ISS, was assigned damage control when the magazine hit the newsstands. He turned to Edith Lynch, Jane's former publicist, for help:

> I called her and said, "What the hell do I do about this?" I was a kid, I was twenty-something years old, working for International Social Service, I didn't know what to do about it. She sort of guided me and everything about what I would say when the press would call. It was a nightmare. But, see, that's the way Jane talked. . . . Those were things she said which, unfortunately, came off really stupid or uninformed or whatever, and she mixed it. When she would get into her religion, everything would go through religion. She didn't have in those days an Edith Lynch around her to be a barrier, to guide her, and guide her not to speak to certain people or to prep her appropriately.[29]

Revisiting the article years later, Cornez observed, "It is clear to me that they [Jane, Kevin Pines, and Dotson Rader] were all drunk, getting more so as their evening together continues. It smacks of the haze so many were in dur-ing those days when drink or drug mixed with the cool or celebrated amongst us and the stories we'd tell later."[30]

Jane and Kevin Pines threatened a defamation lawsuit against *Esquire,* claiming the article was totally inaccurate and filled with misquotes, but this never came to pass.[31]

After spending most of her life in the San Fernando Valley, Jane decided to leave it in 1973. She had recently moved into her apartment in Taos West, but she had spent some time in Santa Barbara with friends and decided the change of scenery would do her good. She purchased a home in the city, about an hour and a half north of Van Nuys. She even started dating again, including Texas native John Peoples, a retired air force lieutenant colonel who was now involved in real estate investments in nearby Santa Maria. The couple had been seeing each other for about a year when they decided to get married. An intimate ceremony took place on January 31, 1974, the bride and groom wearing informal caftans.

The marriage lasted until Peoples's death in 1999, and by all accounts was a good one, though Peoples had to put in a lot of effort to take care of Jane. It seems she never got over the shock and sorrow of losing Roger Barrett, and her bouts with alcoholism and depression would continue. Peoples proved to be a stabilizing force, to the best of his ability. According to Jan Lowell, "She was such a level-leaded, wonderful woman and what destroyed her totally, totally—was she really never got over Roger's death. John Peoples came along, God bless him. He was a helluva guy, he saved her, he really did, and he did it deliberately, he knew what he was getting into. Friends had told him about her, he knew about her, he went after her and he wooed her and he got her. He saved her life. If he hadn't come along, she would have been dead years ago. I liked him."[32]

After she married Peoples, the Howard Hughes contract finally concluded, officially marking the end of Jane's thirty-year professional relationship with the enigmatic mogul. She hadn't made a movie for Hughes since *Underwater!* and couldn't remember the last time she had seen him, but she had always remained fiercely loyal to her boss. When the original term of her deal to make the five pictures had passed, "I voluntarily extended the period two years against my agents' advice. 'Why give him the extension when you don't need to?' they said. I told them Howard had played square with me and I would play square with him."[33] A few years after the term of her contract expired, Jane ran into Noah Dietrich. "I'd still like to make a picture for Howard," she told him. "And even though the time limit has expired, I'd do it for nothing."[34] As he became increasingly eccentric and his lifestyle more mysterious, the media constantly tried to get Hughes gossip out of Jane, but she wouldn't budge. "He's gone a long way out of his way to avoid publicity," she said in the early 1970s, "so I'm not about to be the one to give it to him."[35] Hughes died in 1976, and even then, Jane had no public comment. Learning of his death, Jane "thought back to the first time I had ever seen Howard and what he had been in my life, how he had changed it, what a good friend he had been, how loyal and 'as good as his word.' I loved him."[36]

25

Path and Detours

Jane had experienced years of uncertainty, but marriage to John Peoples brought some much-needed normalcy to her life. And yet, there were still more challenges to come. Taos West was running in the red, mainly because Jane's brother was undercharging for rent and too much of a softy to make increases. Between the losses on Taos West and the end of the Hughes paychecks, Jane was in need of money, so she did separate engagements of *Catch Me if You Can* in Boston and Dallas in 1974 and 1975. John finally convinced Jane to buy out Tom Russell's share of Taos West, and the couple managed to get the apartments in the black, which eased some of the pressure to work.

WAIF was also facing new challenges. By the 1970s ISS had scaled back its operations and was phasing out adoption programs, so the organization severed ties with WAIF. At that point WAIF also decided to change course and incorporate as a nonprofit. Rather than launching its own adoption programs, WAIF partnered with established organizations like the Child Welfare League of America and UNICEF to assist existing programs. When WAIF incorporated in 1977–1978, the board needed to find an executive director. That was when Gerry Cornez started working with Jane, though he had met her a number of years before when he was working for ISS. He later remembered his first encounter with Jane.

> One day in the early '70s when Jane was on Broadway in *Company*, the rumor went through the office that she was coming to meet with the executive director. We were working in Bangladesh and places like that and they were going to update her on stuff. To go from the elevators to his office you had walk through the reception area and into the elevator lobby and pass that to the bathroom. I have to tell you, I went to the bathroom about forty-two times that day hoping that I would just happen to bump into Jane Russell. I mean, the receptionist couldn't figure out what the hell I was doing.

And I did—I bumped into her, and I have to also tell you that I didn't know the difference between Jane Russell and Rosalind Russell. I didn't really know who she was. I was twenty-one years old and didn't go see a lot of Jane Russell movies, I guess; maybe I wasn't allowed to, I don't know. She just sort of smiled and said hi as we passed and I sort of smiled and shaking in my boots. There she was in this suit with a miniskirt and high boots and a hat on, a really stunning-looking stovepipe hat but turned to the corner and sitting cockeyed on her head, as it was supposed to be, and these long eyelashes and this flared nose—I mean, she was gorgeous. She was absolutely gorgeous. And all I could tell you at that point was I didn't know who Jane Russell was, but I knew I'd just seen, pardon my French, a goddamn movie star. I had never seen a movie star in my life but this was a movie star; the way she walked, the way she dressed, the way she looked. I mean, it was a movie star. And I just floated back to my little desk in the typing pool and I don't think I got any work done for a week. But, anyway, that's how I met Jane Russell.[1]

A short time later, Cornez met her again:

I remember going to see *Company* on Broadway and went and waited with throngs of people at the stage door and when she came out she was signing autographs and her manager was with her and he had no time for any of this and he was pushing people and saying, "Come on, Jane, come on, Janie, come on, come on, we got to party, we're due somewhere, blah blah blah blah blah blah." And then I just said, "Hi, I work for International Social Service," and she just stopped everything and she started to talk to me. He was so pissed at me because it was something that was of interest to her and she didn't really care when she got to the party. . . . We had like a fifteen-minute conversation, which lasted me for at least five years. I mean, it was wonderful. I saw that side of her who truly, truly cared, that this was so much a part of her life. It wasn't just like, oh, yes, sign up a celebrity to come and give a little speech and let them go on their way. This was something that was hers. I got such respect for her at that point.[2]

When Cornez took on the role of executive director, he spent a great deal of time with Jane as WAIF transitioned from fundraising to advocacy at the

Jane in the role of Elizabeth for a stock production of *Catch Me if You Can* in Boston, 1974.

national level. One of the biggest challenges came in 1981 when Jane had to testify before Congress to save the Adoption Assistance and Child Welfare Act of 1980, Public Law 96-272. The act authorized federal funding for adoption and foster care assistance and was passed by Congress unanimously during Jimmy Carter's last year in office. Before it could be enacted, however, Ronald Reagan took office and appointed David Stockman as the director of the Office of Management and Budget. Stockman was vehemently opposed to government social safety nets and froze the legislation. Jumping into action, Jane and Gerry went to Washington to unfreeze the funds. On March 11, 1981, Jane testified in defense of the act on Capitol Hill. The scene was straight out of a Hollywood drama, as Cornez later described:

> All of a sudden, the klieg lights went on and paparazzi jumped forward and microphones appeared and everything and they said, "Jane Russell has come to testify." In those days, in the 1980s, it wasn't done as often as it is now with every celebrity having a cause and going to Washington. This stuff appeared in fourteen hundred newspapers

overnight, pictures of Jane Russell testifying, and it was picked up by the *Today Show* and *Good Morning America,* and all of the news programs and the nightly news programs all covered Jane in one fell swoop. We spent several days in Washington going from senator to representative to whomever we could meet with and we made five, six, seven trips back and forth to Washington, even when the cameras were not rolling at all and continued to have these meetings.[3]

After the appearance, Jane worked relentlessly, contacting members of Congress to push the legislation through. "I don't know whether I'm a left-wing Republican or a right-wing Democrat," she said, "but when it comes to kids, I'm all for this legislation."[4] When the bill went to conference for a vote, Pete Stark, congressperson from California, said, "There's nobody in this room who hasn't heard from, met with, gotten calls from Jane Russell. This is Jane Russell's law. If you told her you were going to vote for it, now is the time to vote for it."[5]

The bill passed.

WAIF would continue to advocate for children until 2000, when Jane finally decided to retire from it. Despite everything the organization had accomplished since its inception, Cornez felt more could have been done, especially early on, but ISS and the United Nations never knew how to capitalize on Jane's celebrity to elevate their cause. The UN would invite Jane to lunch once a year as a token gesture, but that was about it. According to Cornez, "She said, 'I can't tell you how many times we went to that delegates' dining room and they patted me on the back and sent me on my way.' That's the way they treated her."[6] WAIF was one of the most important endeavors of Jane's life, yet now remains one of the least known.

In the 1970s Jane would have to endure two more harrowing personal episodes. The first came in 1976 when Buck Waterfield was arrested on suspicion of attempted murder. After the divorce Buck had remained with his father but, much like Thomas, had started to butt heads with Robert when he became a teenager. According to Jane, he "hit the streets" when he was fifteen.[7] Buck had moved to Cuyama, California, which Jane described as the "wild west," and gotten married when he was nineteen. A few months later, according to Sergeant Don Dicus of the Santa Maria Sheriff's Station, "Waterfield and two juveniles reportedly had been driving around the Cuyama Valley on Saturday night, shooting at signs, gates and other spur-of-the-moment targets with a 9mm automatic handgun."[8] One of these targets was the Hay Baler Bar, where one of the bullets struck twenty-six-year-old Oscar Hernandez in the back of the head as he was dancing. He died a few days later. Waterfield was arrested.

John Peoples bailed him out, and Jane came to her son's defense, blaming the environment of the town. "They sell and serve liquor to minors up there. I was shocked at the amount of liquor I found in his home—and in the homes of other young people who live in the Cuyama area. . . . He was only doing what he had seen everybody in Cuyama do."[9] Jane wanted to support her son in person, but felt she was in between a rock and a hard place because of her celebrity. "At the beginning of the trial his attorney (Paul Caruso) told me to stay away because it might look like pressure was being put on the court by the presence of a well-known name. So I stayed out of sight. Then I was accused of deserting Buck. So I started going to the trial and then I was accused of trying to influence the court."[10] The incident gave Jane and Robert a chance to battle each other once again, but they eventually rallied around their son. Buck was eventually convicted of involuntary manslaughter and sentenced to nine months in jail and five years' probation.[11]

Jane also had her own run-in with the law during this time. In 1976 she had been arrested, convicted of driving while intoxicated, and given probation. "I was drunk then, I admit it," she said of the incident.[12] Two years later, less than two blocks from her home, she ran her Mercedes into the side of a truck. It was morning. The other driver was fine and Jane was uninjured, but her car was totaled. The Santa Barbara police arrested her for drunk driving. Jane protested. "I wasn't drunk and no one was hurt. I had a drink the night before, but I wasn't drunk at 10:30 am in the morning." Jane hadn't just had "a" drink the night before—she had been drunk and was severely hungover at the time of the crash. Her protests had no impact on the police or the judge, who sentenced her to four days in jail, suspended her license for a year, and gave her two years' probation. Jane did her four days in June 1978 without too much complaint, though she was aghast at having to wake up early every morning. She also could have done without the embarrassing publicity. Even though she maintained her innocence in that particular incident, she came to view the punishment as a mild price to pay for a lifetime of similar behavior. "Four days in jail, two years' probation, and no driver's license for a year—all because of those other times."[13] As for her drinking, she proclaimed, "I've stopped now and I won't touch it again. I find that my husband, John, and I get along better without it."[14]

The following Valentine's Day, while John Peoples was in Los Angeles on business, Jane was asleep when an intruder entered the house. He crawled

Jane and third husband Robert Peoples. (INTERFOTO/Alamy Stock Photo)

into the bed with her. She managed to maintain her composure and started praying out loud and then speaking in tongues. According to Jane, this seemed to have a calming effect on the intruder, and she managed to break away to another part of the house to call the police. By the time they arrived, the intruder was gone. Though shaken up, Jane was physically unharmed.

By the end of the decade, Jane had had enough of Santa Barbara, and John was inclined to agree. Thomas Waterfield had moved to Prescott, Arizona, in the mid-1970s and co-founded a music band called Toucan Eddy. Tracy, who had married and divorced, had also ended up in Prescott with her son, Jaime. As Jane and John were trying to figure out what their next chapter would be, they went to Prescott to visit the kids, and ended up taking a drive that brought them to Sedona, an hour or so away. They both immediately fell in love with the picturesque city, and Jane was thrilled with the idea of being near her grandson. They decided to sell everything and make the move. The Valley girl was leaving California.

26

Living Legend

When Jane moved to Arizona in the early 1980s, she ingratiated herself into the community, even serving as grand marshal of the annual Sedona St. Patrick's Day Parade in 1981.[1] Jane and John also opened a restaurant and bar called Dude's Far Western, named after Peoples's son from a previous marriage. The venue hosted live entertainment, including musician Ray Starling and Eartha Kitt.[2] After only three years, however, it closed; Jane noted, "Trouble was that the young people would listen to the music all night and buy a couple of wines. We couldn't make a go of it."[3]

Jane and John were living a quiet, comfortable life in Sedona, but when she received an offer to appear on the prime-time television series *The Yellow Rose,* she decided to take it. Tracy had gotten remarried and given birth to twin girls, so Jane took the job in order to give her daughter a financial boost. "I'm not broke or on poverty row," Jane explained. "I'm working so I can leave my children and grandchildren a nice legacy. Oh sure, they're doing OK, but they're all in their 30s and it's time for them to buy houses and put money into businesses. I want to give them something before they die. I don't want them to have to wait until I'm gone to enjoy the good things in life."[4]

The Yellow Rose was a sweeping soap opera about feuding Texas cattle families, starring Sam Elliott, Cybill Shepherd, and Chuck Connors. It was cut from the same cloth as *Dallas* and other evening network shows like *Falcon Crest, Dynasty,* and *The Colbys,* which featured golden age actors like Barbara Bel Geddes, Jane Wyman, Joan Collins, and Barbara Stanwyck. The ratings on the NBC show had been lackluster, so "I'm supposed to be a shot in the arm for *Yellow Rose,*" Jane said. "We'll soon find out whether I'm the vitamin shot they're looking for—or the arsenic."[5] Jane was cast to play Rose Hollister, the long-lost mother of Sam Elliott and sister of Chuck Connors. Her guest-starring appearances were limited, and her scenes mostly with Sam Elliott, but they played off each other well. At sixty-one, she still had that

Jane poses with *Yellow Rose* co-stars Sam Elliott, Edward Albert, Cybil Shepherd, and Tom Schanley. (MediaPunch Inc/Alamy Stock Photo)

dominating movie star presence, and she also got to prove that she was still more than capable of mounting and riding a horse. Age and adversity had not slowed down Jane Russell. Two years after appearing in *The Yellow Rose*, Jane would have one last on-screen acting job, playing a Jane Russell–like actress, with a twist, on a single episode of the show *Hunter*.

While in Sedona, Jane also worked on her autobiography in earnest. She was originally contracted to write the book for Simon & Schuster in 1977, when she was still in Santa Barbara. Jan and Bob Lowell, who had helped pen Shelley Winters's best-selling autobiography, had been brought on to assist Jane. "We met Jane," Jan Lowell later recalled, "and it was love at first sight with all of us. We stayed almost two months in a small motel in Santa Barbara not far from her house. We went over there every day. Jane had broken her ankle or something and for most of the time she was in bed. She would lie in her bed with her foot up and we talked and taped. There was a coffee machine in the bathroom. Jane and I were both big smokers so we would smoke, drink coffee, and talk and tape."[6]

Jane had some fun with the couple when she sent them to speak with Robert Mitchum, who lived in the area. As Jan Lowell recounted:

We went over to meet Mitch at his house and he was charming. He had just come back from lunch and he was slightly buzzed. We sat out on his patio with our tape recorder and we talked and he told us funny stories and it was lovely. And then he said, "Listen, you guys aren't going to write that kind of sexy, who-I-slept-with Shelley Winters sort of crappy book, are you?" And we sort of cringed and we said, which was truthful, "No, no, we're not, of course not." We figured, "Oh my God, he doesn't know that we wrote it." We were kind of embarrassed. We said, "No, no, no, we're writing a book about Jane and Jane is above all a lady." She really was.

We left there after a while, very embarrassed about that, cringing, kind of. As we were driving up to Jane's house, she's hanging out the kitchen window laughing her head off. I got out of the car and I said, "What's so funny?" She said, "Did he tell you that he hoped you weren't going to write the kind of book that was written about Shelley Winters?" And we said, "Yes." She said, "Oh, you poor thing, I shouldn't have done it but I told him you had written the Shelley Winters book." I said, "Jane, that's a dirty trick!" She said, "I know, I couldn't resist." Yeah, she was funny. She had a great sense of humor. I really, really liked that lady.

When the Lowells finished working with Jane, "we went back to Italy with a million tapes and tons of photos and old, old movie magazines and articles and we sat for I don't know how long and put it all together into the book," said Jan.[7] The publisher, which had hoped Jane's story would prove to be as titillating as Shelley Winters's, was disappointed with the result, convinced it would not be a best seller. "Jane wanted to tell her story," said Jan, "and her story really was how God had saved her life and how she couldn't live without God."[8]

Jane took the rejected manuscript back from the publisher just as she was leaving Santa Barbara for Sedona. She invited the Lowells to fly in from their home in Rome to assist her with revising the memoir. "Well, at that point," remembered Jan, "we had been seven months in L.A. with Shelley and then a year and a half later, two months in Santa Barbara with Jane and I had reached the point where I looked at my husband and said, 'No more movie stars. Please, God, no more movie stars!' And I said, 'Jane, I love you, but I just can't do it.'" Jane finished it the way she wanted and *Jane Russell: My Path and My Detours* was published in 1985 by Franklin Watts.

Jane's autobiography may not be as scandalous as Shelley Winters's, but it is frank and honest. Jane made no attempt to sugarcoat the painful parts of her life or to make herself out to be a saint. As to why Jane chose to share so many intimate details, Jan Lowell was at a loss. "Why does one want to expose all of this stuff? I have no idea."[9] Jane claimed she hoped others could avoid the "detours" she had made: "I wrote the book because I thought it would help some people."[10] Jane did change the names of people still living to avoid embarrassing them, but she was forthcoming about the domestic violence she had endured during her marriage to Robert Waterfield. It's possible she felt empowered to reveal this aspect of the relationship since Waterfield had passed away two years before the book's release. He had lived in the Sherman Oaks home until he got remarried in 1976, again in Las Vegas, to a woman named Jan Green. Always one to appreciate the humor of things, when Jane first met Bob and Jan Lowell she "did a double take," said Jan. "She looked at us and said, 'Jesus, I have one Bob and Jan in my life, I'm not sure I want another.'"[11] As for the spectacular Mid-Century Modern home Jane had designed and shared with Waterfield for twenty years, it was demolished in 1996 after sustaining damage in the Northridge earthquake two years before.

Even though Jane had been candid about her abortion and her abusive husband in the book, these were not aspects she wanted to dwell on when she made the rounds of talk shows and local news to promote it. An appearance on Joan Rivers's show became especially awkward when Rivers continued to press Jane about the 1942 abortion, a topic that had been declared off limits to the show's producer prior to Jane's appearance. Jane, although visibly uncomfortable and clearly rankled, managed to maintain her composure during the show, but she was incensed and later threatened a lawsuit.[12]

After spending five years in Sedona, Jane was content to remain settled for the most part, though she had reunited with Connie Haines and Beryl Davis to play some shows around Arizona. John Peoples, on the other hand, had grown tired of the Grand Canyon State. "Jane loves it here," he admitted. "For me it's the pits. I want to get back to Santa Barbara."[13] Jane discounted his sentiments, saying, "Don't take him too seriously when he talks about this place. When we were in New York lately, we could have stayed five days but he couldn't wait to get back here after one."[14] Even so, Jane finally relented, and the couple moved back to the Santa Barbara area, settling in the nearby community of Montecito. The property, one and a half acres with a creek running through it, included a four-bedroom main house, a guesthouse, and an additional apartment above the garage.

Jane arrives at the Academy Awards in 1983. She would continue to make personal appearances until the final weeks of her life.

In 1988 Jane revisited an early ambition when she launched a clothing line bearing her name. Jane Russell Classic Evenings was a line of loungewear and sleepwear designed for middle-income, full-figured women. "I'm so sick of Madonna-type clothes I could croak," she sighed. "People want glamour again, and that's what my line is about: sexy nightgowns, caftans, pajamas—

all for the full-figured gal, naturally."[15] Russell even toured the factory in Lancaster, Pennsylvania, where the clothes were manufactured. "We want to make things for women who are in the mainstream of life and can't find things in stores that will fit."[16] In addition to the clothing, the Jane Russell Collection jewelry line was also launched.

It was during this period that Jane started to assume the role of "living legend," a part she would play for the rest of her life. Many of her contemporaries had passed away, and as the myths of Marilyn Monroe and Howard Hughes continued to grow, Jane was one of the few living links to both. "Movie star" may have not been a role Jane aggressively pursued during the course of her career, but it was one she later embraced as people sought her out as a bridge to the past. When Martin Scorsese made his Howard Hughes biopic *The Aviator*, Leonardo DiCaprio, who portrayed Hughes, sought out Jane and met with her in order to prepare for the role. She was interviewed often for newspapers, magazines, television programs, documentaries, book introductions, film screenings, and so on, often being asked the same questions and often telling the same stories, but usually displaying characteristic patience, humor, and grace. She accepted invitations to film festivals, autograph shows, award shows, charity functions, and countless other personal appearances.

She was often asked about film content after the demise of the Production Code in the late 1960s. "I suppose *The Outlaw* looks like Little Bo Peep compared with some movies today," she would joke. "I'm very glad I'm not starting out in pictures today. I simply wouldn't play."[17] Ironically, when *The Outlaw* was given a rating by the Motion Picture Association of America in 1976, the film that had caused so much controversy was now rated G for general audiences.

Jane and John remained in Montecito, but in April 1999, as Jane recounted, "He had a massive heart attack when he was cutting the hedge. His son, who lived with us, came rushing into the house. I ran out and I felt absolutely sure that he'd already died. The doctors got him to the hospital and restarted his heart but his brain was dead. He never opened his eyes again."[18] John Calvin Peoples was just shy of his seventy-second birthday. He and Jane had been married for twenty-five years. Two months later, Jane put their property on the market for $2.7 million.[19]

For a short time after, Jane continued to live with Peoples's son in Montecito, but "then the next year his son, who had been looking after me, also died." Jane said. "I just went home and started drinking so that I didn't have to think. I didn't care what happened to me."[20] The drinking got out of control; one day Jane was found unconscious in her home and taken to a hospital. When she woke up, she found all three of her children at her bedside. They staged an intervention. "It was my 79th birthday and they said if I'd agree to go into a rehabilitation clinic the Lord would go with me."[21] Jane kept her bargain, and by all accounts, she remained sober for the rest of her life.

After his run-in with the law, Buck Waterfield had gradually gotten his life together and settled down in Santa Maria, around seventy miles north of Santa Barbara, with his second wife, Etta. Now Buck insisted that Jane move to Santa Maria as well, so she purchased a home at 2430 Ridgemark Drive. Jane began forming a circle of friends in the area, including Mary Hudson, mother of pop star Katy Perry, who had her own ministry. Jane also became friends with Yvonne Bracamontes, who was much younger than Jane and ministered to prison inmates. They had met when Yvonne, who had no idea who Jane Russell was, attended a Bible study at the actress's house. Yvonne was more concerned with ministry than movie stars, and the pair hit it off immediately. As Jane got older, she suffered from macular degeneration, so Bracamontes ended up driving her around town, and would eventually accompany her to various engagements as well. "It was like *Driving Miss Daisy*," Bracamontes laughs, "and it was really, really, really awesome. I got to meet all her friends. I've gone to parties where I was the only one that wasn't famous there. People would ask, 'Are you Jane's publicist?'" She continued, "I'm a Latina and I just didn't fit wherever she took me. But she was so awesome. She would never, never treat me like I was less [of a person]. . . . She was like that. And she would let everybody know, I don't care how famous they were, that I was her friend."[22]

Yvonne recalled one visit to the Playboy Mansion, where Jane had been invited. When she dropped Jane off at the door, she said, "Look, lady, if I'm going to be dropping you off over here, you'd better get some of those bunnies saved!" She continued, "She would go in a room where there was a piano and a lot of the bunnies would go in there and talk to her, and she would be able to talk to them. Not tearing them down, but loving them and just letting them hear about her stardom and letting the girls know that they can do it too, and they were more than just this. I mean she would say it in a way that they would receive it. And she was good at that. She was really great at that." When Jane visited prisons with Bracamontes to minister to the inmates, according to Yvonne, she would stand in front of the group and reference her 1978 arrest. "'Hey, well, I'm one of you guys!' And everybody would start laughing. But she would make them feel comfortable right away because she wanted them to know 'I'm nothing greater than you. I'm just a woman saved by grace.'"[23]

Bible study and personal appearances weren't enough to completely fill Jane's time. In 2006 she developed a stage act and started regularly performing at a local hotel. "I miss performing," she admitted. "I always loved singing and for me this is fun. There isn't much for older people to do here in Santa Maria, where I live, so some friends and I decided it would be fun to have some of our kind of music and we sing songs from the swinging Forties."[24] In addition to her loss of sight, Jane's hearing had also begun to deteriorate, so performing was a respite from the ailments of aging. "I've also been losing my hearing for more than a decade," she said, "and that's frustrating. Sometimes I really feel my age. But I can still kick up my heels, and sing and dance."[25] A standard of her act was "Big Bad Jane," a takeoff of the Jimmy Dean song "Big Bad John," with updated lyrics by songstress Peggy Lee.

Connie Haines had passed away in 2008, and Beryl Davis was suffering from Alzheimer's. Jane would visit Beryl often, sometimes bringing her to Santa Maria, where the pair would revisit their musical past. According to Yvonne Bracamontes, "Jane would bring her down here and Beryl would not miss a beat out of any songs she would sing. I mean, all those songs! It's weird that people who have Alzheimer's—they just don't forget the music."[26]

Jane continued to make television appearances, including some on the Trinity Broadcasting Network. Jane had long identified as a Republican, and her beliefs moved further to the right as she got older. In 2003 she did an interview with the *London Daily Mail,* which quoted her as saying, "These days I'm a teetotaling, mean-spirited, Rightwing, narrow-minded, conservative, Christian bigot but not a racist. You can be bigoted about anything. It just means you don't have an open mind."[27] Like the *Esquire* article, the quote was a mind-boggling contradiction of the Jane Russell described by people in her inner circle. "She didn't mean 'bigoted' the way it came out. That was the problem. She meant it some other way," according to Bracamontes.[28] "From my more subjective perch," said Gerry Cornez, "I see her ending that 'These days . . . bigot' quote with a wink! I am a Boston Kennedy Democrat who worked with her, traveled with her, stayed at her house and she at mine and never heard a bigoted word pass her lips. Thus I am saddened that quote has come to identify her in any way or could be construed as part of today's conservative Christian dogma."[29] No matter what Jane meant, in an era of the internet and extreme political polarization, the quote, misleadingly truncated after the word *bigot,* has made the rounds and done much to damage Jane's legacy.

In one of her last appearances, Jane accepted a Lifetime Achievement Award at the Fort Lauderdale International Film Festival in November 2010. (JR Davis-PHOTOlink.net)

At the end of her life, Jane's personal appearance schedule was as robust as ever. In November 2010, she attended the Hollywood Walk of Fame's 50th Anniversary Celebration, followed by a sold-out screening of *Gentlemen Prefer Blondes* at the Fort Lauderdale International Film Festival, where she received a Lifetime Achievement Award. Two months later she flew back to Florida for an appearance at the Crest Theatre in Delray Beach, where she reminisced about her long career and even performed a few songs. The next day she spoke at Palm Beach's Paramount Church, which was trying to raise funds for capital improvements on its building, a converted movie palace. According to Bracamontes, "That weekend she got sick in Florida. Somebody was trying to get John Travolta to give her a ride but his airplane wasn't equipped with medical stuff. So they had to get a medical plane."[30] Jane made it home to Santa Maria, where in mid-February 2011, despite her ailing health, she hosted a hundredth birthday celebration for the late president Ronald Reagan. She was still scheduled for her regular "Swinging Forties" slot, ongoing since 2006, at the Radisson Hotel.

By the end of the month, Jane's health had worsened. On February 28, 2011, she passed away from respiratory complications. "All of the family was right there with her when she passed," Buck Waterfield told the local newspaper. "She was at home and that's where she wanted to be."[31] Jane hadn't made a movie in over forty years, but her death made headlines around the globe.

The legacy Jane Russell left behind is a complicated one: a Hollywood sex symbol who studied the Bible when the cameras weren't rolling; a world-recognized, highly paid movie star who wasn't necessarily a top box office draw; a dedicated advocate of orphaned children who aligned with a political party that challenged the social safety net programs she championed. What is indisputable is that she was a commanding presence on the silver screen at a time when the studio system dominated it. Her career was hampered in many ways by Howard Hughes, but she also benefited from her association with him, which gave her large paychecks and high billing. Very few actresses could have overcome the barrage of "mean . . . moody . . . magnificent" publicity, but Jane Russell did. Not only did she go on to have a notable, if not sterling, career, she was able to use the controversy and celebrity it brought her to benefit others, which she did indefatigably until the end of her life. She herself often regarded her success in movies as accidental, but there's no denying that Jane Russell possessed something that set her apart, some aura that made her a large-than-life personality and an unforgettable human being.

Acknowledgments

My name may be on the cover of this book, but I received a lot of help and support along the way to publication, and I would like to express my sincere thanks and appreciation to those who have lent their time, talent, and support over the past few years.

The internet is an astounding source of information, but no biography is written without good old analog research. Special thanks to the folks at the Margaret Herrick Library at the University of California, Los Angeles the New York Public Library, and the Clip & Still Licensing Department, Twentieth Century-Fox.

As was the case with my Ann Dvorak book, much of this research was conducted at the Los Angeles Public Library's Central Library, where I am fortunate enough to work. The collections at Central are nothing short of treasure troves made accessible by my many colleagues, past and present: Emma Roberts, Mary McCoy, Glen Creason, Cindy McNaughton, Debbie Savage, Kelly Wallace, Nick Beyelia, Terri Garst, Fernando Saucedo, Wendy Horowitz, Sye Gutierrez, Valeria Baragan, Linda Rudell-Betts, Greg Reynolds, Bob Timmermann, Jim Sherman, Sheryn Morris, David Kelly, Pam Quon, Matthew Mattson, Joyce Cooper, Ani Boyadjian, and Kim Creighton.

Writing a book about Jane gave me an excuse to do one of my favorite things: movie memorabilia shopping. Thanks to the following memorabilia dealers, who helped me by keeping an eye out for all things Jane: Roy Windham of Baby Jane of Hollywood, Danny Schwartz of Baseball Cards & Movie Collectibles, Jeffrey Mantor of Larry Edmunds, Jerry Ohlinger's Movie Materials, and Morris Everett of the Last Moving Picture Company.

Thanks to Anne Dean Dotson, Patrick McGilligan, and Ashley Runyon at the University Press of Kentucky for encouraging me to hit the keyboard again. I am also so appreciative of Gerry Cornez, Yvonne Bracamontes, and the late Jan Lowell, who graciously shared their time and memories of Jane. I am especially grateful to Lawrence Williams, who knows more about Jane

Russell than I could ever hope to, and who generously shared his extensive knowledge to ensure that her story was told accurately on these pages.

I am fortunate to be consistently propped up by loving family and friends who always lend encouragement and support. Love and thanks to the Rices— my parents, Louise and Fran; siblings C. J., Casey, Carly, and Susan "Soupcan" Bansmer; Uncle Al; and my stepmom Yvonne Joyce. I am grateful as well as to the Tokar clan, my wonderful in-laws Maureen and Jeremy, and all the other Fialkovs. My grandparents Mary and Al are no longer around, but they remain an inspiration, and I will always be indebted to my grandma Betty "Nonnie" Rice for introducing me to *Gentlemen Prefer Blondes*.

Hugs to my friends Nova Meza, Erik Larson, Tony Pinizzotto, Garland Testa, Tanya Whitehouse, Stephen Lewis, Michelle Morgan, Sherri Snyder, Mark Vieira, Joan Renner, Amy Inouye, David Davis, Tom Zimmerman, Glynn Martin, Cindy Olnick, Lynell George, Steve and Christy McAvoy, Dennis Kopp, Alan Rode, Danny Reid, Margot Gerber, Sera Sacks, Mary Mallory, Chris and Heidi Ryder, Tony Fleecs, Shannon Forrey, Jim Ratay, and the Toluca Moms: Jennifer Raim, Ilana Turner, Jess Finn, and Sara Reddy.

Extra special thanks to Laura Wagner, who's always too generous with her time and mind-boggling depth of film knowledge.

I am so lucky to have Darin Barnes in my life; he never met a movie memorabilia challenge he could resist. Who am I writing about next?

My husband, Joshua Hale Fialkov, is always so supportive of me, no matter how often I overextend myself. Thank you for always being my biggest champion.

Finally, to my amazing daughter, Gable: I know some of these evenings have been long while I worked on this book, but I hope this makes you proud. I am so happy to have someone to share my love of classic film with.

Filmography

The Outlaw (1943)
Howard Hughes Productions. Directed by Howard Hughes. Jane Russell as Rio. Cast: Jack Beutel, Walter Huston, Thomas Mitchell, Mimi Aguglia, Joe Sawyer. (Premiered in San Francisco in 1943, distributed by United Artists in 1946 and RKO in 1950.)

Young Widow (1946)
Hunt Stromberg Productions. Directed by Edwin L. Marin. Jane Russell as Joan Kenwood. Cast: Louis Hayward, Faith Domergue, Marie Wilson, Penny Singleton, Kent Taylor, Connie Gilchrist, Cora Witherspoon, Steve Brodie.

The Paleface (1948)
Paramount Pictures. Directed by Norman Z. McLeod. Jane Russell as Calamity Jane. Cast: Bob Hope, Robert Armstrong, Iris Adrian, Robert Watson, Jack Searle, Iron Eyes Cody.

Double Dynamite (1951)
RKO. Directed by Irving Cummings. Jane Russell as Mildred. Cast: Groucho Marx, Frank Sinatra, Don McGuire, Howard Freeman, Nestor Paiva, Frank Orth, Harry Hayden. (Filmed in 1948.)

His Kind of Woman (1951)
RKO. Directed by John Farrow. Jane Russell as Lenore Brent. Cast: Robert Mitchum, Vincent Price, Tim Holt, Charles McGraw, Marjorie Reynolds, Raymond Burr, Leslye Banning, Jim Backus.

The Las Vegas Story (1952)
RKO. Directed by Robert Stevenson. Jane Russell as Linda Rollins. Cast: Victor Mature, Vincent Price, Hoagy Carmichael, Brad Dexter, Gordon Oliver, Jay C. Flippen, Will Wright, Colleen Miller.

Macao (1952)

RKO. Directed by Josef von Sternberg, Nicholas Ray. Jane Russell as Julie Benson. Cast: Robert Mitchum, William Bendix, Gloria Grahame, Thomas Gomez, Brad Dexter, Edward Ashley, Philip Ahn.

Montana Belle (1952)

RKO. Directed by Allan Dwan. Jane Russell as Belle Starr. Cast: George Brent, Scott Brady, Forrest Tucker, Andy Devine, Jack Lambert, John Litel, Rory Malinson, Roy Barcroft. (Originally filmed by Fidelity Pictures in 1948 but not released.)

Son of Paleface (1952)

Paramount Pictures. Directed by Frank Tashlin. Jane Russell as Mike "The Torch" Delroy. Cast: Bob Hope, Roy Rogers, Bill Williams, Lloyd Corrigan, Paul E. Burns, Douglas Dumbrille, Harry Von Sell, Iron Eyes Cody.

The Road to Bali (1952)

Paramount Pictures. Directed by Hal Walker. Jane Russell as self (unbilled cameo). Cast: Bob Hope, Bing Crosby, Dorothy Lamour.

Gentlemen Prefer Blondes (1953)

Twentieth Century-Fox. Directed by Howard Hawks. Jane Russell as Dorothy Shaw. Cast: Marilyn Monroe, Charles Coburn, Elliott Reed, Tommy Noonan, George Winslow, Marcel Dalio, Taylor Holmes, Norma Varden.

The French Line (1953)

RKO. Directed by Lloyd Bacon. Jane Russell as Mary Carson. Cast: Gilbert Roland, Arthur Hunnicutt, Mary McCarty, Joyce MacKenzie, Paula Corday, Craig Stevens.

Underwater! (1955)

RKO. Directed by John Sturges. Jane Russell as Theresa Gray. Cast: Richard Egan, Gilbert Roland, Lori Nelson, Robert Keith, Joseph Calleia, Eugene Iglesias, Ric Roman, Max Wagner.

Foxfire (1955)

Universal-International. Directed by Joseph Pevney. Jane Russell as Amanda Lawrence. Cast: Jeff Chandler, Dan Duryea, Mara Corday, Robert F. Simon, Friesa Inescort, Barton MacLane.

The Tall Men (1955)
Twentieth Century-Fox. Directed by Raoul Walsh. Jane Russell as Nella Turner. Cast: Clark Gable, Robert Ryan, Cameron Mitchell, Juan Garcia, Harry Shannon, Emile Meyer.

Gentlemen Marry Brunettes (1955)
Russ-Field Productions. Directed by Richard Sale. Jane Russell as Bonnie Jones. Cast: Jeanne Crain, Alan Young, Scott Brady, Rudy Vallee, Guy Middleton, Eric Pohlman, Ferdy Mayne.

Hot Blood (1956)
Columbia Pictures. Directed by Nicholas Ray. Jane Russell as Annie Caldash. Cast: Cornel Wilde, Luther Adler, Joseph Calleia, Mikhail Rasummy, Jamie Russell, Wally Russell, Richard Deacon.

The Revolt of Mamie Stover (1956)
Twentieth Century-Fox. Directed by Raoul Walsh. Jane Russell as Mamie Stover. Cast: Richard Egan, Agnes Moorehead, Joan Leslie, Jorja Curtright, Michael Pate, Richard Coogan, Alan Reed, Jean Wiles, Margia Dean.

The Fuzzy Pink Nightgown (1957)
Russ-Field Productions. Directed by Norman Taurog. Jane Russell as Laurel Stevens. Cast: Ralph Meeker, Keenan Wynn, Una Merkel, Fred Clark, Adolph Menjou, Benay Venuta, Robert H. Harris.

Fate Is the Hunter (1964)
Twentieth Century-Fox. Directed by Ralph Nelson. Jane Russell as herself. Cast: Glenn Ford, Nancy Kwan, Rod Taylor, Suzanne Pleshette, Wally Cox, Nehemiah Persoff, Mark Stevens, Max Showalter, Constance Towers, Howard St. John, Robert Wilkie, Dort Clark, Mary Wickes, Dorothy Malone.

Johnny Reno (1966)
Paramount Pictures. Directed by R. G. Springsteen. Jane Russell as Nona Williams. Cast: Dana Andrews, Lon Chaney Jr., John Agar, Lyle Bettger, Tom Drake, Richard Arlen, Robert Lowery.

Waco (1966)
Paramount Pictures. Directed by R. G. Springsteen. Jane Russell as Jill Stone. Cast: Howard Keel, Bran Donlevy, Wendell Corey, Terry Moore, John Smith, John Agar, Gene Evans, Richard Arlen, Ben Cooper, DeForest Kelley, Jeff Richards.

The Born Losers (1967)
American International. Directed by Tom Laughlin (credited as T. C. Frank). Jane Russell as Mrs. Shorn. Cast: Tom Laughlin, Elizabeth James, Jeremy Slate, William Wellman Jr., Robert Tessier, Jeff Cooper, Edwin Cook, Paul Prokop.

Cauliflower Cupids (1970)
Starlite Films. Directed by Peter Savage (credited as Peter Petrella). Jane Russell as Nira DiLaurento. Cast: Peter Savage, Alan Dale, Lee Meridith, Betty Bruce, Rocky Graziano, Jake LaMotta, Tony Zale, Willie Pep, Paddy DeMarco, Petey Scalzo. (Filmed in 1966 under the title *The Honorable Frauds.*)

Darker Than Amber (1970)
Cinema Center Films. Directed by Robert Clouse. Jane Russell as Alabama Tigress. Cast: Rod Taylor, Suzy Kendall, Janet MacLachlan, Theodore Bikel.

Notes

Abbreviations

ELP	Edith Lynch Papers, Margaret Herrick Library, Center for Motion Picture Study, Academy of Motion Picture Arts and Sciences, Beverly Hills, CA.
FBI	Jane Russell File, Federal Bureau of Investigation.
FOX	Clip & Still Licensing Department, Twentieth Century-Fox, Century City, CA.
HHP	Hedda Hopper Papers, Margaret Herrick Library, Center for Motion Picture Study, Academy of Motion Picture Arts and Sciences, Beverly Hills, CA.
LACSC	Los Angeles County Superior Court.
LAPL	Adoption vertical file, Social Sciences, Philosophy, & Religion Department, Los Angeles Public Library.
PCA	Production Code Administration Files, Margaret Herrick Library, Academy of Motion Picture Arts and Sciences, Beverly Hills, CA.
PPPR	Paramount Pictures Production Records, Margaret Herrick Library, Center for Motion Picture Study, Academy of Motion Picture Arts and Sciences, Beverly Hills, CA.
RBP	Russell Birdwell Papers, boxes 41 and 48, University of California, Los Angeles (UCLA).
RKO	RKO Radio Pictures Studio Records (Collection PASC 3), UCLA Library Special Collections, Charles E. Young Research Library, University of California, Los Angeles.
WGC	William Gordon Collection, Margaret Herrick Library, Center for Motion Picture Study, Academy of Motion Picture Arts and Sciences, Beverly Hills, CA.

Introduction

1. Audio commentary, *The Outlaw,* 2009.
2. Lester, *When Hollywood Was Fun,* 54.
3. Russell, *Jane Russell,* 19.
4. Wilkie, "Catch Me Cookin'!" 2.

1. From Bemidji to Burbank

1. Jacobi Russell, *Oh, Lord, What Next?* 41.

2. Jane Russell, birth certificate, June 21, 1921, file no. 1921-01564, Minnesota Historical Society, St. Paul, copy in possession of author.

3. Jacobi Russell, *Oh, Lord, What Next?* 42.

4. Ibid.

5. Ibid., 114–15.

6. "Ontario Births, 1869–1912," s.v. "Amelia Hyatt, June 18, 1871," FamilySearch.org (accessed June, 1, 2019).

7. "Ontario, County Marriage Registers, 1858–1869," s.v. "Ernest A. Jacobi and Ellen Stevensen," FamilySearch.org (accessed June 1, 2019).

8. Jacobi Russell, *Oh, Lord, What Next?* 30.

9. *Plymouth Theatre Magazine,* January 6, 1913, http://www.performingartsarchive.com/Other-shows/Disraeli_Boston_1913/Disraeli_Boston_1913.htm.

10. Jacobi Russell, *Oh, Lord, What Next?* 31.

11. Daddy Long Legs advertisement, *East Liverpool Evening Review,* February 6, 1918, 10.

12. Jacobi Russell, *Oh, Lord, What Next?* 136.

13. Ibid., 137.

14. Ibid., 33.

15. Ibid.

16. Ibid., 34.

17. Ibid., 37.

18. William Roy Russell, death certificate, June 30, 1920, file no. 495, Provincial Archives of Alberta, Edmonton, copy in possession of author.

19. Jacobi Russell, *Oh, Lord, What Next?* 45.

2. Valley Girl

1. Jacobi Russell, *Oh, Lord, What Next?* 45.

2. *Jane Russell: Body and Soul.*

3. Jacobi Russell, *Oh, Lord, What Next?* 95.

4. DeVane, "Sensational Cinderella," 50.

5. *Jane Russell: Body and Soul.*

6. Russell, *Oh, Lord, What Next?* 48.

7. Ibid., 95.

8. DeVane, "Sensational Cinderella," 50.

9. Ibid.

10. Ibid.

11. Ibid., 51.

12. "Students' Recital Saturday Night at Woman's Club," *Van Nuys News,* October 18, 1937, 4.

13. Jacobi Russell, *Oh, Lord, What Next?* 57.

14. Ibid., 49.

15. Ibid., 46.

16. Jacobi Russell, *Oh, Lord, What Next?* 99.

17. Russell, *Jane Russell,* 33.

18. "Organized Allied Youth Club at High School," *Van Nuys News,* February 21, 1938, 3.3.

19. "Youthful Thespians Enact Play," *Van Nuys News,* January 19, 1939, 1.

20. "Kiwanians to See Famous Picture," *Van Nuys News,* May 8, 1939, 1.

21. Henry, "Jane Russell's Teen-Age Escapades!" 72.

22. Ibid.

23. Ibid.

3. Daughter Grows Up

1. Jacobi Russell, *Oh, Lord, What Next?* 58.

2. Ibid., 59.

3. Ibid., 60.

4. Ibid., 62.

5. Russell, *Jane Russell,* 40.

6. Jacobi Russell, *Oh, Lord, What Next?* 63.

7. Russell, *Jane Russell,* 41.

8. Jacobi Russell, *Oh, Lord, What Next?* 64.

9. *Scene by Scene.*

10. Jacobi Russell, *Oh, Lord, What Next?* 64.

11. "Room for Rent," *Van Nuys News,* September 22, 1938, 2.6.

12. *Scene by Scene.*

13. Jacobi Russell, *Oh, Lord, What Next?* 65.

14. *Jane Russell: Body and Soul.*

15. *Scene by Scene.*

16. Ibid.

17. Russell, *Jane Russell,* 38.

18. Emerson, "Heart Affair," 96.

19. Ibid.

20. Ibid.

21. Ibid.

22. *San Fernando Valley City Directory* (Los Angeles: Los Angeles Directory, 1923, 1924, 1926, 1928), https://rescarta.lapl.org/.

23. "California, County Birth and Death Records, 1800–1994," s.v. Staton Waterfield, death certificate number 3340, March 17, 1930, FamilySearch.org (accessed June 5, 2019).

24. Emerson, "Heart Affair," 96.

25. Sher, "The Bob Waterfield Story," 72.

26. Ibid.

27. David Condon, "In the Wake of the News," *Chicago Tribune,* August 2, 1966, 49.

28. Ibid.

29. Ibid.

30. Sher, "The Bob Waterfield Story," 72.

31. Ibid., 28,

32. Ibid.

33. Ibid., 72.

34. Jacobi Russell, *Oh, Lord, What Next?* 101.

35. Russell, *Jane Russell,* 46.

36. Ibid.

37. Jacobi Russell, *Oh, Lord, What Next?* 101.

38. Russell, *Jane Russell,* 50.

39. Emerson, "Heart Affair," 96.

40. Benjamin, "Censorable Jane," 44.

41. Emerson, "Heart Affair," 96.

42. Jacobi Russell, *Oh, Lord, What Next?* 101.

43. DeVane, "Sensational Cinderella," 51.

44. Jacobi Russell, *Oh, Lord, What Next?* 102.

45. DeVane, "Sensational Cinderella," 51.

4. Accidental Aspiring Actress

1. Jacobi Russell, *Oh, Lord, What Next?* 103.

2. Jane Russell, U.S. Social Security Act, Application for Account Number, August 4, 1939, United States Social Security Administration, copy in possession of author.

3. Advertisement, *Los Angeles Times,* September 23, 1938, 9.

4. Russell, *Jane Russell,* 6.

5. Jacobi Russell, *Oh, Lord, What Next?* 107.

6. Benjamin, "Censorable Jane," 72.

7. DeVane, "Sensational Cinderella," 51.

8. "Mme. Ouspenskaya Opens Drama Studio in Hollywood," *Los Angeles Times,* January 28, 1940, D7.

9. Russell, *Jane Russell,* 7.

10. Ibid.

11. Benjamin, "Censorable Jane," 70.

12. Russell, *Jane Russell,* 7.

13. Ibid., 8.

14. Advertisement, *Modern Screen,* October 1940, 73.

15. Jacobi Russell, *Oh, Lord, What Next?* 104.

16. *Jane Russell Uncut, Part One.*

17. Russell, *Jane Russell,* 9.

18. Ibid.

5. The Howards

1. Joseph I. Breen, "Re: THE OUTLAW—Howard W. Hawks— Howard Hughes," April 19, 1940, *The Outlaw* file, PCA.

2. Ibid.

3. McCarthy, *Howard Hawks*, 292.

4. Stull, "16mm Sound Tests Pick Two New Stars," 494.

5. Ibid.

6. Maltin, *The Art of the Cinematographer*, 109.

7. Dietrich, *Howard*, 153.

8. DeVane, "Sensational Cinderella," 51.

9. Sheridan, "The Superstar Singing for Her Supper," 24.

10. Russell, *Jane Russell*, 11.

11. Jacobi Russell, *Oh, Lord, What Next?* 104.

12. *Jane Russell: Body and Soul.*

13. Russell, *Jane Russell*, 11.

14. Ibid.

15. Stull, "16mm Sound Tests Pick Two New Stars," 462.

16. Ibid.

17. Russell, *Jane Russell*, 12.

18. Ibid.

19. Ibid, 14–15.

20. Maltin, *The Art of the Cinematographer*, 110.

21. McCarthy, *Howard Hawks*, 295.

22. *Jane Russell Uncut, Part One.*

23. Agreement between Hughes Productions and Jane Russell, signed by Jane Russell October 8, 1940, no. 460352, exhibit A (LACSC)

24. Audio commentary, *The Outlaw*, 2009.

25. *Jane Russell Uncut, Part One.*

26. Jacobi Russell, *Oh, Lord, What Next?* 105.

6. Shooting an Outlaw

1. Russell, *Jane Russell*, 17.

2. Emerson, "Heart Affair," 96.

3. DeVane, "Sensational Cinderella," 51.

4. Jacobi Russell, *Oh, Lord, What Next?* 106.

5. Ibid., 107.

6. Ibid.

7. Ibid.

8. Benjamin, "Censorable Jane," 72.

9. Russell, *Jane Russell*, 17.

10. McCarthy, *Howard Hawks*, 295.

11. Ibid., 16.

12. Louella Parsons, "Howard Hughes Signs Two 'Unknowns' for Picture Leads," *San Francisco Examiner*, November 23, 1940, 15.

13. Edwin Schallert, "John Payne Awarded 'Lucky Baldwin' Lead," *Los Angeles Times*, November 27, 1940, 15.

14. "Howard Hughes Starts New Film in Arizona," *Tucson Daily Citizen,* November 27, 1940, 8.

15. "Starlet Arrived for Hughes Film," *Arizona Republic,* November 28, 1940, 41.

16. McCarthy, *Howard Hawks,* 296.

17. Ibid., 297.

18. Russell, *Jane Russell,* 19.

19. "Winslow Girl Chosen Queen," *Arizona Republic,* December 9, 1940, 5.

20. Dietrich, *Howard,* 153.

21. Victor Boesen to Dale Armstrong, memo, September 8, 1941, RBP.

22. McCarthy, *Howard Hawks,* 296.

23. Dietrich, *Howard,* 153.

24. Audio commentary, *The Outlaw,* 2009.

25. McCarthy, *Howard Hawks,* 297.

26. Audio commentary, *The Outlaw,* 2009.

27. Ibid.

28. Ibid.

29. Victor Boesen to Dale Armstrong, memo, September 11, 1941, RBP.

30. "January Start Looms for British Film," *Boxoffice,* December 21, 1940, 8.

31. Maltin, *The Art of the Cinematographer,* 110.

32. "Howard Hughes, Film Producer, Injured Seriously in Auto Crash," *Los Angeles Times,* December 25, 1940, 1.

33. Paul Harrison, "Howard Hughes' Two New Finds Envy of Filmdom, but if They Achieve Fame, They'll Have Earned It," *Sandusky Star Journal,* January 16, 1941, 4.

34. Audio commentary, *The Outlaw,* 2009.

35. Boesen to Armstrong, September 11, 1941.

36. Ibid.

37. Ibid.

38. Ibid.

39. Audio commentary, *The Outlaw,* 2009.

40. Boesen to Armstrong, September 11, 1941.

41. Ibid.

42. Ibid.

43. Boesen to Armstrong, September 8, 1941.

44. Victor Boesen to Dale Armstrong, memo, October 24, 1941, RBP.

45. Victor Boesen to Dale Armstrong, memo, September 16, 1941, RBP; audio commentary, *The Outlaw,* 2009.

46. Ibid.

47. Boesen to Armstrong, September 11, 1941.

48. Ibid.

49. Audio commentary, *The Outlaw,* 2009.

50. "Mother's Dream of Actress Winning Stardom Comes True," *Los Angeles Times,* February 26, 1941, 12.

51. Jacobi Russell, *Oh, Lord, What Next?* 105–6.

52. Douglas W. Churchill, "Ghost of Billy the Kid Does a Double-take," *New York Times,* March 30, 1941, X5.

53. Dietrich, *Howard,* 153.

7. Motionless Picture Actress

Little could Birdwell know how prophetic those words would be.

1. Keats, *Howard Hughes,* 135.

2. Ibid.

3. "Los Angeles City, California, Birth Records 1906–1930," s.v. "Russell J. Birdwell, June 20, 1924," FamilySearch.org (accessed October 8, 2019).

4. "Birdwell Convicted of Attack," *Los Angeles Times,* September 27, 1923, 2.1.

5. "Services Set for Hollywood Publicist Russell Birdwell," *Los Angeles Times,* December 20, 1977, D1.

6. "Texas Death Records, 1890–1976," s.v. "Dorothy Birdwell, December 8, 1930," FamilySearch.org (accessed October 8, 2019); "Los Angeles City, California, Index of Deaths, 1877–1962 and Death Records, 1930–1963," s.v. "Russell J. Birdwell, August 13, 1946," FamilySearch.org (accessed October 8, 2019).

7. Russell Birdwell to Charles E. McCarthy, letter, January 19, 1941, RBP.

8. Russell Birdwell to George Class, memo, December 5, 1940, RBP.

9. Lester, *When Hollywood Was Fun,* 54.

10. Audio commentary, *The Outlaw,* 2009.

11. Russell, *Jane Russell,* 19.

12. Louella Parsons, "Photographs of Jane Russell Arouse League of Decency," *Waterloo Daily Courier,* January 24, 1941, 13.

13. Levis Green to Hedda Hopper, letter, March 11, 1941. HHP.

14. Hedda Hopper to Levis Green, letter, March 27, 1941, HHP.

15. Jacobi Russell, *Oh, Lord, What Next?* 108.

16. *Magazine Circulation and Rate Trends,* 12.

17. "Jane Russell, a Howard Hughes Find, Is 1941's Best New Prospect," *Life,* January 20, 1941, 42–45.

18. "Register Squawk on S.A. Buildup of Jane Russell," *Variety,* January 29, 1941, 3.

19. "Will Hollywood's Jane Russell Be a Dark-Haired Harlow?" *Oakland Tribune Magazine,* February 9, 1941, 1.

20. Russell Birdwell to A. M. Botsford, letter, February 14, 1942, RBP.

21. Russell, *Jane Russell,* 59.

22. "*Click* Discovers the Real Jane Russell on a Dude Ranch," *Click,* November 1941, 23.

23. Jacobi Russell, *Oh, Lord, What Next?* 108.

24. James Montgomery Flagg, "Jane Russell in Bathing Suit Starts Blitz of Photographers," *Boston Daily Globe,* February 26, 1941, 29.

25. Myer P. Beck to Russell Birdwell, memo, April 7, 1942, RBP.

26. Allen, "Glamour by Hurrell," 26.

27. Ibid.

28. Ibid.

29. Vieira, *George Hurrell's Hollywood,* 277.

30. Ibid.

31. John Wentworth to Russell Birdwell, letter, February 15, 1942, RBP.

32. Ibid.

33. Melba Howe to Dale Armstrong, memo, March 7, 1942, RBP.

34. John Wentworth to Russell Birdwell, memo, March 7, 1942, RBP.

35. Melba Howe to Russell Birdwell, memo, March 7, 1942, RBP.

36. Dale Armstrong to Russell Birdwell, memo, March 2, 1942, RBP.

37. Vieira, *George Hurrell's Hollywood,* 278.

38. DeVane, "Sensational Cinderella," 50.

39. Russell, *Jane Russell,* 117.

40. *Jane Russell Uncut, Part One.*

41. Dale Armstrong to Myer Beck, memo, October 30, 1941, RBP.

42. Russell Birdwell to Howard Hughes, letter, January 2, 1942, RBP.

43. Lowrance, Dee, "Publicity's Lucky Star," *Arizona Republic,* August 29, 1942, 2.

44. Paul Keenan to Russell Birdwell, letter, undated, RBP.

45. L. J. Schelper and T. M. O'Connell to Jane Russell, letter, April 9, 1942, RBP.

46. Jacobi Russell, *Oh, Lord, What Next?* 108.

47. Ibid.

48. *Jane Russell Uncut, Part One.*

49. *Jane Russell Uncut, Part Two.*

50. Russell, *Jane Russell,* 62.

51. Ibid.

52. Victor Boesen to Dale Armstrong, memo, September 8, 1941, RBP.

53. Bob Lantz to Russell Birdwell, letter, May 22, 1942, RBP.

54. Dale Armstrong to Russell Birdwell, memo, June 20, 1942, RBP.

55. Ibid.

56. Melba Howe to Russell Birdwell, memo, June 20, 1942, RBP.

57. Russell, *Jane Russell,* 63.

58. Dale Armstrong to Russell Birdwell, memo, June 26, 1942, RBP.

59. Dale Armstrong to Russell Birdwell, memo, June 23, 1942, RBP.

60. Dale Armstrong to Russell Birdwell, memo, July 23, 1942, RBP.

61. Ibid.

62. Jan Lowell to author, telephone conversation, March 25, 2017.

63. Russell Birdwell to Lee Murrin, April 11, 1942, RBP.

8. Mean . . . Moody . . . Magnificent

1. Geoffrey Shurlock to Joseph I. Breen, memo, December 31, 1940, *The Outlaw* file, PCA.

2. Joseph I. Breen to Howard Hughes, letter, March 28, 1941, *The Outlaw* file, PCA.

3. Ibid.

4. Ibid.

5. Joseph I. Breen to Will H. Hays, letter, March 28, 1941, *The Outlaw* file, PCA.

6. Joseph I. Breen to Will H. Hays, letter, March 29, 1941, *The Outlaw* file, PCA.

7. Joseph I. Breen to Howard Hughes, letter, April 8, 1941, *The Outlaw* file, PCA.

8. Carl E. Milliken to Howard Hughes, May 16, 1941, *The Outlaw* file, PCA.

9. Keats, *Howard Hughes,* 161.

10. Joseph I. Breen to Howard Hughes, letter, May 23, 1941, *The Outlaw* file, PCA.

11. Russell Birdwell to A. M. Botsford, letter, February 14, 1942, RBP.

12. Russell Birdwell to Captain Cotton-Ninchin, letter, January 27, 1942, RBP.

13. Nancy Tree to Russell Birdwell, telegram, February 20, 1942, RBP.

14. Russell Birdwell to Lee Murrin, letter, February 25, 1942, RBP.

15. Dale Armstrong to Russell Birdwell, memo, March 6, 1942, RBP.

16. Ibid.

17. Dale Armstrong to Russell Birdwell, memo, March 17, 1942, RBP.

18. Russell Birdwell to Byer P. Beck, memo, May 11, 1942, RBP.

19. Ibid.

20. Audio commentary, *The Outlaw,* 2009.

21. George McCall to Russell Birdwell, memo, November 10, 1942, RBP.

22. Russell, *Jane Russell,* 73.

23. Advertisement, *Tucson Daily Citizen,* December 2, 1942, 7.

24. George McCall to Russell Birdwell, memo, December 7, 1942, RBP.

25. Ibid.

26. "Hughes Offers Newest Stars," *Arizona Daily Star,* December 1, 1942, 4.

27. McCall to Birdwell, December 7, 1942.

28. Angelo J. Rossi to Howard Hughes, letter, December 29, 1942, RBP.

29. Advertisement, *San Francisco Examiner,* January 22, 1943, 9.

30. Louella O. Parsons, "Columbia Will Produce Film Based on Life of De Foucould," *San Francisco Examiner,* February 3, 1943, 6.

31. "*The Outlaw* Will Premiere at the Geary," *San Francisco Examiner,* January 29, 1943, 8.

32. Jacobi Russell, *Oh, Lord, What Next?* 108–9.

33. Henry, "Jane Russell's Teen-Age Escapades!" 72.

34. Ibid.

35. Ibid.

36. Russell, *Jane Russell,* 73.

37. *Jane Russell: Body and Soul.*

38. "Film Reviews: *The Outlaw,*" *Variety,* February 10, 1943, 8.

39. Alexander Fried, "*Outlaw,* Howard Hughes Film, Opens Run at Geary," *San Francisco Examiner,* February 8, 1943, 8.

40. Louella O. Parsons, "Young Stars Sparkle in *The Outlaw,*" *San Francisco Examiner,* February 12, 1943, 12.

41. "Stage Epilog to *Outlaw,*" *Variety,* February 10, 1943, 8.

42. Fried, "*Outlaw,* Howard Hughes Film," 8.

43. "*The Outlaw* Continues Its Run at the Geary," *San Francisco Examiner*, February 18, 1943, 13.

44. Jacobi Russell, *Oh, Lord, What Next?* 109.

45. Ibid.

46. "Sex Bally on *Outlaw* was Biz Hypo in S.F.," *Variety*, March 31, 1943, 15.

47. "Jane Russell Billboard Picture 'Too Risque' for Bay City," *San Pedro News-Pilot*, February 19, 1943, 1.

48. "*The Outlaw* Proves Sex Has Not Been Rationed," *Variety*, February 17, 1943, 21.

49. Mary E. Miller to Will Hays, letter, April 21, 1943, *The Outlaw* file, PCA.

50. Memo, July 7, 1943, *The Outlaw* file, PCA.

51. Geoffrey Shurlock, memo, April 7, 1943, *The Outlaw* File, PCA.

52. Dietrich, *Howard*, 153.

53. Clarence Keske to "Gentlemen," letter, December 3, 1944, *The Outlaw* file, PCA.

54. Joseph I. Breen to Pvt. Clarence Keske, letter, December 20, 1944, *The Outlaw* file, PCA.

55. Advertisement, *Salt Lake City Deseret News*, March 15, 1946, 16.

56. Virginia MacPhereson, "Public Will See *Outlaw* After Delay of Four Years," *Waterloo Daily Courier*, January 3, 1946, 12.

57. Darryl Zanuck to Joseph I. Breen, letter, April 2, 1946, *The Outlaw* file, PCA.

58. "Archbishop Cantwell Hits Film as Offensive," *Los Angeles Times*, April 5, 1946, A9.

59. MPAA Executive Committee to Howard Hughes, letter, April 9, 1946, *The Outlaw* file, PCA.

60. "Hughes Film Ads Draw M.P.A. Fire," *Los Angeles Times*, April 12, 1946, 1.

61. "Hughes Files $5,000,000 Damage Suit on *Outlaw*," *Los Angeles Times*, April 23, 1946, 2.

62. Hughes Tool Company vs. Motion Picture Association of America, Inc., Temporary Restraining Order, *The Outlaw* file, PCA.

63. "Howard Hughes Near Death After Plane Hits Four Houses," *Los Angeles Times*, July 8, 1946, 1.

64. Joseph I. Breen to Francis Harmon, letter, September 5, 1946, *The Outlaw* file, PCA.

65. Photograph, *The Outlaw*—Misc Openings and Exploitations File, Howard Hughes Collection, 1927–1957, Margaret Herrick Library.

66. Philip K. Scheuer, "*Outlaw* Odd Opus," *Los Angeles Times*, April 4, 1946, A3.

67. Schumach, *The Face on the Cutting Room Floor*, 61.

68. Bazin, *What Is Cinema?* 166.

69. Ibid.

70. Scheuer, "*Outlaw* Odd Opus," A3.

71. Bazin, *What Is Cinema?* 166.

72. Ibid., 164.

73. Ibid., 166.

74. Audio commentary, *The Outlaw*, 2018.

75. Joseph I. Breen to Rupert Allen, letter, March 15, 1954, *The Outlaw* file, PCA.

76. Thomas, *Howard Hughes in Hollywood,* 88.

77. Russell, *Jane Russell,* 19.

9. Mrs. Robert Waterfield

1. Russell, *Jane Russell,* 67.

2. Ibid.

3. Jacobi Russell, *Oh, Lord, What Next?* 111.

4. Henry, "Jane Russell's Teen-Age Escapades!" 74.

5. Jacobi Russell, *Oh, Lord, What Next?* 112.

6. Russell, *Jane Russell,* 75.

7. Henry, "Jane Russell's Teen-Age Escapades!" 74.

8. Jane Russell and Robert Waterfield, marriage certificate, April 24, 1923, file no. 164371, Clark County Recorder, copy in possession of author.

9. Henry, "Jane Russell's Teen-Age Escapades!" 74.

10. Ibid.

11. "Jane Russell, Actress, Weds," *Hanford Sentinel,* April 26, 1943, 1.

12. DeVane, "Sensational Cinderella," 51.

13. "Bob Waterfield to Fort Benning Soon," *Miami Daily News-Record,* May 21, 1943, 5.

14. Louella O. Parsons, "Schenck Signs George Jessel as Associate Film Producer," *San Francisco Examiner,* June 1, 1943, 10.

15. Liza, "Miss Curves Is Here Again," 111.

16. "Remember Jane Russell? (She Got Terrific Movie Build-up)," *Hanford Morning Journal,* July 14, 1944, 7.

17. Russell, *Jane Russell,* 79.

18. Benjamin, "Censorable Jane," 70.

19. Jacobi Russell, *Oh, Lord, What Next?* 113.

20. Russell, *Jane Russell,* 81.

21. Harrison Carroll, "Behind the Scenes Hollywood," *Sant Rosa Press Democrat,* October 21, 1943, 14.

22. "Bob Waterfield Back at UCLA," *Los Angeles Times,* June 16, 1944, A11.

23. "Remember Jane Russell?" 7.

24. Sheilah Graham, "Jane Russell, *Outlaw* Star, Starts Work on *Young Widow,*" *Atlanta Constitution,* December 10, 1944, 3-D.

25. Ibid.

26. Jacobi Russell, *Oh, Lord, What Next?* 112.

27. Graham, "Jane Russell, *Outlaw* Star," 3-D.

28. Philip K. Scheuer, "Pin-up Girl Has Hollywood Abuzz," *Los Angeles Times,* May 6, 1945, B3.

29. "Selznick, Small Move to CSU Lots," *Variety,* April 18, 1945, 5.

30. "Dieterle on U Loanout," *Variety,* May 16, 1945, 9.

31. Edwin Schallert, "*Tracy* Cast Gathers; Warners Seek *Widow*," *Los Angeles Times,* May 24, 1945, A2.

32. "Hollywood Chatter," *Variety,* June 27, 1945, 55.

33. Liza, "Miss Curves Is Here Again," 111.

34. Ibid.

35. Ibid.

36. Ibid.

37. "*Young Widow* Humor Best," *Los Angeles Times,* February 22, 1946 A3; "Film Reviews," *Variety,* February 20, 1946, 8.

38. *Jane Russell Uncut, Part One.*

39. "UCLA Grid Star Signed," *Massillon Evening Independent,* June 15, 1945, 12.

40. Sulecki, *The Cleveland Rams,* 139.

41. "Bob Waterfield," *Life,* December 17, 1945, 49–52.

42. "Waterfield Signs for $20,000 Per," *San Francisco Examiner,* December 18, 1945, 19.

43. Russell, *Jane Russell,* 85.

44. Sid Feder, "Big Pro Transfer," *San Francisco Examiner,* January 13, 1946, 19.

10. Kick-starting a Career

1. "Vaudeville Reviews," *Billboard,* March 23, 1946, 50.

2. "Jane Russell's S.A. Keeps *Outlaw* Hot in Chi," *Variety,* March 27, 1946, 17.

3. "Follow-up Reviews," *Billboard,* April 27, 1946.

4. Dale Armstrong to Russell Birdwell, memo, August 7, 1942, RBP.

5. George Frazier, "Jocks, Jukes, and Disks," *Variety,* April 2, 1947, 44.

6. "Night Club Reviews," *Billboard,* March 15, 1947, 36.

7. Ibid.

8. Russell, *Jane Russell,* 99.

9. "To the Winnah!" *Miami News,* March 4, 1947, 5-B.

10. "Jane Russell Takes $12,500 for Stint at Latin Quarter," *Miami News,* March 29, 1947, 1.

11. "Jane Russell 'Shows' Gratis—and $15,000 Boss Cries Out," *Montgomery Advertiser,* March 9, 1947, 9.

12. "Jane Russell Takes $12,500 for Stint at Latin Quarter," 1.

13. Ibid.

14. "Jane Russell Heads Vaude Package Set for Golden Gate S.F.," *Variety,* May 21, 1947, 51.

15. Hedda Hopper, "Home Is Where Jane's Heart Is," *Chicago Tribune,* October 24, 1948, 13.

16. Ibid.

17. "Jane Russell Signs New Film," *Baltimore Sun,* January 7, 1947, 13.

18. Edwin Schallert, "Jane Russell to Be Real 'Outlaw' Now," *Los Angeles Times,* August 10, 1947, pt. 3, 3.

19. Dorothy Raymer, "Show Time," *Miami Daily News,* March 7, 1947, 10-A.

20. "Status of Future Productions," July 22, 1947, *The Paleface* Budgets Folder, PPPR.

21. William Davidson to Richard L. Johnson, memo, June 11, 1947, *The Paleface* Budgets Folder, PPPR.

22. Russell, *Jane Russell,* 96.

23. Graffis, "South America—Take It Away!" 107.

24. "Official Production Budget," *The Paleface* Budgets Folder, PPPR.

25. Ibid.

26. Schallert, "Jane Russell to Be Real 'Outlaw' Now," pt. 3, 1.

27. *Scene by Scene: Jane Russell.*

28. *Jane Russell Uncut, Part Two.*

29. Quirk, *Bob Hope,* 183.

30. "Bob Hope to Do *The Outlaw,*" *Monrovia News-Post,* October 4, 1947, 1.

31. *Jane Russell Uncut, Part Two.*

32. Ibid.

33. "Film Reviews," *Variety,* October 20, 1948, 11.

34. "*The Paleface* Hilarious Burlesque: Top Xmas Fare," *Hollywood Reporter,* December 20, 1948.

35. "Britain Won—and the Fizz Went Flat!" *Picturegoer,* April 23, 1949, 9.

36. Pollock, "Faith of a Beauty," 107.

37. Russell, "Let's Put out the Lights."

38. "Disk Revs," *Variety,* December 24, 1947, 40.

39. "Nat'l Orange Show," *Billboard,* March 27, 1948, 58.

40. Edwin Schallert, "*Born Yesterday* Leads New Project Parade," *Los Angeles Times,* July 12, 1948, 17.

41. *Jane Russell Uncut, Part Two.*

42. Ibid.

43. Lasky, *RKO,* 229.

44. Dietrich, *Howard,* 238.

45. Ibid.

46. "Film Reviews," *Variety,* October 29, 1952, 6.

47. "Star Stand-in Is Sub at *Montana* Opening," *Boxoffice,* January 3, 1953, 3.

48. "Jane Russell Art Goes to GIs Prior to Payday," *Boxoffice,* May 30, 1953, 33.

49. Marx, *The Groucho Phile,* 257.

50. Jane Russell, interview by Stan Taffel, August 14, 2007, transcript, Screen Actors Guild Foundation, Los Angeles.

51. Marx, "When You Say Russell—Whistle!" 64.

52. Marx, *The Groucho Phile,* 257.

53. Reynolds, "Is Sex Necessary?" 87.

54. O'Brien, *The Frank Sinatra Film Guide.*

55. Marx, *The Groucho Letters,* 34.

56. Ibid., 198.

57. Reynolds, "Is Sex Necessary?" 87.

58. Marx, *The Groucho Phile,* 257.

59. *Jane Russell Uncut, Part Two.*

11. House in the Clouds

1. Russell, *Jane Russell,* 95.

2. Peterson, "House in the Clouds," 77.

3. Ibid.

4. Ibid.

5. Ibid.

6. Ibid.

7. Russell, "Take My Word for It," 80.

8. Reynolds, "Is Sex Necessary?" 87.

9. Russell, "Take My Word for It," 80.

10. Wilkie, "Catch Me Cookin!" 78.

11. Bruce, "Jane Takes a Look Back," 66.

12. Ibid.

13. "Application to Erect a New Building," 14888 Round Valley Drive, February 14, 1947, City of Los Angeles, Department of Building and Safety.

14. Peterson, "House in the Clouds," 51.

15. Russell, "Take My Word for It," 80.

16. Sher, "The Bob Waterfield Story," 72.

17. Reynolds, "Is Sex Necessary?" 87.

18. Wilkie, "Catch Me Cookin!" 78.

19. Sher, "The Bob Waterfield Story," 29.

20. Hedda Hopper, "Jane Russell Sticks to 'Old Gang' of Hers," *Los Angeles Times,* July 15, 1951, D3.

21. Ibid.

22. Ibid.

23. Ibid.

24. Russell, "Take My Word for It," 80.

25. Thompson, *Bob Hope,* 101–2.

26. Berg, Louis, "What a Jane!" *Los Angeles Times,* August 12, 1951, G14.

27. Thompson, *Bob Hope,* 102.

28. "Vaudeville Reviews," *Variety,* April 16, 1949, 55.

29. "Chatter," *Variety,* September 28, 1949, 70.

30. "Jane Russell Clicks," *Variety,* September 28, 1949, 2.

31. "Round the Halls," *Variety,* September 29, 1949, 5.

32. Bruce, "Jane Takes a Look Back," 29.

33. Ibid., 29, 66.

12. Mitch

1. *TCM Private Screenings.*

2. "Production Report," *His Kind of Woman* file, RKO.

3. Fleischer, *Just Tell Me When to Cry,* 57.

4. Advertisement, *Life,* July 23, 1951, 54–55.

5. *TCM Private Screenings.*

6. Jewell, *Slow Fade to Black*, 135.

7. *TCM Private Screenings*.

8. "Production Report," *His Kind of Woman* file, RKO.

9. Daniel Siegal, "Artist Worked for Howard Hughes, Influenced Other Creatives," *La Canada Valley Sun*, September 12, 2012, https://www.latimes.com/socal/la-canada-valley-sun/community/tn-vsl-0913-artist-painted-hughes-story.html.

10. Ibid.

11. Herb Rau, "Censorship," *Miami News*, September 18, 1951, 12-A.

12. Virginia MacPherson, ". . . Around Hollywood," *Medford Mail Tribune*, September 3, 1951, 10.

13. Ibid.

14. Ibid.

15. "Mighty Sign to Publicize Hughes Film," *Los Angeles Times*, September 12, 1951, 23.

16. Walt Hackett, "Colossal Unveiling Party Turns out to Be Big Bust," *Lansing State Journal*, October 7, 1951, 15.

17. *TCM Private Screenings*.

18. "Authorization Request," April 26, 1950, *His Kind of Woman* file, RKO.

19. *Jane Russell Uncut, Part Two*.

20. Ibid.

21. *Scene by Scene*.

22. Russell, *Jane Russell*, 1.

23. Audio commentary, *Macao*.

24. Roberts, *Mitchum*, 91.

25. Ibid.

26. Ibid.

27. *TCM Private Screenings*.

28. "Production Report," October 19, 1950, *Macao* file, RKO.

29. *TCM Private Screenings*.

30. Audio commentary, *Macao*.

31. Von Sternberg, *Fun in a Chinese Laundry*, 283.

32. Jervis and Woulfe, *Glamour and Mischief!* 128.

33. Dietrich, *Howard*, 159.

34. Jervis and Woulfe, *Glamour and Mischief!* 128.

35. Ibid., 129.

36. Ibid.

37. Ibid.

38. Ibid.

39. Dietrich, *Howard*, 157.

40. Jervis and Woulfe, *Glamour and Mischief!* 133.

41. Patricia Clary, "Such a Momentous Day: Jane, Lana in Sweaters," *Asheville Citizen-Times*, September 11, 1950, 7.

42. Memo, July 6, 1950, *Macao* file, RKO.

43. "La Russell Oomphy in 21-lb Gown," *Pasadena Independent,* September 15, 1950, 15.

44. Dietrich, *Howard,* 157.

45. Jervis and Woulfe, *Glamour and Mischief!* 133.

46. Server, *Robert Mitchum: "Baby I Don't Care,"* 222.

47. "Film Reviews," *Variety,* March 19, 1952, 6.

48. Jewell, *Slow Fade to Black,* 135.

49. "Production $718 *Macao,"* *Macao* file, RKO.

50. Audio commentary, *Macao.*

51. Ibid.

52. Celestine Sibley, "What's Wrong with Marriage? 'Women!' Says Jane Russell," *Atlanta Journal and Constitution,"* August 19, 1951.

53. *Scene by Scene.*

54. *Conversational Interview with Jane Russell.*

55. Russell, *Jane Russell,* 175.

56. *Jane Russell Uncut, Part Two.*

13. Wing-Ding Tonight

1. *Scene by Scene.*

2. Jervis and Woulfe, *Glamour and Mischief!* 102.

3. "Production Report," *The Las Vegas Story* file, RKO.

4. Jewell, *Slow Fade to Black,* 123–24.

5. "Film Reviews," *Variety,* January 9, 1952, 6.

6. "Jane Russell, Bob to Adopt Baby," *Baltimore Evening Sun,* June 7, 1951, 3.

7. Russell, *Jane Russell,* 126.

8. Hedda Hopper, "Her Friends Call Jane Russell a Lame Brain, but—," *Hartford Courant,* July 15, 1951, 10.

14. International Uproar

1. Russell, *Jane Russell,* 130.

2. Ibid.

3. Jacobi Russell, *Oh, Lord, What Next?* 147.

4. Ibid.

5. Ibid.

6. Ibid, 148.

7. Ibid.

8. *Late Night America.*

9. Russell, *Jane Russell,* 131.

10. "Jane Russell Seems to Adopt British Baby," *Salem Capitol Journal,* October 29, 1951, 3.

11. Jacobi Russell, *Oh, Lord, What Next?* 151.

12. Ibid.

13. Russell, *Jane Russell,* 132.

14. John Edgar Hoover to Commissioner, Immigration and Naturalization Service, letter, December 26, 1951, FBI.

15. R. M. MacColl, "Jane Russell Tells Why Baby Flew Out," *London Daily Express,* November 8, 1951, 1.

16. Russell, *Jane Russell,* 132.

17. MacColl, "Jane Russell Tells Why Baby Flew Out," 1.

18. "British Royalty at Command Performance," *Newark Advocate,* November 5, 1951, 7.

19. "The Royal Film Performance, Splendours of Dress," *Guardian,* November 6, 1951, 7.

20. Russell, *Jane Russell,* 156.

21. Ibid., 158.

22. "Adoring London Fan Gives Jane Russell Her Baby Boy," *Valley Morning Star,* November 7, 1951, 1.

23. "Passenger Manifest, Trans World Airlines, Inc.," November 6, 1951, New York, Passenger and Crew Lists (including Castle Garden and Ellis Island), 1820–1957, Ancestry.com (accessed July 25, 2015).

24. "Jane Russell Flies Home with a Baby Boy from Battersea," *London Daily Express,* November 7, 1951, 1.

25. MacColl, "Jane Russell Tells Why Baby Flew Out," 1.

26. "Jane Russell Back with Baby Given by English Mother," *St. Louis Dispatch,* November 7, 1951, 1.

27. MacColl, "Jane Russell Tells Why Baby Flew Out," 1.

28. Russell, *Jane Russell,* 159.

29. "Jane Russell Bringing London Baby to U.S.," *Los Angeles Times,* November 7, 1951, 1.

30. Jacobi Russell, *Oh, Lord, What Next?* 160.

31. Ibid.

32. Ibid.

33. "Asks Actress Be Investigated for 'Importing' Baby," *New Philadelphia (OH) Daily Times,* November 10, 1951, 2.

34. Mary Louise Muir, *Jane Russell and the Springtown Mother,* BBC Radio 4, March 27, 2015.

35. "Asks Actress be Investigated for 'Importing' Baby," 2.

36. Ferriter, *Occasions of Sin,* 331.

37. "Irish Orphans Fly in, Meet New Parents," *New York Times,* March 18, 1950, 30.

38. A. H. Belmont to V. P. Keay, memo, December 14, 1951, FBI.

39. J. Edgar Hoover to Commissioner, Immigration and Naturalization Service, letter, December 26, 1951, FBI.

40. "Parliament to Study Jane Russell's Baby," *New York Times,* November 10, 1951, 10.

41. Jacobi Russell, *Oh, Lord, What Next?* 161.

42. Russell, *Jane Russell,* 135.

43. "Parents Charged for Giving Baby to Jane Russell," *Tampa Times,* April 1952, 16.

44. "Kin in Adoption Case Lodge Beef against Jane Russell," *Los Angeles Daily News,* April 19, 1952.

45. "Jane Russell Very Nice Woman, Says Court as Parents Go Free," *Binghamton Press and Sun-Bulletin,* April 24, 1952, 1.

46. Ibid.

47. Ibid.

48. "Clears Way for Jane Russell to Adopt," *Chicago Tribune,* April 25, 1952.

49. Martha Martin, "And Now There Are Two," *New York Daily News,* December 23, 1951, 3.

50. Ibid.

51. "Jane's Friends May Adopt Him," *London Daily Express,* November 12, 1951, 1.

52. "Jane Russell 'Wants to Keep' British-Born 16-Months Baby," *Santa Maria Times,* January 2, 1952, 4.

53. Ibid.

54. Ibid.

55. "United States of America, Petition for Naturalization," March 26, 1955, U.S. Naturalization Record Indexes, 1791–1992, Ancestry.com (accessed April 20, 2017).

56. "She Helps U.S. Couples Adopt Foreign Babies," *Parade,* March 13, 1955,

57. Ellen Barr, "From Hollywood Back to Derry," *Derry Journal,* March 17, 2013, https://www.derryjournal.com/news/people/from-hollywood-back-to-derry-1-4907104.

58. Ibid.

59. "In Hospital," *London Daily Express,* April 3, 1968, 1.

60. Ibid.

15. What Happened in Vegas

1. "Books Provided," *Las Vegas Review Journal,* February 12, 1952, 3.

2. "Vegas Set for Big Premiere," *Las Vegas Review Journal,* February 11, 1952, 1.

3. Russell, *Jane Russell,* 124.

4. "Jane Russell's Eye Hits Door; Hubby Hits Trail," *Los Angeles Mirror,* February 13, 1952, 2.

5. Ibid.

6. Carroll, Harrison, "Waterfield Menaces Comedian," *Los Angeles Herald,* February 12, 1952.

7. "Waterfield Sees Red at Blue's Gags about Jane Russell," *Los Angeles Examiner,* February 12, 1952.

8. Russell, *Jane Russell,* 124.

9. Ibid.

10. "Expense Memo," February 12, 1952, ELP.

11. "Actress Denies Spat with Mate; He Meets Her at Plane," *Los Angeles Examiner,* February 14, 1952.

12. "Jane Russell Nurses 'Shiner' Following Tiff in Nightclub," *Pittsburgh Sun-Telegraph*, February 13, 1952, 3.

13. "Jane Russell Back Home with Her Black Eye," *Los Angeles Times*, February 14, 1952, 2.

14. "Lumpy Jaw, Eye Mouse Shine above Other Russell Charms," unidentified newspaper clipping.

15. "Jane's 'Shiner' Stirs Filmland," *Hollywood Citizen News*, February 13, 1952, 14.

16. Edith Lynch to Dick Maha, "Expense Memo," February 13, 1952, ELP.

17. Russell, *Jane Russell*, 124.

18. "Jane Russell's Black Eye? 'Twas 'Wind and Car Door,'" *Los Angeles Examiner*, February 14, 1952.

19. "Jane Russell Back Home with Her Black Eye," 2.

20. "Jane Russell's Black Eye?"

21. *Late Night America*.

22. Russell, *Jane Russell*, 124.

23. Jan Lowell to author, telephone conversation, March 25, 2017.

24. *Scene by Scene*.

25. "Jane Russell in Court with 'Black' Eye, Adopts Baby," *Los Angeles Evening Herald and Express*, February 15, 2952.

26. "Jane Russell Says Woman Accused of Theft 'Honest,'" *Los Angeles Examiner*, February 21, 1952.

27. "Production Call Sheet," June 19, 1952, *Road to Bali* files, PPPR.

16. Blondes

1. Brooks Atkinson, "First Night at the Theatre," *New York Times*, December 9, 1949, 35.

2. "Synopsis of Contract for Purchase of Literary Material," March 10, 1952, *Gentlemen Prefer Blondes* file, FOX.

3. Hedda Hopper, "Ginger Hopes to Be 'Blonde' with Grable," *Los Angeles Times*, March 11, 1952, B6.

4. Kobal, *People Will Talk*, 496.

5. Ibid.

6. Ibid.

7. Lew Schreiber to Jack Codd, memo, February 28, 1957, Jane Russell file, FOX.

8. *Sally Jessy Raphael*, Universal Television, 1992.

9. McCarthy, *Howard Hawks*, 504.

10. *Sally Jessy Raphael*.

11. Kobal, *People Will Talk*, 604.

12. Russell, *Jane Russell*, 137.

13. Morgan, *Marilyn Monroe*, 164.

14. Lawrence Perry, "The Broadway Beat," *Shreveport Times*, June 7, 1953, 4-E.

15. Churchill and Churchill, "I Didn't Say That," 62.

16. Joseph I. Breen to Colonel Jason Joy, letter, November 4, 1952, *Gentlemen Prefer Blondes* file, PCA.

17. *Jane Russell Uncut, Part Three.*

18. Kobal, *People Will Talk,* 604–5.

19. Ibid., 604.

20. *Jane Russell Uncut, Part Three.*

21. Ibid.

22. McCarthy, *Howard Hawks,* 507.

23. *Jane Russell Uncut, Part Three.*

24. *Scene by Scene.*

25. Ibid.

26. Merryman, "Marilyn Lets Her Hair Down," 34.

27. R. A. Klune to All Departments, memo, November 10, 1952, *Gentlemen Prefer Blondes* file, FOX.

28. *The Discovery of Marilyn Monroe.*

29. Kobal, *People Will Talk,* 604.

30. Merryman, "Marilyn Lets Her Hair Down," 34.

31. Skolsky, "I Love Marilyn," 62.

32. Bawden and Miller, *You Ain't Heard Nothing Yet,* 183.

33. Bruce, "The Inside Story of the Marilyn-Jane Feud," 61.

34. Skolsky, "I Love Marilyn," 62.

35. Kobal, *People Will Talk,* 496.

36. Churchill and Churchill, "I Didn't Say That!" 62.

37. Ibid.

38. McCarthy, *Howard Hawks,* 507.

39. Ibid.

40. Ibid.

41. Ibid.

42. Kobal, *People Will Talk,* 496.

43. Ibid.

44. *Scene by Scene.*

45. Bruce, "The Inside Story of the Marilyn-Jane Feud," 61.

46. Lew Schreiber to Frank Ferguson, memo, February 13, 1953, Jane Russell file, FOX.

47. Summers, *Goddess,* 119.

48. Russell, *Jane Russell,* 139.

49. "Interview with Jane Russell," YouTube, https://www.youtube.com/watch?v=NdokE07ERc4&t=295s (accessed March 11, 2020).

50. Jane Russell to Marilyn Monroe, letter, undated, https://www.bidsquare.com/online-auctions/juliens/jane-russell-handwritten-letter-to-marilyn-monroe-135385 (accessed March 10, 2020).

51. Haspiel, *Marilyn,* 93.

52. Kendall, "Jane Russell Speaks Out," 29.

53. Harry J. McIntyre to Frank H. Ferguson, Esq., letter, June 25, 1953, *Gentlemen Prefer Blondes* file, FOX.

54. Lew Schreiber to Frank Ferguson and Jack Codd, memo, August 5, 1957, Jane Russell file, FOX.

17. A Woman of Faith

1. Sid Ross and Kay Sullivan, "They Sold Me Like a Can of Tomatoes," *Parade Magazine,* November 15, 1953.

2. "Classifieds," *Van Nuys News,* July 2, 1943, pt. 2, 9.

3. *Interview with Jane Russell,* YouTube, https://www.youtube.com/watch?v=NdokE07ERc4&t=295s (accessed March 11, 2020).

4. *Christian Celebrity Showcase.*

5. Ibid.

6. *Interview with Jane Russell.*

7. Ibid.

8. St. Johns, "Do Lord . . . Do Lord!" 28.

9. Ibid.

10. Ibid.

11. *Christian Celebrity Showcase.*

12. Jacobi Russell, *Oh, Lord, What Next?* 169.

13. Isabel Moore, "Jane Russell's Other Life," *American Weekly,* May 25, 1952, 22.

14. *Jane Russell Uncut, Part Three.*

15. *Christian Celebrity Showcase.*

16. Virginia Everett, "New Chapel Completed in the Canyon," *Valley Times,* June 21, 1958, 8.

17. *Christian Celebrity Showcase.*

18. "A New Religious Film Aimed at Realism," *Valley Times,* August 6, 1960, 9.

19. Jan Lowell to author, telephone conversation, March 25, 2017.

20. Moore, "Jane Russell's Other Life," 22.

21. Ibid.

22. *Interview with Jane Russell.*

23. Lowell to author, telephone conversation, March 25, 2017.

24. Gerry Cornez to author, telephone conversation, August 20, 2016.

25. Lowell to author, telephone conversation, March 25, 2017.

26. Cornez to author, telephone conversation, August 20, 2016.

27. Pollock, "Faith of a Beauty," 108.

18. J. R. in 3D

1. "Hughes Recovers RKO," *Variety,* February 11, 1953, 3.

2. "Production Report," May 25, 1953, *The French Line* file, RKO.

3. Jervis and Woulfe, *Glamour and Mischief!* 170.

4. Ibid., 172.

5. Ibid.

6. Ibid., 173.

7. Ibid., 190.

8. Ibid.

9. Ibid., 191

10. *Jane Russell Uncut, Part Three.*

11. "Production Report," July 25, 1953, *The French Line* file, RKO.

12. Jervis and Woulfe, *Glamour and Mischief!* 179.

13. Ibid., 193.

14. Ibid.

15. "*The French Line,* Estimated Cost of Lost Time Due to Miss Russell's Illness," *The French Line* file, RKO.

16. Jervis and Woulfe, *Glamour and Mischief!* 193.

17. Ibid.

18. Ibid., 196.

19. Ibid.

20. "Production Report," August 20, 1953, *The French Line* file, RKO.

21. Joseph I. Breen to William Feeder, letter, April 15, 1953, *The French Line* file, PCA.

22. "List of Unacceptable Items *French Line,*" November 18, 1953, *The French Line* file, PCA.

23. Vizzard, *See No Evil,* 174–75.

24. Keats, *Howard Hughes,* 269.

25. Russell, *Jane Russell,* 146.

26. Ibid.

27. "Jane Russell Backs Censor in Film Row," *Los Angeles Times,* December 29, 1953, 2.

28. Bob Thomas, "Jane Russell Rebels over *French Line,*" *Hollywood Citizen,* December 18, 1953.

29. "Jane Russell's New Picture Gets Free Publicity," *Neosho Daily News,* December 29, 1953, 2.

30. Perry Leiber to Lincoln Quarberg, letter, undated, *The French Line* file, Lincoln Quarberg Collection, Margaret Herrick Library, Center for Motion Picture Study, Academy of Motion Picture Arts and Sciences, Academy of Motion Picture Arts and Sciences, Beverly Hills.

31. "More on Code Reactions," *Boxoffice,* January 23, 1954; "*The French Line* Banned from Memphis Showing," *Boxoffice,* February 6, 1954.

32. Russell, *Jane Russell,* 146.

33. *Jane Russell Uncut, Part Three*

34. "Production Report," October 17, 1953, *Underwater!* file, RKO.

35. Mike Fitzgerald, "An Interview with Lori Nelson," *Western Clippings,* http://www.westernclippings.com/interview/lorinelson_interview.shtml (accessed March 15, 2020).

36. Lovell, *Escape Artist,* 119.

37. Egan, "Jane Russell Got in My Hair," 55.

38. Ibid.

39. *Conversational Interview with Jane Russell.*

40. Ibid.

41. "*Big Rainbow* Shooting to Begin Nov. 25 in Kona," *Honolulu Star-Bulletin,* November 23, 1953, 12.

42. Lovell, *Escape Artist,* 123.

43. "*Big Rainbow* to Fade from Kona Scene This Week," *Hawaii Tribune-Herald,* December 21, 1953, 2.

44. "Production Reports," various dates, *Underwater!* files, RKO.

45. Jervis and Woulfe, *Glamour and Mischief!* 252.

46. Ibid.

47. "Jane Russell a Head in Torso Competition?" *Pasadena Independent,* March 6, 1955, 1.

48. "Lyn Jones Drops Suit against RKO Pictures," *Green Bay Press,* March 21, 1955, 22.

49. Freida Zylstra, "Fly to Florida for Premiere of Water Film," *Chicago Tribune,* January 24, 1955, 34.

50. Ibid.

51. Bernard Watts, "*Underwater:* Ocala's First Big Premiere," *Ocala Star Banner,* https://www.ocala.com/article/LK/20091120/Entertainment/604237053/OS (accessed March 20, 2020).

52. Russell, *Jane Russell,* 157.

53. Bosley Crowther, "Screen: *Underwater!*" *New York Times,* February 10, 1955.

19. WAIF

1. "Sen. Henrickson Promises Aid to Jane Russell," *Ridgewood (NJ) Sunday News,* June 7, 1953, 5.

2. Russell and Pettiss, "International Adoptions," 17.

3. Ibid.

4. Ibid.

5. Iss-ssi.org, History, https://www.iss-ssi.org/index.php/en/home/history#1-iss-history-in-more-details (accessed March 22, 2020).

6. WAIF, "A Salute to Jane Russell and Twenty-Five Years of WAIF," LAPL.

7. Russell and Pettiss, "International Adoptions," 17.

8. WAIF, "A Salute to Jane Russell."

9. Russell and Pettiss, "International Adoptions," 17.

10. Gerry Cornez to author, telephone conversation, August 20, 2016.

11. *Jane Russell Uncut, Part Three.*

12. WAIF, "A Salute to Jane Russell."

13. Jane Russell form letter, undated, author's personal collection.

14. Cornez to author, telephone conversation, August 20, 2016.

15. WAIF, "A Salute to Jane Russell."

16. Russell and Pettiss, "International Adoptions," 17.

17. Ibid.

18. Gerry Cornez to author, email, September 9, 2016.

19. WAIF, "A Salute to Jane Russell."

20. Ibid.

21. Russell and Pettiss, "International Adoptions," 17.

22. Ibid.

23. Cornez to author, telephone conversation, August 20, 2016.

20. Russ-Field

1. Sheilah Graham, "Hollywood," *Pittsburgh Post-Gazette,* November 25, 1953.

2. Louella Parsons, "Jane Russell Quitting Hughes," *Miami Herald,* February 5, 1954, 5-B.

3. Frank Finch, "Waterfield to Retire at End of Campaign," *Los Angeles Times,* December 2, 1952, C1.

4. Frank Finch, "Fans Honor Waterfield Today as Rams, Steelers Tangle," *Los Angeles Times,* December 14, 1952, B6.

5. Ibid.

6. "Production Records," *Underwater!* file, RKO; "Jane Russell into *Dolls* Clark Gable Deal Pends," *Variety,* February 10, 1954, 4.

7. Hedda Hopper, "Drama," *Los Angeles Times,* January 26, 1954, 18.

8. "Dior Look Doesn't Worry Jane Russell's Designer," *Bristol Herald Courier,* August 6, 1954, 22.

9. Bawden and Miller, *You Ain't Heard Nothing Yet,* 185.

10. Ibid.

11. Kat Ellinger, audio commentary, *Foxfire* (Kino Lorber, Universal, 2018).

12. Hedda Hopper, "Rooney Will Portray Old West Minister," *Los Angeles Times,* January 24, 1955, 3.8.

13. Russell, *Jane Russell,* 153.

14. Alan Young to author, March 27, 2016.

15. Russell, *Jane Russell,* 153.

16. Hedda Hopper, "Alan Young, Jeanne Crain Teamed Again," *Los Angeles Times,* September 9, 1954, A12.

17. "Passenger Manifest," Trans World Airlines, September 8, 1954, U.S., Departing Passenger and Crew Lists, 1914–1966, Ancestry.com (accessed April 20, 2017).

18. Louis Berg, "What's This! They Didn't Like Jane in Paris," *Los Angeles Times,* September 18, 1955, H14.

19. Russell, *Jane Russell,* 154.

20. Ibid.

21. Jane Russell to Hedda Hopper, undated, Jane Russell file, HHP.

22. "Christian Dior Fails to Debosom Our Jane," *Times Colonist,* September 17, 1954, 21.

23. A. H. Weiler, "Mayfair Has *Gentlemen Marry Brunettes,*" *New York Times,* October 21, 1955, 31.

24. Bawden and Miller, *You Ain't Heard Nothing Yet,* 185.

25. Dietrich, *Howard,* 159.

26. "Employment Agreement between Hughes Productions and Jane Russell Waterfield," 1954, 4, Jane Russell file, FOX.

27. Ibid., 19.

28. Dietrich, *Howard,* 159.

29. Bob Thomas, "Jane Russell Fabulous Contract with Hughes Considered," *Indiana Gazette,* January 17, 1955, 12.

30. Russell and Moore, audio commentary *The Outlaw,* 2009.

31. Russell, *Jane Russell,* 104.

32. Russell and Moore, audio commentary, *The Outlaw,* 2009.

33. Lew Schreiber to Frank Ferguson, memo, Jane Russell file, FOX, January 17, 1955.

34. "Passenger Manifest," Pam American Airways, January 6, 1955, New York, Passenger and Crew Lists (including Castle Garden and Ellis Island), 1820–1957, Ancestry.com. (accessed April 20, 2017).

35. Hopper, "Rooney Will Portray Old West Minister," 3.8.

36. Russell and Moore, audio commentary, *The Outlaw,* 2009.

37. Bawden and Miller, *You Ain't Heard Nothing Yet,* 185.

38. *Jane Russell Uncut, Part Three.*

39. Ibid.

40. Walsh, *Each Man in His Time,* 361–62.

41. McGilligan, *Nicholas Ray,* 237.

42. Eisenschitz, *Nicholas Ray,* 259.

43. "Jane Russell," transcript, September 4, 1955, HHP.

44. Eisenschitz, *Nicholas Ray,* 261.

45. Ibid.

46. Ibid., 263.

47. Memo, October 4, 1955, *Revolt of Mamie Stover* folder 246, WGC.

48. "Office Production Cast Budget," undated, *Revolt of Mamie Stover* folder, 246, WGC.

49. "Jane Russell Is Intrigued by *Mamie's* Drama Aspects," *Honolulu Star-Bulletin,* December 1, 1955, 4.

50. *Mamie Stover* Shooting Begins," *Honolulu Star-Bulletin,* November 29, 1955, 12.

51. Jane Russell to Hedda Hopper, letter, December 7, 1955, HHP.

52. Ibid.

53. Ibid.

54. Ibid.

55. Ibid.

56. Bosley Crowther, "Screen: *Mamie Stover,*" *New York Times,* May 12, 1956, 12.

57. *Scene by Scene.*

58. Jonathan Yardley, "*Mamie Stover*: Blond Ambition," *Washington Post,* May 31, 2006, C.01.

59. *Scene by Scene.*

60. Ibid.

21. Do Lord

1. "Jane Russell to Help Church Raise Money," *Los Angeles Times,* September 20, 1953, 6.

2. Haines, *For Once in My Life,* 122.

3. Ibid., 123.

4. Ibid., 117–18.

5. "Inside Stuff," *Variety,* May 5, 1954, 44.

6. Haines, *For Once in My Life,* 124.

7. Ibid.

8. Ibid.

9. Ibid., 128.

10. Russell, *Jane Russell,* 174.

11. Erskine Johnson, "Some Fuzzy Goings on in *Pink Nightgown,"* *Lancaster New Era,* January 7, 1957, 16.

12. Russell, *Jane Russell,* 174.

13. Ibid.

14. "*The Fuzzy Pink Nightgown* on View," *New York Times,* October 31, 1957, 41.

15. *Scene by Scene.*

16. Russell, *Jane Russell,* 174.

17. Helen Moore to Edith Lynch, letter, November 19, 1957, folder 38, ELP.

18. Hedda Hopper, "De Toth Buys Story about Negro Soldier," *Los Angeles Times,* April 16, 1957, A8.

19. Telegrams, various, 1957, "Jane Russell's Debut at the Sands Hotel: Photographs and Correspondence," Sands Hotel & Casino Public Relations Records, 1952–1977, MS-00417, Special Collections and Archives, University Libraries, University of Nevada, Las Vegas.

20. Edith Lynch to R. K. Wilson, letter, August 4, 1958, Jane Russell Entertainment Dates folder, ELP.

21. Norman Brokaw to Sam Zagon, letter, September 5, 1958, Jane Russell Entertainment Dates folder, ELP.

22. "Night Club Reviews," *Variety,* November 5, 1958, 69.

23. Business Search—Entity Detail, C0280120, Russ-Field Corporation, https://businesssearch.sos.ca.gov/CBS/Detail (accessed April 4, 2020).

22. On the Stage and Small Screen

1. Vernon Scott, "Good Works Come First," *Tucson Daily Citizen,* August 15, 1959, 14.

2. Dwight Newton, "Jane Russell Knows What Viewers Want: Westerns," *San Francisco Examiner,* January 25, 1959, 2.

3. Marie Torre, "Out of the Air," *East Liverpool Review,* August 26, 1958, 10.

4. Newton, "Jane Russell Knows What Viewers Want," 2.

5. Ibid.

6. Erskine Johnson, "Jane Sings TV Blues—but Hasn't a Worry," *Arizona Daily Sun,* January 23, 1959, 13.

7. Ibid.

8. H. Viggo Anderson, "Girl with a Mission," *Hartford Courant,* August 23, 1959, 7B.

9. Scott, "Good Works Come First," 14.

10. "Actress Jane Russell Plans Another Movie," *Tyler Morning Telegraph,* November 15, 1962, 6.

11. Ibid.

12. Ibid.

13. Ibid.

14. Ibid.

15. Fred Russell, "Passing Show," *Bridgeport Post,* August 26, 1959, 29.

16. "Jane Russell in Stage Debut at Wallingford," *Hartford Courant,* August 26, 1959. 5.

17. Jane Russell to Hedda Hopper, letter, August 26, 1959, HHP.

18. Klawitter and Jones, *Headslap,* 148.

19. Ibid., 192–93.

20. Russell, *Jane Russell,* 200.

21. Ibid., 203.

22. Ibid., 205.

23. Kaufman, *Doris Day,* 366.

24. Haines, *For Once in My Life,* 125.

25. "New Acts," *Variety,* August 14, 1963, 63.

26. James Bacon, "No 'Comeback' for Jane Russell," *Abilene Reporter-News,* July 19, 1963, 7-A.

27. Emery Wister, "Swan Song Bit," *Charlotte News,* April 18, 1964, 1C.

28. Joseph Finnigan, "Cast in Film Role Again, Jane Russell Loyal to Pal," *Allentown (PA) Morning Call,* March 10, 1964, 14.

29. Bob Freund, "Moviemaker A. C. Lyles Brings Back the Veterans," *Fort Lauderdale News and Sun-Sentinel,* January 16, 1966, 5G.

30. Bob Thomas, "Jane Russell's Back in Form," *Hackensack (NJ) Record,* November 2, 1965, 34.

31. "Reviews," *Films and Filming,* August 1966.

32. Freund, "Moviemaker A. C. Lyles Brings Back the Veterans," 5G.

33. Sheilah Graham, "Jane Russell Making Comeback to Movies," *Muncie Star,* October 23, 1966, 18A.

23. Endings, Beginnings, and Endings

1. Earl Wilson, "Jane Russell Still Cashing Fat Check from Hughes," *Charlotte News,* September 6, 1966, 5A.

2. Ibid.

3. "$1,000 Wins Auction," *Variety,* December 6, 1967, 4.

4. "Jane Pines for Dramatic Roles," *Honolulu Advertiser,* December 20, 1967, A20.

5. Audio commentary, *The Born Losers.*

6. Ibid.

7. Ibid.

8. Ibid.

9. Ibid.

10. Russell, *Jane Russell,* 242.

11. Ibid., 222.

12. *Interview with Jane Russell,* YouTube, https://www.youtube.com/watch?v=NdokE07ERc4&t=295s (accessed March 11, 2020).

13. Russell, *Jane Russell,* 224.

14. Complaint for Divorce between Jane Russell Waterfield and Robert Staton Waterfield, signed by Max Fink, February 3, 1968, no. 0702898, 2, LACSC.

15. Answer to Complaint between Jane Russell Waterfield and Robert Staton Waterfield, signed by Paul Caruso, March 6, 1968, no. 0702898, 1, LACSC.

16. Ibid., 2.

17. Ibid.

18. Russell, *Jane Russell,* 226.

19. "She Was a Drunk," *National Enquirer,* September 22, 1968, 1.

20. Stipulation Re Division of Property and Other Liabilities between Jane Russell Waterfield and Robert Staton Waterfield, signed by Max Fink and Paul Caruso, July 30, 1968, no. 0702898, LACSC.

21. Russell, *Jane Russell,* 238.

22. Sulecki, *The Cleveland Rams,* 136.

23. "Current Cafe Engagements," *Van Nuys News,* May 24, 1968, 38.

24. Earl Wilson, "Jane Russell Moves Quickly," *Dayton Daily News,* August 16, 1968, 45.

25. Ibid.

26. "Jane Pines for Dramatic Roles," *Honolulu Advertiser,* December 20, 1967, A20.

24. A Life Off-screen

1. Walt McCaslin, "Plenty of Laughs in *High Buttons,*" *Dayton Journal Herald,* July 23, 1970, 24.

2. Bob Lardine, "There's Lots of Sex Appeal Left," *New York Daily News,* August 29, 1971, 5.

3. Russell, *Jane Russell,* 275.

4. Ibid., 287.

5. Robert Whals, "Jane Joins *Company* Cast," *New York Daily News,* May 2, 1971, C27.

6. Ibid.

7. Russell, *Jane Russell,* 287.

8. "Jane Russell Is Back in Spotlight," *Lebanon Daily News,* October 11, 1971, 15.

9. "Legit Followup," *Variety,* June 23, 1971, 58.

10. "The House That Jane Built," *Everybody's*, April 25, 1962, 16.

11. Bob Thomas, "Jane Russell Presents?" *Santa Cruz Sentinel*, January 30, 1972, 11.

12. Ibid.

13. Ibid.

14. Ibid.

15. Ibid.

16. Jeanne Miller, "Yesterday's Sex Symbol Hates Today's License," *San Francisco Examiner*, March 8, 1973, 21.

17. Ibid.

18. "Jane Russell Proves a Glamorous 'Mame,'" *Oakland Tribune*, March 9, 1973, 50.

19. Gerry Cornez to author, telephone conversation, August 20, 2016.

20. Gerry Cornez to author, email, September 9, 2016.

21. Rader, "The Meditations of Jane Russell," 316.

22. Cornez to author, email, September 9, 2016.

23. *Scene by Scene.*

24. Yvonne Bracamontes to author, telephone conversation, June 11, 2019.

25. Huestis, *Impresario of Castro Street*, loc. 3642.

26. Ibid., loc. 3658.

27. Cornez to author, email, September 9, 2016.

28. Pepper Aarvold to author, email, August 31, 2019.

29. Cornez to author, telephone conversation, August 20, 2016.

30. Ibid.

31. Lee Graham, *Hollywood Studio Magazine*, March 1974.

32. Jan Lowell to author, telephone conversation, March 25, 2017.

33. Bob Thomas, "Jane Russell's Back in Form," *Hackensack (NJ) Record*, November 2, 1965, 34.

34. Dietrich, *Howard*, 160.

35. Miller, "Yesterday's Sex Symbol Hates Today's License," 21.

36. Russell, *Jane Russell*, 298.

25. Path and Detours

1. Gerry Cornez to author, telephone conversation, August 20, 2016.

2. Ibid.

3. Ibid.

4. Ibid.

5. Ibid.

6. Ibid.

7. "Jane Russell Stands by Her Son," *Santa Maria Times*, October 13, 1976.

8. "Three Arrested in Bar Shooting," *Los Angeles Times*, May 4, 1976, 3.

9. "Jane Russell Stands by Her Son."

10. Ibid.

11. "Waterfield Given 9 Months," *Five Cities Times Press Recorder*, January 21, 1977, 7.

12. Junger, "Jane Russell Went to Jail."

13. Ibid.

14. Ibid.

26. Living Legend

1. "Jane Russell Grand Marshall," *Arizona Daily Sun,* January 9, 1981, 3.

2. Hardy Prince, "People and Places," *Arizona Republic,* July 9, 1981, F1; July 28, 1981, C5.

3. Bob Thomas, "Prime Time Soap Bags Jane Russell," *Arizona Daily Star,* January 1, 1984, 5.

4. Ivor Davis, "Jane Russell to Get Tough Again," *Los Angeles Herald Examiner,* January 14, 1984, B5.

5. Ibid., B1.

6. Jan Lowell to author, telephone conversation, March 25, 2017.

7. Ibid.

8. Ibid.

9. Ibid.

10. Marilyn Stasio, "Jane Russell, Symbol & Survivor," *New York Post,* June 10, 1985.

11. Jan Lowell to author, telephone conversation, August 20, 2016.

12. "Joan's Sue-thing Talk," *Miami News,* January 22, 1987, 2A.

13. Hugh McIlvanney, "Gentlemen Prefer Brunettes," *Observer,* May 25, 1985, 19.

14. Ibid.

15. "Jane Russell," *Interview Magazine,* August 1988, 17.

16. John Drybred, "Jane Russell Gives Label Approval," *Intelligencer Journal,* February 15, 1988.

17. Robert Whals, "Jane Joins *Company* Cast," *New York Daily News,* May 2, 1971, C27.

18. Lynda Lee-Potter, "Confessions of a Sex Siren," *Daily Mail,* May 26, 2003, 20.

19. Ruth Ryon, "Hot Property," *Los Angeles Times,* June 20, 1999, K1.

20. Lee-Potter, "Confessions of a Sex Siren," 20.

21. Ibid.

22. Yvonne Bracamontes to author, telephone conversation, June 11, 2019.

23. Ibid.

24. Peter Sheridan, "The Superstar Is Singing for Her Supper," *Daily Express,* March 30, 2006, 25.

25. Ibid.

26. Bracamontes to author, telephone conversation, June 11, 2019.

27. Lee-Potter, "Confessions of a Sex Siren," 20.

28. Bracamontes to author, telephone conversation, June 11, 2019.

29. Gerry Cornez to author, email, September 9, 2016.

30. Bracamontes to author, telephone conversation, June 11, 2019.

31. Marga K. Cooley, "Hollywood Bombshell of the 1940s Dies," *Santa Maria Times,* March 1, 2011, 1.

Bibliography

Printed Sources

Allen, G. T. "Glamour by Hurrell." *U.S. Camera,* January 1942.

Bawden, James, and Ron Miller. *You Ain't Heard Nothing Yet.* Lexington: University Press of Kentucky, 2017.

Bazin, André. *What Is Cinema?* Vol. 2. Berkeley: University of California Press, 1971.

Benjamin, George. "Censorable Jane." *Modern Screen,* September 1941.

"Bob Waterfield." *Life,* December 17, 1945.

Bruce, Jack. "Jane Takes a Look Back." *Screenland,* November 1949.

Bruce, John. "The Inside Story of the Marilyn-Jane Feud." *Screenland Plus TV-Land,* April 1953.

Churchill, Bonnie, and Reba Churchill. "I Didn't Say That!" *Screenland Plus TV-Land,* June 1953.

"*Click* Discovers the Real Jane Russell on a Dude Ranch." *Click,* November 1941.

DeVane, Tom. "Sensational Cinderella." *Hollywood,* May 1941.

Dietrich, Noah. *Howard, the Amazing Mr. Hughes.* Greenwich, CT: Fawcett, 1972.

Dunning, John. *On the Air: The Encyclopedia of Old-Time Radio.* New York: Oxford University Press, 1998.

Egan, Richard. "Jane Russell Got in My Hair." *Screenland Plus TV-Land,* March 1955.

Eisenschitz, Bernard. *Nicholas Ray: An American Journey.* London: Faber & Faber, 1996.

Emerson, Beth. "Heart Affair: The New Romance in John Payne's Life." *Photoplay Combined with Movie Mirror,* January 1943.

Ferriter, Diarmaid. *Occasions of Sin: Sex and Society in Modern Ireland.* London: Profile Books, 2009.

Fleischer, Richard. *Just Tell Me When to Cry.* New York: Carroll & Graf, 1993.

Graffis, Bill. "South America—Take it Away!" *Modern Screen,* November 1947.

Haines, Connie. *For Once in My Life.* New York: Warner Books, 1976.

Haspiel, James. *Marilyn: The Ultimate Look at the Legend.* New York: Henry Holt, 1991.

Henry, Ernestine. "Jane Russell's Teen-Age Escapades!" *Modern Screen,* September 1956.

Huestis, Marc. *Impresario of Castro Street: An Intimate Showbiz Memoir.* San Francisco: Outsider Productions, 2019. Kindle.

Jacobi Russell, Geraldine. *Oh, Lord, What Next?* Tampa: Leroy Jenkins Evangelistic Association, 1965.

"Jane Russell, a Howard Hughes Find, Is 1941's Best New Prospect." *Life,* January 29, 1941.

Jervis, David V., and Michael Woulfe. *Glamour and Mischief! Hollywood's "Undercover Costume Designer" Michael Woulfe Takes a Lighthearted Look at Dressing the Stars of the Golden Age—and Working for Eccentric Howard Hughes.* David Jervis, 2016.

Jewell, Richard B. *Slow Fade to Black: The Decline of RKO Radio Pictures.* Oakland: University of California Press, 2016.

Junger, Victor. "Jane Russell Went to Jail, but Insists She Was Not in Her Cups," *People,* July 31, 1978.

Kaufman, David. *Doris Day: The Untold Story of the Girl Next Door.* London: Virgin Books, 2008.

Keats, John. *Howard Hughes.* London: MacGibbon & Kee, 1967.

Kendall, Robert. "Jane Russell Speaks Out." *Hollywood Then and Now,* October 1988.

Klawitter, John, and Deacon Jones. *Headslap: The Life and Times of Deacon Jones.* Amherst, NY: Prometheus Books, 1996.

Kobal, John. *People Will Talk.* New York: Knopf, 1986.

Lasky, Betty. *RKO: The Biggest Little Major of Them All.* Santa Monica: Roundtable, 1989.

Lester, Gene. *When Hollywood Was Fun.* New York: Birch Lane. 1993.

Liza. "Miss Curves Is Here Again." *Screenland,* October 1945.

Lovell, Glenn. *Escape Artist: The Life and Films of John Sturges.* Madison: University of Wisconsin Press, 2008.

Magazine Circulation Rate and Trends, 1940–1959. New York: Association of National Advertisers, 1960.

Maltin, Leonard. *The Art of the Cinematographer: A Survey and Interviews with Five Masters.* New York: Dover, 1971.

Marx, Groucho. *The Groucho Letters.* New York: Simon & Schuster, 1967.

———. "When You Say Russell—Whistle!" *Screen and Television Guide,* August 1949.

Marx, Julius H. *The Groucho Phile.* New York: Galahad Books, 1976.

McCarthy, Todd. *Howard Hawks, the Gray Fox of Hollywood.* New York: Grove, 1997.

McGilligan, Patrick. *Nicholas Ray: The Glorious Failure of an American Director.* New York: It Books, 2011.

Merryman, Richard. "Marilyn Lets Her Hair Down about Being Famous." *Life,* August 3, 1962.

Moore, Isabel. "Jane Russell's Other Life." *American Weekly,* May 25, 1952.

Morgan, Michelle. *Marilyn Monroe: Private and Confidential.* New York: Skyhorse, 2012.

"New Role for Jane Russell." *Parade,* March 13, 1955.

O'Brien, Daniel. *The Frank Sinatra Film Guide.* London: Pavilion Books, 2014. https://www.google.com/books/edition/The_Frank_Sinatra_Film_Guide/9k2_CAAAQBAJ?hl=en&gbpv=1.

Peterson, Marva. "House in the Clouds." *Modern Screen,* November 1952.

Pollock, Louis. "Faith of a Beauty." *Redbook Magazine,* November 1951.

Quirk, Lawrence J. *Bob Hope: The Road Well-Traveled.* New York: Applause Books, 1998.

Rader, Dotson. "The Meditations of Jane Russell." *Esquire,* December 1973.

Reynolds, John. "It Sex Necessary?" *Modern Screen,* May 1949.

Roberts, Gerald. *Mitchum: In His Own Words.* New York: Proscenium, 2000.

Russell, Jane. *Jane Russell: My Path and My Detours.* New York: Franklin Watts, 1985.

———. "Take My Word for It." *Modern Screen,* September 1952.

Russell, Jane, and Susan T. Pettiss. "International Adoptions: Possibilities and Problems." *Summary of Proceedings: Officers, Committees (American Bar Association. Section of Family Law),* 1961, 15–27, https://www.jstor.org/stable/i40170232.

Schumach, Murray. *The Face on the Cutting Room Floor.* New York: William Morrow, 1964.

Server, Lee. *Robert Mitchum: "Baby I Don't Care."* New York: St Martin's, Griffin, 2002.

Sher, Jack. "The Bob Waterfield Story." *Sport,* November 1951.

Sheridan, Peter. "The Superstar Singing for Her Supper." *Daily Express,* March 30, 2006.

Skolsky, Sidney. "I Love Marilyn." *Modern Screen,* October 1953.

St. Johns, Elaine. "Do Lord . . . Do Lord!" *Cosmopolitan,* August 1954.

Stull, William. "16mm Sound Tests Pick Two New Stars." *American Cinematographer,* October 1941.

Sulecki, James C. *The Cleveland Rams: The NFL Champs Who Left Too Soon, 1936–1945.* Jefferson, NC. McFarland, 2016.

Summers, Anthony. *Goddess: The Secret Lives of Marilyn Monroe* .New York: Macmillan, 1985.

Thomas, Tony. *Howard Hughes in Hollywood.* Secaucus, NJ: Citadel, 1985.

Thompson, Charles. *Bob Hope: Portrait of a Superstar.* New York: St. Martin's, 1981.

Vieira, Mark A. *George Hurrell's Hollywood.* Philadelphia: Running, 2013.

Vizzard, Jack. *See No Evil: Life inside a Hollywood Censor.* New York: Simon & Schuster, 1970.

Von Sternberg, Josef. *Fun in a Chinese Laundry.* New York: Macmillan, 1965.

WAIF. "A Salute to Jane Russell and Twenty-Five Years of WAIF," 1983. Los Angeles Public Library.

Walsh, Raoul. *Each Man in His Time: The Life Story of a Director.* New York: Farrar, Straus & Giroux, 1974.

Wilkie, Jane. "Catch Me Cookin!" *Modern Screen,* February 1954.

Audiovisual Sources

The Born Losers/The Complete Billy Jack Collection. Audio commentary. Shout Factory, 2017.

Christian Celebrity Showcase. Trinity Broadcasting Network, YouTube. https://www.youtube.com/watch?v=pHUXOZv1U9E.

Conversational Interview with Jane Russell, part 1. Audio podcast. Celebrity Network. https://www.celebritynetwork.com/guests/conversation-with-jane-russell.

The Discovery of Marilyn Monroe. Director unknown. Ashley Entertainment, 1991.

Jane Russell: Body and Soul. Directed by Torrie Rosenzweig. A&E Network, 1997.

Jane Russell Uncut, Part One. Turner Classic Movies Backlot video, April 27, 1995. https://www.tcmbacklot.com/player/211.

Jane Russell Uncut, Part Two. Turner Classic Movies Backlot video, April 27, 1995. https://www.tcmbacklot.com/player/278?page=6.

Jane Russell Uncut, Part Three. Turner Classic Movies Backlot video, April 27, 1995. https://www.tcmbacklot.com/player/310?page=6.

Late Night America. Hosted by Dennis Wholey, PBS, October 23, 1985. YouTube. https://www.youtube.com/watch?v=Y47bZwSKtbI.

The Outlaw. Audio commentary. Legend Films, 2009.

The Outlaw. Audio commentary. Kino Lorber, 2018.

Russell, Jane. Audio commentary. *Macao*. Warner Archive Collection, 2016.

———. "Let's Put Out the Lights." Columbia Records, 1947.

Scene by Scene: Jane Russell. Directed by Mark Cousins. BBC, 1999.

TCM Private Screening: Robert Mitchum and Jane Russell. Directed by Tony Barbon. Turner Classic Movies, 1996.

Index

*Page numbers in **bold** refer to illustrations*

Index

Screen Classics

Screen Classics is a series of critical biographies, film histories, and analytical studies focusing on neglected filmmakers and important screen artists and subjects, from the era of silent cinema through the golden age of Hollywood to the international generation of today. Books in the Screen Classics series are intended for scholars and general readers alike. The contributing authors are established figures in their respective fields. This series also serves the purpose of advancing scholarship on film personalities and themes with ties to Kentucky.

Series Editor

Patrick McGilligan

Books in the Series

Saul Bass: Anatomy of Film Design
    Jan-Christopher Horak

Hitchcock Lost and Found: The Forgotten Films
    Alain Kerzoncuf and Charles Barr

Pola Negri: Hollywood's First Femme Fatale
    Mariusz Kotowski

Sidney J. Furie: Life and Films
    Daniel Kremer

Albert Capellani: Pioneer of the Silent Screen
    Christine Leteux

Ridley Scott: A Biography
    Vincent LoBrutto

Mamoulian: Life on Stage and Screen
    David Luhrssen

Maureen O'Hara: The Biography
    Aubrey Malone

My Life as a Mankiewicz: An Insider's Journey through Hollywood
    Tom Mankiewicz and Robert Crane

Hawks on Hawks
    Joseph McBride

Showman of the Screen: Joseph E. Levine and His Revolutions in Film Promotion
    A. T. McKenna

William Wyler: The Life and Films of Hollywood's Most Celebrated Director
    Gabriel Miller

Raoul Walsh: The True Adventures of Hollywood's Legendary Director
    Marilyn Ann Moss

Veit Harlan: The Life and Work of a Nazi Filmmaker
    Frank Noack

Harry Langdon: King of Silent Comedy
    Gabriella Oldham and Mabel Langdon

Charles Walters: The Director Who Made Hollywood Dance
    Brent Phillips

Some Like It Wilder: The Life and Controversial Films of Billy Wilder
    Gene D. Phillips

Ann Dvorak: Hollywood's Forgotten Rebel
    Christina Rice

Mean . . . Moody . . . Magnificent! Jane Russell and the Marketing of a Hollywood Legend
    Christina Rice

About the Author

Christina Rice is a writer, librarian, and archivist who was born and bred in the greater Los Angeles region. While majoring in film at Cal State Fullerton in the 1990s, she began collecting memorabilia relating to actress Ann Dvorak, which eventually lead her to document Dvorak's life and ultimately to write *Ann Dvorak: Hollywood's Forgotten Rebel* (2013). After obtaining an MLIS from San Jose State University in 2004, she began a career as a librarian with the Los Angeles Public Library the following year. Since 2009 she has overseen the library's historic photo collection.

In addition to authoring books on Ann Dvorak and Jane Russell, she has also written numerous issues of the *My Little Pony* comic book series and was a contributor to the Eisner-nominated anthologies *Femme Magnifique* (2018) and *Where We Live* (2018). She lives in Los Angeles with her husband, writer Joshua Hale Fialkov, their daughter, and two adorable dogs.